THE HARLEM UPRISING

THE HARLEM UPRISING

Segregation and Inequality
in Postwar New York City

Christopher Hayes

Columbia University Press
New York

COLUMBIA
UNIVERSITY
PRESS

Columbia University Press gratefully acknowledges the generous support for this book provided by Publisher's Circle member Stephen H. Case.

Columbia University Press
Publishers Since 1893
New York   Chichester, West Sussex
cup.columbia.edu
Copyright © 2021 Columbia University Press
All rights reserved

Library of Congress Cataloging-in-Publication Data
Names: Hayes, Christopher, 1979 August 8- author.
Title: The Harlem uprising : segregation and inequality in postwar New York City / Christopher Hayes.
Description: New York : Columbia University Press, [2021] | Includes bibliographical references and index.
Identifiers: LCCN 2021016648 (print) | LCCN 2021016649 (ebook) | ISBN 9780231181860 (hardcover) | ISBN 9780231181877 (trade paperback) | ISBN 9780231543842 (ebook)
Subjects: LCSH: Harlem Race Riot, New York, N.Y., 1964. | Powell, James, 1949–1964—Death and burial. | African Americans—Civil rights—New York (State)—New York—20th century. | African Americans—Social conditions—New York (State)—New York—History—20th century. | Civil rights movements—New York (State)—New York—History—20th century. | Police—New York (State)—New York. | Harlem (New York, N.Y.)—History—20th century. | Race discrimination—New York (State)—New York. | New York (N.Y.)—Race relations.
Classification: LCC F128.68.H3 H39 2021 (print) | LCC F128.68.H3 (ebook) | DDC 323.1196/07307470904—dc23
LC record available at https://lccn.loc.gov/2021016648
LC ebook record available at https://lccn.loc.gov/2021016649

Cover image: © Neil Libbert / Bridgeman Images
Cover design: Lisa Hamm

Contents

Acknowledgments vii

Introduction   1
1. Living   9
2. Working   29
3. Union Work   44
4. Learning   63
5. The New York City Police Department   84
6. A Death and Protests   107
7. Daybreak: Sunday, July 19   128
8. Spreading Anxiety: Monday, July 20   141
9. Day Four: Tuesday, July 21   158
10. Day Five: Wednesday, July 22   169
11. Day Six: Thursday, July 23   179
12. After   192
13. Reforming the Civilian Complaint Review Board   207
14. A Referendum   219

Epilogue: Insufficient Funds   241

Notes   253
Bibliography   309
Index   327

Acknowledgments

Thank you: Mia Bay, without whom there is none of this—no degree, no career, no book—and that is no hyperbole. Beryl Satter, Ann Fabian, and Brian Purnell for their generosity, patience, and forthrightness. They gave quite a bit to someone who was not so sure of what he was doing but thought he knew. I would be nowhere were it not for their efforts. Philip Leventhal, my editor, whose support, guidance, advice, revising skills, and insight have been invaluable and made this book what it is. My outside readers, for their time and constructive criticism. Michael Haskell for shepherding me through the final stages of this project. Rob Fellman and his eagle eye for details. Those at Columbia University Press who worked on my behalf in anonymity. Bob Schwarz. Paula Voos, Lisa Schur, Adrienne Eaton, Will Brucher, Fran Ryan, Dorothy Sue Cobble, Naomi Williams, Mike Merrill, Todd Vachon, Eugene McElroy, Laura Walkoviak, and all at the Rutgers University Department of Labor Studies and Employment Relations. Ronn Pineo. Johanna Schoen and Dawn Ruskai. Everyone who provided feedback on parts of this book at conferences. J. You.

THE HARLEM UPRISING

Introduction

The real danger of Harlem is not in the infrequent explosions of random lawlessness. The frightening horror of Harlem is the chronic day-to-day quiet violence to the human spirit which exists and is accepted as normal.

—DR. KENNETH CLARK, "BEHIND THE HARLEM RIOTS–TWO VIEWS," 1964

For many African Americans, 1964 was a time of great hope and frustration. The civil rights movement had been winning significant national and regional victories for a decade—*Brown v. Board*, the Montgomery Bus Boycott, desegregation of public spaces through sit-in campaigns, the Freedom Rides, and the Civil Rights Act of 1964 are a few—and the federal government was newly supportive of dismantling the southern apartheid system. These victories all came with challenges, whether states refusing to integrate schools, the lynching of civil rights workers, or terrorists bombing people's homes and churches, but it seemed like the movement was pushing toward restoring Black Americans' constitutional rights, as conferred nearly a century before.

While the millions of Black people living throughout the North applauded these campaigns and what they had won, most of the national victories did not change their lives in significant ways. Black northerners could vote, dine, live, work, and travel as they pleased. Of course, they encountered bigoted individuals who would treat them discourteously or deny them service, but there were no laws mandating the segregation of schools or public accommodations. To the contrary, in the middle of the century, northern cities and states began passing their own antidiscrimination legislation, often well ahead of the federal government. New York City and New York State had some of the earliest and strongest laws against discrimination, beginning with banning discrimination in private employment in 1945. By the late 1950s, there would be laws prohibiting bias in the sale and rental of public and private housing as well. The city's board of education had enthusiastically stated its support for school integration following the *Brown* decision.

Despite this legislation and lack of blatantly racist statutes, Black New Yorkers suffered enormously under the weight of a vast system of structural discrimination that became more robust and destructive through the fifties and into the sixties, just as the national movement was making substantial strides. Banking and real estate policy compelled them to live segregated, unequal lives in places like Harlem, Bedford-Stuyvesant, and Brownsville, and bigoted homeowners and landlords worked diligently to keep out those who had managed to overcome the administrative barriers. The neighborhoods into which the majority of Black New Yorkers were confined were the most overcrowded and contained the oldest housing stock the city had to offer, commonly lacking adequate sanitation and access to quality health care.

The city operated its public schools on the basis of where students lived, resulting in large numbers of segregated institutions, with majority Black schools invariably underfunded, understaffed, overcrowded, and physically decaying. Students tended to learn little of use and fell further behind as they advanced through the grades. Many left high school before graduating, leaving them with no recognized skills in an increasingly education-oriented economy.

Black workers faced a job market offering them low-wage, mostly dead-end service work, with manufacturers leaving the city by the month and white workers wielding an iron grip on construction. The jobs that the city was gaining, in areas like finance, insurance, advertising, and law, required some combination of education, experience, and connections that most Black residents of the city would not have, and for those who did, racist hiring practices at the firm level served as a backstop.

The federal government had given its imprimatur to segregated neighborhoods since the beginning of the New Deal with official, written policies that made homeownership much more difficult for Black people. By denying either mortgage insurance to property in neighborhoods with Black residents or mortgages to Black applicants, these agencies translated American racism into financial and real estate code, leading the way for the private sector. City leaders insisted the schools were segregated by coincidence, based on people's choices of where to live, and there was nothing the Board of Education could or should do to address the situation, aside from building new schools to relieve overcrowding, which really meant building more apartheid schools. Labor unions were free to admit and exclude whomever they chose, and employers hired the same way. Losing out on prospective employment because of the candidate's race was difficult to prove, and the burden fell to the victim of discrimination. Most white New Yorkers met suggestions of affirmative action with deep hostility, and with no incentive to do otherwise, employers in the sectors of the economy offering good wages and opportunities for advancement kept reproducing racially homogenous workplaces.[1]

Black New Yorkers and their allies fought with great determination against racism, both systemic and individual. After all, this was the adopted home of a panoply of prominent figures of the Black Freedom Struggle, from A. Philip Randolph and Marcus Garvey to Ella Baker and Bayard Rustin to Malcolm X and James Farmer. Since World War II, Black people in the city had worked to address disparities in housing, education, employment, health, and policing, but twenty years later, they had made little progress. Yes, they had secured victories against discrimination in employment and housing, but too often those victories never moved beyond the paper on which they were printed. Black life either remained as segregated as ever or became more separate and unequal.[2]

Massive structural forces like capital flight and deindustrialization generated stiff headwinds for civil rights advocates in the city, but they also faced strong opposition from a seemingly unlikely source—Mayor Robert F. Wagner Jr., who served from 1954 to 1965, a liberal Democrat with a progressive pedigree. His Democratic U.S. senator father, Robert F. Wagner Sr., was an influential New Dealer from New York, legendary for his championing of labor rights.[3] The mayor professed active support for civil rights goals, yet his administration practiced a deliberate pattern of delay and defer, generally refusing to actually confront any given crisis head-on, especially those that concerned civil rights advances, which many white New Yorkers perceived to be a zero-sum scenario.

In July 1964, after two decades of agitation and every conceivable method of nonviolent activism and protest, including demonstrations, voting, sitting in, petitioning, political organizing, school boycotts, lawsuits, and more, the city finally exploded. In the midst of the Student Nonviolent Coordinating Committee's Freedom Summer campaign in Mississippi and two weeks after President Lyndon Johnson signed the Civil Rights Act of 1964, an off-duty white police lieutenant shot and killed a fifteen-year-old Black boy.[4] The officer alleged the boy had repeatedly attempted to attack him with a knife; bystanders offered conflicting accounts. The boy, James Powell, was from the Bronx, and the shooting took place in the Yorkville neighborhood in Manhattan's Upper East Side, but protests began in Harlem. Two days later, on July 18, those protests led to conflict with officers at one of Harlem's police stations, and what would be known as the Harlem Riot had begun.

For six days, residents of Harlem and then Bedford-Stuyvesant in Brooklyn fought police, looted stores, and destroyed property. In the end, one man was dead and hundreds injured. Police arrested more than five hundred, and nearly seven hundred businesses were damaged, with costs to the city topping $4 million. In the uprisings' aftermath, the demand for a panel of civilians to review citizens' complaints against police emerged as the most salient local outcome. The city's police resisted this proposed oversight, and when a new mayor, John Lindsay, established a new board with police and civilians serving on it in 1966, the rank-and-file officers' union and its allies waged a successful campaign to prohibit civilians from serving on any police review board by amending the city's charter.

New York's unrest was the first of the urban uprisings that would come to define the 1960s. The July 1964 upheaval in New York City was major news nationally and internationally, shaped political campaigns at every level, and touched off a chain of disturbances throughout the nation's cities. Beginning within days of New York's uprisings, at least six other northern cities experienced similar events before the end of the summer. Hundreds more would come over the course of the decade, forever altering the country's racial and political landscape. The ensuing battle over the composition of the review board determined the mayoral race and who would be police commissioner. The opposing struggles over civilian participation in police review marked a turning point for race relations and the civil rights movement in the city, resulting in heightened bitterness and resentment toward the police as well as increased alienation from white voters among many Black New Yorkers.

Contemporary observers advanced a convincing perspective on why the unrest happened when and where it did. Kenneth Clark, the African American psychologist, professor, and one of the most prominent voices advocating for Harlem and its residents, wrote in 1965 that "in the complex turbulence of the Negro ghetto, and consistent with the affirmative dynamics of the civil rights thrust, success feeds hope and provides the strength and the motivation for further activity. This, in turn, makes existing barriers even more intolerable."[5] Five years later, the journalist Max Lerner traced the origins of the 1960s urban uprisings to the French political scientist Alexis de Tocqueville's observations of American slavery in the 1830s. Should slavery end, the freedpeople would not accept mere freedom but demand full equality, "indignant at being deprived of almost all the rights of citizens." Well over a century later, full equality had not yet come, but African Americans were moving toward it faster than at any point since Reconstruction. This, as Clark and Lerner argue, was precisely the fuel on which the uprisings had run. Both men separately assert that times of quickening social progress lead to a collective sense of optimism, which when denied or delayed have a tendency to drive people to take actions far more aggressive and bold than they would in times of despair.[6] However, proximity to freedom and equality does not fully explain why the unrest happened when and where it did.

The July upheaval should be understood as a product of rising expectations during a time of declining fortunes. During and after World War II, hundreds of thousands of Black people had come to New York City from the South, looking for better lives. They found that they could vote without being murdered and would not be arrested for using a water fountain, but new variations of the same fundamental problems presented themselves. Black New Yorkers needed not equality before the law but equality before the employer, mortgage lender, judge, teacher, and city council, issues that were much harder to organize around and legislate against. Their struggles at home for integrated schools, open and better-quality housing, decent employment opportunities, and both respectful treatment and adequate service from the police left them deeply discouraged with the city.

They received little support from white fellow New Yorkers, many of whom were unable or unwilling to see racial inequality as anything other than the result of a lack of personal responsibility and northern civil rights as anything other than a movement whose victories could only come at white people's expense. Local white politicians tended to speak of racism as a problem at the individual level, as opposed to recognizing deep structural impediments. But as Kenneth Clark explained in 1964, "When one sees so many human casualties, and increasing numbers of human casualties, then one cannot look for the explanation in terms of the individual. One must look for the explanation in terms of a widespread social pathology." Perhaps the most fundamental challenge for activists in the city was getting officials to understand and acknowledge this.[7]

Conclusions

Not only were New York City's uprisings the first of others to come over the next five years, but they also had profound and wide-ranging repercussions. On

July 16, 1964, the same day of the police shooting in New York City that led to the uprisings, the conservative Republican presidential candidate Barry Goldwater delivered a speech accepting the party's nomination; in it he hammered home the need for law-and-order values. While Goldwater had been calling for law and order in reference to escalating crime rates in the nation's cities, the disturbances in New York and those that followed over the summer gave the concept new meaning. Though Goldwater lost the election, his ideology proved victorious, for Democrats and Republicans alike soon had to demonstrate their adherence to law and order through tough anticrime measures and crackdowns on urban unrest, just as one had to be tough on communism. Without the spectacle of the nation's cities on fire and under military occupation, it is unlikely the doctrine of law and order would have permeated politics and culture as far as it did. New York's upheaval also forever changed policing. In September 1964, President Johnson ordered both the Federal Bureau of Investigation and U.S. Army to offer all police departments across the country instruction in riot-control techniques. His order marks the beginning of the process of a national militarization of police forces we still see today.[8]

A historical analysis of the 1966 civilian review board referendum that situates it within the contexts of civil rights, race relations, and liberalism in the city provides a crucial point of departure for understanding the history of postwar New York City. Current scholarship generally dates the dissolution of the city's liberal civil rights coalition to 1968, with the Ocean Hill–Brownsville school decentralization struggle.[9] Moving that point back two years helps us see nuances that have long gone unnoticed. Virtually every civil rights and Black community organization in the city came together to fight to keep the review board that Lindsay created, even though most were unhappy with the new panel because it did not remove police from the process altogether. Black organizations worked with many white religious, civic, legal, political, and civil liberties groups toward the common goal of preserving the new board. New York's civil rights movement had a long history of interracial cooperation. From the communist organizing in Harlem of the 1930s to the citywide rent strikes in the 1960s, Black and white New Yorkers worked side by side. This did not end but forever changed after 1966. The failure to maintain what many proponents of review board reform saw as a panel that posed no threat to the police convinced many Black people and organizations in the city that change within the system was unworkable. The rancorous police-led campaign to defeat civilian participation in police review engendered a deep bitterness in many of the city's Black citizens, feeling many of their white allies had abandoned them, and an increase in hostility from other white New Yorkers.

As Craig Steven Wilder has argued, the frustrations parents and activists experienced in fighting for school desegregation in the 1950s and 1960s "caused a crisis in black Brooklyn, a crisis that could only be answered with greater militancy."[10] The same was true for Black New York as a whole regarding all fronts of the quest for equality. In studying the uprisings, the conditions that participants and activists cited as causes, and the review board referendum campaign, we can see Black New Yorkers growing increasingly impatient with the pace of change in the city. Improbably, social and economic conditions for most African Americans in the city only got worse with time.

Just as city leaders' inefficacy in addressing racial inequality created the conditions for the upheaval, it also convinced many Black New Yorkers that they could move forward only by turning inward and taking control of their communities and social and political institutions. They shifted away from imploring local government to redress their many grievances and abandoned interracial coalitions and appeals to white empathy, believing these strategies had won them little over the past two decades. In New York City, like in Philadelphia, Black Power was not the foil of civil rights but instead a progression of it that the failure of liberal political promises had drawn out.[11] By the time Black Power spread as a distinct ideology in the summer of 1966, Black New Yorkers were ready for it, as they had long been familiar with many of its tenets. All-Black community groups and political organizations had existed in Harlem for decades by that point. New York had been a hotbed of Black nationalism for most of the century. The Ocean Hill–Brownsville crisis was a demonstration of Black Power's strength in New York, not its emergence.[12]

Examining the city during the review board referendum offers us new insights into why liberalism fell from prominence in the city and across the urban North. Many authors have looked at this issue through white residents' eyes and come away with similar, related conclusions. One contention is that white residents feared crime, associated it with African Americans, and saw liberals as enablers. Another says white people watched the 1960s uprisings and saw only crime and opportunism, with liberals again going easy on participants. White observers viewed Black people as using the rebellions as bargaining tactics to win undeserved benefits from liberals who ignored white working people. The rebellions never ended and became a "rolling riot" of urban crime. Third and last, Black Power emerged and ruined the civil rights movement and interracial political coalitions, dividing Black and white. By privileging the white perspective and failing to even attempt to understand life in the communities that were the sites of unrest, such accounts perpetuate the historical silencing of marginalized people and get us no closer to a fuller understanding of the past.[13]

Finally, in analyzing the review board referendum, a new form of police power—political—becomes apparent. While there are many volumes on police brutality, scholars have rarely recognized the more subtle forms of domination police are able to exercise. Books critical of the NYPD focus on violence and methods of coercion, as well as falsified charges, lying, and social repression.[14] These allegations are well documented, but they do not encompass all of the power the police department has deployed. In its effort to destroy the hybrid review board in 1966, the rank-and-file police union, the Patrolmen's Benevolent Association, spent substantial amounts of money and employed public relations professionals. The PBA was able to bring out white voters to defeat a liberal measure, the first time a progressive matter had lost at the polls in the city in decades. Running a racially coded campaign designed to incite fear of crime in white voters, the PBA, with no previous experience in politicking, was more successful than it had anticipated. In less than six months, the twenty-thousand-strong PBA was able to muster 1.3 million voters to ban civilian oversight of police and repudiate one of Mayor Lindsay's core programs. Police power extends beyond how we commonly think of it.

A Note on Language

There are multiple instances of people using racial epithets in the text. In situations in which there are repetitions of the same slur in short order, I have left the first one and partially redacted the others to demonstrate the hatred but eschew gratuitousness. My intent is not to shock but rather to illustrate the racial landscape of the city and the world that Black New Yorkers inhabited. Many white people who policed them and shared the city with them were not shy about using such language in print or in public. In my estimation, choosing to not document these facts would be doing a disservice to those who had to endure this abuse and a favor for those who espoused such despicable sentiments.

1
Living

Now, it's very hot. We don't have air-conditioned apartments in most of these houses up here, so where are we going if we get off the streets? We can't go back in the house because we almost suffocate. So we sit down on the curb, or stand on the sidewalk, or on the steps, things like that, till the wee hours of the morning, especially in the summer when it's too hot to go up.

—ANONYMOUS INTERVIEWEE, IN CLARK, *DARK GHETTO*

Harlem owes its very existence to violence. It grew out of violence. It grew out of the violence of segregation. The formation of the ghetto itself was not a voluntary thing. It was a forced thing. Negroes moved together because they could not live elsewhere.

—JAMES FARMER

Today, white people are eagerly moving back into Central Harlem, an idea that would have been preposterous in the 1960s, when the population was 95 percent Black, nearly three times the proportion it had been in 1920. The hip jazz clubs of the twenties and thirties were long gone, and in the middle of the century, white people went there almost exclusively because work or drug habits required them to. Central Harlem suffered a long decline in population beginning in the 1950s, from which it is still nowhere near recovering, down about ninety thousand residents from its peak of more than 237,000 in 1950. One need not look far to find evidence of racial and economic change there, whether the images of white parents with strollers or the many upscale businesses that have moved in, with a recently built, boutique hotel (itself located diagonally from the NYPD's Twenty-Eighth Precinct) on the same block as the former Hotel Theresa. Proceed east on 125th Street to the next block, and you will find an international fast-fashion retailer and high-end grocery store just feet from where the looting began in July 1964. While Bedford-Stuyvesant may lack the extensive development of Central Harlem, its residential makeup has changed more dramatically. The number of white people living there increased 1,235 percent between 2000 and 2015, while its Black population fell 17 percent during the same time. The neighborhood is now more than one-quarter white, quite a difference from the days when white people could not leave fast enough.[1]

In the twentieth century, both Central Harlem and Bedford-Stuyvesant had been majority-white communities. Through the first decade of the twentieth century, Central Harlem—defined by 110th Street on the south, Third Avenue on the east, the Harlem River to the northeast, and the parks along St. Nicholas, Morningside, and Manhattan Avenues serving as western boundaries—was an upper-middle-class, overwhelmingly white neighborhood with a significant Black population. As a result of housing market problems, racist violence, slum clearance, increasing segregation throughout the city, and growing numbers of Black migrants and immigrants, Harlem's Black population grew quickly and enormously, from 10 percent in 1910 to 70 percent by 1930, peaking at 98 percent in 1950. Bedford-Stuyvesant's population shifted later, still being primarily white in the 1930s but more than two-thirds Black by the end of the 1950s, a trend that continued for decades, topping out at 85 percent Black in 1990, when only 5 percent of the population was white.[2]

While some people lived in these communities by choice, many others lived there because of constrained choices and the forces of structural discrimination and segregation arrayed against them. There were certainly benefits to living in Central Harlem and Bedford-Stuyvesant in these years, whether a more limited experience with face-to-face bigotry or various cultural familiarities some might prefer, from neighbors and churches to restaurants to barbershops and salons. Still, the evils of racism were all around, embodied in many ways—inferior schools; biased policing; higher-priced yet lower-quality merchandise; poverty; worse health outcomes; and, above all, housing. Though residential experiences varied significantly between Central Harlem and Bedford-Stuyvesant, the generally deplorable living conditions remained the same. Overcrowded, crumbling apartments shared with countless rats dominated both communities. Nothing demonstrated segregation and discrimination in New York City more than where people lived—not only were communities highly segregated, but the housing in Black neighborhoods was a constant, unavoidable, physical rendering of what white society thought of African Americans and what it had been able to force them to do.

As disinvested, majority-Black and –Puerto Rican neighborhoods spread throughout the boroughs in the fifties and sixties, the city was vigorously engaging in urban renewal, but not for the benefit of those relegated to places like Central Harlem, Bedford-Stuyvesant, or Brownsville. Slum clearance, as it was alternatively known, was supposed to rid the city of run-down areas and replace them with modern, privately owned and operated housing and commercial space. This process frequently leveled several contiguous blocks at a time, blocks that had been occupied until residents were forced out. These people were some of the most vulnerable in the city, living precarious lives that would only get more stressful and uncertain once caught up in the currents of the city's brand of revitalization. Eventually, their squalid rentals would be replaced with modern residences they would not be able to afford, leaving them on their own to find someplace else.

Throughout the entire process, from living in a substandard dwelling to being pushed out of it, African Americans would find a thoroughly indifferent mayoral administration unwilling to do any more than profess concern. In March 1960, Mayor Robert F. Wagner Jr., a Democrat, received one of his favorite governmental creations—a report. "Building a Better New York," which he had commissioned to analyze housing and urban renewal in the city, informed him that the five boroughs were short 430,000 units of housing, just as they had been in 1950. Also, over the decade, slum housing had predictably slid into worse shape. A year and a half later, the new superagency in charge of housing in the city, the agency the report suggested be created, adjusted these numbers through a technicality in an attempt to show that the mayor's housing programs had actually reduced the housing shortage by 85,000. But in reality, little had changed for the better, despite more than six years of Wagner, who had taken office the first day of 1954. The poor, whose housing urban renewal wiped out, filled up the city's greatly expanding public housing sites, mostly isolated, tenant-dense towers. There was not nearly enough of it, and the city faced an even greater deficit of private residences. Still, Wagner tried to claim victory in the face of a complete standstill. As one of his aides said a few months earlier, "Wagner's first two years in office were his best. He worked and he accomplished more than he ever has since. He set the wheels in motion. It looked good. It was a good beginning—and then that was the end."[3]

New York's Peculiar Approach to Urban Renewal

In 1955, a group of tenements slated for demolition in Central Harlem between Lenox and Fifth Avenues and 132nd and 135th Streets became the focal point for Black New Yorkers' battle against the city's urban renewal practices. The developer Robert Olnick had purchased the buildings and land from the city as part of an urban renewal project in 1952. By 1955, the site, variously known as the Godfrey Nurse Houses, Harlem Estates, and Lenox Terrace, was unchanged. Not only had no demolition or construction taken place, but 1,200 families were still living in the buildings while Olnick, their new landlord, was supposed to be finding them new housing, as required by law. The living conditions, however, were not legal. Residents had to live with falling plaster, walls with no plaster, faulty electrical wiring, leaky plumbing, rat infestations, unsafe gas conditions, holes in walls, and no heat in the winter.[4]

When Mrs. Anna Cox, one of Olnick's tenants, went to court on January 25, 1955, she had been without heat since November. Though she had been complaining every time she paid her twelve-dollar weekly rent, Olnick and his employees ignored Mrs. Cox until she filed a civil complaint in the third week of January. Repairs began as soon as Olnick received the summons and were completed before the scheduled court appearance. Olnick pleaded ignorance, claiming, "I only heard about that complaint Monday," meaning January 24, the day he received the summons.[5]

Mrs. Cox was not alone in her difficult living conditions. Her neighbors had filed hundreds of legitimate complaints with various city agencies. Scores of Olnick's tenants were using kerosene heaters to keep warm, in the absence of functional heat in the buildings. A seventy-year-old woman burned to death in a fire her heater caused. Still, the city's Bureau of Real Estate, tasked with supervising maintenance at urban renewal projects and overseeing landlords' efforts to find tenants new housing, refused to issue summonses to Olnick. The municipal Health Department was not even sending inspectors to investigate complaints. A spokesman explained the agency could not "send one man into those buildings alone because he may run across a vicious dog, or derelicts sleeping in hallways, or badly-lighted halls where he may meet all types of characters.

And we can't send two inspectors in together because we are too short-staffed." Even if the Health Department could find employees to investigate complaints, the spokesman divulged, "Our inspectors have been told not to issue summonses there because the city is involved" with constructing the project.[6]

Olnick denied responsibility altogether, asserting he was "doing everything humanly possible" but that the odds were stacked against him. Explaining one of the dilemmas he faced, he said, "Let me give you an example—there are thirteen families in a building. I relocated nine of them. The building is left with only four families and the vandals rush in. They tear the place apart. I've got fourteen maintenance men working all the time. I'm doing everything I can." Claiming thieves and criminals were responsible for the living conditions, Olnick added, "Don't forget, these buildings were slums before I inherited them." The new landlord portrayed himself as working tirelessly for his tenants against a number of forces out of his control. Though it had been three years since he purchased the property, he maintained, "I'm doing my best to get these people relocated. The sooner I do the sooner this project can begin."[7]

The work he put in was not enough for the tenants or their activist allies. With seemingly no end to the tenants' plight in sight, Harris L. Present, chairman of the City Wide Committee on Housing Relocation Problems, a tenants' rights group, wrote to Mayor Wagner on February 14. Wagner, in office for a year, had been in politics for much of his adult life. The mayor very much attempted to follow in his father's footsteps, endeavoring to govern the city as a progressive reformer.[8] After graduating from Yale and Yale Law, Wagner began his political career as a state assemblyman in 1938 and, after serving in the Army Air Corps for the duration of World War II, returned to politics in 1947. He held the positions of City Tax Commission chairman, Buildings Department commissioner, chairman of the City Planning Commission, and Manhattan borough president and won election to mayor in 1953, a position he held from 1954 through the end of 1965.

For a big-city mayor in the 1950s and early 1960s, Wagner was at the leading edge of progressive. Like his father, he seems to have been genuinely concerned with improving poor and working people's lives. He evinced consistent concern for the many problems Black New Yorkers faced but never succeeded beyond token levels in remediating segregation and its deleterious effects. Wagner adopted a habit of deferring decision making through the use of commissions and panels. Fearful of alienating white voters, the mayor rarely put his civil rights sentiments into action. As a local civil rights leader explained, "You can spend two hours talking to him and come away thinking what a nice man he is. Then, when you get around to figuring out exactly what you've gained, you suddenly realize that he's given you nothing at all."⁹

Present urged the mayor to involve himself with the situation, arguing that the lack of upkeep on Olnick's apartments "has gotten so out of hand" that Olnick's removal from the project may be necessary "so that the tenants remaining on [the] Godfrey Nurse site could at least be living under reasonable conditions." As of the date of Present's letter, the city's Department of Housing and Buildings had filed dozens of complaints against Olnick for the conditions to which he subjected his tenants, resulting in at least forty-four decisions against him. There were twenty-five more pending, as well as many complaints tenants had filed.¹⁰

The Reverend W. Eugene Houston, chairman of the Central Harlem Housing Committee, another tenants' rights group, wrote to Olnick ten days later, on February 24, informing the landlord that the CHHC could "no longer, in good conscience, cooperate with you." As Reverend Houston explained, after working with Olnick for the past two and a half years to resolve the issues at the Godfrey Nurse Houses site, "Our efforts, we feel have been fruitless in the total picture, a situation made all the more galling because we have been obviously misled, and some feel, obviously made dupes of." Recounting a meeting three weeks earlier, Houston said, "You denied knowledge of and even the existence of complaints made by agencies in attendance. . . . As late as February 21 two convictions were handed down against your corporation as a result of tenants' action brought in Magistrate's Court. Various agencies and individuals continually report complaints with regard to lack of heat and other hazardous conditions." Continuing to upbraid Olnick, Houston cited a mutual "understanding that certain legal maneuvers which amount to intimidation would not be again used in your relocation procedures." However, tenants were reporting legal notices from Olnick informing them they had thirty days to move, with "no accompanying interpretation of your responsibility to relocate them." After detailing the extent of his organization's exasperation, the reverend told Olnick, "Consequently we have come to the conclusion that more authoritative action must be taken to resolve the maintenance and relocation problems at the Godfrey Nurse Site."¹¹

The same day, Reverend Houston sent a letter to Mayor Wagner requesting a meeting. The CHHC desired "to discuss with you the terrible conditions, vis. lack of maintenance and relocation problems, on the Godfrey Nurse Site." Houston told the mayor, "For nearly three years we have endeavored to work out the problems through many conferences between the Sponsor [Olnick] and our committee," to no avail, "because of a consistent lack of good faith and the persistent run-a-round we have experienced with the sponsor, Robert C. Olnick." Following its years of efforts, the CHHC was now of the "firm conviction that the present Sponsor should be removed because he has not lived up to the contract calling for maintenance and relocation procedures in accordance with the law." Receiving no response, Houston sent the letter again on March 7. With Wagner refusing to acknowledge Houston, much less intervene, the reverend wrote to the commissioner of the state's Division of Housing on April 18, requesting a hearing on the problems at the Godfrey Nurse Houses. The deputy commissioner, Robert C. Weaver, a former member of Franklin Roosevelt's Black Cabinet, soon-to-be state rent commissioner, and future Department of Housing and Urban Development secretary, responded to Houston, telling him, "While we would welcome any ideas relative to the planning of such a project from organizations such as yours, we are not of the opinion that it is customary to have the type of public hearing which you have proposed." Present, Houston, and their fellow housing activists were finding official avenues of redress quite frustrating.[12]

Olnick's tenants and their allies had little luck in finding elected or appointed officials who would help them directly, and their years of efforts only resulted in marginal, short-term victories. The unwelcome publicity these living conditions drew to municipally overseen urban renewal efforts eventually forced the city to make an example of Olnick. Judges reversed their previous courses of minimal fines and suspended sentences against offending landlords, with various city courts fining Olnick thousands of dollars. In February, a judge offered him the option to avoid a $325 fine by living for sixty days in one of the apartments he controlled. He did not respond.[13] By April, Olnick's actions brought attention to similar conditions at several other renewal projects in Harlem. To stanch the flow of sentiment against his efforts, Robert Moses, the overseer of the city's urban renewal machine, intervened, vowing to "be tough" on Olnick and others who dallied in their legal responsibilities to relocate tenants living in buildings slated for demolition and allowed their facilities to deteriorate so greatly. Aside from the fines and comments from municipal officials that tenants and activists forced, little came from the debacle. As of November 1956, over a year and a half after the powerful Moses pledged discipline for urban renewal landlords, a number of families were still living in the same state at the Godfrey Nurse Houses site. It was business as usual for urban renewal in the city.[14]

While New York State already had a 1938 law on the books permitting slum clearance, a federal law passed a decade later provided the means for New York

City to transform housing.[15] The Housing Act of 1949's Title I provision created a national blueprint for urban renewal. The federal government committed itself to providing municipalities with two-thirds of the costs associated with buying and clearing areas designated as slums. The city and state would pay the rest, then sell off the land to private developers. Congress also renewed and expanded the Federal Housing Act in 1954, making federal money available for a wide variety of other measures, encompassing "conservation, rehabilitation, and comprehensive planning and redevelopment." From 1949 to 1964, New York City received over $265 million of the $4 billion the federal government had released for urban renewal, nearly 7 percent of the total.[16]

The case of Olnick and his tenants could only happen in New York City, with its peculiar approach to urban renewal. Every other city in the country would empty apartment buildings marked for demolition, clear the land, and transfer the lots to developers. Robert Moses, however, was adamant that the sites' new owners receive the buildings not just intact but full of rent-paying tenants. He said it was the only way builders would commit to projects. How developers committed to projects was also odd, as each site usually had only one bidder, done not through a public process but through private meetings with Moses. Razing the buildings and resituating the tenants was then carried out at the new property owners' discretion, effectively creating a class of elite slumlords. With the city's imprimatur and protection, these men and their companies frequently went on collecting rent on decrepit buildings for years before finally getting the clearance underway. Tenants had few choices in alternative accommodations, which made them easy targets for unscrupulous landlords, who could extract month after month of rent from their captive residents and expend virtually no capital in upkeep. Occupants had little power to force repairs on buildings marked for demolition. Developers could get rid of assertive tenants quickly by offering unsuitable apartments in the same building. If anyone being relocated refused any dwelling, regardless of reason, the landlord was legally permitted to evict that person or family.[17]

The city's approach to urban renewal was disastrous for tenants. From 1949 to 1964, the city had christened forty-one Title I projects; by 1964, only three were completed, leaving untold thousands living in condemned buildings for years with nowhere else to go.[18] What did get built was highly segregated. The *New York Amsterdam News* conducted a survey in 1952 that discovered the city had 23,000 private apartments constructed with public money. Black people lived in only twenty-seven of them, twenty of those in one complex.[19] As the 1950s opened, the city was adding 2,500 housing units a year, but in 1953 and 1954, the city lost three thousand apartments a year as landlords began to demolish housing in favor of commercial space, indicative of a trend that would lead to the New York we know today. Urban renewal had displaced 12,000 Manhattan families in 1955, "predominantly among the moderate- and lower-income families, few of whom can pay the monthly rentals of $60 or more per room which are being charged for new developments." Their numbers would rise over the following years.[20] In 1955, the executive director of the New York City Housing Authority accurately predicted the future of Manhattan. He saw it becoming a hub of business and management with only high-rent housing, with poor neighborhoods increasing in the other boroughs.[21]

Urban renewal was also disastrous for the city's finances, money that could have been spent in countless other ways. In 1956, there were ten ongoing Title I projects, including Lenox Terrace. The city had spent nearly 95 million dollars buying up these blighted blocks, reselling them to private developers for just under 25 million dollars. Federal and local taxpayers covered the windfalls to the old slumlords, while the typically impoverished residents of the buildings funded the windfalls to the new slumlords. From 1952, when these projects began, the people in charge of the sites had made what the city's comptroller described as "disappointing" progress four years later. They had relocated about two-thirds of the tenants they took on, 57 percent of commercial tenants, and torn down 44 percent of the buildings. They had only paid half of their 25-million-dollar debt to the city, loans that accrued interest at a rate of only 1.6 percent. In 1957, Title I property owners were behind almost a million dollars in property taxes.[22]

The worst case, as far as plundering was concerned, was Manhattantown, an ambitious project on the Upper West Side that never existed. The city granted approval to the seventeen-building complex in 1951 and spent over sixteen million dollars to acquire the land. It turned over the six blocks to their new owners in 1952, accepting a purchase price of $3.1 million, with just over a million in cash. Within three years, the owners had taken in more than a million dollars through rent and by operating a parking lot on the grounds. A month before the complex was scheduled to be completed, four years after taking ownership, not one building had been started. A year later, in 1957, the developer owed the city $620,000 in back taxes. Wagner had defended Moses, urban renewal, and Manhattantown for years, but continual negative publicity and bad behavior on the developer's part finally led the mayor to concede, "Well, if you want to put it that way—yes, I guess you could say we were conned for five years." The city then arranged for the sale to another developer, for only $1.3 million. The new firm promptly gave consulting jobs to the men who had just sold the property. The company retired the scandal-plagued Manhattantown name and eventually built the luxury rental towers it called Park West Village, with the first residents arriving in 1961.[23]

Private Housing

Olnick's tenants were able to draw attention to their conditions because of their buildings' status as an urban renewal project, but many of their neighbors lived similarly and had no such leverage. In 1964, Central Harlem was the most crowded, run-down, and economically depressed neighborhood in Manhattan. That year, 232,792 people lived within the community's 3.5 square miles. Ninety-five percent of them were Black, and they were 97 percent of all Black people in Manhattan.[24] Their housing was frequently decrepit. Out of the area's 87,369 housing units in 1964, 90 percent of them were in buildings more than thirty-three years old. Forty percent were built before the twentieth century, during the era of "old law" tenements, which meant they still may have had shared bathrooms in the hallway, two per floor of four apartments. Only 10 percent were constructed after 1929. The 1960 U.S. Census listed 11 percent of the community's housing as dilapidated, meaning it "does not provide safe and adequate shelter." An additional 38 percent was classified as deteriorating, meaning it would "need more repair than would be provided in the course of regular maintenance." That left 51 percent of its housing designated "sound," which was far below the figure of 85 percent for the broader city.[25] As the Harlem native and seminal writer James Baldwin told a rent strike rally in 1964, landlords "don't have to repair the houses and the people have to pay the rent."[26]

Because of the many landlords who failed to provide consistent heat, Central Harlem had the highest number of wintertime residential fires and deaths by gas poisoning in the city.[27] Poverty, pestilence, and a lack of access to medical care, among many factors, meant that 5 percent of Harlem's babies died during infancy, versus under 3 percent citywide. People of all ages dealt with much higher incidences of a panoply of diseases—physical, mental, and emotional.[28] For all of this, renters in Central Harlem surrendered 45 percent of their income to the landlord, paying some of the highest rents per square foot in the city, while people in the rest of Manhattan paid an average of 20 percent.[29]

Figure 1.1 "This is home???" Members of NAACP youth and college units inspect a hallway on West 133rd Street in Harlem. This visit was part of their campaign to improve living conditions in Central Harlem. Students found defective plumbing, exposed electrical wires, laths showing through plaster, inadequate heat, poor water pressure and unsuitable fire escapes, all common issues in the area. Taken between 1959 and 1965.

Source: Library of Congress, Prints and Photographs Division, Visual Materials from the NAACP Records, LC-DIG-DS-08058.

Still, Harlem created a history onto which residents could hold. It had a proud, complicated legacy stretching back decades, producing vital components of American culture. Bedford-Stuyvesant had no such past. In the mid-1960s, it was a rootless place, still very much developing, with African Americans moving there in large numbers only in the last two decades. Over that time, Bedford-Stuyvesant had gotten larger, its borders defined by wherever Black people lived contiguously in Central Brooklyn, while the neighborhoods it abutted shrunk.

There was little to identify with the area aside from segregation, poverty, and crime. Jack Newfield, a white journalist who grew up there in the 1950s, described what his old neighborhood was becoming as "the place where people land when they fall out of Harlem; it is where the Wagner Administration used to dump black people after they were uprooted by the urban renewal bulldozer."[30]

Harlem struggled under an immense load of problems, despite its exceptional cadre of leaders and advocates over the years, from A. Philip Randolph, Marcus Garvey, and Queen Mother Audley Moore to Malcolm X, Kenneth Clark, and James Baldwin. But by the 1960s, Harlem no longer attracted leading activists to reside there. A. Philip Randolph would soon leave, and even Malcolm X, minister of the Nation of Islam's Mosque Number 7 at 116th Street and Lenox Avenue, lived in Queens. There were Black politicians, including Assemblyman and Manhattan Borough President Hulan Jack and Congressman Adam Clayton Powell Jr., both representing the area since the 1940s. Bedford-Stuyvesant, in great part because of the burgeoning nature of its growth and being the site of so many displaced people, struggled to develop leadership both at the community and political level. Bertram L. Baker, the first person of African descent to represent Brooklyn at the state level, served the neighborhood for more than two decades and was first elected in 1948. Bedford-Stuyvesant would not get a Black member of Congress until Shirley Chisholm's election over James Farmer in 1968.[31]

Bedford-Stuyvesant offered little to those interested in grassroots activism. Sure, there were mountains of challenges, but the neighborhood had little organizing infrastructure and virtually no traditions of struggle, aside from whatever people brought with them. If the activists and organizations in Harlem working over decades had been unable to secure improvements in their neighborhood, Bedford-Stuyvesant's residents were in a much worse position from which to fight for rights and better lives. This was the neighborhood with the highest infant mortality and lead-poisoning rates in the *nation* in the mid-1960s.[32] It would not be until the early 1960s that a new crop of varied personalities would coalesce as the Brooklyn chapter of the Congress of Racial Equality, quickly transitioning from a militant direct-action organization into a Black Power group within a few years, helping elevate the neighborhood's first homegrown activist of renown, Sonny Carson.[33]

While most Black New Yorkers did not have a great deal of choice as to where they lived, they did not accept their living situations as unchangeable. In 1959, Jesse Gray led fifty or so buildings on 116th Street in a coordinated rent strike for the first time in Harlem's history.[34] Hailing from Louisiana, Gray served in the Merchant Marine, became a member of the National Maritime Union, and made his way to New York City in the 1940s. There he joined the American Labor Party, a worker-centered social democratic political organization. Gray became involved with housing struggles in the 1950s, organizing the Lower Harlem Tenants Council to aid Harlem residents with improving their living conditions and fighting evictions. With a flair for public spectacle, Gray reveled in organizing sensational events, including highlighting the eviction of a wheelchair-bound woman. Tenants emerged from the strike with some concessions, plenty of experience, and the Community Council on Housing, a volunteer group that served tenants who had housing issues but inadequate knowledge of how to address them.[35]

In September 1963, too many people in disinvested neighborhoods were still living in apartments like those of 87 East 111th Street, where the "main hallway smelled of urine. The hallway walls were riddled with gaping holes where rats had chewed through the wood and plaster. Plaster was falling from the hallway ceiling, and the staircase to the second-floor apartments was bent and buckling." Once more, tenants in Harlem began a long-term organized rent strike against their private landlords, with Gray again leading the organizing efforts.[36] The strikes spread throughout Harlem and out into other parts of the city over the next few months, eventually reaching more than two hundred buildings. Activists made ramshackle, captive housing into a major issue over the winter, with numerous pickets; marches; a riotous rent control hearing at City Hall; and Governor Nelson Rockefeller, a Republican, entering the debate when he publicly lambasted Mayor Wagner for allowing any of this to happen in the first place.[37]

After months, the strikes produced municipal reforms and important court cases decided in favor of tenants withholding rent. The effectiveness of the strikes went beyond the participating buildings and reached similarly unscrupulous landlords who made some basic repairs, hoping to ward off such actions from their tenants. The strikes were also successful in that they showed other poor people throughout the city, as well as their counterparts in Cleveland and Chicago, typically regarded as voiceless, that they could find power through sustained, coordinated action. This was Gray's point, as he told Malcolm X's audience at the Audubon Ballroom, in November 1964: "It's always very easy for us to be ready to move and ready to talk and ready to act, but unless we truly get down into the heart of the ghetto and begin to deal with the problem of jobs, schools and the other basic questions, we are going to be unable to deal with any revolutionary perspective, or with any revolution for that matter." Revolution or not, people wanted to live in a decent place, and it was clear that relying on the city to ensure people had that was unworkable. Residents and their allies would have to use the power of mass action.[38]

Rent strike rallies drew hundreds, featuring speakers such as James Baldwin and John Lewis, chairman of the Student Nonviolent Coordinating Committee. Lewis's speech at one public meeting in January 1964 showed that Harlem's issues did not stay local:

> Those of us who live and work in the Deep South have been following the struggle here in Harlem with great interest. This [rent strike movement] represents something very new and meaningful not only to the state of New York but to the whole nation. Some of us have been saying all along that when the masses get moving in Harlem, the masses in the whole nation will move. I think 1964 is the year for us to move and you are moving. At the present time, and I think I am right here, this community is the only community in this nation at the present time that is mobilized and prepared to move.[39]

Lewis's words illuminate the often hard-to-discern national importance that Black New Yorkers' civil rights movement had. Fundamentally a man of the South and a major figure in the national movement, Lewis had his eye on developments in the city before they had garnered much national media attention. His interest in New York predated the July uprisings, the 1966 civilian review board referendum, and the 1968 Ocean Hill–Brownsville school board battle. Lewis shows that many people in the South who had a great deal else about which to worry gave time and thought to different yet related struggles in what was supposed to be another world. This is a testament to the national expanse of the civil rights movement and New York's importance in that web, despite the city's decidedly low visibility in many histories of the movement.

As for Bedford-Stuyvesant, the other site of rebellion, its housing differed from Central Harlem in substantial ways but also maintained many similar characteristics. Earlier in the century, Bedford-Stuyvesant had been a quiet residential area dominated by single-family homes and small multifamily whitestones, with five- or six-floor tenements on main streets.[40] In the 1940s and 1950s, guileful opportunists invaded the neighborhood, greatly accelerating the pace of both neighborhood change and deterioration. Predominantly white speculators would target all-white blocks on which the majority of people owned their homes and employ any variety of fear-inducing tactics, including flooding white homeowners with postcards indicating a buyer was already lined up, spreading rumors of neighbors having already sold their homes to Black people, and paying young Black men to feign street fights.[41] The hope was that enough spectacle and disinformation would lead to paranoia over "losing" the neighborhood, motivating homeowners to sell quickly. The men orchestrating this disarray, euphemistically considered entrepreneurs, would then offer to buy the homes, at a depressed price, all cash.

Many white homeowners worried that if they waited too long, their property values would decline, because of the presence of their new Black neighbors, so they took the offer and unwillingly left their homes. Soon, the block would become segregated in the reverse, moving from all white to mostly or entirely Black. Because African Americans faced profound discrimination in obtaining mortgages and in the real estate market, prospective buyers were plentiful. Almost immediately upon acquiring a home, the speculator would be able to turn it around to a Black purchaser at a profit margin of 50 percent or more and would hold the loan himself, subjecting the buyer to whatever terms and interest rates he chose, unencumbered by the regulations that applied to financial institutions. Missing one mortgage payment could violate the terms of the loan, reverting ownership of the house back to the speculator, who would then sell it again, continuing to reap rewards from his relatively small investment. This was the process of blockbusting—using racialized fears to turn a profit. It worked.

Commercial flight accompanied the previous residents, leaving the people of Bedford-Stuyvesant with even less variety and opportunity than Harlem offered. After years of white people and their money leaving, with poorer people replacing them, most businesses were low-tier services, like luncheonettes, beauty parlors, drycleaners, and shoeshine parlors. The twelve-block subsection of Stuyvesant Heights had one bar or liquor store per block, with a Pratt Institute study finding "a direct relationship between the incidence of derelicts and vagrants and the distance from the liquor stores and bars. The blighting effect of these establishments, both in physical and social terms, is quite evident." These, of course, were not the hip bars one might associate with the Brooklyn of today, and according to residents' comments, they led to problems with public intoxication in almost exclusively residential areas.[42]

As of the 1960s, 90 percent of the housing had been built before the end of the First World War, and fully one-third of it was officially labeled "dilapidated, with inadequate bathroom facilities, wood burning stoves, and a rapidly swelling population of rats and roaches." Twenty percent of that stock, some of the oldest buildings in the city, included shared hallway bathrooms.[43] Shared bathrooms were not uncommon for Black and Puerto Rican tenants in New York, with one-fifth of the former and one-third of the latter living with them in the late 1950s.⁴⁴ Given the combination of apathetic apartment building owners and financially strapped homeowners, the physical environment of Bedford-Stuyvesant deteriorated much faster than it should or otherwise would have. Too many of the Black buyers of the overpriced homes blockbusting initially produced had to carve these homes into "rabbit warrens," or many smaller quarters, which they rented out to afford their inflated mortgage payments.⁴⁵ Other single-family houses contained two or three Black families who moved in together to make ends meet. Sometimes tenants would take in lodgers to make extra money, with some paying for accommodation periods as short as eight hours.⁴⁶

As a result, Bedford-Stuyvesant contained the most overcrowded housing in the city, eclipsing even Central Harlem. Here, you would find a household size of 3.3 people, compared to 2.8 for Brooklyn and 2.7 for the city.⁴⁷ One lifelong Bedford-Stuyvesant resident recalls growing up in the 1950s:

> It was a cold-water flat with a coal stove for heat, and the wind blew right through the place. I used to sleep with my two older brothers in a pull-out couch and, man, I hated to get out of bed. What saved me from freezing was those quilts my mother made. All in all, it was about the same way my friends lived. In the big families, with ten kids, say, they were on relief and the kids would have to go out and steal.⁴⁸

Like Central Harlemites, Black residents of Bedford-Stuyvesant, with no better options available to them, paid very high rents for terrible housing that only continued to fall further into neglect. Also like the people of Harlem, private housing would provide no escape, since of the two hundred thousand units built in Brooklyn between 1946 and 1955, developers allowed only nine hundred nonwhite people to purchase any of it.⁴⁹

Public Housing

Unfortunately, private housing was not alone in its exigencies. New York's public housing in the early-to-mid-1960s was in a catastrophic state. The city had 140,000 public housing units, needing at least 200,000 more.⁵⁰ By 1964, 520,000 New Yorkers lived in public housing, with more than 660,000 on waiting lists.⁵¹ In the preceding years, the city had been building about 3,500 units a year, which means, assuming everything else stayed the same, that its public housing scarcity would be sorted out in seventy-five years. Affordable housing was fundamentally the city's problem, as private enterprise did not build low-cost housing in New York; President Johnson's Housing Act of 1965 pledged funding for a few thousand units annually, but those would take years to arrive.[52]

The City Planning Commission found fewer than 30 percent of 170,000 tenants dislocated through urban renewal were able to gain access to public housing and stated it had no idea what happened to those who did not.[53] The city routinely violated clearance laws, which required it to provide the displaced with new homes, with impunity. Instead, it forced them to find their own places to live, providing them with relocation stipends, which tenants received only if they passively accepted their dislocation and with the threat of revocation hanging over their heads as a stick against resistance. The lack of public housing, coupled with the city's refusal to help ejected tenants find new homes, forced poor Black New Yorkers to do the dirty work of expanding the city's slums by moving into remaining older neighborhoods. Racial tensions increased in tandem as Black and Puerto Rican New Yorkers, both disproportionately displaced groups, moved into older working-class white neighborhoods.

In 1956, 55 percent of all public housing in Manhattan was in Harlem, bolstering urban renewal critics' complaints that the city used its clearance power as a method to remove people of color from integrated areas and place them in already segregated, overcrowded neighborhoods.[54] By 1964, New York City had simultaneously made public housing not just overwhelmingly Black and Puerto Rican but also highly selective. The city revised its list of exclusionary criteria in April, which became known as the "Thirty Hurdles of Public Housing" to those who dealt with it regularly. The list was split into the categories of "Clear and Present Dangers" and "Conditions Indicative of Potential Problems." Applicants possessing qualities from the former group were excluded outright from public housing, while those who demonstrated tendencies consistent with the latter had to submit to a thorough and generally humiliating examination before they could hope to be approved. A number of the hurdles punished people for being poor, such as not having enough furniture, moving often, or not having a steady employment history. Others were morality barriers—single-parent households, couples who cohabitated without being married, or parents who had children out of wedlock. These measures served to eliminate "the vast majority of people who need public housing the most." The final hurdle allowed Housing Authority personnel to reject applicants "for any possible personality problem, as determined by the Authority, and never be told why he has been rejected."⁵⁵ Those who did not qualify were offered no further assistance in finding housing.

Title I projects in Harlem replaced long-established Black communities with monolithic housing projects that warehoused people in an atmosphere inhospitable to social bonding. Many residents of these new housing projects, which were over 90 percent nonwhite, were adrift. Not only did they suffer the daily indignities forced upon them through discrimination and segregation, but when the city took a wrecking ball to their homes, churches, political and social clubs, and shops, they lost many of the institutions and gathering places that would have helped them transition and cope. Their former social networks were often greatly weakened or destroyed, and new ones were hard to build in strange places that offered no sense of community.

Their new residences were not designed with social or economic integration into the local host communities in mind. New York constructed housing projects for the poor on expensive land in already crowded areas. Having spent so much on the land, the municipal government was not willing to put much money into the buildings. The city erected cheaply built high-rise apartment buildings in communities unprepared for such a number of new residents. The businesses and small factories in urban renewal sites had either closed or moved. Most of the people who worked in communities undergoing renewal either no longer had a place to work or had to travel to jobs elsewhere that were often on the lower end of the wage scale.⁵⁶

The city was not living up to the declared vision of federally assisted urban renewal, as decreed through Congress' language in 1949: "the realization as soon as feasible of the goal of a decent home and a suitable living environment for every American family."⁵⁷ Recent scholarship suggests New York's system was "public housing that worked." It worked well for those who were able to gain access to it, but it did not work well for those who needed it the most. It certainly did not work for the many tens of thousands forcibly displaced from their homes so the city could build segregated public housing. The idea of it working is based on the housing authority's solvency and lack of concentrated poverty and crime in massive blocks of towers, stacked to the brim with families relying on public assistance, à la Chicago's Robert Taylor Homes. New York's public housing program was an aberration in that it was not housing for citizens on welfare, like it was in most other major cities. Part of this is because the city never built many large housing projects and also because the city's housing authority was run like a business from the 1940s, as opposed to a charity agency. Public housing in New York was also funded differently than in most other cities, drawing money from the city, state, and federal government, resulting in a much larger budget. Because of the program's ample funding, the maintenance force charged with keeping the buildings in good repair dwarfed those of other cities. Implying that keeping most of those in desperate need of quality housing out of public housing was fundamental to the program's success is an oversimplification. While the New York City Housing Authority may have performed well compared to its peers nationally, it was also clearly a tremendous failure in other arenas. That the city was able to maintain a public housing program much better than others does not mean it is the only way to do so, especially when most other cities all ran their programs the same way.[58]

Conclusion

In 1958, Mayor Wagner told the city he would rid Manhattan's West Side of its slums.[59] The next year, Wagner asserted "there is no longer any excuse for delaying action" on housing conditions in Harlem. He also said that housing was the "number one" problem in the city and revealed his program, which had been "sweated out for months," calling for lower rents, higher fines, and increased inspections.[60] According to the mayor, his administration was "doing more, I believe, than the rest of the country combined" in 1960. The following year saw Wagner waging a "massive attack" on slums, coupled with a six-point program designed to aid and strengthen tenants' rights and power. This was also when he announced "that one of his major goals was to make New York the first big city of the world without slums." Relentless in his fantasy war on slums and armed with new laws that he would not use, in 1962 Wagner swore to run slum landlords out of business. In 1963, he unveiled his "concerted master plan" through which city agencies would cooperate to destroy housing discrimination. But by early 1964, Governor Rockefeller was openly deriding Wagner for standing by while disinvested neighborhoods deteriorated. That same year, the mayor told Congress in 1964 that one in four apartments in the city was in a "deteriorated condition." This was also when the city's Board of Estimate approved Wagner's astonishing new three-year examination "of the whole code-enforcement problem," though he had been in office for ten full years and had been in various positions in the city government since 1947. The same day, the city released a list of 233 buildings that had fifty or more violations pending against their owners.[61] Despite all his committees, declarations, and pledges, housing for the poor and those trapped in the disinvested neighborhoods of New York was demonstrably worse by the time Mayor Wagner exited office in 1965.

It was not as though no one was pushing Wagner to do better. Black New Yorkers had been organizing to claim their rights for two decades by 1964, their achievements profoundly incommensurate with their efforts. Despite living in a state with the earliest and strongest civil rights statutes on the books, Black people in the five boroughs were worse off than they had been twenty years earlier by most measurements. African American neighborhoods typically ranked at the top throughout the city for the highest rents, most street crime, highest unemployment, lowest median income, fewest parks, oldest housing, worst living conditions, cases of tuberculosis, lowest number of licensed teachers, number of remedial classes, high school dropout rates, most overcrowded schools, lack of city services, most inflated prices for the lowest-quality consumer goods, least political representation, and lowest rates of business ownership. In a 1963 interview with Dr. Kenneth Clark, James Baldwin declared, "And people talk about progress, and I look at Harlem which I really know—I know it like I know my hand—and it is much worse there today than it was when I was growing up."[62]

2
Working

> *Negroes are second class citizens because while the Civil War emancipated them from the chains of chattel slavery, it never transformed them into free workers in the labor market or free citizens in public life.*
>
> −A. PHILIP RANDOLPH

> *The masses of Negroes in New York City are more concerned with where they work than where they eat. Jobs are the first issue in the civil rights fight since jobs are the fulcrum upon which progress turns.*
>
> −YOUTH IN THE GHETTO

Better employment opportunities had long drawn people from all over the world to New York City, and this was particularly true of southern African Americans looking to escape racial terror, futureless agricultural production, industrial labor that paid less for a longer day than what could be found in the North, and right-to-work laws keeping unions hobbled. In the middle of the twentieth century, New York had much to offer the unskilled or semiskilled worker: various forms of manufacturing, a large municipal workforce, a vast waterfront, and food and beverage industries, along with higher wages and the potential benefits of collective bargaining.

However, Black workers, whether born in Harlem or Selma, quickly encountered problems at multiple levels in their quests for economic security. There were the frequent encounters with racial discrimination, like employers specifying in job ads that only white people need apply, being denied a job for being Black, or being hired but paid a lower wage. Then there were broader structural issues, such as industries that had long given Black workers a foothold leaving the city or unions institutionalizing discrimination and exclusion, with the city's leaders incapable of taking action or unwilling to do so. In 1964, African American New Yorkers were faring not just worse than their fellow white city dwellers, which one might expect, but also worse than Black workers had ten or even five years earlier, with no improvement in sight.

Black workers who had migrated to the industrial North and West found different opportunities and social realities than those of the South, but not all of what they had hoped for had materialized. While World War II had contributed to a significant and quick rise in African Americans' employment prospects and income, those gains were reversing as the 1950s became the 1960s. This national trend did not except New York City, the Black political and cultural mecca, home to more people of African descent than any other city on the planet. What had been a vital location in establishing and maintaining Franklin Roosevelt's arsenal of democracy during the war was failing to deliver much in the way of opportunities for equal participation in American society to the majority of its Black residents. While they may have enjoyed more freedom from fear than their southern counterparts, the freedom from want was sorely lacking.[3]

Though the nature of work was changing in the 1960s, as it always is, these changes affected Black New Yorkers, and indeed Black people throughout America, much more than their white fellow citizens. Automation, deindustrialization, and the city's economic evolution into a provider of services spared no racial or ethnic group, but white workers were commonly able to advance out of the lower levels of unskilled and semiskilled labor that were most affected. And while manufacturing was on the decline in New York City, all those law, insurance, advertising, accounting, and real estate firms needed office space, much of which would be brand new. In this building boom, unionized construction work tended to be lucrative, especially among the skilled trades, offering some of the best wages and benefits for blue-collar New Yorkers. Like in every other city across the country, the skilled men doing the building were almost all white and making most of the money. They fought hard to keep it that way, using union rules to exclude people of color from their ranks. Black New Yorkers and their allies had fought hard for inclusion in the skilled construction trades, but recalcitrant union locals and national leadership and feckless, indifferent political leadership, from the city to the federal government, made any real advances very difficult. This situation would not change until the 1970s.

The Postwar Black Working Class

World War II was an exceptional time in the history of work in America. With several years in a row of an unemployment rate lower than 2 percent and a dire need for maximum industrial output, American workers, especially African Americans, made substantial gains. Black people left agriculture and sharecropping in the South and headed for better opportunities in northern and western industries, where they rapidly increased their incomes. In many cities during the war years, working-class Black people were able to move out of low-paying, servile occupations, like domestic work, quickly and in large numbers. For example, the Census Bureau found the number of Black women and men in New York working such jobs had declined by about 44 percent each.[4] These gains came slowly and never easily, most notably with A. Philip Randolph's March on Washington Movement forcing FDR to issue Executive Order 8802 in June 1941. The decree barred discrimination based on race, creed, color, or national origin in the federal government or any private company contracting with the federal government and established the temporary Fair Employment Practices Committee to back up the order.

While the end of the war was a joyous occasion for people all over the world, it did have negative economic consequences for working-class Americans. First of all, as the military no longer needed an endless amount of weaponry, aircraft, and supplies, the nation underwent the process of "reconversion," that is, shifting back to a less war-oriented economy. With Germany, Japan, and Italy crushed, war industries in New York quickly began shedding workers. This initiated New York City's transition from a manufacturing hub to becoming the world's first great service city. African Americans felt the effects earliest and suffered the worst. In just one month in the late summer of 1945, nearly 45 percent of African American employees of twenty-five major war plants in the city lost their jobs. Working-class white New Yorkers were losing jobs as well, but their Black colleagues lost them at double the rate, contributing to maintaining the economic disparity between the two groups and reinforcing the idea that skin color was a chief determinant of who deserved what kind of employment and when.[5]

All around the country, Black workers suffered substantial economic regression after the war. Between 1947 and 1949, Black unemployment floated at a level 60 percent above that of white workers, increasing to more than 100 percent greater by 1954, further growing into the early 1960s, reaching a peak of 125 percent in 1962. In the Northeast, Black men had an unemployment rate twice that of white men in 1960, with Black women unemployed at a rate 1.6 times higher.

Though that sounds high—and is—it was about as good as Black people could expect anywhere in the country. Only in the South, where segregationists openly flouted the Constitution, did Black workers, irrespective of gender, have an unemployment rate less than double that of white workers. As great as these differentials were, they were official figures and therefore likely undercounts, with the true unemployment rate for African American women and men about three times higher than that of white workers.[6]

Black workers had, on the whole, always been worse off than white workers. They were paid less, given worse jobs, last hired, and first fired. As those bad jobs got better, cleaner, more automated, and safer, they evolved into white jobs, pushing Black workers out of lines of work that had traditionally been "theirs," like food service. As these jobs acquired a higher status, white workers were more willing to do them, which meant Black workers were facing increasing unemployment or underemployment, since few new job opportunities opened for these displaced African Americans. With automation slashing away at work that had been available to Black people, whether manufacturing or agriculture, and with structural barriers combining with white racial solidarity to keep Black workers out of more skilled jobs, the African American worker was finding an increasingly difficult path after World War II, and white workers pulled away at an ever faster pace. The leverage that working people had during the war, when labor was in short supply, was greatly diminished, meaning that workers in lower-status jobs returned to a situation of difficulty in securing wage gains, while those working in better-paying occupations, with more recognized skills, were winning proportionally larger wage increases, adding to the income gap.[7]

The unskilled jobs most available to African Americans in New York and other northern cities failed to grow along with the increase of the Black population.[8] Black migrants found themselves competing with other Black people, migrant and local, for jobs white people did not want. Northern Black men worked as porters, janitors, and cooks, while white men of the same educational attainment held positions as machinists, managers, foremen, carpenters, and salesmen, with higher pay, potential for promotions, and little real competition from Black workers. Black people *could* do these jobs as well as anyone else, of course, but poor education, barriers to training, and bigoted hiring practices and men on the job successfully worked to keep them out. Clerical workers, truckers, and mechanics were the only men likely to see a substantial racial overlap among their colleagues, though the racial pay differentials were still significant. The segregation and stratification of these jobs, open to men with eighth-grade educations, led to artificially high competition and unemployment for Black workers and little incentive for employers to raise wages for these men, as their supply was plentiful.[9]

The Ignored Postwar Depression

It is then unsurprising that the earnings gap between Black and white workers only grew, beginning as early as 1951.[10] Racial income disparities narrowed massively during the war years, with the average Black worker moving from earning 40 percent of what the average white worker did in 1940 to 60 percent in 1947. However, they were not only unable to hold those gains but watched as the gap began to widen just a few years later.[11] Nationally, Black median income was 53 percent of white median income in 1963, down from 56 percent in the mid-1950s, showing that Black workers were continuing to lose ground even during the time of so many civil rights triumphs, when one might assume economic advancement was progressing as well. Even though the drop was only 3 percent, the fact is that Black income was moving in the wrong direction. During all of the 1950s, in every part of the country, Black men's income fell significantly in comparison to that of white men.[12] Twenty-two states out of the twenty-five, plus the District of Columbia, with one hundred thousand or more African Americans, including New York, saw the racial income gap widen between 1949 and 1959.[13] In New York City in the early 1960s, Black women earned close to what white women did, just 7 percent less, whereas Black men had a far inferior income, only 68 percent of median white male earnings.[14]

Amid America's fantastic economic growth after the war, during which it became the "affluent society," Black workers "experienced the equivalent of a general economic depression."[15] Disparities were such that Herman Miller, head of the Census Bureau's Income Division, testified before the U.S. Senate in 1963 that "the Negro still ranks among the poorest of the poor and that his economic status relative to whites has not improved for nearly 20 years," seeking to dispel the "general impression that the relative economic position of the Negro—particularly with respect to employment opportunities—has improved in recent years." It was true that Black workers had advanced their occupational attainment during that time, at a quicker pace than white workers, but this was mostly the result of migrating to northern and western industrial centers.[16] This migration continued past the wartime boom, with sharecropping rapidly disappearing after 1949, when International Harvester released a mechanical cotton picking machine that did the work of fifty field hands at a cost savings of more than 80 percent.[17]

Between 1947 and 1962, the number of Black families living below the federal poverty threshold decreased only 3 percent; 44 percent of Black families in America lived in poverty in 1962. For white families, those living in poverty had dropped 27 percent during the same period, leaving 17 percent of them below the poverty line of $3,000 a year. Over those fifteen years, the average Black family saw its income more than double, from $1,600 to $3,300. The bad news was that the average white family in 1947 was earning only $100 less than the Black family was in 1962. By then, that white family was bringing in $6,200. As the economist Vivian W. Henderson pointed out in 1967, "People do not spend and save percentages; they spend and save dollars." While large percentage increases in income are always welcomed, white families were increasingly able not just to cover the basics but to move deep into the territory of disposable income, spending on vacations, improvements to the homes they owned, new cars, appliances, and more.[18]

By the numbers, African Americans in New York City seemed to be doing much better than they would if they lived elsewhere. While the city's Black poverty rate was still monstrously high at 27 percent in the early sixties, it was far below the 44 percent national average, and the same was also true of white New Yorkers, 12 percent of whom lived in poverty. Black income was significantly higher in New York than the mean for African Americans elsewhere, averaging $3,811 in 1959. Then, as now, New York was a very expensive place to live, especially for Black people. In an increasingly segregated city, they paid exorbitant rents in captive neighborhoods, and local stores charged higher prices for just about everything. That $500 premium Black New Yorkers earned over the national average did not go very far, if anywhere, and was eaten up by the costs of segregation and poverty. While men like Milton Friedman and Nathan Glazer believed, or at least said they did, that capitalism, democracy, and American ideals would inevitably wipe out such vulgar disparities, Jamestown had been founded in 1607, New York in 1664, the United States in 1776, and slavery abolished just shy of a century before Friedman was writing. That they were no longer in bondage was unlikely to comfort any Black person enduring poverty and the systemic denial of opportunities.[19]

Problems with wages and income were not limited to the lower rungs of the blue-collar workforce. In 1959, an African American college graduate could expect to earn less over their lifetime than a white worker whose education ended at eighth grade.[20] In northern and western states, a Black college graduate would earn 5 percent more throughout life than a white person who only finished elementary school.[21] The white worker who completed high school could expect to earn the same as a Black person with a graduate degree.[22] In fact, as Herman Miller found, "the relative earnings gap between whites and nonwhites increases with educational attainment."[23] These discrepancies became increasingly important during the postwar period, when service industries became the primary employers.[24] It was already clear that white-collar work was the future of the national economy and that unlike manual labor, the well-paying jobs would require higher education. From 1947 to 1963, almost all employment growth, 97 percent, was in white-collar work.[25] As a result of this exclusion from rapidly growing, lucrative occupations, when it came to higher earners in New York, only 4 percent of Black families made more than ten thousand dollars in a year. Four times that number of white families did.[26]

As in every other measure of expansion, the benefits of growth in white-collar jobs were distributed unevenly along racial lines. Nationally, one in six African Americans, or 17 percent, worked in a white-collar role, versus nearly half of white workers.[27] During this same period, the proportion of workers involved in any kind of tangible production, whether mining, manufacturing, construction, or agriculture, fell from 51 percent to 40 percent.[28] New York City saw the same trends. Employment in the service, finance, government, insurance, and real estate sectors would only continue to grow.[29] Opportunities for African Americans to participate in that growth were limited. In 1950, Black New Yorkers were 3.2 percent of retail workers, 0.9 percent of those in banking and finance, and 2.8 percent of the public utilities workforce. Ten years later, those percentages had increased to 7.4, 2.1, and 5.1, respectively. They were still terribly underrepresented, especially in the most lucrative white-collar work.[30]

In Harlem, the story got worse. In the early 1960s, the median neighborhood income was $3,480, about two-thirds of the citywide figure. Half of Harlem families lived on less than four thousand dollars, while 75 percent of all New York families earned more than that. High unemployment certainly contributed to this, with one in seven or eight adult Harlemites out of work. This rate, in the mid-teens, eclipsed the citywide rate of 5 percent in 1960, or one in twenty. For those who did work, 64 percent of men and 74 percent of women in Harlem held unskilled or service jobs, which tended to be near the bottom of the pay scale. For the rest of the city, regardless of race, those respective figures were 38 percent and 37 percent. Just 7 percent of men in Harlem held positions as professionals, managers, technicians, or officials, while 24 percent of men throughout the city could say the same.[31]

Bedford-Stuyvesant occupied a circle even below Harlem's. Men there had a 17.3 percent unemployment rate in the mid-1960s.[32] Residents earned one thousand dollars less per year than the average Brooklyn family, with one-half supporting families on yearly earnings below *three* thousand dollars, less than half of the citywide white median income. They then had to manage the inflated costs of housing, food, and merchandise that came with confinement in segregated communities. Bars, liquor stores, and storefront churches, just as in Central Harlem, were overrepresented in Bedford-Stuyvesant.[33]

Harlem's employment opportunities were limited, and most of its residents had to leave to find work. The bulk of its businesses produced nothing beyond what the community itself consumed. Most businesses were small, with more than half being service-oriented operations in personal care and food. The community had a large department store, which white people unsurprisingly owned, as was true of most of Harlem and its businesses, whether apartment buildings, restaurants, or theaters. One savings and loan was Black owned, with Black proprietors committing to open a bank in the near future. For Harlem's workers, 43 percent of them labored in industries economists anticipated would either stagnate or decline. With all the problems plaguing the Black worker, from underemployment to marginal status, increasing pay disparities, and exclusion from higher-paying fields, the forecasted decline would only make matters worse.[34] Numbers matter, and we can understand quite a bit from them, but as the economist of industrial relations Arthur M. Ross writes, "Statistics seem out of place in discussing a problem with such tremendous moral and ideological dimensions as the Negro's demand for economic citizenship. They cannot convey the despair of a jobless man in his eleventh month of unemployment, or the frustration of a well-educated woman confined to menial tasks, or the demoralization of a teen-ager without career prospects."[35]

These indefinite, quantifiable disparities had profound consequences on Black people and families. Various forms of discrimination forced African Americans to get by on far less than their fellow white Americans, which led to all the attendant problems poor people face—worse health outcomes, little to no savings or wealth, higher stress levels, ruinous debt, a lower sense of self, substance abuse, physical abuse, and unstable living situations—compounded with racial oppression. White people and the financial and governmental entities they built worked hard to keep Black people in segregated neighborhoods for decades, and lower incomes made it difficult to come up with down payments or qualify for mortgages should one overcome the institutional barriers to leaving segregated confinement. In New York City, with its neighborhood schools, poverty and

Blackness were virtually guaranteed to combine in inferior schooling, working to keep the cycle of poverty intact.

African Americans also faced far greater emotional and mental health challenges than white people. As Kenneth Clark described the typical man in Harlem existing at the periphery of the economy, "he has little or no power to change his inferior status, and his entire life is dominated by the reality of his position. Not only does he have a menial job, but he becomes, therefore, a menial person. He sees himself as not quite human and is fixed in this role by his job and his skin."[36] Though people tended to focus on the world through a man's perspective, relegation to a lifetime of menial jobs, regardless of one's abilities, desires, or aspirations, wears people down whatever one's gender. The city planner Martin Meyerson saw indefinite, racialized unemployment as fundamentally different from the generalized unemployment of the Great Depression: "When unemployment gripped people of a wide range of skills and backgrounds, the unemployed probably did not feel the same sense of personal failure as they do when only a selective group is affected."[37]

Whether or not people are aware of the precise figures and percentages, they know that they are not getting ahead. They know that they are not living anything like the lives they see on television or in magazines. They know they are not doing as well as their parents and see that their children are struggling even more than they are. They know finding work is not getting any easier. They know their friends and family members are experiencing the same kinds of frustrations and defeats. It is not that no Black people had broken out of racialized poverty. In 1964, Sammy Davis Jr., Muhammad Ali, Ella Fitzgerald, Sidney Poitier, Harry Belafonte, and Ralph Ellison were all well known. Some of them were even from Harlem. New York City had a few Black politicians throughout the fifties and sixties, including Adam Clayton Powell Jr., Harlem's congressman. But successful Black businesspeople, at least in the legal industries, were rare. The United States presents itself as a land of individualistic opportunity in which each person is free to make her or his success through hard work. Harlem, like so many segregated Black neighborhoods across America, was full of people feeling defeated and frustrated. As James Baldwin, a child of Harlem, raised at 131st Street and Seventh Avenue, explained:

> What I'm trying to get at is that by this time the Negro child has had, effectively, almost all the doors of opportunity slammed in his face, and there are very few things he can do about it. He can more or less accept it with an absolutely inarticulate and dangerous rage inside—all the more dangerous because

it is never expressed. It is precisely those silent people whom white people see every day of their lives—I mean your porter and your maid, who never say anything more than "Yes Sir" and "No, Ma'am." They will tell you it's raining if that is what you want to hear, and they will tell you the sun is shining if *that* is what you want to hear. They really hate you—really hate you because in their eyes (and they're right) you stand between them and life.[38]

The Problem with Industry

In the two decades after the war, New York City gained 122,000 service sector jobs, primarily in finance, law, insurance, and government, but it had hemorrhaged the manufacturing jobs that were central to Black New Yorkers' economic well-being. Between 1954 and 1965, the city lost more than 150,000 manufacturing positions. In early 1965, the New York State Department of Commerce declared that the city had lost 227 manufacturers to other parts of the state since 1960. The city had an overall employment growth rate of 1.6 percent between 1958 and 1963, while the rest of the country averaged 11.1 percent. These problems had been unfolding and worsening for some time, but the municipal government seemed to be continually rediscovering the same problem. The city had killed off anywhere between 18,000 and 50,000 entry-level industrial jobs through its zealous urban renewal. As the chairman of the city's Planning Commission pointed out in 1963, developers had demolished 5.8 million square feet of loft and factory space since 1960.[39]

It was not until 1962 that the Wagner administration created the Department of Commerce and Industrial Development to "foster, retain, attract, and expand business, industry and commerce." Incredibly, the head of the department asserted it "first had to learn the causes of the outflow" before anyone could take action, as though this were some suddenly uncovered crisis. The Department of Commerce and Industrial Development spawned the New York City Industrial Development Corporation in an attempt to persuade new manufacturers to set up shop and old ones to expand with sweet loan deals. Two years later, about ten companies had taken advantage of the financing. The program that was supposed to deliver so much had created or saved two thousand jobs. The city announced four industrial parks to provide modernized facilities for a variety of firms throughout Brooklyn, Queens, and Staten Island, starting in 1959. Only one had even reached the planning stages by 1964. In April of that year, the city hired a Boston-based consulting agency to figure out some way to address industrial flight.[40]

By the time Wagner finished his third and final term at the end of 1965, the city had lost two hundred thousand jobs in twelve years, saving or creating 3,500. Governor Rockefeller demonstrated, through inaction, a similar lack of concern. In the fifties and sixties, the bulk of capital flight was still domestic, with industrialists opening up shop in the emerging New South and Sunbelt. Southern states were quite happy to receive these employers, incentivizing them with generous tax breaks and newly built industrial parks.[41] According to the congressman and soon-to-be mayor John Lindsay, the worst part of the employment decimation "was that it was treated as inevitable. It was not as though a bad policy was being used to fight the loss of economic strength in New York—there was *no* policy." If someone were interested in opening a new business in the city, the process was especially onerous because "there was no single center where a businessman could go for advice on zoning laws, city assistance, the hiring of skilled or unskilled labor, or small-business loans." The Department of Defense announced in May 1964 that it was considering closing the Brooklyn Navy Yard. When it did so later that year, no one in the city government had planned for what to do should those three hundred acres become vacant.[42]

People often overestimate a mayor's power, especially in a large city. Local, state, and federal laws and bureaucracies greatly constrain what is possible for one person to do. Beyond legal limits, the mayor has to navigate various competing bases of power throughout the city and its many agencies. It is not that Wagner could have fixed something so profound as job loss through force of will, signing executive order after executive order, or by making a spectacle of himself by blocking a convoy of trucks leaving a closing factory. He had no power to compel manufacturers and other employers to stay, and the structural issues contributing to deindustrialization and relocation were far larger and more powerful than any one person could handle. But he could have done more than lament what was happening and establish committees and study groups. Over twelve years, his administration did next to nothing. It was not a new problem in 1954, and it was an old problem by 1965.

The Problem with Work

In March 1945, the state of New York passed the Law Against Discrimination, or the Ives-Quinn Law, which prohibited discrimination in private employment based on race, creed, color, or country of origin. To enforce the ban, the bill established the State Commission Against Discrimination, which later became the State Commission for Human Rights. This was the first law of its kind in the country, nearly twenty years before a similar federal measure would be enacted, and the commission would have the largest budget and staff of any such agency in any other state. Authorized to investigate systematic discrimination even in the absence of a complaint, SCAD, and later the SCHR, had teeth and was poised to remediate the rampant racial employment discrimination occurring in the promised land. In 1953, 65 percent of employment agencies in Manhattan were willing to accept job openings that explicitly discriminated on race; 70 percent would do so two years later. Ten years on, the law was not accomplishing what its supporters had hoped. In 1959, the New York State Employment Service recorded applicants' skin color and sorted them as such.[43]

From its inception in July 1945 until the end of 1962, over more than seventeen years, SCAD/SCHR took 7,725 complaints, dismissing 4,198 for lack of jurisdiction or having found no probable cause. It found another 1,620 cases to have no specific cause for the complaint but identified some other discriminatory practices while investigating. Of the 7,725 total complaints workers filed alleging discrimination, only four went the full distance to public hearings, with the state issuing legally binding cease-and-desist orders against the offending employers. All others were settled "through conference, conciliation and persuasion," which was the commission's preferred way of conducting business, according to its general counsel. It certainly had greater powers had it wished to invoke them, especially after its transformation into the SCHR, but time and again it declined to do so.[44]

In 1962 alone, the commission closed 1,392 complaints, finding more than two-thirds showed no evidence of discrimination, a higher proportion than it found in 1950. It found no evidence to substantiate the complaint in another 11 percent of cases, meaning more than 81 percent of all complaints were found to demonstrate no discrimination. One could charitably conclude that the commission was doing its job well, the civil rights movement was triumphing, and white people were becoming less bigoted and more accepting, but none of this explains what was happening. The commission reached agreements with just over two thousand different employers, statewide, over the more than seventeen years between the middle of 1945 and the end of 1962. One could find more than this number of businesses within a single square mile of Manhattan. It was also not making examples of the worst offenders, because only 0.05 percent of cases ever went to a public hearing. Employers were writing plainly discriminatory job ads—and employment agencies were taking them—ten years after the law's implementation. The state's own job service was sorting people by skin color nearly fifteen years after.[45]

Undoubtedly, these thousands of complaints had some effect, and we should not seek to write off the law and those who worked earnestly in the service of combating discrimination. However, like all other remedies that rely on the individual to file a complaint, the law, SCAD, and the SCHR generally waited for someone to be wronged before anyone took action. Then the aggrieved party would have to wait a year and a half to two years for the board to issue a decision.[46] Instead of positive enforcement and checking for compliance, making employers prove they were not discriminating, the state's antidiscrimination mechanism required harm to be done before it took action. This is akin to a police department that does nothing until laws are broken and someone complains. Would we accept law enforcement that as a matter of course drove by a dead body and did nothing because no one called it in? This is exactly what was happening with employment and housing discrimination. When whole industries and trades either entirely or almost entirely exclude groups of people wholesale, something is afoot. Activists, unions, academics, and various government bodies had documented this exclusion beyond any doubt. The victims were clear and many, but the perpetrators remained out of sight and unaccountable. Certainly, what New York was doing about discrimination was better than nothing—and better than any other state—but its approach could not effectively address structural discrimination. Nor was the state interested in doing so.

Finally, in February 1964, nearly two decades after its inception, the SCHR made a landmark ruling in which it moved beyond its piecemeal approach. It found that Local 373 of the United Association of Journeymen and Apprentices of the Plumbing and Pipe Fitting Industry, in Spring Valley, a small but rapidly growing suburb five miles over the New Jersey border and about a thirty-mile drive from Midtown Manhattan, had historically maintained practices to exclude Black men from its membership. A legacy of discrimination was nothing new for unions, especially those in the construction trades. They were generally left alone, with the AFL-CIO occasionally issuing warnings or empty threats. This time, however, a government agency with court-enforceable authority came down on an individual union and ordered it to put one man, Harold Mitchell, at the top of its work referral list.[47]

Mitchell, a Black man, had filed his complaint a year and a half earlier, after a plumbing company that had employed him for a decade fired him when it began a collective bargaining agreement with Local 373. The all-white union demanded the contractor let him go, as it would neither accept nor represent him, regardless of his skills, and the company complied. His former employer was required to pay Mitchell back wages, offer him reemployment, and restore seniority rights for the time since his firing if he returned. As for the union, it had to allow Mitchell to take the journeyman's test at a time of his choosing and score it objectively. In the most significant portion of its ruling, the SCHR ordered the union not just to stop discriminating but to supply the commission with a binding written plan as to what it would do to break its practice of deliberate racial uniformity. Still, the commission did not accept Mitchell's charge that Local 373 had colluded with the contractor to deny him membership.[48]

A few weeks later, the SCHR issued an even stronger ruling, this time against Local 28 of the Sheet Metal Workers Union, in New York City. Instead of addressing a worker's complaint to the commission, the state's attorney general's office requested it investigate allegations of racial discrimination in the selection of apprentices. Until 1946, Local 28's parent union's constitution had held "no Negro could ever become a full member." In 1948, SCAD resolved a complaint against the New York Sheet Metal Workers Union, demanding it eliminate all rules that excluded Black workers. The union complied, though erasing the language did nothing to stop the practice. In 1964, the SCHR found Local 28 had "automatically excluded" Black men over its nearly eight-decade existence and compared the union's selection of apprentices to the practices of medieval guilds. This time, the SCHR demanded, in its words, "affirmative action," instead of more empty promises, and gave Local 28 two months to get rid of its list of nine hundred apprentices, all white, and start over again, this time under the commission's supervision. The union also had to cease requiring that current members sponsor and vouch for new applicants, which was a sure and easy way to perpetuate a monoracial organization. Local 28 denied everything, despite never having had a Black member. Civil rights organizations hailed the decision as finally recognizing the severity of the crisis. The New York City Urban League and the national NAACP demanded the city and state cancel all contracts involving Local 28, but Wagner and Rockefeller ignored them.[49]

The best explanation for why the SCHR, after nearly twenty years, finally took on systemic discrimination, in the construction unions in particular, is the power of protest. In 1963, activists and would-be workers staged militant demonstrations for access to union construction jobs at public works sites in Philadelphia, Harlem, and the Flatbush section of Brooklyn. In May, protests at a school construction site in Philadelphia site drew hundreds. After the demonstrations degenerated into violence, local unions agreed to admit two Black electricians, a Black plumber, and a Black steamfitter. This was token integration, intended for show.[50] The next month, protestors picketed an annex under construction at Harlem Hospital, 135th Street and Lenox Avenue. After a few days of marching, which seemed ineffective, they began civil disobedience in groups, blocking entrances for both workers and vehicles. One group would be arrested, with another waiting to replace it, keeping the campaign alive, raising the stakes and intensifying the pressure. The police presence eventually grew to hundreds of officers. When more violence broke out, the city shut down construction indefinitely out of concerns for "public safety." The administration hoped that with enough time, the issue would fade, as was the Wagner way.[51]

Finally, in July hundreds of demonstrators deliberately had themselves arrested at the site of the new State University of New York's Downstate Medical Center in Flatbush, using nonviolent civil disobedience to press local and state politicians to do something proactive about racial exclusion in the building trades. After weeks of protest and resistance, Governor Rockefeller made a few conciliatory gestures and empty promises that led to no jobs for Black people or Puerto Ricans but did stop the spectacle of respectable citizens and ministers demonstrating in the streets and disrupting construction, blocking and chaining themselves to equipment. After all, such sights were supposed to be southern matters, and northern politicians were quite determined to keep things that way.[52]

When decades of negotiations, backroom deals, and individual remedies seemed to make little, if any, perceptible progress, people decided to increase the pressure. Activists were determined to secure economic opportunities for African American New Yorkers and to knock down discriminatory practices and structures. They needed to draw an unavoidable spotlight on their plight to show the city, and perhaps even the entire country, what was going on in the apparently racially tolerant North. Such tasks were certainly uphill climbs, even if economic justice advocates could capture the nation's sympathy. But before that, they, along with their allies throughout the United States, would have to convince white Americans that structural bias existed and that racial discrimination was prevalent, powerful, and harmful. This was a tough sell to many white New Yorkers, especially those who viewed themselves and their ancestors as having overcome great obstacles as unwelcome immigrants in past decades. Some believed African Americans faced little to no discrimination, instead needing "to undertake the generational processes of economic and educational self-improvement and were in fact doing so."[53] Would civil rights activists be able to combat this way of thinking and show that opportunity did not await all?

3
Union Work

Labor unions were essential to the quick and improbable increase in working-class Americans' quality of life in the 1950s. Only twenty years earlier, the country had been on the brink of ruin, with shantytowns common throughout urban America and interminable breadlines just about wherever people lived in large numbers. Unemployment rates fluctuated between the teens and twenties for the whole decade and were much higher in cities—and as high as 50 percent for Black workers. To think that working-class families would soon own homes, fill them with technological marvels and fine furnishings, buy new cars, and send their children to college would have been ridiculous, a pointless fantasy. But in the 1930s, the Roosevelt administration provided organized labor with moral support and a raft of new laws that finally legitimated organizations that had struggled against capital for decades, establishing a new, elevated foundation on which the labor movement could stand. By 1955, unions represented one-third of all American workers, a movement seventeen million strong. These were incredible advances, but they largely and deliberately kept Black workers at the periphery.[1]

Without question, Black participation in the labor movement had grown enormously since the Depression. In 1935, President Roosevelt signed the National Labor Relations Act, commonly known as the Wagner Act, for Senator Robert F. Wagner of New York, its sponsor. The landmark law guaranteed workers in many industries the right to form unions and bargain collectively; it also included provisions that allowed for unions to discriminate based on race. People understood in 1935 that unions, especially those for skilled craft workers, excluded Black workers and that many types of work had yet to benefit from organization of any kind. Civil rights activists pushed Congress to make the bill more comprehensive, but instead, like the Social Security Act a month later, the NLRA excluded agricultural and domestic workers, fields in which two-thirds of all Black workers labored. For decades thereafter, the National Labor Relations Board, the agency established to enforce the NLRA, not only conferred federal approval onto racially exclusive unions but also refused to do anything about them when Black workers filed complaints. Despite this intentional lack of inclusion and the unwillingness of federal authorities to do much about it, Black workers pushed on. With the help of war employment, relentless activism, and northern migration, the African American working class made significant strides in organizing, rising from 1 percent of union membership in 1935 to about 20 percent twenty years later.[2]

In no place in twentieth-century America did organized labor have more power than in New York City. From 1954 to 1965, Mayor Wagner carried on the family tradition his father began, delivering for organized labor and its constituents time and again. With Wagner in City Hall, as Joshua Freeman writes, the working classes "pushed the city toward a model as close to European social democracy as the country had seen." The mayor, working with labor and sometimes with Rockefeller, presided over a number of transformative and innovative programs, such as public housing for the middle class, health care, and expanded help for poor New Yorkers.[3] In one of his first actions for labor, Wagner issued an executive order in 1954 that began the multiyear process of granting public employees the right to unionize, as he had promised while campaigning. In 1958, he signed another executive order, colloquially known as the Little Wagner Act, which permitted unions to enter into collective bargaining with the city, and so they did. Wagner enjoyed enormous popularity and seemed unstoppable, thanks to his expanded and politically active base. New York's example as one of the first cities to allow public-sector unionization was quite powerful; four years later, John F. Kennedy would do the same for federal workers.[4]

The AFL-CIO and Race

On paper, and depending on who was speaking, the AFL-CIO was a solidly progressive institution. However, there was an enormous disjuncture between what the national leadership wrote and advocated and what its member unions and locals practiced. Organizers formed the CIO as a renegade faction of the

AFL in the 1930s, dissatisfied with its approach to organizing. The AFL, dating to 1886, cultivated craft unionism, in which workers of a particular skill, such as cigar makers, plumbers, printers, and butchers, organized unions that represented only their niche in a field. The CIO advocated industrial unionism, establishing organizations such as the United Automobile Workers and United Steelworkers, making no distinctions among skill. Though craft unions dominated numerically and in terms of power, the AFL contained a few industrial unions long before the CIO emerged, such as International Union of United Brewery, Flour, Cereal, Soft Drink, and Distillery Workers of America, the United Mine Workers of America, and the ILGWU, and became more accepting of them over time. In 1955, after a few years of negotiating, as well as the CIO driving out nearly a dozen leftist unions, which made it more closely resemble the AFL politically, the two federations' leaders, Walter Reuther of the CIO and George Meany of the AFL, finalized a merger. Reasoning that labor organizing would be more successful with a superfederation and that the two organizations had more that united than divided them, they created the AFL-CIO, with Meany unanimously elected its first president, a role he would hold and relish until 1979.

Drafted at its founding convention, the new AFL-CIO constitution included strong civil rights provisions within the federation and advocacy for progressive civil rights legislation at the federal level. Its Committee on Civil Rights would work to deliver on the constitution's vow "to bring about at the earliest possible date the effective implementation of the principle stated in this constitution of non-discrimination," with help from another new body, the Department of Civil Rights. Convention delegates wrote and approved motions to create an in-house apparatus to adjudicate allegations of racial discrimination and to include antidiscrimination clauses by default in all future collective bargaining agreements. The convention also produced several resolutions pressing the federal government to enact stronger racial justice measures, including outlawing the poll tax, passing antilynching legislation, and creating a permanent Fair Employment Practices Committee: the wartime one had expired in 1946, and conservatives in Congress refused to renew it. All three ideas were old, having failed when President Truman pushed for them in 1948. It would be another decade before the Equal Employment Opportunity Commission would supplant the FEPC and federal courts would knock down the poll tax. There has yet to be antilynching legislation at the national level, a disgrace for which the U.S. Senate apologized in 2005.[5]

The new AFL-CIO had an official, progressive agenda that was determined to remove racial discrimination from its ranks. In reality, there were serious differences in racial attitudes that separated the leadership of the two organizations. The CIO's industrial unionism was, by necessity, inclusive. If it were to successfully organize the auto industry, it would need the Black workers, not just the white majority. Those Black workers, because of discrimination and lack of access to the same kinds of training and educational programs as white workers, were often relegated to dirty, dangerous work that paid little, like the lower ranks of production or sweeping floors. The CIO accepted them but did not do nearly enough to change their status. The AFL, with its craft union approach, would either outright exclude African Americans altogether or push them into segregated locals.

As for their leaders, Reuther was much more enthusiastic about social justice than Meany, telling the 1955 founding convention, "I believe that this labor movement of ours will make a great contribution in the field of civil liberties and civil rights." Reuther came from a CIO that encouraged its members to join the NAACP in the 1940s, at a time well before very many white people concerned themselves with basic matters of Black civil rights. It pushed the NLRB to deny recognition to locals that rejected or segregated Black workers. Meany expressed concern over racism but was not terribly interested in doing much within his own organization, instead condemning employers. As A. Philip Randolph would describe him, Meany had done "some creditable things against the evil of Jim Crow. . . . Our only complaint is that he hasn't done enough and has taken too long to do what he has done." The most visible manifestation of these divides came in August 1963, when Reuther was a high-profile participant in the March on Washington, which the AFL-CIO refused to endorse. Though Randolph, one of the federation's vice presidents, was the chairman of the march, Meany pushed most of the executive council, save for Randolph and Reuther, to vote against supporting the event. Apparently, a majority of the federation's leadership feared violence at the march, which they worried would taint their organization. Instead, it released a statement supporting the demonstration's goals, which Reuther characterized as "so anemic that you'd have to give it a blood transfusion to keep it alive on its way to the mimeograph machine."[6]

But one did not have to wait until 1963 to see the AFL-CIO's problems in addressing racism and discrimination. James B. Carey, president of the previously CIO-affiliated International Union of Electrical, Radio and Machine Workers, served as the chairman of the organization's Committee on Civil Rights. An Irish-American from Philadelphia, Carey was determined to advance civil rights both in and out of the federation. Under his watch, several unions made at least some progress, however slowly, including admitting their first

African American members, forcing southern employers to accept antidiscrimination language in hiring contracts, and making a rail workers' union eliminate its written policy limiting membership to white men. Carey believed he had the tools and abilities to accomplish more, but Meany and loyal officials prevented him from doing what was necessary to move against discrimination. Two years after the AFL-CIO's founding, Carey resigned in frustration as chairman of the CCR. The bulk of the federation's leadership wanted to promote an image and reputation of racial consciousness and inclusivity but steadfastly refused to take decisive action within their own organizations and restrained those who wanted to do more.[7]

While Meany's leadership was less than exemplary on racial issues, member unions and locals were often far worse. This was certainly true in the skilled building trades. In 1961, a National Urban League official told Congress that licensed Black journeyman plumbers and electricians numbered fewer than three hundred each, total, in the country.[8] Six years after the AFL-CIO declared its dedication to eliminating racial exclusion, the unions representing electricians and plumbers had a racial makeup one might think was from the Gilded Age. This was a fundamental feature of construction unions and locals, and the excuses the federation deployed to shirk responsibility, like lack of interest and/or ability among workers of color or vestigial prejudice at the local level, were flimsy. While these unions had all eliminated racial restrictions from their constitutions by the early sixties, nearly impenetrable structural barriers to entry remained.

Construction unions totally controlled the process by which they admitted journeymen, those who had successfully completed their training as apprentices and were judged to be competent, independent artisans, with familial bonds typically the best measure of merit. Deliberately limiting supply of a given trade makes plain economic sense, as an abundance of workers would depress wages. Scarcity also benefited those in the skilled trades, as it softened the impact that the peaks and troughs of construction activity have on those doing the constructing. While unions were quite powerful in the middle of the twentieth century, they were still relying upon developers to generate projects and partner contractors to employ their members. In the leaner times that inevitably came with economic downturns, austerity was more bearable across the few than the many, hopefully leading to cut hours instead of cut workers.

Only a select few had access to this protection, and most of them were union members' male relatives. The current tradesman would introduce the young man to his colleagues at the union hall, and as long as the candidate were not incompetent, he could count on receiving the apprenticeship. Once admitted, he would train for three or four years alongside journeymen and take classes at night, earning a decent wage all the while. Unions did not deny that nepotism was the primary way into membership; in fact, they cited it as the best method to recruit qualified candidates, as those who had grown up around a particular line of work already understood its culture, norms, and risks, even if they did not know how actually to do it. The outcome of this practice was the continuation of racial homogeneity.[9]

While being someone's relative was not the only way into a skilled construction union, the other methods also offered locals robust barriers to exclude undesirables. They would recruit from high schools, working with guidance counselors, who commonly steered African American and Puerto Rican students away from skilled trades, believing them to be poor fits. Locals might also advertise apprenticeships in newspapers, but not those that served communities of color. But even if a young man of color were to apply, unions had more barriers.

Much like the literacy tests that kept Black southerners off voting rolls for decades, construction unions' admission criteria were ultimately arbitrary. There were supposedly objective standards, such as a high school diploma, a written exam, and prior experience, but the Joint Apprenticeship Committee responsible for judging applicants, composed of union members and contractors, could decide to waive the diploma requirement, which it would do for white applicants. Or it could disqualify those who had been arrested, even if not convicted, which would be a more common characteristic for applicants of color, not because they were more prone to criminal activity but because racially biased policing is not a new story. Following a successful written exam, applicants then underwent an oral interview, which is easy to make subjective and therefore difficult to pass, should the examiner or committee desire it to be so. Without satisfying every challenge, the applicant could be dismissed.[10]

Construction unions did not need color barriers in their constitutions; the entrance process was effective enough at keeping out men of color. A local could admit a few token men to give the appearance of inclusion and fairness and disarm critics. While one could slough off discrimination as the unfortunate choices of bigoted individuals, as union officials so often did, the fact is that when many individuals, regardless of their personal beliefs, make and repeat the same decisions over time, these decisions transcend individual choice. Collective, embedded choices become ways of doing business and the very definition of structural: developed, maintained, and enduring. George Meany could claim that a local had taken every African American and Puerto Rican who had applied and peddle excuses about lack of interest and ability, but the reality was that construction unions had built up a formidable scheme of exclusion that projected a façade of objectivity and merit.

No one really believed that the unions were acting fairly, but for decades, those who mattered were willing to go along with the performance. As long as the key players did not breach the fourth wall, the pantomime could continue. State antidiscrimination bodies were highly reluctant to act in the face of historical patterns of crude bigotry. The federal government expressed some concern, but before the mid-1960s, taking action would mostly be contained to a few bureaucracies, which would wait for harm to be done first before responding. The National Labor Relations Board had been around since 1935, tasked with enforcing aspects of labor law concerning collective bargaining and unfair labor practices. It could have recognized the damaging effects of systematic exclusion and used various means to coerce unions to be more inclusive, but instead it protected all-white unions and segregated locals until 1962, taking several years more to begin addressing discrimination head-on. The Department of Labor was biased in favor of organized labor and so generally reluctant to deploy what powers it had at its disposal to rectify discrimination. At long last, Title VII of the Civil Rights Act of 1964 generally banned discrimination in private employment and in labor unions, but it would not take effect for another thirteen months after Lyndon Johnson signed the bill in July.[11]

The Problem with Union Work

The city's most powerful unions deliberately marginalized African American and Puerto Rican New Yorkers. While benefiting from municipal unionization, these workers tended to be concentrated in the lowest ranks of city employees, largely excluded from the best jobs, like policing and firefighting, with each profession having its own union. In the city's shrinking but robust textile industry, the International Ladies' Garment Workers Union represented the many thousands of workers in the industry who had organized across specialties, uniting women and men with varying skill sets into one larger union composed of numerous locals. It did not exclude Black workers, but it did engage in practices that created many predominantly segregated locals, keeping them from enjoying the same privileges and potential for upward mobility, both in life and within the union's structure, that their white fellow members enjoyed. While the ILGWU's membership was 40 percent Black and Puerto Rican in the early sixties, its leadership looked and acted as though time had stood still since the union's founding in 1900, when the workers it represented were mostly Italian and Jewish.[12]

In 1947, the ILGWU settled a case with New York's State Commission Against Discrimination, promising to stop excluding African Americans and Puerto Ricans from its all-Italian locals, but nearly twenty years later, two such locals still existed, and they dominated some of the best-paying jobs in the industry. Its members of color typically worked in low-wage work, regarded as unskilled and offering little chance of advancement, pushing carts of clothing through the streets or laboring as shipping clerks in a segregated local. Their local, 60-A, effectively a subsidiary of the mostly white Waist and Dress Pressers Local 60, never received a charter from the ILGWU, despite 60-A having twice the membership and doing completely different jobs than the Pressers. Not having a charter meant that its members were under the authority of the white manager of Local 60, someone who was unlikely to have much concern with representing 60-A's interests. Local 10, the cutters' local, excluded workers of color from its skilled union by denying Black and Puerto Rican workers the ability to enter training programs necessary for admission.[13]

The stories of Locals 60-A and 10 are microillustrations of a macro problem. The ILGWU did not have a single Black officer at the international level, on its twenty-three person General Executive Board, or serving as a vice president. Not one African American or Puerto Rican headed a local. In years when other unions gave heavily to civil rights causes, the ILGWU instead carried on its philanthropic endeavors to the Jewish and Italian causes leadership preferred, ignoring its many members of color.[14]

During an unprecedented building boom and a time of industrial and capital flight, construction unions controlled access to the best blue-collar jobs in New York City, and African American and Puerto Rican workers were all but excluded. In the 1950s and 1960s, these unionized tradesmen built almost two million square feet of office space.[15] It is not that no men of color worked in construction or joined construction unions. They did, but they were almost singularly relegated to types of work that had virtually no room for advancement, like moving materials or various landscaping activities. If organized, these men would typically be in the International Hod Carriers and Building Laborers Union, named for the three-sided half-cube on a stick that they used to carry loads of bricks around job sites. Although the jobs did not require many skills, they were hard and often dangerous. Men would be paid decent wages but were essentially disposable, having to hustle for work constantly. Those employed in the skilled trades had the key advantages of structural support networks and hiring agreements with companies to keep bringing them back, as opposed to seeking out work at the hiring hall. Men classified as laborers may very well have had any number of skills, but if the particular union for your skill refuses to recognize and certify it, then you are effectively unskilled.[16]

In the early 1960s, the city had over 182,000 union members in 121 construction locals. White people were more than 167,000 of those members, meaning that men of color were just 8 percent of that total, at a time when the city was nearly one-quarter African American and Puerto Rican. Almost a third of them were in one union, the various carpenters' and joiners' locals, with bricklayers', masons', and plasterers' locals providing home to many others. Not coincidentally, these were also the trades suffering the highest unemployment. Other unions, like Local 28 of the Sheet Metal Workers Union, with a 3,300-strong membership, had no men of color. Locals 1 and 2 of the plumbers' union had more than seven thousand men in their ranks, twenty-five of them Black.[17]

Given the prominence, connections, and political power that the city's construction unions enjoyed, these matters of discrimination were well known. In 1963, Mayor Wagner appeared to have a moment of recognition, conceding, "Whatever we have been doing in the field of human rights until today is not enough for tomorrow." His labor commissioner, James J. McFadden, directly pressed the matter with the heads of two dozen construction unions, telling them, "Statistic after statistic clearly indicates that right here in New York City many of our Negro and Puerto Rican workers are making little true progress in the vital fields of wages and employment."[18] This was the same year, according to the writer Louis Lomax, that Lyndon Johnson had clandestinely traveled to the city in the summer to meet with representatives of construction unions. Johnson, vice president at the time, was renowned for his persuasive abilities. He met with the union men over several days and unleashed "the treatment" on them, employing his distinct combination of intimidation, flattery, empathy, threats, and pleading to achieve his goals. This man, who would soon do much to convince Congress to back both the Civil Rights Act of 1964 and the Voting Rights Act, was unable to persuade the union representatives to take any action toward inclusion. "I failed," Lomax quoted him as saying. "Nobody can move these people. They simply don't mean to do it."[19] The ardent proponent of union desegregation and long-time NAACP official Herbert Hill described the city's construction union leadership as "undoubtedly the most backward, bigoted, and odious trade union leadership to be found anywhere in the world." That was in 1949, but it could have been in 1959 or 1964.[20]

Fighting Integration

On April 30, 1964, forty-one white union men with Local 2 of the United Association of Plumbers and Pipefitters refused to work on the massive Hunts Point Terminal Market construction project in the Bronx, a 126-acre produce market. That day, three Puerto Rican men and an African American man also showed up for work, but they were not yet members of the union. The plumbing contractor for the job, holding a $1.41 million contract from the city, had brought in the four men of color as per an agreement with the City Commission on Human Rights, the municipal interracial committee charged with addressing discrimination in housing and employment, to try to give more men of color access to construction work. The white union workers stated they would not work on any site with nonunion laborers and argued they had a right to refuse to work altogether. However, both federal law and the union's collective bargaining agreement permitted a contractor to hire qualified workers who did not belong to the union as long as they joined within thirty days, a situation known as the union shop. Local 2, however, was attempting to establish as close to a closed shop as possible, meaning employers could only hire those already belonging to unions, though this practice had been outlawed since the federal Taft-Hartley Act of 1947. In its legal agreements with contractors, Local 2 set out terms of hiring that prioritized years of experience but then included a clause that put members of the local at the top of the list "without regard to prior length of service."[21]

The CCHR and civil rights groups asserted that the men's refusal to work was based in racial prejudice and had nothing to do with labor standards. The union, with sixteen Black members out of 4,100, and the plumbers at the worksite, who verbally assaulted the nonunion men with a variety of racial slurs, all denied race played any part in the controversy. They stated the plumbing contractor had "broken a traditional agreement on hiring practices by taking on nonunion men." One of the white plumbers argued he was not racist, as he had "fought in World War II with Negroes." However, he did not like the idea that the state, under pressure from civil rights groups, was pushing unions to do targeted hiring of racial minorities. He saw civil rights advances to be "getting to the point that if I'm eating steak and someone else is eating chicken, he's got to come into my house and eat steak."[22] Another white union plumber, demonstrating the strict control construction unions exercised over employment, had no problem telling a reporter: "If they [nonunion plumbers] were blond and blue-eyed, we still wouldn't work with them. In fact, if they were whites, they probably would get their heads busted."[23]

The CCHR held a meeting on May 4 in an attempt to reach a settlement, after it became clear the white plumbers would continue in their refusal to work. The commission's chairman, Stanley Lowell, a Harvard-educated Jewish civil rights lawyer with a decade of municipal service experience, met behind closed doors with the plumbing contractor and the president of Local 2, Jack Cohen. One of the union officials present shouted, "You continue in this practice and you will be known as a union-busting committee, not a human relations committee!" After nearly four hours of yelling and "repeated table-banging," a dejected Lowell told the press, "I am not optimistic. I had no success." The contractor concurred, shaking his head in defeat. Cohen, clearly agitated, distributed a prepared written statement declaring the union's history of opposing racial discrimination in employment and, saying nothing, left with his entourage of ten aides.[24]

The plumbers and their union were acting strategically: if they continued to refuse to work on the $25 million project, all other construction would have to stop within a matter of days. While carpenters and electricians had been able to work through the dispute, what they could accomplish was quickly coming to an end. Of the twelve 550-foot-by-150-foot buildings comprising the market, only one had complete plumbing. Without plumbing in place, it was impossible to pour concrete for the foundations, and with no foundations, no further work could be done. The contractor was not going to fire the white union plumbers, as he had a contract to employ them, and the union alleged the company was already breaking it by attempting to force it to accept the four men of color as members. Contractors in the city relied upon unions to provide labor, with one anonymously bemoaning, "I've got to go out of business if I incur the enmity of the unions." Local 2 understood the power it was wielding.[25]

The conflict soon drew in a number of local organizations and figures, including the Congress of Racial Equality, the Urban League, Mayor Wagner, and District Attorney Frank Hogan. Wagner convened a number of meetings with various parties in the conflict, repeatedly trying to broker deals behind the scenes, a preferred strategy. Hogan, at the request of the Congress of Racial Equality, opened an investigation into whether the union was violating state antidiscrimination laws. The Urban League filed charges against Local 2 with the National Labor Relations Board.[26]

After the plumbers had stayed off the job for seven workdays, President Lyndon Johnson intervened. On May 8, he instructed Secretary of Labor W. Willard Wirtz to "see what could be done" to resolve the dispute as soon as possible. Wirtz had some experience in desegregating organized labor. Less than a year earlier, in June, he floated a proposal in which the Department of Labor would go through lists of apprenticeship candidates unions had submitted to the Bureau of Apprenticeship and Training, a federal agency established in the 1930s to connect aspiring tradespeople with appropriate unions. Should those lists reflect a plain disparity between Black and white registrants, the union in question would have to admit more Black workers or be removed from participation in the BAT. Both unions and employers responded negatively, so Wirtz caved to pressure and removed the Department of Labor's analysis of aspiring apprentices. Instead, racial disparities could continue, but unions would just have to show that their acceptance processes were fair. In the city, Local 3 of the International Brotherhood of Electrical Workers, under the progressive leadership of Harry Van Arsdale Jr., admitted three hundred Black and Puerto Rican apprentices in 1963. The Sheet Metal Workers, unsurprisingly, fought Wirtz and the Department of Labor in court for years.[27]

How did this otherwise ordinary local issue gain national prominence in such a short amount of time? In another time and place, it may not have. Construction unions engaging in discriminatory behavior was news to no one, including previous presidential administrations. Even President Eisenhower had attempted to force construction firms contracted with the federal government to hire qualified racial minorities. Members of the Kennedy administration recognized the racial near-exclusivity building trades unions practiced as "an extremely bad situation." Activists, workers, and members of various antidiscrimination agencies had been saying as much for quite some time. The strike at Hunts Point Terminal Market, while pocked with hateful language, was tame. It had none of the mass arrests or bursts of violence other job sites in the past year had seen. Just two weeks earlier, members of various CORE chapters from around the city attempted a "stall-in" to block roadways and subways to the opening of the World's Fair, protesting, among other things, that the construction crews who had built the fair's facilities were almost all white. While it was a sensational story, it led to no positive response from anyone in power. However, with Local 2, Johnson had a few primary concerns that motivated him to act.[28]

The 1964 election was six months away and would have been at the forefront of Johnson's mind. He needed both labor and civil rights out at the polls in full force on November 3. Should Local 2's refusal to work drag on, it would be yet another loss for Black workers, which could depress enthusiasm and voter turnout, however slightly and locally. If he were to broker a skillful win, as he had so many times during his congressional career, his campaign and surrogates could present that as a victory to voters concerned with civil rights and Black advancement without doing too much damage to the organized labor vote, as it would be a one-off event involving no new laws or rules.

Johnson's desire to eclipse his political idol, Franklin Roosevelt, as the greatest reforming president loomed large and was a second significant motivator. He had been working furiously for months to get the votes together to see the Civil Rights Act through Congress, a process Kennedy had begun. Organized labor was a key ally in this task, with its lobbyists working overtime on Capitol Hill, at least partially to ensure the inclusion of union-friendly fair employment practices in the act. In taking up this Hunts Point issue while continuing the long-term work of the Civil Rights Act, the president needed to avoid alienating unionized workers and their leaders in his handling of exclusionary unions, setting himself up for a nearly impossible task.

In fact, Johnson did not have much power to make Local 2 do anything differently, outside of the bully pulpit. While the AFL-CIO's national leadership spoke out against racism, segregation, and discrimination to various degrees, unions are often structured as democratic organizations with varying degrees of decentralization that can prevent parent organizations from exercising a great deal of control over their constituents. Federation officials had moral authority, respect, and a highly visible stage but not much power to wield against member unions that disobeyed them. Even at the local level, disciplining or expelling individuals, much less entire locals, is challenging, because labor law compels unions to represent everyone within equally, regardless of how an individual's behavior or words may damage the union or go against its interests. So however hard Johnson pressed the AFL-CIO to do something about Local 2, aside from browbeating and pleading, there really was not very much the federation's officials could do, either.[29]

Back on Capitol Hill, organized labor advocates were lobbying alongside the National Association for the Advancement of Colored People and national CORE officials. However, the relationship between labor and civil rights was complex. For example, Walter Reuther was a white, fairly reliable civil rights ally. He spoke at the 1963 March on Washington for Jobs and

Freedom and walked arm in arm with national civil rights leaders. A number of labor organizations and unions, mostly notably the UAW, AFL-CIO, and the United Steelworkers, contributed generously and freely to civil rights causes, including bail money for protestors and funding for the Freedom Rides and the NAACP's many legal campaigns, as well as supplying people at the local level for civil rights membership, dues, donations, and activism. However, at the same time, local chapters of civil rights groups were demonstrating against affiliate unions' racial discrimination in New York and other northern urban centers.[30]

The growing strength and assertiveness of the national civil rights movement is the third factor behind Johnson's decision to intervene. During the first half of the Eisenhower years, much of the energy for Black activism was directed into the courts, with some scattered protests. The Montgomery Improvement Association's victorious bus boycott at the end of 1956 presented a new model and direction to the movement. Court victories continued, the federal government took halting steps toward civil rights progress, and grassroots activism kept growing, entering America's living rooms in increasingly stark terms as the Kennedy administration mostly looked on, hoping to keep Black Freedom Struggles out of the spotlight. But Freedom Rides, James Meredith's attempts to gain admission and physical access to the University of Mississippi, and the Southern Christian Leadership Conference's Birmingham Campaign, among many other examples, showed that the movement would not subside. Civil rights organizations grew both in number and size. Tactics became more aggressive and Black people in America less accepting of perpetual inferiority. Coupled with Cold War geopolitics, in which America's adversaries put its heinous racial problems on display whenever the opportunity presented itself, which it so often did, Johnson felt compelled to act.

The New York controversy was "particularly embarrassing" to Johnson and the AFL-CIO's high command for revealing the disjuncture between the AFL-CIO's position and what its affiliates' locals practiced, as well as for pointing out the fractures in the liberal civil rights coalition. The AFL-CIO's constitution prohibited any of its locals from denying benefits or membership to any worker because of skin color. Local 2, along with 116 other unions under the AFL-CIO umbrella, signed pledges with the President's Committee on Equal Employment Opportunity to not discriminate. Place was crucial to the controversy's significance. As part of America's developing Cold War narrative of freedom and race relations, crude discrimination was a southern matter that could and would be eliminated. However, a situation many characterized as prejudice was publicly taking place day after day in New York, not just a northern city but also one of the Democrats' national hubs of power.[31]

CORE began picketing Local 2's office at Fourth Avenue and Twelfth Street on Saturday, May 9, continuing the action for several days. On May 11, eight members from the Bronx and East River chapters of CORE began a sit-in in the building's lobby after union officials refused to speak with them. Some of the union men coming to and from the office responded by stepping on demonstrators' heads and hands and kicking a woman. Police on the scene did nothing. James Farmer, CORE's executive director, joined the several dozen demonstrators on the sidewalk supporting those in the lobby. Displaying his characteristic wit, Farmer said George Meany, himself a member of Local 2, "ought to take his plumber's wrench and lead Local 2 back to work."[32]

CORE responded to the plumbers' violence by blockading the union's office twenty-four hours a day, successfully preventing all union officials and workers from entering. Twenty-seven-year-old Blyden Jackson, chairman of Harlem's East River CORE, vowed, "The day we let them in will be the day they go back to work with the three Puerto Ricans and the Negro up at that Bronx construction site." A number of men tried to break through the human chain of twelve demonstrators locked arm in arm but were unsuccessful. Police broke up these attempts before the workers could assault demonstrators. Though police made clear their willingness to arrest the CORE protesters if the union made a complaint, no complaint was lodged, as the union had to appear as friendly to civil rights as possible, given the claims it was making about the nature of its Bronx job site dispute. Having the demonstrators arrested would play into CORE's tactics and validate what Local 2's critics had been saying about its racial prejudice.[33]

Meany, also involved with brokering an end to the impasse, made Johnson's effort for a united front against Local 2's actions impossible when he came out on May 14 fully in support of the striking plumbers. Declaring the white plumbers "completely justified in refusing to work," Meany asserted, "As far as I'm concerned, they're going to stay off. This union won't work with nonunion men." Further emphasizing his point, he said, "If they were to go to work with those nonunion men, I'd resign from the union." He argued they were operating on a union shop basis, but the situation he was describing was the closed shop, which he well knew was illegal. Still, for Meany, this was unquestionably an issue of labor rights and not civil rights. Privately, he believed the situation in the Bronx was a setup from civil rights activists to embarrass him and the local that gave him his start. "It would be different if we had kept Negroes and Puerto Ricans out," he explained. "But we have no record of this—we've taken every Negro and Puerto Rican who applied." The fewer than twenty men of color in a union over four thousand strong demonstrated that Local 2 did not practice the absolute exclusion of men of color, but the token level of integration was not hard to see.[34]

Getting Meany involved was a poor choice, and it is not clear what positive role anyone thought he would play. For one, Local 2 was Meany's union. It was also his father's union. Meany quit high school to enter the world of plumbing, a world through which he quickly climbed. By the age of forty, in 1934, he was state president of the AFL. Five years later, he was second-in-command in the national AFL and became its leader in 1952. This was a man thoroughly steeped in the world of New York City building trades unions and all that came with it. He had benefited from racial exclusion and worked to maintain it, whether he would have described his acts as such, and he still refused to give an inch of ground on these matters in 1964. There was no way he was going to go against the union he and his father built. And when he, predictably, failed to do that and even endorsed what Local 2 was doing, whatever Johnson, the city, activists, and those four men who showed up to work hoped to accomplish was futile.[35]

Meany did not deny that racism and bigotry existed. Like many white northerners involved in liberal politics, he was quick to cut down white southerners. In 1964, he observed, "We have had striking evidence in the last few days that the Constitution and the Bill of Rights and the civil liberties we all like to boast of do not prevail in certain parts of the country for those people whose skin is a little different color from that of ourselves. . . . This Constitution does not prevail in the Southland." This was a fairly easy position to take, with little risk to him or his organization. He was simply describing what was apparent to anyone watching, and the South had always been much more hostile toward organized labor. For Meany, the South was an exceptional place, the region where racism happens, and it was also mostly contained there. The racism that was in the AFL-CIO was a "bootleg product," as he put it, in violation of policy.[36]

On measures that were more directly related to his majority-white membership and threatened its sense of dominance, Meany was less delicate, even when those members were turning out the bootleg product in plain sight. At the federation's 1959 national convention, A. Philip Randolph, then a national vice president, challenged Meany to suspend two unions that still maintained racial exclusion as official, written policy. Meany refused and shouted at him from the podium, "Who the hell appointed you guardian of all the Negroes in America?"

Randolph responded that he was the only Black person there. He also had been advocating for Black advancement and organizing workers since the 1910s, publishing the socialist *Messenger* magazine, leading the Brotherhood of Sleeping Car Porters, the first all-Black union to gain an AFL charter, and organizing the 1941 March on Washington Movement to integrate defense contracting. Such behavior explains why the historian David Golland describes Meany as a man who "sought to ruffle the fewest rank-and-file feathers while doing the minimum necessary to appease the national civil rights organizations." Was this who Herbert Hill had in mind in 1949?[37]

Victory for Local 2

The white plumbers went back to work on May 18, after three weeks of conflict. The involved parties had worked out a compromise in which the four nonunion men would take apprentice exams, qualifying them for union membership. The issue languished for some time, with the men initially refusing to take the exams, citing the tests as violating labor laws. Three of them changed their minds, took the exam under local and federal pressure to bring a positive ending to the matter, and failed.[38] The NAACP proposed sponsoring the men for ninety days of training. Two of them accepted but subsequently refused to take the exams at the end of their training period, citing concerns of fairness on the part of the union.[39]

For all the outcry, conferences, and public statements, the union won without question. Not only did Local 2 succeed in keeping the four nonunion men off of the job, but construction unions continued to have command over who would have access to the best-paying physical labor in the city, with short workweeks, guaranteed overtime, and many other benefits. It kept these Black and Brown men out of lucrative skilled jobs they could pass down to sons and nephews, ensuring a degree of social mobility for future generations. Instead, as the industrial job market was collapsing in the city, people of color were systematically excluded from trades that allowed white ethnic New Yorkers to gain political power and economic mobility. African American New Yorkers did not dominate any well-paying industry or middle-class profession in the city as so many other ethnic groups did.[40]

Whether or not racial hatred motivated the white plumbers in the Terminal Market dispute, many people—Black, white, and Puerto Rican—believed it did and believed it to be emblematic of a broad trend in organized labor. The ways the plumbers and their leaders behaved did little to help dispel such ideas. Racial epithets and the nearly complete lack of men of color in Locals 1 and 2 spoke for themselves, regardless of however Meany tried to explain it away. The plumbers' refusal to work, which the *New York Times* characterized as "a sordid combination of bigotry, sophistry and intraunion politics," fostered existing resentment in the city's African American and Puerto Rican population toward organized labor, as well as a lack of faith in the government—local, state, and federal—and conventional means of protest to effectively address their worsening crisis in employment.[41]

In addition to offering the best wages and opportunities for working-class New Yorkers, labor unions provided other important social goods, though also unequally. Expanded social programs and public hospitals were helpful to poor New Yorkers, which African Americans disproportionately were. However, most of the housing cooperatives that unions sponsored, despite their race-blind open-occupancy policies, were overwhelmingly white. The expansive, subsidized health care that unions won was reserved for members and their families, helping keep them in better health. And, of course, Black New Yorkers mostly missed out on wage gains, shorter workdays, and safer workplaces.[42]

Wagner's refusal to take a stand on racial justice in the Local 2 controversy is demonstrative of his priorities and approach across twelve years in office. The white working class had an active ally and defender in him, while the Black working class merely had a concerned ear. It is not possible to argue that the mayor was unaware of what was happening to the vast working-class communities of color in his city. It is also not true that he did not know what to do. For example, when Stanley Lowell, the head of the City Commission on Human Rights, suggested in 1963 that the city adopt a policy of "preferential treatment" for integrating its labor force, he faced vicious public attacks and no support from the Wagner administration. While affirmative action has become a dirty, poisonous phrase in some quarters, many progressive and mainstream figures, including JFK and LBJ, saw it as a way to rectify centuries of denied opportunities and suppressed abilities. Whether Wagner favored or opposed such a policy is ultimately beside the point. What matters is that this is one more instance of him doing nothing, acting on perhaps his most valued piece of advice from his father—"When in doubt, don't." Eventually, the thinking went, whatever dilemma was at hand would subside, and his popularity would endure. For at least eight years, it worked. At some point during his third term, it ceased to provide benefits that outweighed the negatives.[43]

The Black working class had allies in organized labor but not nearly enough to counter their enemies or those indifferent to them. As was too often the case in the history of social justice in the United States, it would take a federal law, coming after decades of struggle and loss, to give these workers what they needed to force many unions, locals, and employers to become less exclusionary and bigoted. While the Civil Rights Act of 1964 was a momentous achievement for African Americans and their allies and Title VII vital to integrating organized labor, it was already clear in 1964 that the future of work would be outside of manual labor, in fields that required many levels of quality education. Given that reality, the children of Harlem and Bedford-Stuyvesant faced a bleak tomorrow.

4
Learning

In May 1954, the U.S. Supreme Court struck down the constitutionality of "separate but equal" public education, which had thrived with the court's imprimatur since 1896. Its unanimous decision in *Brown v. Board of Education of Topeka* reverberated throughout the nation, as educational segregation was an American problem, not a southern one. The New York City Board of Education, applauding the *Brown* decision, trumpeted the case as a "legal and moral reaffirmation of our fundamental educational principles." At the end of the year, the board unanimously passed a resolution creating its Commission on Integration, charged with exploring how the city might go about integrating its schools.[1] As the state had outlawed legally mandated school segregation since 1920, the racial separation students in New York City public schools experienced came through a combination of residential segregation, zoning, Board of Education decisions as to where schools would be built, and the city's refusal to take meaningful action.

Complaints of overcrowded, segregated public schools in the city date back to at least the 1930s.[2] Up to the Great Depression, Black New Yorkers attended integrated schools. As the city's Black population and residential segregation increased, educational segregation emerged and, with it, inferior Black schools.[3] The city organized its public schools as neighborhood schools, which meant students learned where they lived. Students were zoned into schools based on their addresses, leaving parents virtually no choice in the matter. Given the increasing residential segregation in the city in the middle decades of the century, it followed that schools would also be segregated. That a growing number of public schools had predominantly Black and Puerto Rican student bodies was obvious; what to do about segregation and the fact that it was worsening was not.

Parents utilized every peaceful means at their disposal, from conferences and pickets to withdrawing their students and citywide boycotts. It seemed that nothing could convince the Board of Education to act upon the principles it claimed to hold.

A 1955 report from a New York University research center confirmed what so many Black and Puerto Rican parents throughout the city already knew to be true. It demonstrated that New York's predominantly white schools, by any standard, were significantly more capable and functional than those schools with largely Black and/or Puerto Rican student bodies. White schools had smaller class sizes, younger buildings, better maintenance services, and newer equipment. Majority-minority schools spent about twenty dollars per child, while white schools expended over sixty-five dollars. Ten times as many white schools could count 80 percent of their educational staff as tenured.[4] One Harlem school had two teachers licensed to teach junior high school out of twenty-three eighth-grade classes. Segregated Black schools commonly saw many full-time teachers leave for less challenging schools after taking principal's tests and other supervisory examinations as soon as regulations allowed.[5] Unsurprisingly, pupils in segregated Black or Puerto Rican schools performed well below their white peers.[6]

What the NYU study documented so thoroughly conveys the essence of pushing for school desegregation. For most parents and activists pursuing integration, putting Black and Puerto Rican children in the same room with their white peers for its own sake was not the goal, or even a goal. People reasoned that distributing children of various races and ethnicities more equitably through the city's schools would result in an overall increase in the quality of education and initiate rapid infusions of money into the sorely underfunded previously majority-minority schools. They knew that the city and white parents would not stand for middle-class white children attending school in run-down buildings, in overcrowded, chaotic classrooms, with inexperienced, and often indifferent, teachers at the front of the room. As long as neighborhood schools remained what they were, nothing significant was likely to change.

Recognition

Mayor Wagner created a committee charged with better utilizing school buildings to relieve overcrowding in February 1955, a year into his first term. At that time, Wagner publicly stated that students, most of whom were Black or Puerto Rican, in 225 of the city's 566 elementary schools learned in overcrowded facilities while the rest of the schools offered an incredible eighty thousand empty seats.[7] He vowed to pursue integration no matter the obstructions.

By the fall of 1955, the Urban League of Greater New York was already pushing the Board of Education to implement an "emergency program to desegregate New York City's Public Schools." The chapter called for "immediate attention to correct the shocking inferiority of educational standards, teacher quality and turnover, aspirational levels, physical and instructional equipment and over-all capital expenditures in presently de facto segregated Negro and Puerto Rican schools." In its letter to Charles Silver, president of the city's Board of Education, the group proposed broad reforms to diminish educational segregation, including rezoning neighborhood schools to include children of varied race and ethnicity, busing children "to increase integration in 'core areas' where geographic zoning could not achieve the purpose," and the board working with the city's housing and planning bodies to tear down residential segregation.[8]

Busing elicited an especially virulent reaction from certain elements of white New York. In February 1957, Silver issued a press release to make clear that the school system was neither engaged in nor considering transporting children in order to achieve any measure of integration but only to help children get to school who live too far away from the nearest facility or to relieve overcrowding.[9] The board declined to implement any of the Urban League's suggestions at this time, and it should not have been surprised to learn of such conditions in Harlem, as the African American sociologist E. Franklin Frazier had detailed the same kinds of deficiencies in a report the city had commissioned him to write in 1935.[10]

Dr. Kenneth Clark, a relentless integrationist, began organizing against segregation in the city's public schools in 1954, taking impetus from the *Brown* decision and the psychological damage he and his wife saw segregation do to Black children firsthand. His work against racially separate schools was a perfect fit, given his background and accomplishments. Clark grew up in Harlem and personally witnessed its changing demographics. He began school with classmates in PS 5 at 140th Street and Edgecombe Avenue who were primarily the first-generation daughters and sons of Irish and Jewish immigrants. By the time he left for college in the early 1930s, the neighborhood's schools were filled with students who mostly looked like him and were already suffering neglect. As he later related:

I grew up in Harlem. I saw Harlem deteriorate, disintegrate. I saw classmates who went to school with me in the elementary and junior high schools in Harlem, many of whom were much brighter than I, end up in prisons, or worse. I don't know what specific things made the difference. The only thing that I know is that statistically, too many of my classmates and an even greater number of youngsters who come after me have been lost to any meaningful or constructive role in our society.

Basil Paterson, a lawyer, NAACP official, and influential Democratic politician, grew up Black in Harlem, about a decade later than Clark did, and experienced what the doctor had begun to witness on his way out: "As a graduate of the New York City public school system, I well remember the struggle to survive, and possibly excel, that confronted me and my ghetto junior high school classmates when we entered high school." Clark's mother, raising him as a single parent, arranged to have him attend George Washington High School at 193rd Street in Washington Heights, considerably farther north in Manhattan.[11]

Clark earned bachelor's and master's degrees from Howard University, the premier historically Black institution of higher learning. There he met his future wife, Mamie Phipps, who grew up in Arkansas and provided a conduit for Clark to understand southern Black life. They both earned doctorates in psychology from Columbia University in the 1940s, he the first African American to do so and she the second. In 1950, they left the city for good, moving to predominantly white Westchester County. The Clarks said their children only had one chance at education, and they knew very well the conditions in New York City public schools.[12]

The Clarks were outliers. Most African American families in New York City lacked the opportunities that would have allowed them to bring their children to better environments. Instead, they were stuck in a city whose schools were declining rapidly. By 1959, one-third of public school children throughout the city were Black, while Black students comprised two-thirds of Manhattan's public school attendees. White parents were removing their children from the city's public schools by the thousands in the late 1950s and early 1960s, placing them in private schools, which were not subject to the *Brown* decision. At the same time, the city's population of Black children was growing rapidly. These factors, combined with the Board of Education's refusal to integrate its schools, produced a substantial growth in educational segregation.[13] Forty-five percent of all Black and Puerto Rican students in junior high learned in segregated facilities.[14] The board's own figures show that between 1960 and 1965, the

Figure 4.1 Kenneth and Mamie Clark, date unknown.

Source: Library of Congress, Prints and Photographs Division, LC-USZ62-112521.

number of predominantly Black and Puerto Rican schools went from 118 to 201, accounting for 23 percent of all schools by 1965. Puerto Rican pupils tended to go to integrated or mostly white schools much more than their African American peers. Most Black students attended schools that were 70 to 90 percent Black and Puerto Rican, and most white students were enrolled in schools in which they made up 90 percent or more of the student population.[15]

Decades before charter schools, public and private were the only choices. Harlem had twenty-four public schools for its 32,000 pupils. In its twenty elementary schools, 90 percent of students were African American, 9 percent were Puerto Rican, and the other three hundred or so were white, likely children of long-time residents of East Harlem who had resided there from the time it was heavily Italian and Jewish and had yet to leave. The remaining four schools were junior high schools, where 96 percent of students were African American, fewer than 4 percent were Puerto Rican, and white students accounted for not even 1 percent. Harlem had no public high schools. It had two private high schools and six Catholic schools, which enrolled only 10 percent of Harlem's children. Across Manhattan, only two-thirds of children attended public school.[16] Brooklyn's schools were so segregated that seventy thousand African American and

Puerto Rican students between the ages of five and eleven would have to be transported up to ten miles and fifty minutes each way to reach schools in which their attendance would achieve meaningful integration.[17]

In addition to the challenges of old buildings, overcrowded classrooms, insufficient supplies, and inexperienced teachers, Black students faced bigoted instructors. The city's school system, the largest in the country, only had 544 Black teachers out of the over fifty thousand educators it employed in 1955, and 312 of them were substitutes.[18] Many of their predominantly white teachers believed in the inability of Black students to learn, as well as in their profound otherness. They assigned blame to different factors—genetics, socialization, psychology, parents who did not value education—but agreed that their classrooms were full of uneducable pupils. As a white former teacher at PS 170 in Harlem revealed: "The first day of school I was told that all I was expected to do my first year was keep my children quiet—not teach them. I was told that this was all I had to worry about—keeping the classes in order—nothing else. Really, all we were expected to do was to get the children to walk through the halls more or less quietly. If we could do that, we had succeeded."[19]

Albert Shanker, president of the United Federation of Teachers, stated that his rank-and-file members found it "impossible to teach" in half of the city's schools because "so much retardation has taken place that pupils have lost hope for learning."[20] Their assumptions were wrong, but continuing to work as though students were inferior would make them inferior, and it did. More than half of Harlem's students who began high school in 1959 did not graduate.[21] Parents would find few allies within the school system.

Activism

Parents and students faced headwinds not only from within the school system but also from the civil rights establishment. In 1956, the NAACP was the nation's foremost civil rights organization, a status it would soon lose to more adventurous and confrontational groups, such as the Southern Christian Leadership Conference, CORE, and the Student Nonviolent Coordinating Committee. Within the NAACP, heavy friction sometimes characterized relationships between the national organization and local branches. The Brooklyn chapter of the NAACP pressed hard after *Brown* for the Board of Education to desegregate Brooklyn's schools, focusing initially on PS 258, a school that had opened the previous year in Bedford-Stuyvesant. The school was 98 percent Black, though the neighborhood in which it was situated was not yet segregated. The Brooklyn chapters of the NAACP and Urban League organized a December conference to address school segregation, with a focus on the ways zoning was being used to maintain and expand educational segregation, as well as how it could be used "as a positive and deliberate means to achieve public school integration, overcoming the restrictions of residential segregation." A few weeks earlier, NAACP representatives from seven chapters throughout the city met privately to discuss school segregation. Several of those at the meeting attacked the national NAACP office for neglecting problems the Brooklyn branch had been raising.[22]

In fact, the national office was deliberate in its neglect and hostile to the work the Brooklyn branch was doing and proposing. Executive Secretary Roy Wilkins wrote to a number of local and national NAACP leaders, laying out the organization's positions on school segregation. He chided the Brooklyn members for their focus on zoning. Wilkins said that since one of the thrusts of the attack on southern segregation was the use of zoning to maintain apartheid schools, it would be hypocritical to encourage New York, or any northern city, to use zoning for positive purposes. Further, Wilkins was concerned "that we do not press a northern program that will have the effect of stymying [sic] beginnings in the South," as "the chief task is getting the southern program underway." The national NAACP seemed unable at this time to appreciate the gravity of the northern situation, despite the fact that Wilkins had lived in New York City since the 1930s. He emphasized that "there are nearly 2,000,000 Negro children still attending cruelly inferior schools" in the South and argued that addressing their exigencies is "infinitely more important than the desegregation of one school in Brooklyn, N.Y." As for all of the focus on the Board of Education in allowing segregated schools to operate in such poor conditions, Wilkins opined that "some responsibility rests with parents and with the community" for how these schools function and that segregation "is only one problem in the educational picture." In what would prove to be a great error in judgment, he advised the local chapters to relax, for "in the North we have time, freedom, allies and power to achieve our ends."[23]

Many involved in the battle for quality education disagreed with Wilkins's assessment, and Black New Yorkers' action against their children's segregated schools would greatly intensify as the decade came to an end. In August 1957, Black parents, teachers, and civil rights leaders presented Mayor Wagner with a list of the ways that the Board of Education was failing Black students. "I want you to know," the mayor assured them, "that I will do everything in my power to see that every child in the city gets an equal opportunity for a good education." He pledged to "follow up on the issues . . . and get in touch with the Board of Education immediately." The group gave the mayor one month to produce something tangible and pledged to return as demonstrators should he fail.[24] When the city took no action, hundreds of African American and Puerto Rican parents picketed City Hall a month later, demanding an end to "the substandard conditions existing in schools attended by our children, and the delayed implementation of the recommendations of the [Board of Education's] Commission on Integration." Wagner again met with some of them, including the longtime NAACP activist and national organizer Ella Baker, who had recently begun her tenure at the Southern Christian Leadership Conference, and scheduled what proved to be a fruitless conference between protest leaders and Board of Education personnel the following week.[25]

By the time school began in September 1958, the Board of Education's report on integration had been out for three months. The report recognized activists' claims:

> A substantial amount of *de facto* segregation has grown up in the New York City school system . . . as a consequence of the prevailing *residential* segregation of white and Negro families. Inequality of educational opportunity has inevitably resulted. Increasingly, the schools in the colored neighborhoods of Greater New York have tended to be older, less well equipped and more crowded than the schools in the white neighborhoods; the quality of the teaching provided in these predominately colored schools has also suffered.

The report went on to acknowledge "the steady deterioration during the preceding twenty years of the education available to Negro and Puerto Rican children; the disastrously rapid turnover of teachers in the 'difficult' segregated schools of the Negro and Puerto Rican neighborhoods; the paucity of classes for the intellectually gifted," and other issues. The city, the report advised, "could not afford to ignore these conditions, nor could it be in the least complacent or self-righteous." But, the city did ignore the conditions, complacently and self-righteously. On the same page, the Board of Education congratulated itself and President Silver for "his determination to permit no lapse in the continuity of the integration program. During the next two years [from taking office in 1954], his dedication and dynamic leadership proved to be major factors in the successful development of the program."[26]

While the board developed a program, parents and activists consistently derided it as inadequate, and the board rarely followed through on even the moderate promises it had made, often shrinking in the face of hostility from white parents. To move toward integrated public schools in the city, the report recommended rezoning, just as the Brooklyn NAACP activists had two years earlier and the Urban League a year before that, along with careful site selection in building future schools and transferring teachers throughout the city so that disinvested schools would enjoy more competent instruction. How much the educational establishment in the city actively believed in what the report put forth is hard to say, but these admissions and proposals were now part of the school system's official positions.

The report elicited intense opposition from white New Yorkers. Parents objected to anything that would move their children or move children from other neighborhoods into the schools they attended, and teachers opposed their transfers. White parents in Brooklyn and Queens were quick to respond and determined to resist measures like rezoning and busing, even going so far as to threaten violence. These patterns would continue for years and succeed over and over. New York's overwhelmingly white public school teachers strenuously opposed the commission's idea that experienced teachers should be equitably distributed throughout the school system, with one teachers' group likening such a fate to "sentencing them to Siberia." The only educators who supported this idea were the tiny Negro Teachers Association and the soon-to-be-extinct communist Teachers Union. Responding to the public and professional outcry, the Board of Education quickly scuttled these plans. Kenneth Clark, chair of one of the commission's subcommittees, told the board that "anticipations of violence, real or fancied, cannot be accepted as valid excuse for inaction," an assertion that could be applied to its wavering integration decisions for the next decade.[27]

In the meantime, majority-minority schools were still in dire straits, with little hope for improvement in the near future. In the fall of 1958, at least nine different African American parents refused to send their children to three "inferior, below-standard, segregated" Harlem junior high schools, and the parents of seven African American children in Bedford-Stuyvesant did the same. Parents quickly arranged daily six-hour tutoring sessions for their children, led by volunteer teachers. Responding to a plea from the parents' lawyer, the State Education Commissioner refused to intervene in the case, declaring the state could only involve itself in a local matter if the Board of Education asked it to. The city superintendent of schools, Dr. John Theobald, also declined to assist the students. When seven of their mothers met with him, asking for the children to be reassigned to more adequate and integrated schools, Theobald refused, maintaining he was able to act only on the basis of "educational grounds." In October, four of the parents filed a million-dollar lawsuit against the city for its alleged "sinister and discriminatory purpose in the perpetuation of racial segregation." The following day, Theobald asked the New York State Education Department to study "the problems and needs of schools in so-called difficult areas," which included the three Harlem junior high schools parents were boycotting.[28]

By the middle of November, the city had issued eight of the students' mothers with summonses for refusing to send their children to their Harlem schools.[29] Four were found guilty, one was placed on parole after returning her child to the offending school, another had her charges dismissed on a technicality, and two had their charges dismissed.[30] While the judge who found the four guilty said he had to decide the case without considering the quality of the students' education, Justice Justine Wise Polier, who dismissed the charges against two of the mothers, asserted they were doing the right thing given the fact of their children receiving "inferior educational opportunities by reason of racial discrimination." Polier held that the parents "have the constitutionally guaranteed right to elect no education for their children rather than to subject them to discriminatorily inferior education." She castigated the Board of Education for contending "that one arm of the state—this court—must blindly enforce the unconstitutional denial of constitutional rights by another arm of this state—the Board of Education."[31]

Polier's decision not only galvanized parents and activists but also convinced state legislators that the city's school system needed to be investigated for racial discrimination. Superintendent Theobald retorted, "Only a lack of understanding of the facts would lead anyone to say that New York City discriminates against Negro and Puerto Rican children."[32] Black parents in the city disagreed. Taking Polier's decision as a legal affirmation of what they already knew, they used the case to build momentum for their struggle to desegregate and integrate New York City's public schools.[33] Even Roy Wilkins, NAACP's head and a committed moderate, had grown impatient with the Board of Education, writing in 1959 to Charles Silver, its president, to denounce the board's retreat from transferring four hundred students from overcrowded schools in Bedford-Stuyvesant to underutilized schools four miles away in Glendale, Queens. In Bedford-Stuyvesant, schools were operating on two- and even three-session days, meaning schools were so overcrowded that a full school day would be divided into halves or thirds, with students attending in shifts of a few hours a day, guaranteeing a terrible outcome. The white members of the Glendale Taxpayers Association hired a lawyer to intervene with the Board of Education on their behalf, to prevent the partial filling of some of the 2,600 empty seats in Glendale. As would be the case with similar groups opposed to any measure that changed the racial makeup of schools, such as the Parents and Taxpayers Coordinating Council, white parents saw the local schools as theirs and "just don't like the idea of strangers coming into their neighborhood." It is worth noting that the taxes they paid covered all public schools in the city, not just the ones in their neighborhoods.[34]

The mothers' boycott would be the first of several that African American parents and civil rights activists would lead over the next few years to force the Board of Education to improve their children's learning environments. The Parents' Workshop for Equality in New York City Schools, a grassroots group that empowered parents to challenge Board of Education policies, was crucial to these protests. After its threatened boycott in 1960 resulted in some African American children transferring out of their inferior schools, the group organized parents in Harlem, Bedford-Stuyvesant, and Williamsburg, in Brooklyn, to lead a five-day boycott at the start of the 1961 school year in which hundreds of mostly Black children stayed home from segregated schools. The parents succeeded in securing transfers for their children.[35] Similar scenes would play out throughout 1961 and 1962, including sit-ins at the Board of Education headquarters in Brooklyn.[36]

In October 1962, Jerome and Elaine Bibuld, an interracial couple, moved into Park Slope from Crown Heights, both sections of Brooklyn. After a short time, they refused to allow their three children to attend PS 282, their top choice out of several designated neighborhood schools. PS 282 was the best of several bad options, with students learning far below grade level, yet the other schools were even worse. The Board of Education rebuffed their request to transfer the Bibuld children to a more functional and better-equipped school outside of their district. After a month and a half of homeschooling, the parents were summoned to Family Court for keeping their children out of school, a sign of neglect. If convicted, the Bibulds could spend several years in prison and lose custody of their children. The Board of Education allowed them to temporarily attend a better school, PS 200, but they were not allowed to enroll, and the family received at least one phoned-in threat to their children for going to the school. The Family Court judge convicted the parents but delayed sentencing repeatedly.[37]

All along, a Brooklyn CORE campaign using publicity to embarrass the school system, including a week-long sit-in at 110 Livingston Street, the Board of Education headquarters, coerced school administrators into allowing the children to enroll in PS 130. Though the school was outside of their district, it met the Bibulds' expectations. The children began attending in the first week of February, and the judge dismissed all charges against the parents the following week. It was a real victory and provided a possible way forward for other families in similar situations. One family's successful boycott helped energize a growing movement and increased the pressure on the Board of Education. Still, just three children out of hundreds of thousands in deficient learning environments were able to switch schools, and this was no way to achieve progress. The family endured months of stress, harassment, and legal problems that threatened total ruin, with no guarantee that anything would work out. Once more, hard-fought individual remedies were all that seemed to be obtainable.[38]

In 1963, the Parents' Workshop joined with a new grassroots activist group focused on school desegregation, the Harlem Parents Committee, and several chapters of CORE and the NAACP to form the New York Citywide Committee for Integrated Schools.[39] Its goal was "to see that the 1954 Supreme Court Decision is applied in New York to wipe out the last vestiges of 'de facto' segregated schools."[40] Building on the work of Drs. Clark, the Urban League, member organizations, and the Harlem Neighborhoods Association, the committee pressured the board to take real steps to integrate schools.[41] In June, the New York State Commissioner of Education requested that every board of education in the state submit a plan to remediate segregation in its schools. The city's board did so in August, in which it proposed a voluntary transfer program available to all students and the rezoning of one pair of junior high schools, as well as possible future rezoning and pairing. Nearly ten years after *Brown*, when the board supposedly had begun addressing integration in earnest, it did not have much to say for itself.[42]

After Calvin Gross, the new superintendent of schools, told civil rights leaders at a late August 1963 meeting that he would not permit involuntary student transfers to take place to integrate schools or even provide a desegregation timetable, the NYCCIS announced that it would be organizing a school boycott in all five boroughs at an unspecified date later in the school year. The group vowed to "launch a large scale citizens' effort to eliminate the illegal and immoral Jim Crow School System of New York City."[43] The strike would also serve a second purpose—exerting economic coercion. Milton Galamison, a Presbyterian minister in Bedford-Stuyvesant and NAACP leader, chaired the NYCCIS, which along with the Harlem Parents Committee believed keeping students out of school for an indefinite amount of time was the only way to win. His strategy was predicated on low attendance decimating the state's financial aid to the board the following year, as the state calculated it using a formula that prioritized daily attendance figures. However, more moderate influences within the committee won out, and the NYCCIS decided on an initial one-day boycott. With the civil rights mastermind Bayard Rustin contributing his organizing services, Galamison secured substantial attention for the movement.[44]

Rustin, a New Yorker since 1937, could claim a lengthy list of civil rights activism and leadership: cofounder of CORE, early Freedom Rider, essential to the formation of the Southern Christian Leadership Conference, key advisor to Martin Luther King Jr., and organizer of the March on Washington for Jobs and Freedom eleven months earlier. Despite all this, he was generally relegated to the background for two reasons: he was a gay man who, while not publicly out, made no attempt to conceal it, with a decade-old "public morals" conviction related to his sexuality, and he had been a member of the Communist Party for a few years in his twenties. Actors ranging from Adam Clayton Powell Jr. to Strom Thurmond and J. Edgar Hoover had threatened to use his homosexuality as a weapon against him and those with whom he worked, including Dr. King. Rustin's adversaries hoped that claims, both real and manufactured, would split this most dedicated activist for freedom, peace, and justice from the movements and organizations to which he contributed his talents.[45]

Throughout the summer and the 1963–1964 school year, many groups, parents, children, and activists continued to pressure the Board of Education to finally act in the face of this looming threat. They maintained a high profile for their cause through pickets; sit-ins; rallies featuring nationally known figures like the National Director of CORE, James Farmer, and the legendary jazz vocalist and actress Abbey Lincoln; leafleting; provisional freedom schools; meetings; conferences; civil disobedience; and other methods.[46] Once the NYCCIS announced its boycott, the school board reacted with immediate promises to draw up formal desegregation plans, giving several dates by which it would provide these plans and falling through on all of them.[47] Given the board's history, as well as Board of Education President James Donovan's November 1963 statement that "this is a Board of Education, not a board of integration, nor a board of transportation," few were surprised.[48]

As battling the Board of Education went on, activists continually pushed up against an educational apparatus that was unresponsive and resistant to outside

Figure 4.2 Flier advertising rally in support of school desegregation, 1963.

Source: Harlem Neighborhoods Association records, Schomburg Center for Research in Black Culture, New York Public Library.

influence. Public education in New York City was a highly centralized system. The board wielded near-total control over public schooling and had a very low degree of accountability to anyone. The mayor appointed its unpaid nine members, two each from Manhattan, Queens, Brooklyn, and the Bronx and one from Staten Island. Additionally, board membership had to be split equally among Jews, Catholics, and Protestants. Members served for seven years and could not be fired. They could only lose their appointments if the mayor brought charges against them for malfeasance, with those charges found to be substantiated at a hearing. The board selected the city superintendent of schools, who was almost always an insider drawn from the four dozen associate and assistant superintendents, all of whom a previous superintendent selected and could count on the board approving. When his six-year term was up, he could count on reappointment until he hit the age ceiling at seventy years old.[49]

The superintendent would also nominate, and expect to have approved, candidates to fill any vacancies in the school system's force of nine hundred principals, as well as numerous other administrators. Unsurprisingly, almost all of these people were white, with just six African Americans among the more than 1,200 upper-level administrators, and only three principals in 1965. Principals and assistant superintendents received tenure after three years, permanently attaching them to the bureaucracy. The five borough presidents assigned five unsalaried members to each of a total of fifty-four local school boards across the city, which provided politicians and those with influence over them some say in the city's educational system, but local school boards had unclear authority and responsibilities. Each board was also part of a district that a Board of Education–approved assistant superintendent oversaw, subjecting it to centralized supervision.[50]

With the cry of "Boycott Jim Crow Schools," the Harlem Parents Committee urged every mother and father of a school-age child to "Join the thousands of Harlem parents who refuse to send their children to inferior Jim Crow Schools."[51] By this time, the Harlem Parents Committee was also leading a struggle for "a commitment to a *new* educational concept, an educational concept which is nurtured in true democracy and cultural pluralism; that is to say: outlaw all history and philosophy of public education that has excluded the Negro and other minority groups' true role in the evolution of our society."[52] The 1963–1964 boycott movement had many components to it, drawing from liberal, progressive, and radical traditions. Its revolutionary demands for public education that discarded Euro- and Anglocentric models of history in favor of one that taught Black and Puerto Rican history in a proportional

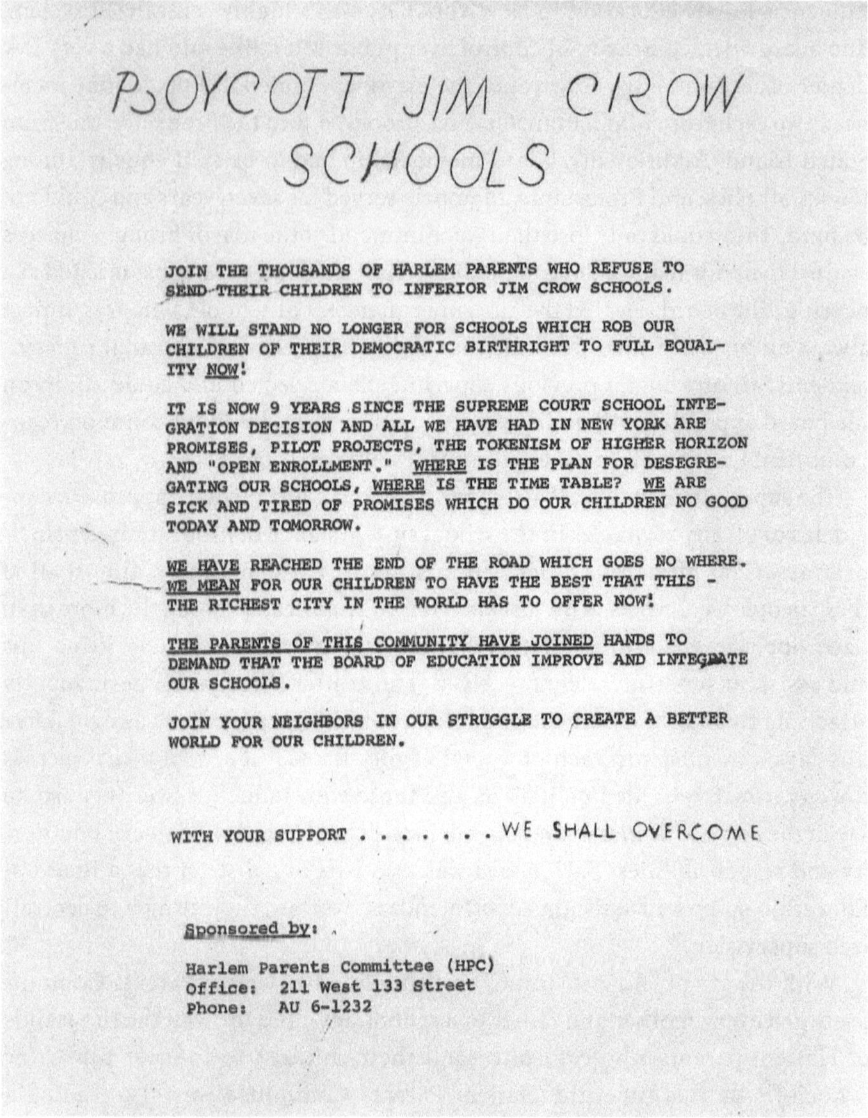

BOYCOTT JIM CROW SCHOOLS

JOIN THE THOUSANDS OF HARLEM PARENTS WHO REFUSE TO SEND THEIR CHILDREN TO INFERIOR JIM CROW SCHOOLS.

WE WILL STAND NO LONGER FOR SCHOOLS WHICH ROB OUR CHILDREN OF THEIR DEMOCRATIC BIRTHRIGHT TO FULL EQUALITY NOW!

IT IS NOW 9 YEARS SINCE THE SUPREME COURT SCHOOL INTEGRATION DECISION AND ALL WE HAVE HAD IN NEW YORK ARE PROMISES, PILOT PROJECTS, THE TOKENISM OF HIGHER HORIZON AND "OPEN ENROLLMENT." WHERE IS THE PLAN FOR DESEGREGATING OUR SCHOOLS, WHERE IS THE TIME TABLE? WE ARE SICK AND TIRED OF PROMISES WHICH DO OUR CHILDREN NO GOOD TODAY AND TOMORROW.

WE HAVE REACHED THE END OF THE ROAD WHICH GOES NO WHERE. WE MEAN FOR OUR CHILDREN TO HAVE THE BEST THAT THIS – THE RICHEST CITY IN THE WORLD HAS TO OFFER NOW!

THE PARENTS OF THIS COMMUNITY HAVE JOINED HANDS TO DEMAND THAT THE BOARD OF EDUCATION IMPROVE AND INTEGRATE OUR SCHOOLS.

JOIN YOUR NEIGHBORS IN OUR STRUGGLE TO CREATE A BETTER WORLD FOR OUR CHILDREN.

WITH YOUR SUPPORT . . . . WE SHALL OVERCOME

Sponsored by:

Harlem Parents Committee (HPC)
Office: 211 West 133 Street
Phone: AU 6-1232

Figure 4.3 School boycott flier, 1963.

Source: Harlem Neighborhoods Association records, Schomburg Center for Research in Black Culture, New York Public Library.

Figure 4.4 Malcolm X speaking at a school boycott rally in Harlem in 1964. Jesse Gray is seated.

Source: Library of Congress, Prints and Photographs Division, NYWT&S Collection, LC-USZ62-114814.

way anticipated similar calls from Black and Brown Power activists by several years.

The New York Citywide Committee for Integrated Schools' one-day boycott on February 3, 1964, kept over 360,000 students out of public school beyond the one hundred thousand who stayed at home on any given day.[53] Overall, the absentees constituted 45 percent of the school system's total enrollment of slightly over one million children. The teachers' union, the United Federation of Teachers, did not endorse the boycott, but almost triple the number of teachers was nevertheless absent. On a day when temperatures never topped twenty degrees, thousands of parents and their children spent the day picketing over a third of the city's schools, culminating their demonstrations in a march 3,500 strong to the Board of Education headquarters in Brooklyn.[54] Four days later, and a world away, the Beatles landed at John F. Kennedy International Airport in Queens, scheduled to play *The Ed Sullivan Show* in two days.

Outcomes

Under pressure from civil rights leaders and elected officials, the Board of Education provided several options in the early 1960s to address overcrowding and segregation. The Open Enrollment plan in 1959, allowing students in overcrowded schools to leave them for the many white schools with room, was its first offering. By 1966, 22,300 pupils had participated in the program, or fewer than 5 percent of eligible children. This low participation rate can largely be attributed to the fact that neither schools nor the school system made much of an effort to promote the program. Parents who did know had to apply and worry about providing transportation for their children, as the board would not.[55] The Free Choice Transfer Plan, an extension of the Open Enrollment plan, gave graduating fifth-graders the choice of either continuing to their designated schools or attending an underpopulated white school. Again, schools advertised the program poorly, and numerous principals of the children's neighborhood schools gave talks to parents on the many downsides of the program. Overall, voluntary transfer programs only offered opportunity at the individual level, as the schools students left behind in Central Harlem would remain segregated, and no white parents would choose to transfer their children into Harlem, Bedford-Stuyvesant, or Brownsville.

In January 1964, the Board of Education, pushed by the threatened Black and Puerto Rican student boycott, announced that it would begin instituting "pairings," or the "Princeton Plan," in which it would rezone and consolidate two nearby elementary schools, one largely Black and the other mostly white. The schools would then exchange students for three years at a time, so that each student would spend half of her or his six elementary school years in each school. The board initially had twenty-one pairings, but it reconsidered at the urging of white parents and school officials at every level, soon reducing it to four. Those four likely had impact at the individual level for the students who participated but had almost no effect on the overall situation, as the original twenty-one pairings would have reduced racial segregation by just 1 percent. In terms of new schools for the 1964–1965 school year, the school board planned to construct thirty-nine of its 106 building projects in areas that would guarantee 90 percent or more African American and Puerto Rican enrollment. The Board of Education continued this course for the rest of the decade.[56]

Those initial pairings, even though significantly reduced, were still too much for tens of thousands of white parents throughout the city. In September 1964, white parents had their own boycott, this one for maintaining segregation.

Parents and Taxpayers, an organization that lawyers for homeowners' groups had founded in September 1963 to resist integration in Jackson Heights, Queens, professed to stand for the principle of neighborhood schools. Within weeks of its founding, the group claimed fifteen affiliates and three hundred thousand members. These white parents drew on the civil rights movement for tactical inspiration, promising they would employ litigation, pickets, boycotts, and civil disobedience to achieve their goal of defeating integration.[57] Upward of 15,000 of them marched from the Board of Education headquarters in Brooklyn to City Hall in Manhattan in March 1964 to protest soon-to-be-announced integration measures.[58] By then, Parents and Taxpayers was claiming half a million members spread across one hundred chapters.[59] As the school year progressed and African American parents' pressure and demands on the school board increased, white parents in Brooklyn and the Bronx took inspiration from Parents and Taxpayers and formed similar groups. Over two days in September, 27 percent and 23 percent of the city's public school students stayed home to protest integration through school pairing, while parents picketed schools and the Board of Education headquarters.[60]

After all parents and activists had done, by 1964 New York City's public schools were failing to provide for their Black students more than ever before. As an educator explained, teaching in Central Harlem frequently looked like this:

> When I came to school "X," I had never seen anything like that school. I cried, they behaved so badly. I soon learned that the boys like to be beaten; like to be spoken to in the way in which they are accustomed, and when I learned to say things to them that, to me, would be absolutely insulting and to hit them when they needed it, I got along all right and they began to like me. Somehow that made them feel that I liked them. I talk to them in the terms and in the way to which they are accustomed, and they like it.[61]

Because of similar approaches and many underqualified teachers, gaps between white and Black students' achievement scores were growing in the early 1960s. In 1962, African American eighth graders averaged three and a half grades behind their white peers on standardized exams. As they progressed through the city's schools, Black students fell further behind. In 1963, nearly seventy thousand Black junior high students were more than two grade levels behind, while ten thousand Black seventh graders were unable to get through a third-grade book. African American third graders were 13 to 39 percent below grade level in reading comprehension that year; 60 to 93 percent of sixth graders could say the same. In 1964, three-quarters of students in Central Harlem's junior high schools tested below grade level in reading comprehension and word knowledge.[62] More than 80 percent tested below grade level in math.[63] Students in Bedford-Stuyvesant regularly tested two grade levels behind their white peers in both reading and math scores.[64] By 1964, Bedford-Stuyvesant schools, compared to any area in Brooklyn, featured the most overcrowding, half-day sessions, substitute teachers, nonresident educators, and least experienced teachers.[65]

In April 1964, Calvin Gross, the superintendent of New York City schools, convened a meeting with Roy Wilkins, James Farmer, Milton Galamison, and other civil rights activists to discuss desegregation. Gross focused on quality education in schools, an approach activists had long derided as a form of separate but equal. As Kenneth Clark and most others involved in the fight argued, standards in segregated schools undoubtedly needed to be raised but this must happen in tandem with integration; neither would be sufficient on its own. If one switched the date of the meeting ten years earlier, to just after *Brown*, that context would make more sense and be less frustrating for those in attendance. Gross spoke and the Board of Education acted as though they had just begun to consider the issues of inferior education and racial segregation. Not only did he lack a timetable for integration months after the board had to submit plans to the state, but Gross would not even so much as commit to *producing* a timetable.[66]

The same month that leaders met with Superintendent Gross, the State Education Commissioner's Advisory Committee on Human Relations and Community Tensions issued a lengthy, critical report in which it labeled the city Board of Education as continually hewing to a "pattern of building on sites within the most segregated areas." Unable to find faith in the school system's ability to integrate itself, the state declared:

> We must conclude that nothing undertaken by the New York City Board of Education since 1954, and nothing proposed since 1963, has contributed or will contribute in any meaningful degree to desegregating the public schools of the City. Each past effort, each current plan, and each projected proposal, is either not aimed at reducing segregation or is developed in too limited a fashion to stimulate even slight progress toward desegregation.

Black and Puerto Rican parents, students, activists, and their white allies had been right all along. The board had made little progress on either rezoning neighborhood schools for integration or transferring experienced teachers to neglected schools, two of its own Commission on Integration's proposals from 1958. Contrary to the Board of Education's claims, the state report found in 1964 that segregation had increased in the city's schools since 1958, with seventy-eight primary and intermediate schools becoming segregated. The city did not prevent even one school moving toward segregation from becoming so. Its plan for building in the immediate future reinforced "substantially the historic pattern of building on sites within the most segregated areas." At the elementary school level, where more than one-fifth of schools were segregated, "the Board has done nothing and proposed no plan that would reduce current levels, or stem the rising tide of segregation." Despite ten years, a litany of promises, and school integration proponents' best efforts, including multiple boycotts, sit-ins, conferences, pickets, legal intervention, and more, schools were more segregated, and students of color were worse off than they were in 1954.[67]

These years of struggle took a toll on those seeking change and pushed them to exhaustion not just with the Board of Education but with the city in general and the established avenues of reform. It seemed as though nothing would move New York City school administrators, nor would those running the city intervene. With all other options exhausted, significant numbers of parents and activists came to accept segregated schools as unavoidable for the time being. Instead, they moved to take control over the schools in their neighborhoods, wanting to decide who ran them, who the teachers were, and what they taught. In 1968, this predominantly Black movement would collide dramatically with the mostly white and heavily Jewish teachers union in the Ocean Hill–Brownsville area of Brooklyn. As for the students who came of age in these schools in the 1950s and 1960s, they experienced poor teaching and deplorable facilities firsthand. They saw their parents fight to secure better educations for them only to come away defeated again and again. Black students in New York City's schools during these years learned that accepted methods of protest did not work.

5
The New York City Police Department

> *Yet, with extremely rare exceptions, even those who themselves engage in no corrupt activities are involved in corruption in the sense that they take no steps to prevent what they know or suspect to be going on about them.*
>
> —THE KNAPP COMMISSION REPORT ON POLICE CORRUPTION

By the early 1960s, the New York City Police Department was thoroughly corrupt, a condition that had accelerated over time. This corruption operated across a very wide spectrum. At one end were actions many people would judge to be harmless, such as accepting free meals from restaurants on an officer's beat or cash payments at Christmas. Beat cops typically had spots, often in commercial spaces, where they could sleep while on the job. Traffic officers commonly accepted bribes from tow truck drivers to funnel them work, to get a leg up in a competitive industry. Moving from graft into crime, the first officers responding to a burglary might loot the store that had been broken into and pass off the missing items as part of the initial crime, and those entering a home in which someone had just died would frequently take what they liked. In neighborhoods with high rates of visible crime, like Harlem, officers assigned to vice squads systemically extorted protection money from drug dealers, sex traffickers, and those running gambling operations. These practices were not new in the 1960s; they had been standard procedures for decades. What was new, however, was the expansion into stealing drug money and the drugs themselves, which netted officers in that line of policing enormous profits.

When discussing issues of policing, physical violence receives a significant amount of attention, and for good reasons. The police have a legal monopoly on violence and force and are charged to use it judiciously. However, as has been the case to varying degrees throughout the history of policing, some officers employ force wantonly. Being on the receiving end of an unnecessary, unjustified use of force is one of the most humiliating experiences a person can have—not just when in public or in front of one's family, but even if done behind closed doors. It is a situation of powerlessness. Resisting force is a survival instinct, but doing so when the force is applied by a police officer can lead to death, because the officer has permission to escalate until the threat, real or manufactured, is eliminated. Some encounters end with no significant physical injuries, and others end in death, with almost anything in between—stitches, casts, gunshot wounds, and blindness—possible. The humiliation and emotional trauma can continue long after the encounter, because there is rarely anything the victim of an overzealous officer can do to hold the perpetrator accountable, especially since the interaction often ends with an arrest, legitimate or not, which serves to justify the officer's behavior. Victims can and do pursue lawsuits, but doing so requires time, money, and access to the legal system, as well as potential encounters with one's attacker. Many times, even though a wrong has been done, there is no real recourse.

As the NYPD was 95 percent white and at least 99 percent male in the mid-1960s, any officer-involved beating or shooting anywhere in the city was almost certain to be done at a white man's hands.[1] In neighborhoods like Central Harlem, Brownsville, Bedford-Stuyvesant, or Crown Heights, with overwhelmingly Black populations and a heavy police presence, residents would see an ever-changing cast of white policemen getting physical, justified or otherwise, with neighbors. The police violence residents witnessed or experienced, much of which was incontrovertibly racially motivated, reinforced concepts of state oppression and racial targeting, some of the same realities that had convinced families who lived in these neighborhoods to leave the South. Where else could they go?

Police violence was unquestionably a serious problem in New York City in the 1950s and 1960s, particularly for African Americans and Puerto Ricans. Paul Chevigny, Marilynn S. Johnson, and Clarence Taylor have thoroughly documented some of the NYPD's acts of aggression against New Yorkers.[2] Police officers who have written of their service during the 1960s provide firsthand accounts of how violent the city's police could be, particularly when protected from public view: "The squad room was a very violent room. They don't do it as much anymore, but in the time I was a detective it was just part of the job: knock the shit out of a guy, kick him in the ass. You learn this as you're coming up the line. You see other people do it, and you find that this is the way to interrogate people." As far as interrogations were concerned, virtually nothing was out of bounds, post–third degree and pre-Miranda, including two men beating the suspect with pillows, a technique that leaves no marks. As former detective Bill Phillips explains, "He did the crime anyway. I guess I was a believer that if these guys did something, whatever means you could use to extract it, short of hanging him out the window or murdering the guy, it was OK."[3]

Officers saved their most unreserved violence for men who resisted policemen. Once such suspects were brought back to the precinct, officers would attack with abandon, as in one instance in East Harlem in the 1960s:

I've seen a guy brought in, cop fighter, handcuffed, hung up in the squad room on one of those mesh cages. Then the cops beat the shit out of him. They let him hang there all day. This was the Twenty-Fifth Precinct. Hanging there like Jesus Christ. Guys coming on duty beat the shit out of him. Guys going off duty beat the shit out of him. He's hanging there. Guys walk in, pow, kick him in the balls, bust his fucking head. Unmerciful . . . I've seen cops put a guy in a room, break sticks over his head, kick him in the balls, bounce him off the walls, let him lay there in his own blood and vomit, just because he smacked some other cop.[4]

A different detective, Robert Leuci, describes a similar scene, this time replete with a crown of thorns, in the Bronx. Every man who observed these situations was expected to join in, as a demonstration of his commitment to the brotherhood and silence of the force.[5]

There are other ways to think about police brutality. As damaging to individuals and communities as unjustified police violence is, what was far more destructive to people's presents and futures was the lack of responsible policing so many Black New Yorkers endured. People in Central Harlem repeatedly articulated that they wanted *more* policing, not less.[6] Though it may seem paradoxical, with complaints of police brutality figuring prominently in activists' rhetoric, the preponderance of New York's Black residents lived in areas with high rates of violent and property crime. They desired more policing to address the increasing rates of street crime that poverty and lack of opportunity breed, and they wanted that policing to be respectful and professional. More policing and less police violence and discourtesy are not mutually exclusive, or at least they should not be. But to achieve both would be exceedingly difficult.

What many Harlemites knew, and the wider world would eventually find out, was that the city's police force did not just ignore crime, especially drug dealing, sex trafficking, and gambling. Some residents of the city's disinvested areas accused the police of apathy, viewing the white officers as indifferent to street crime in poor Black and Brown neighborhoods. A white, twenty-year veteran of the NYPD who retired in 1961 confirmed this:

> In busy precincts covering sections inhabited by Negroes and Puerto Ricans, the sphere of inaction is large. Incidents that would cause commotion and consternation in quiet precincts seem so common in ghetto neighborhoods that they are often not reported. The police rationalize this avoidance of duty with theories that the victim would refuse to prosecute because violence has become the accepted way of life for his community, and that any other course would result in a great loss of time in court, which would reduce the efficiency of other police functions.[7]

Dr. King, a man who was fundamentally of the South, understood this as well in 1965:

> The most grievous charge against municipal police is not brutality, though it exists. Permissive crime in ghettos is the nightmare of the slum family. Permissive crime is the name for the organized crime that flourishes in the ghetto—designed, directed, and cultivated by white national crime syndicates operating numbers, narcotics, and prostitution rackets freely in the protected sanctuaries of the ghettos. Because no one, including the police, cares particularly about ghetto crime, it pervades every area of life. The Negro child who learns too little about books in his pathetic schools, learns too much about crime in the streets around him. Even when he and his family resist its corruption, its presence is a source of fear and of moral debilitation.[8]

This was all true and accurate. Yes, organized crime networks viewed segregated Black and Brown neighborhoods as safe spaces for all manner of criminal activity. No, the police did not do very much about it. And yes, this was immeasurably destructive to the people who had to endure such an environment. And the situation was even worse than King described. King either did not know just how protected these sanctuaries were, or he did but was mindful of how explosive his claims would be.

In fact, a vested interest, not callousness, made the city's impoverished, racially separate neighborhoods so rife with violence and addiction. The NYPD's squads dedicated to suppressing drug dealing and gambling instead saw opportunities for personal enrichment and chose to foster and protect such activities in certain neighborhoods. Central Harlem became the epicenter of the nation's booming heroin problem in the 1950s and 1960s because some people, chiefly white organized crime figures and law enforcement officers from the units that were supposed to be combating the drug trade, decided it would be. On top of the worsening structural challenges Black New Yorkers faced, people whom residential segregation, failing schools, and a retreating job market had hemmed into neighborhoods that already had significant challenges, the police and crime bosses actively made life for them much worse than it had to be. Nowhere was this more acute than in Harlem.

The policing that Harlemites received in the 1960s was profoundly destructive to their well-being, the health of their neighborhood, and their children's futures. Thriving on corruption and lawlessness, the pernicious, cynical ways that the NYPD operated there were neither an aberration nor the product of a small number of wayward officers. Corruption and lawlessness had always characterized the NYPD to varying degrees, though both had been reined in intermittently over the decades, either because of massive scandals broken into the open or reformist commissioners.[9] Without question, officers continued to practice lower-level corruption—accepting free meals, soliciting bribes from tow truck drivers and undertakers—across the city and years, without pause. The combination of policing described in this chapter, however, was reserved exclusively for Central Harlem. It was highly organized, with officers assigned to Harlem's streets the foot soldiers of criminal enterprises they and their commanders built on top of extant organizational structures within the NYPD. Nowhere else in the city did the police not only permit but systematically participate in gambling, sex trafficking, and drug dealing operations. Departmental and municipal leaders allowed this destructive policing to flourish until, beginning in 1971, public hearings on police corruption and criminality humiliated the city, marking the end of the accepting attitude from the top toward such widespread malfeasance and exploitation. The brutal acts the city's police officers perpetrated on Harlem and its residents, though lacking the spectacle of a public beating, were years-long episodes of great violence that harmed every fiber of the community.

The NYPD in 1964

In 1964, the NYPD had just under 27,000 officers.[10] They were almost all white and nearly entirely male, with women numbering in the low hundreds. This was also the year women in the department won the opportunity, through a lawsuit, to take the written test to become a sergeant. They were still relegated to serve in the gender-segregated Bureau of Policewomen and would not be able to walk a beat or ride in a radio car, as about 70 percent of officers did, until 1973.[11] The average new officer in the 1950s and 1960s was a young, white man from an upper-working-class ethnic background, with a high-school education. Most of them sought out police work for job security, with only a single-digit percentage following their fathers into the force.[12]

Once candidates passed a written exam, a physical, and background check, they would attend the NYPD academy for two months. There they took classes with experienced, college-educated officers in law and government, the fundamentals of policing, how to conduct themselves with civilians, and first aid, and they were trained in martial arts and weapons use. While in the academy, the department put cadets under a curfew and forbade them to visit establishments that sold alcohol. This was no mere honor pledge: the NYPD had officers assigned to follow cadets to check for compliance. Those who satisfactorily completed their coursework graduated and became trainees, earning a salary of $6,365 in 1964, significantly higher than the median city income of $5,103.[13]

However, as much as the NYPD stressed professionalism at the academy and strove to put its best-educated, by-the-book officers at the head of the class, there were almost immediate conflicts between theory and practice. For one, the bulk of cadets, required to live in or near the city when they applied, would have had a good understanding of how officers conducted themselves in public. This dissonance led to "a basic lack of respect for the instructors, since the men already had personal experience with how different real police work was from the picture painted in the classroom." Cadets would do their work and meet the requirements to graduate, performing their dedication to the curricular ideals, but were already prone to disregarding the classroom instruction that was designed to increase the ethicality, competence, and rectitude with which an officer carried out his or her duties.[14]

This jettisoning of rules accelerated once the cadets went to work. Rookie officers spent the next four to six months paired with older patrolmen, for on-the-job training, at which point they would immediately begin unlearning all the ideas about professionalism and ethics they had taken in at the academy. As a former long-time officer and academy instructor wrote, "The more experienced men tell him that in order to become a real policeman, he'll have to forget everything he is learning at the Academy." His experienced colleagues would mock him for abiding by the theory and rules stressed at the academy, impressing on the rookie that policing is about the authority of the individual, a man empowered to make decisions as he sees fit in the moment. This new officer would now learn how police work was done in the real world.[15]

Asleep

In 1911, the state of New York mandated that the NYPD schedule its officers into three shifts, or platoons—8 AM to 4 PM, 4 PM to midnight, and midnight to 8 AM. The state had tried to change this arrangement of shifts on a number of occasions since, but the PBA had defeated state efforts a total of eight times, always killing the bill in committee.[16] Among other issues, one of the problems with the three-platoon structure was that the overnight shift fell when most people would be sleeping. Accordingly, NYPD officers frequently looked at this shift as a time to do just that. One officer, recalling his first night on patrol, describes his veteran partner driving to what was then the city's Jamaica Bay bird sanctuary in Queens and informing him it was time to sleep for a few hours: "Larry opened the car door and stepped outside, took off his tunic and gun belt and tossed them in the backseat, walked off a few feet and urinated in the weeds. Then he let himself into the car's backseat, blew up his pillow, and set the alarm clock. Using his tunic as a blanket, he was snoring in less than a minute."[17] His partner, Larry, referred to the practice as "heaving." Some officers working that shift were so bold as to go to their homes to sleep.[18]

Phillips, while assigned to the Twenty-Fifth Precinct, covering East Harlem, describes the culture of policing the city at night in the 1960s:

> All the cars used to line up; the guys would take off their shoes and go to sleep. The first time I saw it, I couldn't believe it. Well, fuck it. I'll sleep too. They start calling the cars, nobody answers. The fucking sergeant gets pissed, comes in the park blowing the fucking siren; everybody out of the park. It was unreal, fucking unreal. The next night, the same thing; everybody's in there sleeping.[19]

Officers did need to worry about the sergeant on duty, their next-in-command. He would figure out the common spots men would go to sleep and roust them out. When on the job under a sergeant who tried to ensure his men were actually working, officers would get creative, finding back rooms of restaurants and retail establishments or basements of apartment buildings where they could "coop," or hide while working; they would sleep, play cards, or do whatever else they wanted. At the Twenty-Fifth, the sergeants, who were responsible for ensuring those under them were doing their jobs, would also sometimes get caught sleeping in an out-of-the-way place. While stationed at the Nineteenth Precinct on the Upper East Side, the same officer described a work environment in which "a lot of the guys were card players and they'd sit all night eating pizza, drinking beer and playing cards."[20]

Graft

The dereliction of duty in which many officers engaged damaged the city's social fabric and confidence in citizens' leaders to do anything about the seemingly ceaseless escalation in street crime. Heaving and cooping, though, generally took place out of sight. Some New Yorkers surely understood such practices took place, but only a small number really knew how common they were. What more New Yorkers would have understood was the low-level graft, the steady diet of corruption on which the New York Police Department functioned, because pettier forms of bribery, by necessity, involved members of the public.

The breadth of this graft was remarkable. At the most basic level, eateries served free meals to officers on the beat or in the stationhouse. This took place throughout the city, with police officers taking thousands of free meals a day, and not just as a courtesy. NYPD officers commonly moved past accepting into expecting. Establishments that police favored heavily would suffer under the weight of demand and entitlement, being in no position to deny the perquisite. Refusing to serve was not an option; neither was asking for a small payment in exchange for the meal. One restaurant, which offered two-dollar chicken dinners for delivery, found itself bringing dozens of these meals to its local precinct every week. To reduce the financial pain of giving away hundreds of dollars a month, the owner began charging officers fifty cents for each dinner. Immediately, he found his drivers getting ticketed every time they made a delivery, racking up $600 in fines in one week.[21]

Meals were not enough. Businesses would need to give more. They offered—had to offer—more than just coffee and chicken. The police would be able to demand, and receive, any number of goods and services, from cigarettes, alcohol, and groceries to dry cleaning. At Christmas, nearly every business in the precinct was expected to give one large payment, usually several hundred dollars, to the stationhouse, along with individual payments to beat cops. The large payments would be pooled and doled out back at the precinct, while officers got to keep their personal payments. Ranking officers centralized collection of precinct-level payments, employing a lower-status policeman to serve as his graft collector, or bagman. The bagman would get a separate payment for that work, in addition to the payments all officers would receive once the money had been divided. In other instances, captains might have had their own private sources of revenue, from which they excluded the rest of the precinct.[22]

Those involved were not rogue elements of the police force. In May 1970, the city's Commission to Investigate Alleged Police Corruption, commonly known as the Knapp Commission for its chairman, Whitman Knapp, began studying NYPD corruption. As it wrote in its December 1972 final report, "Almost all policemen either solicited or accepted such favors in one form or another." What all this amounted to—the free food and other goods, soliciting cash payments, and punishing those who refused to fully comply—was a police department-run protection racket. This is one of the ways organized crime operations were making money in the city at the same time. The NYPD, from a fairly high level on down, was running a parallel effort, one with even more powerful threats than violence. Those same officers who smiled in your face when serving them dinner could and would make your life miserable the next day if you crossed them. The city's police force conducted itself with a sense of entitlement. It was their city, and officers could do as they wish. Residents owed them whatever they wanted.[23]

Many officers saw violations of the law as opportunities to make extra money. Some were relatively minor, such as stores selling beer on Sundays. The police would commonly allow such conduct to continue, provided owners paid regular bribes. If clubs wanted to stay open past the city-mandated closing time, serve alcohol to minors, flout occupancy limits, and encourage patrons to violate parking rules, they could do that, again, provided their operators paid off the police.[24] Other businesses, facing the challenge of parking in a crowded city, saw bribery as a line item in a budget. As veteran city reporters wrote in *The Nation* in 1959, "Some of the largest and most reputable papers in the city pay off the police to make sure that their delivery trucks don't get tickets when they clutter the streets at edition time." They claimed the corruption began at the highest level in the precinct, with the captains, the men who oversaw each stationhouse.[25] The Knapp Commission found that the many small payments officers would receive, either individually or shared, added "substantially to a patrolman's income."²⁶ One officer confessed he averaged between sixty and one hundred dollars per month in illicit income and expected $250 at Christmas.²⁷

Police payoffs did not stop with quality-of-life offenses or infringements of lesser codes. Graft thoroughly pervaded the legal system, from the street to the courtroom. Officers would accept money in exchange for not issuing tickets to drivers for violations ranging from running red lights to drunk driving.²⁸ In other instances, officers would refer those they had arrested to lawyers who would split the legal bill. If an officer arrested someone who had paid a bail bondsman and failed to show for the court appearance, he might demand payment from the bondsman for returning the defendant.²⁹ Others would promise to speak with the district attorney on a defendant's behalf, in an effort to have the charges reduced. What they were really doing was taking advantage of the plea-bargaining system, in which prosecutors offer defendants reduced sentences and penalties in exchange for a guilty plea, with the goal of not expending the resources a trial requires. Such arrangements were already common in the 1960s, save for egregious offenses. Experienced officers knew prosecutors were likely to pursue a plea bargain as it was, so no intervention would be required. Those they were arresting would be less likely to know the frequency with which plea deals were offered; officers were able to take advantage of this knowledge gap and exploit people's fears for profit.³⁰

For arrestees who were unable or unwilling to bribe themselves out of the initial offense, court appearances offered plentiful opportunities for defendants to escape conviction. One common method of throwing a case would be for the arresting officer to lie on the stand in exchange for payment. Phillips accepted money from an arrestee's relative to lie, did just that, and succeeded in having the case dismissed.³¹ Leuci claims he "never met one, not one defense lawyer whose practice was made up mostly of narcotics defendants who didn't offer me some sort of dirty deal if I would help his clients." While such behavior is a direct contravention of a police officer's job, the perversion of justice extended well beyond defense lawyers and individual officers. Assistant district attorneys also pressured officers to change their testimony, but for a conviction. Finally, judges who had paid tens of thousands of dollars into the old political club system in exchange for appointments to municipal judgeships could and would expect to make the investment back through corrupt arrangements with defendants and their lawyers. Stationed in Brooklyn, Leuci describes the city criminal court there as "a marketplace, not a hall of justice."³²

The culture of graft was so normalized and extensive that the police typically bribed one another to get any number of tasks completed or goals met.

According to every one of the dozens of police officers who testified before the Knapp Commission, this was how the NYPD's gears turned. Entry-level payoffs would be five dollars to a uniformed clerical officer in order to have reports typed up in a timely fashion. An officer desiring the required form to seek a departmental citation would need to pay a five-dollar bribe to get it. The man who determined schedules and assignments could earn up to two hundred dollars in payments from his colleagues who wanted to patrol sectors that offered more opportunities for illicit income or who wanted certain days off. Lieutenants would sell permanent assignments—typically those that were most lucrative—for five hundred dollars.[33]

Theft

For some on the force, what they took in from bribery, protection money, and free goods and services was insufficient. Officers frequently burglarized businesses that had already been broken into. Happening upon a freshly burgled delicatessen in the Nineteenth Precinct, Bill Phillips went searching for money inside and found a paper bag containing cash and checks. Nervous about his first crime of this nature, he reported the break-in and rushed to a nearby basement he used to sleep on the job. After pocketing the cash and tearing up and flushing the checks, Phillips returned to the scene, where he found two officers stealing the deli's television. After telling Phillips, "Don't worry, nobody's around," they loaded their loot into the trunk and drove away. Eventually, he would join other officers breaking into safes at burgled businesses, stealing and dividing up hundreds of dollars.[34] Waverly Logan, an officer stationed in Brooklyn, witnessed the second burglary of a business in which he "saw cops all over the place stuffing clothes down their pants and up their shirts. The sergeant never came in because, as one cop told Logan, the owner would take care of him later."[35] Some officers went beyond revictimizing those whose property had been stolen to enabling criminals not on the force to orchestrate high-value thefts. The Knapp Commission found officers working as guards for organized car thieves and that crime networks stealing commercial trucks packed with goods "almost always received police protection in one form or another."[36]

The recently deceased were even easier targets. Officers hastened to respond to calls of people who had died in their homes, as one never knew what might be inside. As Phillips recalls, "I know fellows made up to fifteen, eighteen thousand dollars on DOA's.... The only thing you have to bargain with is your conscience. But very few people I know wouldn't take this type of money. In fact, when you receive a call for a DOA.... Radio cars race to the scene. The cars try to beat the sergeant there and the sergeant tries to beat the cars." Indeed, Leuci witnessed a sergeant strip a man of all his valuables, using soap from the kitchen to remove the rings from his "still-warm" fingers, while accomplices kept the man's wife occupied elsewhere in the apartment. If a person were not quite dead, officers might ride along with the ambulance to await the inevitable. Should death come quickly, those officers would take the person's keys, return to the deceased's home, and plunder it.[37]

Numbers

By the 1960s, Harlem had been a hotbed of the numbers game for decades. A form of gambling also called the policy racket, players visited a designated betting location, chose one to three numbers, wrote them on a slip in triplicate, and placed a bet between a quarter and a dollar. An intermediary, known as a runner, would then gather up the day's slips and bets and deliver them to the operation's headquarters, or bank. The winning numbers, derived from financial figures at a chosen horse track that day, and therefore publicly verifiable, would pay out at rates of six to one, sixty to one, or six hundred to one, depending on how many numbers a winning gambler chose. The operation would keep a 40 percent cut of the winnings, and the runner would expect a tip from the winner.[38] While its importance has greatly diminished with the advent of state lotteries, numbers was a core feature of Harlem. Kenneth Clark described numbers as "a vital and indestructible part of Harlem's economy."[39] The novelist and native Harlemite Claude Brown agrees—"Numbers was the thing; it sort of ran the community."[40] It was also against the law and thus the province of external organized crime syndicates.

The NYPD had a unit dedicated to suppressing gambling, the Public Morals Division, with more than 3,500 officers in it. Like the rest of the department, the PMD was profoundly corrupt, but at an elevated level. Its corruption was more organized and far more lucrative than what the typical beat cop would encounter. This was a unit in which men, provided they avoided the occasional anticorruption sweep, would serve five or six years, go back to patrol, and use their ill-gotten gains as a retirement fund. The men at the heart of numbers extortion were part of a small group of 450 plainclothesmen, from patrolmen to captains, who wore regular clothing in an effort to not be so easily identified as police officers. But instead of running a protection racket victimizing legitimate businesses, these officers ran a protection racket targeting illegal enterprises. Systemically profiting from those breaking the law presented even less of a moral challenge to those who thought little of accepting free meals, cash payments, and merchandise on demand. Even though the money they extorted from the numbers operators came from the payer, who was engaging in criminal activity, officers rationalized it was "clean" money, since a majority of people both on and off the force viewed gambling as harmless, a classic victimless crime. And there was a great deal of money to be made.[41]

Corruption in the PMD was as old as numbers and the unit itself, going back at least into the Depression, and was clear to anyone who wanted to know about it. There had been corruption investigations into the NYPD in 1894, 1911, 1932, and 1950. The 1950 investigation failed to root out the organized extortion of numbers operators. Throughout the 1950s and 1960s, the officers assigned to stamp out illegal gambling operations instead worked to keep them in business on a "regular, highly systematic basis."[42] Commissioner Stephen P. Kennedy, running the NYPD from 1955 to 1961, was a strict disciplinarian and serious in his campaigns against corruption. He demoted, disciplined, reassigned, and fired many officers, across ranks, who had been either caught in or suspected of corruption. Like much of the public, and certainly in Harlem, Kennedy knew the police were deeply involved with numbers, so he targeted Harlem for more intense enforcement. Kennedy swapped in many rookies, with the idea they would not yet be familiar with the institutionalized corruption veterans knew so well. He also sent in handpicked teams to conduct enforcement, bypassing the PMD. Still, in 1959, a Manhattan grand jury determined the NYPD's Tenth Inspection Division, covering the Twenty-Fifth, Twenty-Eighth, and Thirty-Second Precincts in Central and East Harlem, was at least failing to enforce gambling laws, with the police likely benefiting financially from this. Kennedy fired and transferred more officers.[43]

The same year, two veteran city journalists wrote a special issue of *The Nation* focused on the manifold crises New York City was facing, from housing and employment to competent leadership and financial stewardship. The authors expressed a total lack of confidence that police corruption would change:

"Big Cop Shake-up in Harlem," the headlines will scream. In fifteen years in New York, the writing half of this team has written the same phony story so many times that he is now positively afflicted with nausea. The story will explain that the police commissioner is angry, he is getting tough, he is bouncing commanders out of Harlem and bringing fresh blood in. This is supposed to be drastic action. But is it? Is anybody ever prosecuted? Do any of the bribe-taking cops—and common sense says their number must be legion—ever go to jail? The public knows better. All that happens, usually, is that the bribe-takers are given new areas to cultivate.[44]

The following year, Adam Clayton Powell, then in his eighth congressional term and amassing increasing power, repeatedly attacked NYPD corruption on the floor of the House of Representatives. He accused the NYPD of sending "the dregs of the police force" to serve in Harlem. Powell kept up his assault on corruption in appearances at Harlem rallies and on television, calling out major figures by name, including Louie the Gimp and Slim Brown, as well as a handful of lawyers and bail bondsmen who counted numbers operators as steady clients, all with mafia backing. The *New York Post*, then a reputable newspaper conducting investigative journalism, looked into the congressman's accusations and confirmed each. The numbers racket plodded on. But despite Kennedy's efforts, Powell's attacks, and journalists' investigations, extorting policy operations "persisted in virtually unchanged form."[45]

As the authors of *The Nation*'s special issue in October 1959 pointed out, for numbers operations to maintain customers, they needed to operate out of a regular location, whether a candy store, basement, hair salon, or apartment.[46] PMD officers should have been able to find out what places housed policy rackets pretty quickly, given the high foot traffic and number of people who would seem to have no other business at one of these sites. Smart police work and intelligence gathering would have led to rapid identification of numbers joints. This is exactly what happened, but once identified, the police went to work extorting the operators, as opposed to shutting them down. Unlike other instances of benefiting from crime—taking a bribe from a speeder or stealing a television from a burglarized business—policy graft was not the result of sudden opportunity. Instead, it was organized and ordinary, utterly pedestrian, and typically conflict-free.

Once identified, the PMD put numbers enterprises on what was referred to as "the pad," meaning they would now be expected to pay fixed amounts every two to four weeks. The protection money from all of the operations would be pooled and divided. Each man received his share, or "nut," which ranged from three to four hundred dollars in Midtown Manhattan to fifteen hundred dollars in Harlem. One Harlem division extorted forty different policy facilities simultaneously, with each paying one hundred dollars a day, every day. Payments followed a hierarchical, ordered structure, with the men in charge of each unit getting one-and-a-half times the base nut. New men received nothing for two months but were compensated with two months' of coerced gains when eventually assigned to a new post.[47] Officers also received individual payments, just as legitimate businesses in the precinct paid.

Those on the operational side of numbers knew exactly who the enforcement side was, both the uniformed officers and those in civilian clothes. The gambling and bribery were done in plain sight. As Michael Armstrong, the chief counsel for the Knapp Commission recalled, "Any kid on any corner in Harlem could report seeing police officers being paid off by gamblers."[48] When Bill Phillips first began working in Harlem, strangers approached him and gave him between twenty and forty dollars, which was an essential feature of his time there. Running the protection scheme, not busting gambling dens, became the job.[49] While operators were inclined to pay, a successful extortion racket required keeping track of who had paid and which operations had shut down, moved, or sprung up. PMD units and other police competed with one another to get a numbers den on the pad. The men doing this work were highly motivated and resourceful—but they were putting their efforts into cultivating crime. Over the course of six months, Phillips made six thousand dollars in graft, as did every other man in his squad.[50] Robert Leuci describes numbers extortion as "the backbone and heart of corruption in New York City" and claims the money "went all the way up, right through police headquarters into the mayor's office."[51]

Of course, the Public Morals Division still had to make arrests, or else its total corruption would be too apparent. Those who were targeted had little to fear. PMD cases had their own division within the municipal courts, known as the Gamblers Part. While it was a criminal court, the sentences it handed out were lenient to nonexistent. Many arrests were dismissed, and most of the convicted had to pay small fines. This situation owed more to the fact that everyone involved—arresting officers, judges, prosecutors, defense attorneys—was willing to exchange money than to the contemporary social view of gambling.[52]

Corruption bred corruption. Almost all of those who were not corrupt became corrupt in short order. Very few policemen stayed honest in the 1960s. Some pursued as much illegal money as they could find, others took the standard precinct payments, while a good number accepted graft only for certain occasions—vacations, Christmas. Most policemen fell into those categories. Some lied about what they had done, boasting of nonexistent scores, hoping to impress their colleagues. A marginal number took nothing at all, getting by only on their salaries. And those men all kept quiet, despite their colleagues frequently refusing to work or socialize with them. They went along with the culture of corruption, perhaps doing their best to ignore it, keeping the wall of silence unbreached.

People could discount numbers as harmless and lament the corruption as regrettable, but in the early 1960s, a much more nefarious and destabilizing corruption was emerging in the NYPD. What had previously been taboo—profiting off of the drug trade—was now becoming an increasingly acceptable method of making money. It was less organized than policy protection, much more fruitful for those willing to engage, and in no way victimless.[53]

Heroin

In 1963, the Federal Bureau of Narcotics, since transformed into the Drug Enforcement Administration, determined that New York City had half of the total 48,535 heroin addicts in the United States. Organized crime syndicates had run heroin smuggling and distribution operations out of East Harlem since the 1940s, so it follows that the city would have a relatively high number of addicts. Heroin use had long flourished in New York, always centered in Central Harlem, where policing and political corruption had concentrated it. The most recent heroin contagion had burned itself out in the early 1950s but left deep marks long after.[54] As Claude Brown recalled about his time growing up in Harlem and becoming a heroin addict, "If anyone had asked me around the latter part of 1957 just what I thought had made the greatest impression on my generation in Harlem, I would have said, 'Drugs . . .' It seemed as though most of the cats that we'd come up with just hadn't made it. Almost everybody was dead or in jail."[55]

As late as 1962, NYPD officers, even those otherwise entirely corrupt, regarded drug money as "dirty" and refused to put dealers on the pad or to take bribes to let those caught with drugs go. Nor would they steal money or product from them. In just a few years, that would all change.[56] Men on the force who had grown up during the Depression and World War II had a dim view of drugs, associating them with ruin and the lowest element of society. Officers joining the NYPD in 1963, who would have been born in 1942 or a few years earlier, were living in a society in which the taboos surrounding drugs had diminished.[57] Plus, there was a great deal of money at hand, far more than what "clean" graft could provide.

NYPD officers referred to Harlem as the "Gold Coast" for all the money one could make through corruption. The nearly eight hundred men who were tasked with targeting drug dealing were detectives in the Narcotics Division, and they were almost all corrupt.[58] Working in teams of four, they began to take dealers' money when arresting them, reasoning they had not earned it and would just use it to bail themselves out. This money was irregular in both frequency and amount, the result of sudden opportunity. As more officers became open to profiting from the drug trade and realized just how much money there was to be had, they worked to make this income more regular. Soon they began using combinations of informants, burglaries, and unsanctioned wiretaps to determine who had significant quantities of cash and when. Armed with this knowledge, they could then raid a dealer and take his money, knowing he would be unable to complain to anyone.[59] In three-quarters of Narcotics Division raids, officers arrested no one. The men supervising drug squads were not fools. While they may not have known all the details or been in on it themselves, they had a general idea of what was happening—outright criminal activity—but did nothing about it, time and again.[60]

Quickly, their tactics degenerated into stealing money, drugs, or both and either arresting the dealer or letting him go. One could take some money, turning in the rest as evidence to be used in the criminal proceedings against the suspect. This was Bill Phillips's preferred approach. Waverly Logan favored a more aggressive technique: "When you're new, you turn in all the money. But when you're working on the job a while, you turn in no money. That's been my experience, that you don't voucher no money, or you voucher very little of what you made when a boss is there, and the boss is straight." And even when one had submitted all the confiscated cash, no one would believe you.[61] Other options included taking most of his money and all of his drugs and arresting him, taking most of his money and all of his drugs and letting him go, and taking all of his money but no drugs, so the dealer would have more money for the officer to take the next time.[62]

Stolen drugs served several purposes, none of which seems to have been personal use. Typically stored in officers' personal departmental lockers, drugs could be sold to addicts or given to informants to sell in lieu of cash. A detective could also keep some to plant on future arrestees, a process called "flaking." If one were to catch someone with a quantity of drugs not meeting the threshold for a distribution charge, planting more drugs on the person would upgrade the arrest from a misdemeanor to a felony, accelerating the officer's pace toward promotions, commendations, and pay increases. Flaking a suspect could also put the arresting officer in a position to extract a substantial bribe from someone eager to stay away from felony charges, whether real or augmented.[63]

The corruption involved with numbers was simple. It seems quaint when compared with what the police would innovate with the heroin trade. Detectives put some dealers on the pad, provided they paid the highest bribes yet seen. Some detectives in the elite narcotics squads could make three thousand dollars a month, per man, from one dealer. Because drug dealing is much more competitive, resource intensive, and violent than numbers, officers would have to engage in far more unsavory endeavors to keep those fire hoses of cash open. Putting a dealer on the pad means you have a vested interest in him succeeding, staying out of prison, and staying alive. These men needed protection—and who is better positioned to do so than the police? When a shipment would come in, officers would provide muscle to guard against a rival's attack. To help move drugs around with a reduced risk of their colleagues intervening, these men would rent cars for traffickers, in the name of official NYPD business, to transport drugs, so that other officers would either not pull them over or let them go soon after doing so. Corrupt officers would inform dealers about raids other law enforcement entities, including different parts of the NYPD, were planning. To shield these men from arrest, they would falsely list dealers who bribed well as informants in departmental files.[64]

As more officers pursued more money, their morals vanished. There was virtually nothing out of bounds for some of these men, all of which accelerated the devastation heroin dealing and use wrought upon Harlem. Not only were there profits to be had in extorting drug dealers, and stealing, selling, or bartering their drugs; there was also profit in selling dealers confidential information, like names of informants, information investigators had compiled on people, and locations of wiretaps. These officers were actively sabotaging the organization for which they worked. These were grave professional and legal transgressions—and the human cost was even worse. Drug dealers were not interested in learning the names of informants so they could stop talking to them. Informants had already begun a relationship with the police, which meant they had to be dealt with definitively. Several dozen informants would wind up murdered in the 1960s in New York City, dead through the betrayal of the men who were supposed to protect them but instead traded their lives for money.[65] Some officers went even further, personally kidnapping witnesses to prevent them from testifying against a dealer they were extorting and even offering hitmen to take care of witnesses permanently.[66]

The decisions these officers made, collectively and as individuals, had devastating consequences for the people of Harlem. The NYPD had long permitted heroin markets to exist in the Black neighborhoods of the city, along with the crime that accompanied it, from theft and robbery to support habits to the physical violence that dealing drugs often entails. Standing by while this happened, adopting a containment policy on heroin, was a severe dereliction of duty.

But by 1964, one could not speak of heroin simply existing. New York City was undoubtedly in the grips of a burgeoning heroin epidemic, and Harlem was its epicenter. Rates of street crimes like robberies, muggings, shoplifting, and burglary rose by hundreds of percentage points over the course of just a few years. African Americans throughout the city experienced the highest rates of violent crime, at two to three times what white New Yorkers endured, with poverty and rates of heroin use compounding the problem. Some parts of Central Harlem had almost 20 percent of residents on heroin. These people were already likely to be poor, and if not, their habits would quickly guarantee it. Their addictions compelled them to obtain the next fix however they could, which often manifested in crimes of convenience, with users victimizing their neighbors and passersby for a few dollars. As a direct outcome, the Twenty-Eighth Precinct soon became one of the most violent in the city.[67] The results had the NYPD actively fought the heroin trade are unknowable, but they surely would have produced a better quality of life for the people of Harlem than officers protecting traffickers and dealers and then engaging in both pursuits themselves. These men choosing to violate their oaths inflamed and accelerated a social decay that would take decades to repair. These neighborhoods and their residents are still recovering.

This would all get much worse, very quickly, in the few years following 1964. The police became more actively involved, more organized, and more corrupt in their dealings with heroin. The largest single cash haul anyone could verify officers taking for themselves was eighty thousand dollars, split three ways, which the Knapp Commission described as "by no means unique." Officers stationed in Harlem, particularly at the Twenty-Eighth and Thirty-Second Precincts, began trading drugs for stolen merchandise to local addicts, soon evolving into a steal-to-order arrangement.[68] There was more heroin, it was flowing more freely, and there were far more addicts, most of whom were Black or Puerto Rican. The plague of heroin in New York City was racialized and intentional, and there was almost no one to fight it. Parents, family members, friends, and health care practitioners were left to deal with it on their own. The NYPD and Lucchese crime family, not two organizations that are supposed to work in concert, conspired to flood Central and East Harlem with internationally trafficked heroin. It worked. The FBN, which should have served as a check on the NYPD, instead cooperated and competed with the city's police, with its agents in the New York office almost entirely corrupt as well.

The greatest score of all would not be from a dealer, or even a wholesaler, but the police department itself. Between 1969 and 1972, still-unknown people stole 261 pounds of heroin and 137 pounds of cocaine, with a street value of more than seventy million dollars *at the time*, from the department's Property Clerk Division, the office in charge of holding evidence and confiscated property. This included the entirety of the "French Connection" haul from 1962 and in total accounted for one-fifth of all heroin and cocaine the NYPD had seized since 1961. The absconders did not steal nearly four hundred pounds of drugs outright. Instead, they followed procedure, requesting the evidence and signing it out, but they all forged the signature of one detective and replaced the drugs with flour and cornstarch. The drugs made their way back out onto the streets from which they had come, greatly enriching a small number of law enforcement personnel and fueling the crime and misery inevitably attached to such substances.[69]

Colony

As history has shown over the last fifty years, eliminating drug use, addiction, dealing, and distribution chiefly through zealous law enforcement and incarceration is an unsuccessful strategy. However, those NYPD officers nurturing the heroin plague were not acting out of a libertarian devotion to individual choice and responsibility. They acted out of selfishness and racial animus, motivated to extract as much money from communities like Central and East Harlem as they could. These were brutal acts that perpetrated a great violence on Black neighborhoods, the people who lived in them, and their institutions.

It is clear that many officers had, at best, no respect for places like Harlem and Bedford-Stuyvesant. Others had outright antipathy both for the neighborhoods and the people who lived in them. Many studies have demonstrated that the New York Police Department had deep-seated issues with racial prejudice and hatred during these years.[70] As Bill Phillips described his former place of work, the Twenty-Fifth Precinct: "The whole fucking Harlem stinks. Every hallway smells of piss, garbage, smelly fucking people. I hated the fucking place." While working with federal agents on an anticorruption investigation and wearing a wire, Phillips repeatedly used the phrase "that fucking nigger" to describe any Black person. When one of the agents challenged his language, Phillips informed him, "That's the way New York cops talk."[71] Leuci writes that he and his colleagues typically referred to Black people as "yoms," an Anglicized abbreviation and corruption of "melanzana," the Italian word for eggplant.[72] As Anthony Russo, a labor official for seven mayors, from La Guardia to Koch, explained, "Hell, it's simple. These guys don't live in the city anymore and don't care what happens to it. And a lot of them hate the blacks and Puerto Ricans."[73]

African American and Puerto Rican officers were not necessarily more sensitive to the neighborhood. As Claude Brown recalls of childhood acquaintances who had joined the NYPD: "They seemed to be exploiting Harlem too, once they got in there. These were the same cats who had come up in Harlem. They didn't care anymore either. They just wanted to go out there and get some of that money too."[74] Waverly Logan would eventually wind up in an all-Black and –Puerto Rican undercover unit working in Harlem; like every other unit there, it, too, was thoroughly corrupt. Skin color was no armor against malfeasance.[75]

By 1964, Kenneth Clark had come to view Central Harlem as a colony.[76] The neighborhood had become fundamentally a place of extraction. People lived isolated lives that outsiders dominated. Most of those who called it home owned virtually nothing—not their apartments, not businesses, and not even the successful gambling and drug-dealing operations. Harlem's economy was highly unbalanced: the bulk of the money people spent went out, and far less came in. Residents had a disproportionately weak political voice. The city's residential segregation diluted African Americans' electoral strength and representation, as most politicians aspiring to represent New Yorkers at the municipal or state level did not have to appeal to a diverse group of voters. While their congressman enjoyed great popularity in his district, some Harlemites saw Powell as someone who failed to deliver to his constituents, instead taking advantage of them for his own ends, a man "who was always making those pretty promises that never amounted to anything, those bullshit promises."[77] Businesspeople, politicians, organized crime syndicates, and the police all saw Harlem as a place of opportunity. It was a neighborhood that could be used for one's own benefit, taking advantage of a captive population, one with a deliberately diminished capacity to stand up for itself.[78]

Those assigned and sworn to protect the people of New York City contravened their missions in ways small and large, almost to a man. Some of them attempted to justify what they practiced as economic necessity, claiming their salaries, whether as entry-level patrolmen or detectives with nearly a decade on the force, insufficient for men with families.[79] These tens of thousands of men, over years, betrayed their city and those who counted on them. At its worst, the corruption so many of them pursued turned entire neighborhoods into booming drug markets, casting all those contained within, already feeling the forces of educational and residential segregation and economic discrimination, into lives steeped in crime, violence, and the slow decay of addiction. Harlem was the place where these factors collided and coalesced in the most violent and poisonous ways. Most residents took no part in any of these activities, but it was not possible to live in Central Harlem and not experience them. Many members of the New York Police Department, through not just ignoring but working to expand drug distribution and addiction for their own benefit, perpetrated long-term social and economic violence on the city's most vulnerable communities. Dirty cops saw it as "paradise."[80]

Conclusion

For decades, it was easy for citizens not exposed to police corruption to dismiss charges of it as propaganda that enemies of the police had manufactured or, when undeniably true, the work of a few renegade actors. When someone like Representative Powell spoke up, those who did not want to believe his accusations could find convenient reasons to do so, given Powell's brash manner, flashy lifestyle, and bombastic public pronouncements.[81] Whenever the public learned that the accusations (including Powell's) were true, then the department would reflexively cast the guilty officers out as "rotten apples." As the Knapp Commission found, the idea of corrupt police as individual exceptions was not simply an offhanded explanation but a vital method of maintaining morale and public confidence in the police force. It also was an impediment to structural change, as NYPD leadership would have to acknowledge organized, extensive corruption throughout the city in order to more fully address these problems.[82] The steady denials came also from on high, from elected and appointed leaders whose words carried significant weight, certainly more than what an average citizen had—and a disparity even greater when that person was Black, Brown, or poor.

While Central Harlemites could not have known the scale and depth of the NYPD's corruption, they understood it was happening. They watched officers take bribes in the middle of the day. They knew policy operators had no reason to fear the police. They saw as heroin came ripping back into their community in the early 1960s. Bayard Rustin knew this corruption well, and stated it plainly, on television:

> I have seen in New York City, prostitutes arrested on the street, supposedly, taken around the corner, they give the officer so much money, and he lets them go. I have seen dope addicts in Harlem, stopped on the street, supposedly arrested, taken around the corner, their money taken away from them, and they're sent down the street. Now, no young Negro in Harlem can have any respect for police when he sees that kind of thing going on, and then this officer dares to come to him and accuse him of a crime because he's shooting crap in the street. And there's a double resentment when they know the police—many of them, not all, but many of them in Harlem—themselves engage in the most criminal forms of bribery.

And as Basil Paterson, a leader of Black Democratic politics in Harlem, explained, "You can't very well expect people to cooperate with the police, and I don't know how police can function properly unless they're getting cooperation from the people of the community, when the people of the community have no respect for law enforcement, and for good reason."[83]

By 1964, it would have been difficult for the people of Harlem to feel as though outsiders and people in power really cared about them. They had been living increasingly segregated lives, experiencing declining fortunes, with no better tomorrow in sight. Children had little hope to do better than their parents. Jobs were vanishing. Schools were getting worse by the year. The police were corrupt in a multitude of ways, and too many of them were unnecessarily violent. As Claude Brown concluded:

> Harlem was getting fucked over by everybody, the politicians, the police, the businessmen, everybody. There were a lot of things that we knew about but didn't think about when we weren't high: how nobody cared too much about cleaning up the junkies or making drugs legal so they'd stop robbing people, since it was just Harlem and East Harlem; how nobody gave a fuck about some niggers and some Puerto Ricans, so that's why nothing was going to be done about it.[84]

Was he wrong?

6

A Death and Protests

It seemed as though Harlem's history is made on Saturday nights. . . . People know you shouldn't bother with Negroes on Saturday night, because for some reason or another, Negroes just don't mind dying on Saturday night. They seem ready to die, so they're not going to take but so much stuff.

–CLAUDE BROWN, MANCHILD IN THE PROMISED LAND

There are in this country tremendous reservoirs of bitterness which have never been able to find an outlet, but may find an outlet soon.

–JAMES BALDWIN, OCTOBER 1963

New York's experience with the July uprisings and how people acted and reacted provides us with insights into the local and national civil rights movements as well as African American New Yorkers' attitudes toward integration-oriented movement goals. From the moment of the shooting, we can see the anger African Americans in New York, especially the young, had been carrying with them and the forthrightness with which they expressed it. Unlike cities in which the southern movement was strong, nonviolence did not predominate as a strategy in New York. Black New Yorkers did not embrace violence, but some found physical attacks on the police appropriate, especially in the face of what they characterized as police murder. Black high-school students at the scene of James Powell's death had no compunction about throwing cans, bottles, concrete, and whatever else they could find at officers. This is a trend that would continue throughout the uprisings, with thousands of Central Harlem and Bedford-Stuyvesant residents fighting the police. Some citizens claimed they used physical force only as self-defense against rampaging officers, but their actions violated the tenets of nonviolence nonetheless. Many more citizens willfully attacked the police from afar, lobbing projectiles at them, while others did so from strategic locations such as rooftops and windows. These were tactics of warfare. Night after night, people waited for their chances to attack the police. Black New Yorkers set the model for the urban upheaval to come in other cities.[1]

Black New Yorkers' physical attacks on police demonstrate how little restraining influence national civil rights groups like CORE and the NAACP had in the city. No doubt many Black southerners also wished to physically resist the police, but they rarely did so, partially because of how strong and organized the nonviolent movement was at the local level. New York activists, by contrast, knew the tactics that were so successful in the South, such as sit-ins, boycotts, and provoking white violence, were not effective in the city. Black New Yorkers and their white allies had used these tactics for several decades but won little. For example, they sat in at municipal offices and union halls, picketed stores in Black neighborhoods whose owners would not hire Black workers, and boycotted schools to secure desegregation. The tactics were largely ineffective because there were no discriminatory laws to defeat or crudely racist officials to expose to the world, as was the case in the South. While southern activists had clear targets in Jim Crow laws, there was no written system of oppression in the North. Northern segregation was diffuse, not centralized.[2]

Though the heads of three major national civil rights organizations lived in or around the city, they and their groups never dominated activism in New York, nor did their ideologies of gradualism and integration.[3] They were unable to offer Black New Yorkers many tangible achievements in terms of jobs, better housing, or desegregated education, which precluded the established groups from building a strong base in the city's Black neighborhoods they could have used to quiet the chaos once it began.

In fact, during the uprisings many residents of Central Harlem and Bedford-Stuyvesant vocally rejected anyone preaching nonviolence and restraint, not just on the streets but also at demonstrations, mass meetings, and Powell's funeral. Groups of people regularly shouted down as Uncle Toms and liberals those pleading for calm or speaking of voter registration, whether the national

Figure 6.1 The "Big Six" national civil rights leaders meet at the Hotel Commodore in New York City in 1963. From left: John Lewis, Student Nonviolent Coordinating Committee; Whitney Young Jr., Urban League; A. Philip Randolph, AFL-CIO; Dr. Martin Luther King Jr., Southern Christian Leadership Conference; James Farmer, Congress of Racial Equality; Roy Wilkins, National Association for the Advancement of Colored People.

Source: Library of Congress, Prints and Photographs Division, NYWT&S Collection, LC-USZ62-126847.

movement veteran Bayard Rustin or an unknown local worker. The same people enthusiastically applauded militant and Black nationalist speakers who excoriated the police and advocated guerilla warfare.

Throughout the disorder and from the moment of the shooting, demonstrators, witnesses, and participants drew continual links between the civil rights movements in New York City and in the South. The connections they expressed show that while there were distinct regional wings of the movement, African Americans commonly viewed it as one struggle. People from school children to seasoned organizers frequently referred to race relations in the city as being equivalent to or worse than Mississippi, the state widely understood to have the

110 A Death and Protests

Figure 6.2 15,000 demonstrators in a Harlem solidarity march for voting rights and racial justice, on March 14, 1965, one week after state and local law enforcement brutalized marchers in Selma, Alabama. While the northern and southern movements were distinct, they were closely connected.

Source: Library of Congress, Prints and Photographs Division, NYWT&S Collection, LC-USZ62-135695.

worst record on civil rights in the country, to see the most violence against African Americans, and to be the most dangerous place to do civil rights work. New York was supposed to be different, but many people were not so sure. The southern movement and the violence its participants faced were frequently on the minds of many of New York's Black citizens in 1964, both as a comparison and a source of anger. What happened in the South mattered in the North.

Killing

Thursday, July 16, 1964, started out as an ordinary summer day in Manhattan's Yorkville neighborhood. It was hot and humid, as it typically is in the city in

July, with the temperature already at 76 degrees by nine AM and reaching 85 before the end of the day. That morning, James Powell and Thomas Gilligan crossed paths through coincidence, forever changing the city's history. Powell, a fifteen-year-old African American boy from the Bronx, was attending summer school at Robert F. Wagner Junior High School on East Seventy-Sixth Street, between Second and Third Avenues in the city's Yorkville neighborhood. He had enrolled in a supplemental reading course that began ten days earlier. The previous summer, he worked as a local youth organizer for the March on Washington for Jobs and Freedom, which he attended along with 55,000 others from the city.[4] Neighbors and friends characterized Powell as "a nice guy" who stayed out of trouble.[5]

Gilligan, thirty-six years old, having spent the last seventeen of those with the New York Police Department, had the day off from his job as a lieutenant in Brooklyn's Fourteenth Division. A military veteran, the lieutenant was a decorated member of the police force, awarded with nineteen citations for outstanding police work, four of them for disarming men with guns. While in a television repair shop across from the school, he heard some commotion outside. Powell and two other students, waiting for school to start, had gotten into an altercation with an apartment building superintendent, Patrick Lynch, after he had sprayed them with a hose.[6] The boys, unhappy with being sprayed, chased him back into his building, where he locked himself in his first-floor apartment and called the police.[7]

According to the NYPD, Gilligan emerged from the repair shop to investigate the noise and saw Powell and his two friends "banging on an apartment door with a garbage can lid."[8] Gilligan's later testimony before a grand jury was in conflict with this, asserting that what he saw was much more serious: Powell running after Lynch with a three-and-a-half-inch pocketknife. In the lieutenant's version of events, he stood in front of the apartment building, displaying his badge and gun to Powell with the verbal warning "I'm a police officer. Come out and drop it." Despite having a gun pointed at him, Powell responded by charging head-on out of the building hallway, knife drawn. Powell, five feet six inches tall and 122 pounds, lunged at Gilligan once, grazing his arm and drawing blood.[9] The lieutenant, six feet tall and weighing two hundred pounds, fired a warning shot, but Powell persisted in his attack. Gilligan then fired three shots at Powell.[10] The first missed; the second, proving fatal, initially struck him in the right wrist, severed an artery just above his heart, and came to rest in his left lung; and the third passed through his abdomen, striking the largest vein there.[11] By 9:20 AM, James Powell was dead.

Other witnesses provided a different account of the morning's events. Some students claimed Patrick Lynch, the apartment building superintendent, called the boys "dirty niggers," following with the proclamation "I'll wash you clean" as he deliberately sprayed them.[12] Others quoted him as saying "I'm going to wash all the black off you."[13] A nurse who witnessed the shooting said she saw Lynch "spraying a bunch of colored kids and as the kids moved back, he went after them with more water."[14] Lynch pleaded otherwise, quietly asserting he had never had problems with any of the students, calling them a "good bunch" he let sit on his building's steps to eat lunch every day. He swore that he did not speak a mean word to the boys and had accidentally sprayed them after he "asked them 10 times to move."[15] Some of Powell's schoolmates reported he and his two friends threw garbage can lids and bottles at Lynch.

A fourteen-year-old girl who was also waiting for school to start that morning told a reporter, "I saw the boy [Powell] go into the building and he didn't have any knife then. When he came out, he was even laughing and kind of like running." As other students contended, "when he came out of the hallway, he didn't have a knife." Gilligan appeared unannounced and, with no warning, shot Powell. The aforementioned nurse corroborated this: "This tall man with black hair [Gilligan] came out of the radio shop and he had a little black revolver. . . . As the boy came out, he shot him twice and then the boy fell to the sidewalk, and this man stood there for maybe 10 minutes just staring at the body. The boy never had any words with the man."[16] He then kicked Powell's body or turned it over with his foot, depending on the account. One of the two boys Lynch had sprayed along with Powell maintained Gilligan called Powell a "dirty nigger" after killing him.[17] Noticing students crowding around him, he waved his gun around to convince them to move across the street.[18]

Of all those who witnessed the incident, only one or two backed Gilligan's assertion that Powell had a knife. Gilligan also had an insignificant cut on his finger.[19] One of the dead boy's friends claimed he had been holding a knife for Powell that morning, which Powell took from him before the shooting but never used.[20] Lynch, whom Powell had supposedly menaced with the knife, said he never saw anyone with a knife when interviewed the next day but "had been told about it."[21] A teacher found a knife eight feet away from Powell's body, between two parked cars, but the police never definitively connected it to Powell, nor did they say much about it publicly.[22] They also refused to allow reporters on the scene to photograph it.[23] An NAACP investigation gathering information from fifty witnesses concluded Powell was holding a soda can and was walking away from Gilligan when shot.²⁴ The FBI, in its report to President Johnson, accepted the lieutenant's account verbatim.

The FBI's investigation into the incident also drew very different conclusions about Powell. According to its findings, "he had begun indiscriminate fighting as early as 7 years of age." He was described as a terrible student, missing thirty-two days in the 1963–1964 school year. When he did attend, "he was repeatedly accused of bullying other students, picking pockets and even fighting in the guidance office." Agents reported he was a member of a gang and had once been hospitalized for a stab wound to his leg. And they said he had been arrested at least twice, with one resulting in probation for assault; the other arrest's conclusion, for attempted robbery, was unclear. This was all ruinous to Powell's reputation and would likely serve to justify in many people's minds Gilligan's taking of his life, either because the boy was so violent that the officer had no choice or because Powell was an incorrigible animal who needed to be removed from the planet. Most significant of all, because of Powell's age, the bureau had no access to his official record. Where did it get this information, then? "Inquiry in the neighborhood in which the deceased boy lived," the agency wrote. Whether all true, partially true, or nothing but rumor, this would be the final word on James Powell for many people, at a time when the FBI enjoyed broad and deep trust.²⁵

Within minutes of the shooting, a large, mostly Black crowd gathered at the scene of the shooting in this overwhelmingly white neighborhood to boisterously protest Powell's death. These were young people arriving for school; teachers managed to maintain order in the twenty-five classes already in progress inside the building. The few police on the scene pushed them away from the area and told them to go either into the school or home. This response not only failed to disperse them but elicited cans, bottles, and chunks of cement sailing through the air in the direction of the patrolmen. The crowd grew to an estimated size of three hundred, despite the best efforts of several teachers and Max Francke, the summer school principal. Using a police megaphone, Francke urged the students to clear the area, but none of them heeded his pleas. As the crowd grew, so did the intensity of emotions, with "young girls [becoming] hysterical, tears streaming down their cheeks." Some students reportedly screamed, "This is worse than Mississippi!" evincing a visceral sense of the interconnectedness of civil rights struggles throughout the country and the violence African Americans faced at the hands of white people, particularly police. An African American teen girl, in what would become the most sensational quote of the morning, taunted police: "Come on, shoot another nigger!"²⁶

It took about one hundred steel-helmeted police two hours to disperse the crowd.[27] Most of the students belatedly filed into the school. Some walked around the surrounding area engaging in petty vandalism, such as pushing over flowerpots, and a group of young people went into the Seventy-Seventh Street and Lexington Avenue subway station two blocks away, banging on train doors and disturbing a newspaper stand. Nearly two hours after Gilligan shot Powell, East Seventy-Sixth Street was once again clear. One police officer was hit in the head with a soda can and received treatment at a hospital. The police took three "screaming girls" into custody and released them "after they had calmed down."[28] For the next twenty-four hours, the police kept a "special detail" of twenty-five patrolmen in the three blocks around the school to guard against further protest.[29]

Francke, the older white principal of the summer school, was exceptionally sympathetic toward the protesting students and saw both Patrick Lynch, the building superintendent, and the police as sharing substantial responsibility for what had transpired that morning. The students' reaction in the street, in Francke's analysis, was "produced because a white adult," Lynch, "didn't use his good sense." Francke viewed Lynch as having hosed the students "with malice aforethought." The principal further indicted Lynch as causing the entire chain of events, implying he was partially responsible for Powell's death: "What could have been handled very promptly and efficiently [the students sitting on the apartment building steps] by the school turned into a tragedy."[30] An important part of this becoming a "tragedy" was a white man aggressively using a hose against Black youth, which the world had seen Sheriff Bull Connor deploy in painful detail just one year earlier in Birmingham, Alabama. Francke argued the police could have prevented the school children from massing in the street and confronting the police "if someone had acted sensibly. If only a couple of police cars had arrived, and if the boy [Powell] could have been removed immediately, along with the lieutenant and key witnesses, none of the disturbance would have occurred."[31] Francke also defended the general population of the summer school students, protesting, "They gave up a summer's vacation because they wanted to improve themselves. These children are not hooligans. They're dedicated to improving themselves and we never had any trouble with them."[32]

Within two hours after the shooting, representatives from the national office of the Congress of Racial Equality, the city's East River chapter of CORE, and the New York branch of the NAACP arrived at the NYPD's nearby Nineteenth Precinct on East Sixty-Seventh Street, all with similar demands. As with all homicides, District Attorney Alexander Herman's office launched an investigation into the shooting, but civil rights groups and many individual citizens wanted more. After meeting with police and hearing the official version of Powell's shooting, the groups emerged with joint demands for a more probing investigation.[33] Blyden Jackson, East River CORE's chairman, told reporters the shooting required a "civil investigation . . . independent of the police."[34] His organization announced a demonstration for noon on the next day, Friday, July 17, at the Nineteenth Precinct, to push the city to create a "disciplined and impartial committee" to review the shooting.[35] The local NAACP declared its insistence for "an immediate investigation by the District Attorney aimed at a possible murder indictment."[36] In a letter to Mayor Wagner, the New York Civil Liberties Union reasoned "that a 6-foot, 220-pound man should be able to relieve a 15-year-old-boy of a pocketknife without killing him or even resorting to the use of firearms."[37]

Protest

Friday, July 17 brought with it another day of heat and humidity. At 8 AM, when around seventy-five people, again mostly Black and young, gathered to march and sing in protest in front of the school where Gilligan shot Powell on East Seventy-Sixth Street, it was already 74 degrees, with the relative humidity the same number. The NYPD was aware of the CORE-organized demonstration ahead of time and sent fifty police to wait for the students two hours before it began. Initially with nightsticks at the ready, a member of the City Commission on Human Rights convinced the officers' superiors it would be in everyone's best interest to keep the weapons out of sight. The students picketed for four hours without incident, chanting such slogans as "Killer cops must go!" and holding signs reading "Save Us From Our Protectors" and "Stop Killer Cops." While the protesting students "jeered and hooted" at the police monitoring them, there were no physical interactions between the two groups.[38]

When the summer school session let out at noon, 150 students joined the demonstrators. By this time, it was 86 degrees. Downtown CORE's chairman Chris Sprowal worked diligently to keep the protests within the law, giving police no legal excuse to act against the picketers. He urged them, via megaphone, "to behave like ladies and gentlemen." Sprowal asserted, "People around here just want you to get into trouble so they can point and say, 'See, I told you so.' But we're going to fool them, and we're going to show them that we've had some training." Within a few minutes, the much larger group marched nine blocks to the Nineteenth Precinct, where it was corralled behind a barrier down the street. Police explained that with a firehouse, the Soviet Mission to the United Nations, and the Kennedy Child Study Center all on the same stretch of East Sixty-Seventh Street as the stationhouse, over a hundred people demonstrating would be too chaotic and disorderly. Eventually, police allowed twenty-five from the group to picket in front of the police station. After an hour, the protesters went home. Sprowal left them with the imploration that they continue picketing the school until Powell's funeral, at which time they should "empty the school" to pack the boy's funeral service. As the demonstration wound down, a white man yelled, "He deserved killing!" at a group of students leaving. When a few of them went after him, police grabbed the man and told him to leave the area.[39]

The CORE-led demonstration attracted people from other strains of the city's ideologically diverse Black Freedom Struggle. Several CORE staffers reported observing three men from Malcolm X's post–Nation of Islam political group, the Organization of Afro-American Unity, interviewing students. Members of the communist Progressive Labor Party were also at the scene and eager to organize. A fifteen-year-old Black boy, claiming to be from Monroe, North Carolina, home of the African American armed-self-defense icon Robert F. Williams, told students, "In Monroe, if the cops shoot a Negro, we arm ourselves and get that cop worse than he got us." Someone from CORE was quick to counter the boy's claims in the interest of heading off any further violence, asserting that "the situation is different" in Monroe. He told the crowd that Monroe police were on the front lines of propping up de jure segregation, while in New York City "not all police are racists, although racists predominate."[40]

Resistance

Tensions in Central Harlem had grown markedly by Saturday, July 18, when James Powell's body was first put on display for public viewing. Though not mutilated, Powell in an open casket echoed Emmett Till's Chicago funeral in 1955, with his mother wanting the world to see her son as he was. Over three hundred people attended the afternoon viewing at a funeral home in Harlem, on Seventh Avenue between 132nd and 133rd Streets.[41] By 6:30 PM, large crowds began gathering in Central Harlem in front of the Hotel Theresa on 125th Street at Seventh Avenue for a CORE-sponsored protest rally. The temperature read 89 degrees; the sun would not set for another two hours. Seventeen-year-old Judith Howell from Bronx CORE opened the rally by declaring, "James Powell was shot because he was black." She then argued, "We got a civil rights bill, and along with the bill we got Barry Goldwater and a dead black boy." By the time she was done, the crowd had grown to more than two hundred, not all of whom were friendly. Some members of the audience sought to invalidate the speakers' messages with exclamations like "White people dictate your policy!" criticizing the interracial nature of CORE's leadership and membership. In his address to this group, which contained hostile radical elements, Downtown CORE's chairman Chris Sprowal revealed a more militant attitude than he had a day earlier. He fulminated, "It is time to let the man know that if he does something to us we are going to do something back. If you say 'You kick me once, I'm going to kick you twice,' we might get some respect."[42] Reporters quoted Sprowal as telling the audience, "I belong to a nonviolent organization, but I'm not nonviolent. When a cop shoots me, I will shoot him back," to which some of those in attendance responded, "That's right, brother," and "Blood for blood."[43]

Once the CORE rally was finished, people stayed to listen to speakers from James Lawson's United African Nationalist Movement and the Harlem Progressive Labor Movement. The final speaker, Reverend Nelson C. Dukes, from Fountain Spring Baptist Church in Harlem, ended the gathering with a twenty-minute speech that roused the crowd to action. The people responded well to his call for a march to the NYPD's Twenty-Eighth Precinct at West 123rd Street and Eighth Avenue to demand Lieutenant Gilligan's arrest, shouting, "Let's go!" and "Let's do it now!"[44] Roughly 150 of them began the march around 8:45 PM.[45] Though the sun had set, the oppressive heat persisted in the mid-80s, and the stone facades that had been soaking up sun all day and the poor ventilation of Harlem's tenements and row houses ensured that interior temperatures were much higher. They gathered another hundred people on their way to the station, two blocks away, chanting the slogans "We want freedom," "We want protection," and "Down with police brutality."[46]

Some from the crowd attempted to gain entry to the stationhouse to demand Gilligan's arrest for murder. Five policemen locked arms to keep the demonstrators out. Additional police forced the protesters across the street. Many more residents had gathered near the precinct, both to participate and to watch.[47] A few citizens sporadically threw bottles and garbage can lids at the police, who responded by putting on helmets and sweeping rooftops for those throwing objects. Some people in the protest group shouted, "[Police Commissioner Michael] Murphy must be removed"; others castigated the twenty police in front of them as "Killers, murderers," and "Murphy's rats."[48]

The Reverend Dukes, Ernest Russell of East River CORE, and a few others formally presented their demands to Inspector Thomas Pendergast, in charge of the precinct at the time. They wanted Commissioner Murphy to appear at the station and publicly announce that Lieutenant Gilligan was being suspended. The spokespeople said the demonstrators would not move until then. At 9:20, the police began setting up barricades to keep the protesters away from the station. Demonstrators and police scuffled when the police tried to confine them. Inspector Pendergast ordered the men under his command to begin arresting anyone in the crowd who was showing outward signs of resistance. Sixteen of the demonstrators, including two who had spoken at the earlier CORE rally, immediately sat down on the sidewalk in nonviolent civil disobedience. Police took them "roughly" and as quickly as possible into the station to try to head off what they realized was on the verge of sliding out of control. Predictably, those in the street were unhappy with this action and became more agitated. They increased both their verbal and physical assaults on police, still mainly throwing bottles, debris, and garbage can lids. Many more police emerged from the station, anticipating battle. One of them took a bottle to the head and was hospitalized. Reverend Dukes lamented, "This has got out of hand. If I knew this was going to happen, I wouldn't have said anything."[49]

Police pushed demonstrators to the ends of the block, away from the stationhouse. A bus arrived carrying forty-eight officers from the NYPD's Tactical Patrol Force, a unit of two hundred men trained in martial arts, all under thirty years old and standing over six feet tall. Inspector Pendergast ordered them to charge and club those who remained in the streets, though the TPF may have in fact been armed with axe handles, as a former member recalls.[50]

Demonstrators, spectators, and bystanders were now fighting with police—some in self-defense, some on the attack. All the while, residents continued raining down bottles and garbage can lids on police.[51] The volleys from the rooftops helped fan a physical response to police attempts at crowd control. Roughly a hundred more Tactical Patrol men disembarked from two buses and immediately joined in the battle; this was an overwhelming show of force.[52] Ed James, an African American photographer for the *New York Post*, wrote the next day of witnessing the following scene: "A young Negro, trying to run, fell. A cop beat him with his club until his head bled and then handcuffed him. Those who didn't run fast enough got the club."[53] The police managed to quickly clear the section of 123rd Street that housed the precinct and establish barricades at either end. They set up a mobile police emergency truck to block Seventh Avenue, ringed by riot-ready police. A growing crowd of Harlemites, all Black, easily surpassing five hundred, surrounded the increasingly uneasy police.[54]

Shortly after 10 PM, with the temperature stubbornly at 80 degrees and the relative humidity quickly rising past 65 percent, the new police official in charge, Deputy Chief Inspector Harry Taylor, was gathering manpower in the form of off-duty police and reinforcements from other precincts in all five boroughs. Taylor ordered the Tactical Patrol Force to break up the crowd surrounding the emergency truck, which they did by jumping over barricades and running into the gathered people, nightsticks swinging, replete with the battle cry of "Charge!" While the police dispersed the mob, they were not successful in getting them to go back into their homes; rather, those in the street broke into smaller and more inflamed groups that spread about the neighborhood. Police began shooting at 10:30, firing into the air in response to a Molotov cocktail thrown at a police car filled with five patrolmen. What would become known as the Harlem Riot was now in full swing, radiating outward from West 123rd Street and Eighth Avenue.[55]

A few blocks north and one east, the corner of 125th Street and Lenox Avenue was ground zero for the turmoil on the first night. People had begun looting there by 11 PM, and it would not take long until it was described as a "disaster area ... littered with broken glass and debris" where "screaming crowds occupied each corner, pushing toward a ring of police cars and patrolmen crouched behind them. The police fired volley after volley into the air and over roofs as the crowd raced wildly back and forth." More police came and began charging the crowd, indiscriminately clubbing anyone in the way, regardless of whether they resisted or fought. One detective advised a reporter to not believe charges of police brutality stemming from the tumult, explaining, "We asked them to move. They didn't. They became abusive. We had to get a little tough."[56] Another officer later freely admitted to engaging in illegal violence, or "instant justice," during the uprisings. While patrolling the streets, he and his band of fellow policemen "entered any store that had broken windows and if we found anyone inside we would beat them to the ground with our axe handles, then move on to the next store without making any arrests."[57]

Within just a few hours, Central Harlem was a place with "smears of blood up and down the sidewalks," where "spent cartridges littered the pavement."[58] These cartridges were remnants of a sound that repeated so often throughout the night that "it sounded like an endless chain of firecrackers."[59] People had torn the protective gates away from many stores in the area, including grocery stores, an insurance agency, men's clothing stores, pawnshops, and liquor stores, so that they could smash the windows and gain entry.[60]

The disturbance spread rapidly during the night, drawing in thousands to participate in one way or another, some voluntarily, some clearly not of their own volition. As patrons from the nearly fifteen-hundred-seat Apollo Theater on 125th Street between Seventh and Eighth Avenues left a performance, they were met with people on the street speaking of police beatings and shootings. The same was true for people getting off the subway at 125th Street and Eighth Avenue. Throughout the night, people fought with police, looted stores, smashed windows, set trash cans alight, and vandalized cars. Others made the actions a spectator event, laughing and applauding as police and more active citizen participants chased and fought one another in a high-stakes version of cat and mouse. Those who sought respite from the calamity would typically flee into buildings, places where most police, at least in these circumstances, feared to tread. In what would become an oft-repeated scene over the next week, someone claiming a position of authority, in this case a police officer, told neighborhood residents to go home, to which someone in the crowd responded with some variation of "We are home—this is our home."[61]

As the night of July 18 wore on, it became undeniably clear that parts of Harlem were experiencing a severe disturbance. The cycle of bottle throwing, looting, vandalism, massing of police, police violence against anyone in the area, and scattering crowds continued for hours across an eight-block section of Central Harlem between Eighth and Lenox Avenues and 123rd and 127th Streets. Anxious police closed off the streets of Harlem to vehicular traffic between 110th and 135th Streets and Lenox and Eighth Avenues.[62] They kept pedestrians from 125th Street between Fifth and Eighth Avenues, beginning at 1 AM. Also at that time, the police called in fire trucks to block streets and requested Transit Authority police to guard Harlem subway stations and keep city buses out of the area.[63] At the upheaval's height, the NYPD had at least fifty squad cars in the area.[64]

The police response quickly intensified. A Black sergeant told the men in his command, five Black and five white, that they had to "be extra careful," advising them, "You're gonna be called a whole lot of names and you're gonna be provoked. I want you to lean over backward. But if anybody puts his hand on you, crack his skull. Try to do this thing peacefully, but if you have to, go hard."[65] Many did indeed go hard, with one reporter noting that "those who attempted to pass these corners [that police were occupying] were often greeted with a shout and a curse, and maybe a shove." An African American

Figure 6.3 Spectators to the uprisings jeer and taunt police on Lenox Avenue. They are mostly male and a variety of ages.

Source: Library of Congress, Prints and Photographs Division, NYWT&S Collection, LC-USZ62-136929.

man, one of many experiencing the same treatment, "who did not move along quickly enough from a corner was shoved hard by an officer and then hit in the back with a nightstick." A nearby police officer, momentarily mindful of public relations, told the reporter, "I hope you're not quoting all my comments. We just have to be firm with these [Black] people." Another warned against wading too deeply into the crowds, cautioning that the newsman would be in danger not from those residents in the streets but police gunfire.[66]

No longer using their guns to practice crowd control, the police in Harlem had begun firing at rooftops, aiming to stop the frequent barrage of bottles, bricks, garbage can lids, and whatever else was available.[67] In doing so, the NYPD had decided to skip a step in standardized police methods of crowd control, moving from nightsticks to live ammunition without first attempting to use tear gas. The NYPD's decision was in noticeable contrast to the number of police forces in the South who had rejected gunfire in favor of fire hoses, tear gas, and dogs to subdue and disperse African American demonstrators over the past year.[68] Surely southern law enforcement had earned its reputation for violence, cruelty, and inhumanity, but its methods of suppressing crowds were generally less lethal. A Swedish reporter for the evening newspaper *Expressen* who was in the thick of the upheaval accused the police of firing with deadly intent: "A water-filled bottle smashed on the pavement and more than 10 policemen drew their revolvers and fired almost simultaneously. . . . They were shooting to kill, not to scare. I was standing in the middle of them and I could not have made a mistake."[69] A photographer for the *New York Post* made a similar statement, contending that after an hour or two of being in the disorder, "the cops were still firing, but they were aiming and firing lower."[70]

The hundreds of police striving desperately to repress the uprising in Central Harlem had exhausted their ammunition by 3 AM. Two policemen, one with a machine gun and the other a shotgun, drove a truck laden with replenishments down from the Bronx and through the streets of Harlem, delivering munitions to their visibly relieved brothers.[71] The temperature had fallen to 74 degrees, but the humidity was peaking at over 80 percent. By 4:30 AM, the area had quieted considerably, and the disturbances in the streets appeared to cease for the night.[72]

After a nearly two-hour lull, crowds began forming again, increasing in size until by 7 in the morning on July 19, physical violence between the police and people on the street resumed to the point that "it appeared for several minutes that the situation might become worse than it had been during the night." This continued until about 8:15, when reinforcements arrived. Demonstrating curiously different methods than they had throughout the night, the police helped quiet the situation rather than intensify it. They walked slowly through the crowds, with no weapons in their hands and refraining from shoving anyone, simply instructing people to keep walking. Within half an hour, though there was much debris and evidence of a night of chaos, the sidewalks and streets were flowing as they usually did on Sunday mornings.[73]

Violence

During the course of the night, at least thirty-two stores were looted, most white owned.[74] Over seven hours, the police, numbering over five hundred, had shot fifteen people, killing one; beaten hundreds; and arrested at least thirty. One arrestee was Charles Humber. Though claiming he was on assignment for *Life* and had the credentials to prove it, he was accused of "failure to move along when ordered to by police." They beat many Harlemites for being on the street, guilty of running.[75] The *New York Times* reported that "scores of persons with bloodied heads were seen throughout the eight-block area" where the uprising took place. Twelve of the NYPD's own had been injured, including one who had the misfortune of taking a Molotov cocktail to the leg.[76]

While the NYPD inspector who headed the Tactical Patrol Force reminded his men to shoot only if someone's life were in danger, imparting upon them that "in this country we don't shoot people for crimes against property," not every officer shared his sentiments.[77] At least two of the gunshot victims were men whom police had shot in the back, both unarmed and reported at the time as in critical condition. One, Abe Rick, twenty-five years old, was accused of being in the process of stealing two watches from a pawnshop. The other, Thessolonia Cutler, thirty-four, was standing in a doorway.[78] Police shot an unarmed woman who had stolen shoes, with an officer on the scene taking delight in watching her "bleeding in the street . . . all over those shiny new shoes."[79] That night's sole documented fatality came when a police officer shot Jay Jenkins, a forty-one-year-old Black man from Central Harlem, in the forehead while he was allegedly in the process of tossing brick after brick down from a rooftop.[80]

Those who took to the streets also injured a few white people that night, in what would be an exceedingly rare occurrence over the next week. A CBS photographer was knocked out and had his arm broken.[81] In another instance, a group of Central Harlem residents attacked two white people driving through the area who were stopped at a red light at 3:30 Sunday morning. The twenty-four-year-old female passenger, a British woman, suffered several cuts to her head and reported her purse, keys, immigration papers, and $25 in cash stolen. The male driver, twenty-nine, received a dislocated shoulder. Both were hospitalized after police came to their aid.[82]

A reporter for the *New York Amsterdam News* provided the following firsthand account of an incident of police violence that night:

> You rush inside a bar at 125th St., and 7th Ave, and witness Police Car 1938 drop off a Negro male, blood rushing from his eyes and his white shirt and handkerchief dripping with his life.
>
> A friendly passing male seeks to help him, but his female companion frenziedly grabs at him to let the man alone as the helmeted Cossacks rush to yell

at the crowd to "move on, get the hell out of here." The police car, with a Negro and a white officer, speeds away having dispatched its passenger.

The bleeding victim sat crying for minutes on the sidewalk until a waiter from the restaurant went out and dragged him inside the bowling alley, away from possible further bruises.

The reporter went on to describe the atmosphere in Central Harlem that night: residents of all ages stood on the street in small groups "wondering what the cops are going to do next, and why." That evening, he said, "Negroes were not fighting Negroes, they were defending themselves against the hordes of blue shirts, helmets, billies, and gun shots."[83]

Not surprisingly, many Harlemites suffered serious injuries that night. Harlem Hospital reported treating seventy-five people for bruises, cuts, and stab wounds and seven for gunshots, while another hospital in Harlem, Sydenham, admitted thirty people for various injuries and also another seven who had been shot. Louis Smith, a CORE field secretary who had just returned to New York from Mississippi, referred to the scene in Harlem Hospital's emergency room as "worse than anything I ever saw in Mississippi. Even the ambulance driver cried.... They had to mop the blood off of the floor of the ward."[84]

Melvin Drummond, a twenty-four-year-old Black Central Harlemite who was on his way home from working for the Peace Corps in Europe, related the story of his beating to the *New York Herald Tribune*. He claimed that as he exited the subway station at 125th Street and Lenox Avenue, he entered a crowd. As a police sergeant was telling everyone to keep walking, someone threw a bottle. Drummond unexpectedly received a blow to the back of the head from a policeman's club. Then, four or five more police joined in beating the now handcuffed man until another sergeant told them, "Stop hitting this man; he didn't do anything."[85] Despite being someone who "didn't do anything," the police charged him with "felonious assault and interfering with an officer attempting to make an arrest."[86]

Drummond's account of his arrest describes what is known as a "cover charge," a lie to excuse police misconduct. As the veteran New York civil liberties lawyer Paul Chevigny argues, "The New York police are sophisticated enough in drawing charges and making them stick not to need an actual act of physical violence to arrest anyone. If they feel that a man is a troublemaker, they can, unfortunately, charge him with resisting arrest, without the necessity of risking injury to an officer." Though the man very likely may have committed no crime and violated no order, he was now in the hands of the legal system and would have a difficult and expensive time extricating himself without a permanent record. Chevigny continues:

> Once they have arrested him, of course, lying becomes an inevitable part of the procedure of making the quarrel look like a crime, and thus the lie is the chief abuse with which we must come to grips. If the police simply hit a man and let him go, there would be an abuse of the authority . . . but not the compound abuse of hitting a man and then dragging him to court on criminal charges, really a more serious injury than a blow. One's head heals up, after all, but a criminal record never goes away. There is no more embittering experience in the legal system than to be abused by the police and then to be tried and convicted on false evidence.

Chevigny identifies enduring this experience as one that "feeds the impulse to riot," for "once respect for the legal process is gone, grievances can only be expressed by force." The charges Drummond faced, "together with a story to establish them, constitute the system for covering street abuses." Drummond's story describes what countless Black New Yorkers experienced at the hands of a police officer, a significant factor driving so many Harlemites out into the streets during the tumult. In Drummond's account, the officers attacked him for no good reason, and then once they were done, they arrested him to protect themselves from accusations of wrongdoing. The police concocted cover charges to inoculate themselves from legal charges, lawsuits, and complaints with the city's Civilian Complaint Review Board, which would all be viewed as highly suspect coming from someone who was now a convicted felon, as a result of his encounter with the police.[87]

Ed James, the *New York Post* photographer, spent all of Saturday night in Harlem covering the events, trying to navigate the streets safely without being perceived as with either the police or the people in the streets. As a member of the press, he was able to gain access to the Twenty-Eighth Precinct, where "the cops brought in several men; all were bleeding. One Negro broke and ran. He was a youngster. The cop caught him twice and rapped him twice on the head. I heard him screaming from inside the stationhouse." Later, out on the street, he saw "a cop club a Negro to the ground and another cop crack him on the legs, but he didn't move."[88] Edward Cumberbatch, a Black journalist also with the *Post*, witnessed a group of ten African American teenagers shouting "We want Malcolm X!" face to face with as many police, then watched as one of the boys tripped when police chased them and "saw three cops pound his skull and back with clubs." The teens, though young, were obviously politically aware and believed Malcolm X, who had ministered from a temple in Harlem and called New York home for a decade, would bring some kind of clarity to the streets of Harlem. The press often portrayed the neighborhood's youth as utterly apathetic and alienated. While this may have been the case for most electoral politics and for common social institutions such as school and church, it was untrue when it came to grassroots leaders who offered people hope and dignity.[89]

James Farmer, national director of CORE, was witness to part of the evening's events. Farmer was a long-time pacifist and believer in civil disobedience who had helped found the organization in 1942. He became the group's first African American national director in 1961 and was instrumental in planning student sit-ins and the 1961 Freedom Rides throughout the South. By this time, Farmer, a Texan who now lived in New York City, was a nationally known and respected civil rights leader. CORE staffers called Farmer at his Greenwich Village apartment from their 125th Street office very late at night to inform him of the convulsions gripping the streets of Central Harlem. They told him of hundreds of Black youth in the streets, smashing windows, throwing bottles and bricks, and "cops up here shooting like cowboys." When he arrived at the office, he found just what was described to him, including police who had decided "to shoot into hotel windows and tenement houses" in the heat of Saturday night's action, claiming bricks and bottles were being tossed out of them.[90] On WABC television the next day, he declared that Saturday evening was a "blood orgy on the part of the police." He provided his most serious accusation when he told the audience, "I saw a woman who walked up to the police and asked them for their assistance in getting a taxicab so that she might go home. This woman was shot in the groin and is now in Harlem Hospital." Police officials fervently denied Farmer's accusations at every turn. According to the *New York Times*, Harlem Hospital had treated a woman that night for "a superficial gunshot wound in the left thigh."[91]

Barbara Barksdale, twenty-three, charged that a police officer shot at her five times, hitting her once in the left thigh. Intending to pick up her four-month-old son from her husband's aunt's apartment, Barksdale decided it was too dangerous to bring the boy into the street and attempted to take a bus home. Buses had stopped running where she was, on 128th Street near Lenox Avenue. Hoping a policeman would help her find a cab, she instead "saw this cop cross over from the traffic island. He came at me with his gun in his hand." She ran and he gave chase, finding her behind a parked car. According to Barksdale, the white officer then shot at her and beat an African American teenage boy who tried to aid her. She screamed, "You shot me! You shot me!" The policeman responded, "Well, lay down and die then." She saw the officer as "hating all of us Negroes" when he shot her.[92]

A nineteen-year-old African American man chastised Black police for what he perceived as their eager participation in subduing the unrest: "Some of the Negro cops, I suppose, got to prove to the white cops they're not biased. So they overdo it."[93] In a related but more extreme vein, an African American woman supposedly told a Black police officer in Harlem that night, "If you were my husband, I'd beat you to death."[94]

This night of rage, destruction, and crude materialism drew a twenty-nine year old LeRoi Jones, already a well-known playwright and poet, back to New York from Buffalo, where he had been working as a visiting lecturer. Writing decades later as Amiri Baraka, he described the calamity in the streets of Harlem as "the first shots of a war, which I not only knew would break out but one that I had to get into because I felt I had helped start." Baraka claims to have retrieved a .45 caliber handgun he had stashed in a mistress' apartment, "put it in my gas mask bag, and split." What came after, he does not reveal, nor are there any accounts that mention Baraka during the uprisings.[95]

What would tomorrow bring?

7
Daybreak: Sunday, July 19

The problems that churn in the guts of the black masses of Harlem are so real, so visceral, so true that they will no longer listen to the voices of moderation. No longer are they willing to follow Negro leaders who cannot produce results.

—LOUIS LOMAX, APRIL 12, 1964

The night of destruction, violence, protest, hostility, and joy frightened city leaders, who were now eager to meet with civil rights leaders and offer palliatives but still unwilling to do much of substance. Elected and appointed politicians and officials tried throughout the following day and night to prevent another night of disorder. Civil rights activists used the day for meetings as well, holding one particularly tense rally packed with frustrated attendees who no longer wanted to hear about nonviolence and voting. James Powell's funeral service in the evening attracted large crowds and verged on chaos. Shortly thereafter, the streets again popped with people, bottles, gunfire, shattering glass, and shouts, revealing that the day's efforts to make the disorder a one-night event had been inadequate.

Flailing to prevent further unrest, Deputy Police Commissioner Philip Walsh met with a small hodgepodge of leading Harlem citizens, including the executive director of the City Commission on Human Rights, a criminal court judge, James Lawson of the United African Nationalist Movement, and Bishop Alvin Childs, the recently elected unofficial mayor of Harlem.[1] Commissioner Murphy arrived to meet with the men around 4:30 in the morning on Sunday, July 19.

Their meeting ended after he drew up a missive that he requested be read at every Harlem church service later that morning. The commissioner held a 7 AM press conference, at which he read his statement, which was also distributed to the media.[2]

Murphy, not in touch with the city's civil rights movement, understood the uprisings as linked solely to Gilligan shooting Powell, as opposed to that incident being the breaking point for so many African American New Yorkers who had run out of patience for the daily inequality and indignities they suffered. He assured New Yorkers that he had "ordered the civilian complaint review board to step in at once" and that "extra investigators were assigned to get all the witnesses and obtain the truth, which is what we all want." After spelling out the intended depth and speed of the district attorney's impending investigation of Gilligan's actions, he got to his main point: "Some persons have used this unfortunate incident as an excuse for looting and for vicious, unprovoked attacks against police. These crimes have been met by swift and necessary police action. In our estimation this is a crime problem and not a social problem."[3]

Temperature Rising

Commissioner Murphy's message did not reach many of the active participants in the uprisings, as they were unlikely to be found at a church service. And even for those who were churchgoers, at least one clergyman, the Reverend Richard A. Hildebrand, president of the New York NAACP, followed his reading of the commissioner's statement with:

> I'm sure we're as anxious as the Police Commissioner to stop violence. But in order to maintain peace, the Commissioner must do something to restore confidence in the police department. Whether it is true or not we read in the papers about policemen who get rich off the crime and violence that goes on in our community and it does appear that they are overzealous when it comes to brutality against Negroes. So who has respect for the police?

Reverend Hildebrand finished his sermon in stifling heat, warned those in his flock at Bethel AME on West 132nd Street in Harlem to take care of themselves, and announced the cancellation of his evening service, anticipating a second night of unrest.[4] The temperature, both inside and outside, was soaring, on its way to a high of 91.

Ten blocks and an ideological world away from Reverend Hildebrand's church, the Harlem rent strike leader Jesse Gray addressed an emergency meeting of five hundred people billed as "Is Harlem Mississippi?" at the Mount Morris Ascension Presbyterian Church at 122nd Street and Mount Morris Park West in Harlem. It was not only bystanders making the comparison any longer; now a mass meeting was devoted to the similarity life in Harlem bore to that in Mississippi. With a bandaged and swollen face he said the police had inflicted the previous night after recognizing him, Gray charged, "We have one of the most corrupt, rotten police departments in this country. Murphy is nothing but a crumbsnatcher and a stoolie." Gray continued, "Last night the police looked no better than German storm troops," referencing Hitler's private armies responsible for securing his rise to power and terrorizing and murdering dissidents and Jews, with which many in attendance were still familiar.[5]

Significantly escalating the intensity of his rhetoric, he declared, "There is only one thing that can correct the situation, and that's guerilla warfare," though he later explained he was referring to employing the tactic in Mississippi, not Harlem. Mapping out his vision for a local protective and activist force, Gray asked for "100 skilled black revolutionaries who are ready to die" to step forward as platoon captains, who would then each recruit another one hundred men until they had amassed a force of "50,000 well organized Negroes" who would "determine what will happen in New York City." Gray lambasted the city's police department as "deeply rooted with hatred and racism." The audience reacted with thunderous, prolonged applause. Gray finished by telling those in attendance he intended to head a demonstration at the United Nations to request the organization's assistance against "police terror in the United States." Gray was known as a militant, but his statements during the uprisings represented perhaps his most inflammatory.[6]

Marshall England, head of New York CORE, found himself in the unfortunate position of following Gray in the pulpit. Visibly crying, he mustered the suddenly irrelevant and hopelessly inadequate utterance that the "Negro people must vote and organize." He was immediately booed, with several in the crowd calling out the correction that "We are black men, not Negroes!" Amid a "roar of jeers," England left as quickly as he had appeared, realizing he had no place at the meeting.[7]

Inserting himself into the storm to redirect its energy, Edward "Pork Chop" Davis, the head of the African Freedom Movement, a popular Black nationalist street speaker in Harlem, and a mainstay at Lewis Michaux's National

Memorial African Bookstore on 125th Street, calmed the riled audience with the dictate that "You are not going to solve the problem by an emotional outburst or by undirected violence." He scolded local civil rights organizations for counterproductive infighting when they could instead be organizing for Black freedom, which many in the crowd thoroughly applauded. Concluding his remarks, Davis injected further militancy into the meeting when he declared, "All you black people that have been in the armed services and know anything about guerilla warfare should come to the aid of our people."[8]

Yosef Ben-Jochannan, a radical Black nationalist and Afrocentric scholar of Egypt, attacked the Black church in his remarks and was reported to have received the loudest applause of any speaker that afternoon. He went after the plentiful storefront churches of Harlem, criticizing their proprietors for buying up old buildings and "instead of building a factory or some place to live, which we need desperately," opening yet another church, used only on Sundays, whose main purpose he perceived to be to separate worshippers from their money. Ben-Jochannan reserved particular vitriol for the men leading these churches, positing that no matter how long one is a dedicated, paying member of the institution, when that individual dies, "the minister doesn't come to the funeral and if he does it will be just to the funeral parlor. He may come for a minute or two, but he certainly won't waste his gas to go to the burial ground and say a mass when they are throwing dirt on you."[9]

What Ben-Jochannan really wanted to target was all the money African Americans spent on religion, arguing they should engage in more proactive pursuits of justice and freedom. Moving beyond local institutions, he criticized religion in general and African Americans' reliance upon it for deliverance. Going back into the days of slavery and nodding to the growing Nation of Islam, Ben-Jochannan declared:

> I say the black man has called upon Jesus Christ for so many years here in America—and now he starts calling on Mohammed and there are many who are calling on Moses—and at no time within this period has the black man's situation changed, nor has the black man any freedom. It is obvious that someone didn't hear his call or isn't interested in that call—either Jesus, Moses or Mohammed.

To hammer this point home, Ben-Jochannan asked his audience to consider the scenario of him asking a dead man in a funeral parlor for help. They would laugh at him, he concluded. However, "You won't laugh at me when I ask for help from someone where the bones are all deteriorated," referring to the aforementioned religious figures, men who died "over thousands of years ago." He culminated with a call for self-reliance, arguing that only Black people could secure freedom for themselves, rather than asking "dead people to come back and help us."[10]

James Farmer made a surprise appearance. His arrival elicited a chorus of jeers from the audience, but he seemed unperturbed, telling them, "That kid James Powell was my son and your son and the son of every black man."[11] In reference to the Alabama city made infamous the previous year for its especially violent and racist police department, he termed Saturday night "New York's night of Birmingham horror." While not in Mississippi, Birmingham, or "Bombingham," as it had come to be known for its level and character of racial violence, the national head of CORE likened the police in the streets of Harlem to those of that southern city. Describing the police in Harlem as "hysterical," Farmer pointed his finger high, declaring, "The police commissioner, in the posture which he had adopted in the last few months of self-congratulations for the Police Department, must assume part of the responsibility" for his officers' behavior and violence.[12] Farmer related firsthand accounts of several instances of police violence the previous night: wantonly shooting a Black woman point-blank, beating customers in a grocery store, and firing guns into the Hotel Theresa.[13] He also repeated the by then already common demand that Lieutenant Gilligan be arrested for murder, at which point a number of those in attendance responded by rising from their seats and asking the rest of the room, "Let's go, what are we waiting for?" Farmer, striving to prevent further bloodshed, admonished them: "If you go out of here," he calmly stated, "one running one way, one running another, it will be slaughter." Everyone remained in the room.[14]

Bayard Rustin was the final speaker. His presence and oratory drew a bitterly negative reaction from those gathered in the church. In this space, his civil rights credentials were a liability. To these people, in this place, at this time, he was a member of the old-guard pacifist movement—weak, ineffectual, eager to compromise, and accommodating. He was also unapologetically gay at a time when society and law found homosexuality amoral, repugnant, and deviant. Rustin, of course, had faced far worse in the nation's jails and at the hands of violent police and racist thugs. Cutting through their boos and insults with sober determination, Rustin asserted his authority: "There is nobody in this room who cares more than I do that a young boy was shot down like an animal. . . . There is nobody that has gone to jail more often than I have." Continuing for as long as the crowd permitted, he told his audience, "I am not ready to die. I want no Negro to die. I want no human being to die or be brutalized."

Contributing to these "monstrous deeds" through retributive violence "is to make an animal of me as the police were animals."¹⁵ And, like Farmer, Rustin warned the audience against violence for practical reasons: "Those people who think that we can use guns and knives against tanks and bazookas, they are the ignorant ones."¹⁶ Like Gray, he also sought one hundred men to join him in the streets, but working nonviolently "to end the brutality toward all men." Rustin's appeal for radical nonviolence brought further hostility, to the point that he was booed from the pulpit, ending the rally. A group of men with violent intentions surrounded him and attempted to prevent him from leaving, but another larger group intervened and allowed him to leave safely.¹⁷

The latter group, which Rustin estimated to number about seventy-five men and youth, spent the next four nights walking the streets of Harlem, trying to disperse crowds, convince the police to allow innocent arrestees to go, and tending to the injured, taking them either to the CORE office on 125th Street for first aid or to Harlem Hospital if the wounds were more serious. Surely Rustin and his group had an impact and likely prevented more people from getting hurt or killed, but they were ultimately ineffective in the city in which he had lived for decades. Some people probably listened to him and went back into their homes or at least ceased whatever activity in which they were engaged, perhaps out of concern for their safety and freedom or because they had a moment of clarity and decided what they were doing was wrong. However, neither Rustin nor anyone else pressing for calm was able to speak with authority to those in the streets those nights. This was an explosion that could only burn itself out, highly resistant to anyone preaching restraint. Rustin and those working with him never built any further following during those nights and do not seem to have curbed the looting and violence by any appreciable level. Even Rustin describes his efforts with phrases like "we did what we could" and "had some minor success." These advocates for nonviolence and peace were in hostile territory, encountering resistance from civilians and police alike.¹⁸

While Stokely Carmichael would not introduce the phrase "Black Power" to the masses for another two years, this rally featured all the core components of that slippery ideology. A number of New York–based speakers and several hundred attendees, most of whom likely lived in Harlem, embodied these ideas before they were bundled and named. Several of those addressing the crowd spoke favorably of armed self-defense and guerilla war in pursuit of freedom, seeing no use for nonviolence in Harlem, if there ever were any. While it may be tempting to write off these men and others who agreed with them as radicals detached from reality, the nation's foremost peace activist understood the nature of their frustration. As he spent more time in the North, Martin Luther King Jr. came to understand that "it cannot be taken for granted that Negroes will adhere to nonviolence under any conditions. When there is rocklike intransigence or sophisticated manipulation that mocks the empty-handed petitioner, rage replaces reason. Nonviolence is a powerful demand for reason and justice. If it is rudely rebuked it is not transformed into resignation and passivity."[19] Even King, the face of nonviolent resistance in the United States and winner of the 1963 Nobel Peace Prize for his efforts, could see what would drive people into the streets of Harlem and Bedford-Stuyvesant.

Nonviolence was never a given for those seeking racial justice in the North, and certainly not in New York City, the adopted home of people like Marcus Garvey and Malcolm X, men who preached adamantly about the dignity to be found in self-defense, along with any number of lesser-remembered Black nationalists and radicals. Instead, nonviolence was a tool in a box, and one not utilized often. Peaceful demonstrations ending without violence are not the same thing as nonviolence, a confrontational strategy that seeks out conflict with repressive authorities to highlight the illegitimacy of their rule. It requires significant dedication and sacrifice from adherents, including accepting violence with no attempt to defend oneself. Whether Harlem was or was not Mississippi, it was not a good place to find people willing to take a beating and respond by curling up in the fetal position.

Even James Farmer, a committed pacifist and transplanted New Yorker, had to appeal to people's sense of self-preservation to prevent them from going to battle. He skipped over the morality and justness of nonviolent resistance. Bayard Rustin pressed the philosophical evils of violence, and it got him threatened with just what he was denouncing. The self-reliance and racial solidarity that would be so essential to Black Power were well received that afternoon, in contrast to the messages of interracial cooperation and integration that mainstream organizations had long stressed. Again, even though Farmer was squarely within the latter camp and never abandoned these positions, he seemed to know his audience and so avoided the rhetorical places England and Rustin went. The people gathered in this church did not come for more of the same. If they ever had much support for the peaceful, gradualist strategies that the major civil rights organizations championed, those beliefs had fallen away today. They wanted freedom now.

Though the rally was held in a church, that was about the only religious aspect of it. The men who spoke represented no religious organizations. There were no prayers offered, no benedictions given, and the men themselves were not overtly religious. They called on no deity or prophet for deliverance. In fact, the only talk mentioning the spiritual life was in opposition to it, demanding that Black people deal with the here and now and stop worrying about the afterlife and what long-dead religious figures may be able to do for them. No, this was a rally about the physical reality confronting African Americans in 1964, after a night of significant protest, destruction, and violence.

None of this was new for New York. Its civil rights movement had never been primarily religious, nor had it relied heavily upon the mass marches, sit-ins, and jail fillings that worked so well for the southern movement. To be sure, New Yorkers marched, sat in, and got arrested for civil rights, but those tactics would only take them so far. As James Farmer later explained, "The northern problems don't lend themselves quite so easily to the kind of drama which we engaged in, in the early sixties. A Freedom Ride is probably not going to close the educational gap. A series of sit-ins probably will not increase life expectancy and close that gap, and so on."[20] Dr. King knew this in 1965. Reflecting on the Watts rebellion, he wrote: "Our movement has been essentially regional, not national—the confrontation of opposing forces met in the climactic engagements only in the South. The issues and their solution were similarly regional and the changes affected only the areas of combat."[21] Indeed, de facto segregation has proved to be a hard target, given the liberal countenance of the urban North. While the outcomes of segregation were quite apparent, what drove it was not easy to discern, rendering mass protest rather ineffective.[22] Kenneth Clark agreed and argued for sustained, direct contact with those in the city's power structure as the best chance for progress.[23]

Back in the established, plodding realm of the movement, the news of the uprising horrified Roy Wilkins, executive secretary of the NAACP, who was vacationing in the quiet splendor of Wyoming. He implored, "I don't care how angry the Negroes are. For the sake of the city and its people and getting to a solution to see that this kind of thing [Powell's death] doesn't happen again, we've all got to keep our heads. We can't leave it to the bottle droppers and rock throwers."[24] Wilkins had much about which to be anxious: the well-being of Black New Yorkers; the image of the NAACP as the leading African American voice for progress; his position as one of the country's eminent Black leaders, with access to the halls of power; the continued advancement of the civil rights struggle nationally and the ability to continue to get support for civil rights from local and federal authorities, as well as sympathetic white people. However, he had very little currency with many people in Harlem, especially those out in the streets the night before.

Sunday night, local courts began the lengthy process of prosecuting citizens arrested in the uprisings. The city arraigned over thirty people in connection with the ferment that night, all of whom were arrested Saturday night into Sunday morning, on such charges as felonious assault, burglary, resisting arrest, and inciting to riot. Those on the front lines of the judicial system were also busy that day, with four hundred police officers from all five boroughs occupying Central Harlem, still wearing their steel helmets and keeping their holsters unsecured for quicker access to their pistols.[25]

The Second Night

Shortly before Powell's 8 PM funeral service on Sunday, July 19, more than one thousand people thronged the street outside while 150 mourners gathered inside the Levy and Delaney Funeral Home at 132nd Street and Seventh Avenue in Harlem. It was still 85 degrees outside, with the humidity climbing past 60 percent. Dozens of police watched, waiting for confrontation, which would not take long. The police were anxious about the large crowd outside the funeral home, especially given the previous night's tumult and the symbolic importance of the funeral. Some of the crowd heckled the police to their faces, including a Black teenager who said of two Black officers on the scene, "Look at those Uncle Toms." A Black man nearby confirmed that "Whitey can always get some of us to do his dirty work." Police began trying to get people to move away from the funeral home, instead of working to prevent the buildup in the first place.[26]

Verbal attempts at dispersal quickly gave way to the police shoving the mourners with their nightsticks, which caused a stampede of attendees, including the Manhattan deputy borough president and one of Governor Rockefeller's former personal assistants. Some members of the crowd responded to the police by showering the patrolmen with a hail of bottles. The police then "charged into crowds, waving nightsticks" to extinguish the incipient uprising as citizens "pour[ed] out from behind barricades." In the chaos of the dispersal, one of the aforementioned Black officers, Lieutenant Robert H. Johnson, defused a confrontation between a local woman walking home and a white officer who was physically preventing her from doing so. After the officer shoved and threatened her with his nightstick, the woman faced off against him, on the brink of greater violence. Johnson intervened, allowing the woman to keep walking the way she was going without further violence or intimidation. The officers' gunshots into the air and three buses full of Tactical Patrol Force officers, the NYPD's combat unit, managed to quell the disturbance for a little while longer. Police also stopped and repelled a group of perhaps one hundred Black youth as they tried to cross Seventh Avenue to reach the funeral home, a number of them armed with large pieces of wood. One member of the group managed to land a bottle on a police sergeant before they fled and dispersed.[27]

Meanwhile, inside the funeral home, the Reverend Theodore Kerrison softly eulogized James Powell against an aural backdrop of gunshots and smashing bottles outside. Annie Powell, James's mother, "was near collapse and sobbed hysterically" as the service concluded. Bayard Rustin, who had attended the funeral along with the Reverend Milton Galamison, the organizer of the year's school boycotts, had arranged for a sound truck to be parked on the street in front of the funeral home to try to calm the expected crowds. Rustin, again pleading forcefully with Harlemites to refrain from a second night of tumult, spoke from the truck: "I urge you to go home. We know there has been an injustice done. The thing we need to do most is respect this woman whose son was shot." Members of the crowd denounced him as an Uncle Tom.[28]

Unfazed, Rustin responded, "I'm prepared to be a Tom if it's the only way I can save women and children from being shot down in the street, and if you're not willing to do the same, you're fools." A number of those in the vicinity had no patience for such advice and again responded with scornful boos. A few other speakers followed Rustin with similar warnings, but the dominant voices surrounding them shut them down with demands for Malcolm X. Malcolm X, like Harlem's congressman Adam Clayton Powell Jr. and Mayor Wagner, was out of the country when the uprising began. Reached for comment the next day while attending the Organization of African Unity meeting in Cairo, he expressed surprise "that the trouble has been contained to the degree it has." Attributing the outbreak to the NYPD's use of "outright scare tactics," Malcolm credited the city with having "used wiser methods than any other city to deal with racial problems" until Commissioner Murphy entered his role in 1961, since which time "for some strange reason, tactics have changed." He advised Commissioner Murphy and others that police scare tactics, on which he did not elaborate, "won't work, because the Negro is not afraid. If the tactics are not changed, this could escalate into something very, very serious." As usual, his insight was on the mark, but he left his allies and followers with no advice, just another warning to the ruling elite.[29]

Rustin left the funeral and, after accompanying an injured resident to the hospital, went to the Twenty-Eighth Precinct on 123rd Street with James Farmer. There he told the chief inspector, "There is a social necessity for his [Gilligan's] suspension now, without prejudice. Only when the Negro leadership is able to go to the people of Harlem with a suspension in their hands will they be able to take the first step toward the conclusion of these tragic occurrences." Police politely brushed aside the wisdom of a dedicated activist seeking peace, to which he responded with the prescient warning, "I don't think it's a quieting crowd. Resentment is still boiling up. This situation is going to become even more violent."[30]

As night fell, so did the temperature, dropping to an overnight low of 78 degrees, while the humidity ascended to 72 percent. The police worked frantically in anticipation of another night of unrest, cordoning off fifty-seven blocks of Central Harlem, between 116th and 135th Streets and Eighth and Lenox Avenues, the same vicinity but a slightly smaller area than they had occupied the night before. On this night, police took the action before any real disturbance, calling it "a temporary measure occasioned by the crowds that gathered for the Powell funeral." Police commanders mobilized the entirety of their force, nearly 27,000 officers, to work indefinite twelve-hour on-and-off shifts until they deemed the situation in Harlem sufficiently under control. The Transit Authority directed its drivers on the IND line of the subway system to deny all service to passengers at the 125th Street station in Central Harlem until around midnight. The agency also increased police presence on trains passing through Harlem and stations there.[31]

As many had feared, the previous night's activities commenced once again, though they turned out to be less intense. A reporter for the *New York Times* described the essence of the citizen/police conflict that night as "missiles and gasoline-filled bottles thrown at the police, with shots returned." Police shot at least seven people and reported twelve others injured, though that number was surely much higher, given the frequently mentioned beatings they were doling out.[32] The city's police officers also responded in kind, reported to have "picked up bricks, bottles and stones that had been thrown at them and threw them back at the rooftops."[33]

Journalists described Harlem Hospital as "a battle-zone field hospital" where "every 15 or 20 minutes an ambulance sirened up to the emergency entrance with another blood-spattered, moaning stretcher case." Police officers dropped off arrestees they had injured, while some of their other victims walked in with "T-shirts soaked crimson, open slashes on heads and faces leaking blood freely."[34] Doris Berry, an African American woman from Central Harlem, claimed a white policeman deliberately shot her in the knee while in the street looking for her mother. Berry said, "I thought he was just shooting blanks until I got hit in the leg. The cops just left me there. I had to find a taxi to get to the hospital."[35]

Figure 7.1 Aggressive policing on Seventh Avenue and 126th Street during the uprisings.

Source: Library of Congress, Prints and Photographs Division, NYWT&S Collection, LC-USZ62-136896.

A white police officer shot two African American teenagers toward the end of that night's upheaval, shortly after midnight. Officer William O'Carroll said he witnessed John Vaughan attempting to break into a television store at 118th Street and Third Avenue. O'Carroll stated that he ordered Vaughan to stop, but the boy ran. He fired a warning shot, which struck Ava Robles, a thirteen-year-old African American girl, who had been sitting on her fire escape, in her leg and lodged in her back. After Vaughan kept running, O'Carroll admittedly shot him in the back. The bullet exited through his stomach and critically injured the boy.[36] *New York Post* reporters were present when Vaughan arrived at Harlem Hospital, unconscious and bleeding profusely. A group of about twenty-five local residents witnessed this and screamed "Rotten butcher bastards!" at police on site.[37]

Shortly after midnight, the police department issued a press release stating that "groups of hoodlums are still roaming the streets but the situation is improving very rapidly." Around the same time, most bars and restaurants in Central Harlem shut their doors hours before they usually would in a concerted effort to get people to their homes earlier and in a less drunken state. By 1:30 AM, the streets of Harlem were again quiet.[38]

The list of people police had arrested during the past two nights runs the gamut from a thirty-six-year-old photographer for *Life* to a twenty-year-old Army private to a forty-nine-year-old man to a sixteen-year-old-boy. All were African American. The *Life* photographer, Frank Dandridge, husband of the notable Maryland civil rights activist Gloria Richardson, was arrested late Saturday night when he refused to stop photographing a woman in the process of being arrested. He quickly posted $500 bail and was freed pending a hearing nearly two months later. The private was arrested and charged with resisting arrest, disorderly conduct, and assault. Police charged the forty-nine-year-old man with looting, and the same was true for the sixteen-year-old boy. Of the forty-three people reported arrested those two nights, nearly all were from Central Harlem, with five giving addresses in the Bronx, one in Brooklyn, and another in Newark, New Jersey. Most were charged with some combination of disorderly conduct, resisting arrest, burglary, and assault. Police charged an eighteen-year-old man with receiving stolen property when he picked up a pair of pants from the ground. A twenty-four-year-old woman was charged with assault and inciting a riot, though her $500 bail makes the charges seem much less serious than the $1,000 to $5,000 many defendants were facing for looting. A nineteen-year-old man was charged with attempting to take a policeman's nightstick from him.[39]

The next day, New Yorkers outside of Central Harlem would awake to discover that another night of tumult had taken place in its streets. The revolt now threatened to become an event of indeterminate length. Anxieties throughout the city as well as urban centers across the country heightened substantially. No one knew what would come next, and many feared the worst. City leaders desperate to quell the chaos scrambled for solutions and explanations. Civil rights leaders, concerned both for their status as men who were able to control local African American populations and the physical safety of those people, were similarly frantic in their search for relative calm. That night, July 20, would show that any hopes for an immediate cessation were in vain and that the disorder would spread beyond the confines of Central Harlem.

8
Spreading Anxiety: Monday, July 20

Does anyone believe that a much decorated policeman with seventeen years' experience on the force and nineteen citations had to shoot down and kill a 15-year-old school boy under the circumstances admitted to by the Police Department last Thursday? Nobody in Harlem does.

—*NEW YORK AMSTERDAM NEWS* EDITORIAL

By Monday, July 20, New York's uprisings had become international news, with papers across Europe covering the situation in front-page stories. When unrest broke out in the Bedford-Stuyvesant section of Brooklyn later that night, this marked a transition into something unprecedented. No longer contained to Central Harlem, the revolts threatened to spread to every poor Black neighborhood in the city, and city leaders expected as much. While the city had experienced uprisings in Central Harlem in 1935 and 1943, they neither lasted nearly so long nor moved beyond the neighborhood. Once the city's upheaval crossed the East River into Brooklyn, President Johnson involved himself and ordered the director of the FBI to do so as well. The disorder was now causing concern and prompting policy changes at the highest levels of government.[1]

The city government struggled to address the tumult. City leaders knew they could not respond with crushing force from the police. They expected this would only serve to escalate tensions in the streets and elicit an increase in violence. They understood a policy of shooting looters would bring condemnation locally, nationally, and abroad, especially with southern police violence a prominent current issue. Unrestrained, lethal violence against people in the streets would also jeopardize delicate political alliances within the Democratic Party. Mayor Wagner and President Johnson were both Democrats and relied on each other for support, and overt police violence locally would put Johnson in a position in which it would be difficult for him to not condemn what was happening. The city knew it had to use its police with some restraint and accompany physical force with promises of police reforms and social programs. The solutions the city offered to its Black citizens' economic and social woes did not extend far beyond what it had promised and failed to deliver on in previous years. Once again, there were more panels and committees set up to study problems, even though civil rights activists had been identifying the issues plaguing their communities for years. The Wagner administration's response to the turmoil and the circumstances creating it convinced many Black New Yorkers the city would never listen to them.

Day Three: Monday, July 20

On Monday morning, the twentieth, James Powell was laid to rest. When the Powell family arrived at the Levy and Delaney Funeral Home at 9 AM, approximately one hundred police were already standing outside in the warm and humid morning. It was 78 degrees, as it had been all night. They were also met with the drone of a hovering police helicopter, watching for wider signs of trouble. Mrs. Annie Powell, James's mother, left the car crying out, "My baby, my baby, oh my God, I want to see my baby." Tears streamed down her face, and two men physically supported her.[2]

About one hundred Black people had gathered outside the home, along with a significant number of photographers and reporters. There were a few minor disturbances at the funeral home this morning: an African American woman, reacting to the sight of Powell's coffin leaving the building, exclaimed, "Oh, why did they have to shoot the boy!" and made a fleeting attempt to attack a nearby white policeman. A sympathetic Black man held her back, trying to calm her, saying, "There's nothing you can do." The procession then departed for a small service at Ferncliff Cemetery in Hartsdale, New York. Located about fifteen miles north of the city, the Powell family had a plot there where the boy's father, Harold, had been interred three years earlier. Before roughly twelve family members and close friends—as well as the watchful eyes of three Black Westchester County sheriff's officers—Powell's coffin was lowered above his father's.

Mrs. Powell shouted, "Oh God, look how I brought my boy to you! Harold, Harold, look how they've sent you my baby!"[3]

Back in the city, Paul R. Screvane, City Council president and acting mayor while Mayor Wagner was vacationing in Spain, held two meetings with a number of government officials and civil rights leaders. Screvane, who maintained "that as long as people can sit down and discuss the problems, something can be worked out," quickly amassed a contingent of city officials to meet with the activists, including Deputy Mayor Edward Cavanagh Jr.; Manhattan Borough President Edward Dudley; Cleveland Robinson, a member of the City Commission on Human Rights; Madison Jones, the executive director of the City Commission on Human Rights; Commissioner Murphy, and several of the mayor's aides.[4] They first met with a nine-member delegation that James Farmer headed, including L. Joseph Overton, from the national Negro American Labor Council; Alexander Allen, representing the Urban League; the Reverend Dr. Eugene Callender, from the NAACP; and Percy Sutton, a CORE lawyer. That group demanded the immediate suspension of Lieutenant Gilligan, his arrest for murder, an independent civilian review board to take and investigate complaints against the police, Mayor Wagner's return, and an increase in the number of Black police in Harlem, where Farmer said "practically all" officers were white.[5] At this meeting, Farmer claimed to have information that Lieutenant Gilligan, a former military man, was receiving mental health treatment at a Veterans Administration hospital, implying he was unfit for service.[6] Reverend Hildebrand from Bethel AME led the second meeting, accompanied by eight others. They pressed upon the municipal contingent the need to implement their three-point program: "the formation of a committee from outside the city government solely to investigate the Powell shooting, the relieving of Lieutenant Gilligan of duty for the present and the assignment of more Negro policemen to Harlem in all ranks."[7]

Much like Mayor Wagner, Screvane was a gracious and amiable host but did not respond to the groups' demands in any substantial way. After the meetings, Screvane announced a grand jury would begin considering an indictment of Gilligan for murder the next day, Tuesday, July 21. In his statement, Screvane attempted to use the grand jury to quiet Harlem's anger, promising "all the facts will be brought out and the grand jury's judgment as to Gilligan's guilt or innocence will be promptly given, with all the safeguards provided by law." This was the city's standard procedure whenever a police officer killed someone. The only difference was the quickness with which the district attorney convened the jury, described as "somewhat speedier than usual."[8]

Screvane also revealed a series of measures, which he called "programs of action," designed to mollify the anger in the streets. First, Deputy Mayor Cavanagh was to undertake a review of the Civilian Complaint Review Board's procedures and all cases before it charging police brutality. He would send the results of his work to the mayor, who would then discuss the findings with the police commissioner. Next on the list, the police department would temporarily increase the number of African American police in Harlem and remove their white colleagues from the area. Commissioner Murphy described this measure as just "to meet a special circumstance at a special time," reiterating its impermanent nature. Third, the city would establish a body of high-ranking police officials, known as the Community Affairs Committee, which would "meet regularly with community leaders at designated places within Harlem and other communities." The fourth program aimed to aggressively recruit racial minorities to work on the police force, as "part of the city's anti-poverty program." Finally, the city sought to relieve pressure in Black and Puerto Rican neighborhoods through "the encouragement of the submission of complaints and protests" to sundry municipal offices throughout the city. Citizens would be able to address a complaint to any city agency or department, as well as the mayor, and hand it in at one of many designated municipal government appendages acting as couriers.[9]

These responses politely denied the civil rights groups' demands with a paternalist hand, taking little action in the face of massive problems. Regarding Deputy Mayor Cavanagh's impending review process, which may seem to be the most significant step of the lot, this was nothing new. The review board already reported to the commissioner, who approved of its conduct, as was true for the mayor. And of course, it was a far cry from an independent civilian review board, the demand for which the uprisings were rapidly increasing. As for Mayor Wagner's return, it was not until the third night of ferment that Screvane called him in Spain and strongly suggested he come back. The city was unwilling to accede to any demands from civil rights groups. Commissioner Murphy could have suspended Lieutenant Gilligan as a temporary measure to quiet the panic in the streets of the city, but he refused. Wagner could have created an independent review board with the stroke of a pen, but he was as intransigent as Murphy, merely more genial.[10] People like Wagner and Murphy refused to accept moderate civil rights leaders' advice. Groups like the NAACP, CORE, HARYOU, the Harlem Neighborhoods Association, and small grassroots organizations had long apprised city leaders of the major issues in their communities, but endless committees and studies were substituted for progress. Various city agencies could have taken real steps to alleviate the deplorable housing conditions by penalizing slumlords or could have integrated schools in a meaningful way, but with Wagner's blessing they had not.

Cleveland Robinson, the forty-eight-year-old Jamaican-born member of the City Commission on Human Rights; labor leader with the thirty-thousand-strong District 65 of the Retail, Wholesale, and Department Store Employees Union; and national co-chairman of the 1963 March on Washington for Jobs and Freedom, provided a broad, critical analysis of the general social and economic situation in Harlem. Viewing the uprisings from a holistic perspective, he told reporters Harlem faced "not just the question of police brutality but the whole social structure—housing, education, lack of jobs." Turning to why people were looting and fighting police, Robinson asserted, "It's important to know that the people in the streets acting unlawfully and seizing the opportunity to vent pent-up emotions are leaderless. They don't even have faith in Negro leadership." Given this lack of leadership, Robinson continued, "This is not the time for street rallies and open demonstrations for the simple reason that there is that element which is leaderless and uncontrolled." Finally, he addressed the matter of corrupt policing in the community, relating that many Black New Yorkers felt "Harlem is a lucrative field for police who are paid off and who do not pay attention to crime."[11]

The senior civil rights and labor dignitary A. Philip Randolph, with the additional authority conferred by living in Harlem for fifty years, provided a statement to the press that day from Los Angeles. Randolph pleaded futilely for those participating in the uprisings to stop, bluntly stating: "Violence and bloodshed is not the remedy. It will destroy our community and hurt and set back the Negro cause. It only plays into the hands of our enemies." Randolph then changed his focus to the national stage and the coming presidential election and expressed his worry that continued unrest "could elect [Republican candidate] Senator Goldwater, who voted against civil rights legislation, president, which would be the greatest disaster to befall Negroes since slavery."[12] Randolph's message, like those from other civil rights leaders, had only limited impact at best, given that many Black New Yorkers had scant interest in disciplined nonviolence as a local strategy and, as Robinson argued, a lack of faith in Black leadership. The bulk of the people in the streets the past few nights were out as individuals acting with no defined social goals, so political appeals to them were of little meaning.

Jesse Gray, on the other hand, had no interest in trying to tamp down the unrest. People from most political and ideological perspectives criticized him for inflaming tensions and keeping the uprisings stoked. One such measure was the rally against police brutality he held at United Nations headquarters on the afternoon of July 20, with an estimated attendance of 250. Gray told the people "there will be more demonstrations and riots whether we like it or not." He was right. Other groups were also encouraging further action the same day. The Harlem Defense Council, a group sharing office space with the militant communist Progressive Labor Movement at 336 Lenox Avenue, began distributing leaflets throughout the community during the day, demanding residents "defend each block from the cops" and calling for a demonstration against police brutality at the Thirty-Second Precinct on 135th Street for Saturday, July 25.[13]

James Farmer, CORE's national director, made attempts to reach Governor Rockefeller, hosting Roy Wilkins on the family ranch in Wyoming, to request the deployment of the National Guard to Harlem. Farmer asserted the force was necessary "to protect the people of Harlem," given the NYPD's inability to do its job with professionalism and regard for citizens. This is notable not just for what it said about Farmer's view of the police but much more for the fact that in the urban upheaval to come throughout the country, especially in places like Watts, Newark, and Detroit, the calling up of the National Guard became synonymous with intense violence. Farmer seems to have believed the National Guard would have done a better and more impartial job of maintaining order in the streets of Harlem. At this time, military intervention still had a positive connotation, such as in Little Rock, Arkansas, in 1957 to integrate its Central High School or to keep James Meredith enrolled at the University of Mississippi in 1962.[14] In Los Angeles, LAPD Chief William H. Parker drew the same conclusion from an opposite ideological perspective. Before the annual gathering of the National Conference of Police Associations, Parker told his audience, "Perhaps it would be better if the Harlem situation was turned over to the military. Officers are working 12 hours a day amid bloody battles and it's too much to expect of them on a non-relieved basis." The chief received a standing ovation.[15]

An African American resident of Brooklyn, Barbara Benson, wrote a letter to the editor of the *New York Times* on this day, endeavoring to explain, without justifying, what had been happening in the streets of Harlem for the last two nights. Conveying a Black woman's seldom-heard perspective, Benson expressed a deep sorrow at the physical and political damage the chaos in Harlem had already done, particularly concerned it would strengthen Barry Goldwater's message and chance to win in November. Still, she argued, "one must be capable of comprehending the underlying causes for this upheaval." For her, the police were the primary explanatory factor, on a number of levels. She wrote of the indignity stop-and-frisk does to its targets and of officers' reflexive urge to break up groups of Black people congregating in public. The police, in her telling, "are sadistic in their administration of the law, insatiable in their beatings, unable to discern men from children, and irrational in their fear of the black man." She articulated police violence and harassment to be a Black issue, irrespective of gender, class, profession, or education. The risk was constant, to the extent that she feared involving herself with the police, even in the case of an emergency. Hers was a common fear, one everyone from Black celebrities to ordinary citizens to politicians voiced, borne out by experience. Benson was clear that she wrote "not to condone these horrible riots," instead trying to reveal what led to the uprisings, "so that we can all work toward solutions."[16]

Someone who was not interested in solutions, the white mayor of Notasulga, Alabama, James Rea, gleefully telegrammed President Johnson, requesting the deployment of federal troops to Harlem "to protect the lives and property of the white minority in the area and to restore law and order." Five months earlier, emulating what the governor of his state, George Wallace, had done at the University of Alabama in June 1963, Rea had gone to great lengths to prohibit six Black students from entering a local high school, including passing several ordinances and then physically blocking the entrance to the school. Since Rea was disobeying federal law, federal officials became involved to secure the students' enrollment. The mayor told Johnson "that since you alerted several thousand soldiers for possible use in our community last February, you should be willing to send some to Harlem, where a large number of persons have been killed and injured." He communicated that residents of his town were "greatly alarmed at the apparent breakdown of law and order" in Harlem, though neither Rea nor white Notasulgans had seemed as concerned when, three months earlier, arsonists had destroyed the high school the Black students were attending.[17]

Store and business owners in Harlem estimated that day that they had sustained at least $50,000 worth of property damage from the two nights of unrest. Some said they would stay closed until the tumultuous atmosphere of the past few days quieted down; others said that they needed to get their businesses up and running as quickly as possible in order to maintain a cash flow. Police had forty-six local businesses on record as having been damaged on the nights of July 18 and 19, with five looted. White people owned every one. Worst hit was the A&P supermarket at Eighth Avenue (since renamed Frederick Douglass Boulevard) and 131st Street, which someone had tried to burn down with a Molotov cocktail. Though police quickly extinguished the fire, looters had shattered 439 square feet of quarter-inch plate-glass windows, which would cost $15,000 to replace. The white manager of the store sounded hopeful about the community in which he worked, voicing his certainty that "winos and junkies" were responsible for the damage, not local families. An African American teen nearby told a *New York Times* reporter, "The only thing I regret is that they broke into the cleaners and took clothes. They are just harming our people who live in this neighborhood when they do that. I don't care about the bar [two bars in the area were extensively damaged]. It's owned by whitey anyway."[18]

About a mile southeast, a number of young Puerto Rican men in East Harlem were conducting peace patrols to try to make sure the chaos did not spread eastward. The twenty-five young men came together Sunday night, after some of the helmeted police fighting in Central Harlem ventured into their community of about eighty thousand. One of the founders of the patrol, Victor Alicea, a twenty-four-year-old Columbia University graduate student, described the general reaction to that incursion: "When we see helmets, we think of war." In Alicea's analysis, "It was very unwise of the cops to walk through here wearing helmets when there was no violence. They were coming to the worst conclusions about us." Fearing the aggressive police presence would only serve to touch off a forceful community response, he and some concerned friends got together to walk and drive the streets from dusk to dawn, doing what they could to keep tensions down. One peace patrolman, Anibal Solivan, a twenty-one-year-old Columbia pre-law major, said the group's main point was to communicate to the youth in the streets that "we can never win against the cops. With a war against the cops, we've been telling these kids, you win nothing but publicity—bad publicity. The kind of publicity that will hurt us, will make some say of us we're a bunch of animals."[19]

It worked. There were no uprisings in East Harlem. The streets stayed quiet. Still, Solivan cautioned, "Violence is a tool that we do not want to use, but it could have been very bad here Sunday, when the cops started walking through here wearing helmets."[20] For these men, like many civil rights activists, especially in the North, nonviolence was conditional, one tactic among many and not by any means a core principle. Self-defense and self-preservation were the highest obligations.

That day, many Harlemites gathered on stoops and corners, in barbershops, beauty salons, restaurants, and bars to socialize as they usually did, especially in the summer. This was the season when repressive heat and humidity pushed people out of their tenements, which had terrible airflow and brick exteriors that radiated heat inward. Air conditioning was not even a possibility. Many conversations quickly turned to the upheaval in the streets, as they had the day before. Today, though, was not the day after a one-time flare-up, like the previous disturbances had been in 1935 and 1943. There had now been two nights of unrest, which made it a major event. People were expecting it but did not know what to expect. The streets were electric.

The Third Night: Spreading Conflict

Following a second day of intense yet ultimately fruitless meetings between city officials and designated Black leaders, Harlem rose up for a third time, this time, before the sun set. Newspapers reported that sometime in the early evening, around 6 PM, a group of Black Harlemites, mostly teens, took to the streets and initiated an ad hoc march from 125th Street and Seventh Avenue that spanned fifteen blocks or so. The police boxed them in, containing the group from the front and back. On 116th Street, some people on the sidewalks began throwing bottles at police, who then converged on the march and ended it by force, even though no one in the march was throwing bottles. Another group of African Americans, estimated to number around fifty, congregated at 127th Street and Seventh Avenue. Elements of the crowd threw bottles at some of the police officers who had been occupying Harlem that day. The police scattered them by force as well.[21]

At 6:30 PM, two fires broke out on Seventh Avenue between 125th and 126th Streets. The first was on the second-floor balcony of a movie theatre, the RKO Alhambra, and was quickly extinguished. The second was on the second floor of 2105 Seventh Avenue, notable at the time for its first-floor tenant—Lewis Michaux and his National Memorial African Bookstore, also known as "The House of Common Sense and Home of Proper Propaganda." Michaux's store was a Harlem landmark, having been in operation since 1930, functioning as the hub of cultural and intellectual dissemination in the community. The shop served as Malcolm X's usual street speaking location for several years, where he would draw throngs of listeners. Housing several hundred thousand books, as well as works on and by Black people throughout the diaspora of every other medium available at the time, his store was known throughout the world and had received visits from several African heads of state, including Kwame Nkrumah of Ghana and Congo's Patrice Lumumba. Whether this fire was intentionally set is unknown, but it was extinguished before it did any real damage.[22]

150 Spreading Anxiety: Monday, July 20

Figure 8.1 Police pointing their revolvers at Harlem rooftops during the unrest.

Source: Library of Congress, Prints and Photographs Division, NYWT&S Collection, LC-USZ62-136928.

Around 8 PM on Monday, July 20, several small groups of African American marchers took to the streets, walking Seventh Avenue with 125th Street as their center, perhaps just to demonstrate that the streets were theirs. This area was where the most looting and fighting had taken place over the past two nights and had therefore attracted the heaviest police presence and response. Others on the street began taunting police and throwing a few bottles their way. The police responded with truncheons and revolvers in their hands, holding their fire for the time being. A few people set fires in garbage cans and buildings, but nothing came of them.[23]

A few minutes past 9 PM, a group of African American teens, estimated to number around 150, marched down 125th Street, chanting, "We want justice!" Some carried signs with a large picture of Lieutenant Gilligan with the caption

"WANTED FOR MURDER—GILLIGAN, THE COP." Six police cars followed them until the group disbanded without incident.[24]

By 9:30 PM, the streets of Harlem were once again full of people interested in the uprisings for a variety of reasons—airing grievances, releasing anger and hostility, taking property for personal gain, fighting the police, or simply witnessing those more actively participating in it all. The temperature had fallen to 71 degrees; the humidity ascended to just short of 100 percent. Police met a rapidly growing group of one thousand or more young Central Harlemites marching the length of 125th Street. At Second Avenue, police "indiscriminately" clubbed the crowd off of the streets; they also shot over people's heads, which made it easy for people to think they were being shot at. Rumors spread accordingly. Preparing for a third night of confrontation, the police blocked off

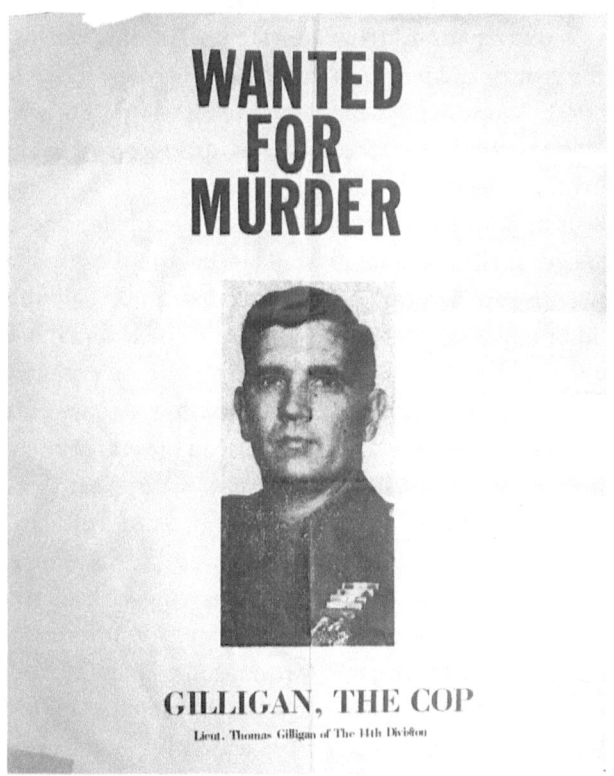

Figure 8.2 "Wanted for Murder—Gilligan the Cop" flier, 1963–1964.

Source: Arnie Goldwag Brooklyn Congress of Racial Equality (CORE) collection, ARC.002, Brooklyn Historical Society.

125th Street between Amsterdam and Fifth Avenues with the help of fire trucks and the area between Fifth and Lenox Avenues, from 116th Street to 135th Streets.[25] Civil rights activists endeavoring to clear the streets drove a sound truck through the area, urging those within earshot to "return to your homes." They encountered stiff resistance when a group of African American teens set upon the truck and rocked it back and forth in an effort to flip it. Upward of one hundred policemen and fifteen patrol cars scattered the attackers with gunshots.[26]

Around 10:45 PM, James Farmer saw several hundred mostly young, African American people, along with large numbers of police in riot gear, approach CORE headquarters on West 125th Street. He described them as "two mobs, two armies." Farmer, watching from the second floor of the building, dispatched a CORE member to talk to them, who reported back that the young people wanted to raid the office because there were white CORE members inside. At this point, according to Farmer, the disturbances were "anti-white. It was the 'Get Whitey' period." In an effort to prevent this violence, he walked outside into the crowd, and before he could say much, the youth let him know where they stood: "Now, Mr. Farmer, don't tell us about no nonviolence, we don't want to hear that shit. Don't tell us about turning no other cheek. We ain't gonna turn no other cheek."[27]

While dozens of police stood across the street, ready for battle, he did just that, telling the group Mayor Wagner would be back in the city soon. He spoke about meeting with Paul Screvane and, more importantly, said that Lieutenant Gilligan would be appearing before a grand jury, which would decide whether to indict him for crimes related to Powell's death. These announcements had little effect upon the people gathered before him. It was more of the same—be patient, give the system a chance. Whether those in the crowd knew much about Paul Screvane or Robert Wagner was irrelevant; it was clear that they had no trust in the men who ran the city, because they had done little to improve the lives of these young people, their parents, and the people they knew. Farmer had nothing of substance left to say to these people looking for leadership. Like others the previous nights, he told them to go home. And like those others had heard, people in the crowd told him, "We're not going home. We are home." That was not something Farmer, who lived downtown, could say for himself.[28]

At the behest of L. Joseph Overton, a trade unionist and former president of the New York City chapter of the NAACP, Farmer joined with Bayard Rustin in a final effort to lead the people gathered in front of the CORE office away from the area. Careful to let the police know what they were doing, the three men walked arm in arm at the front of the group in the classic style of so many civil rights marches before, chanting "We want freedom" and "We want justice." The idea was to march the young people, organized two abreast, around the neighborhood until they were tired. As individuals passed their homes, ideally they would fall out of the march and go inside, off the streets. The march was both a way to release some pressure and to get people home while trying to keep the risk of physical violence low. Farmer was committed to marching for hours, whatever amount of time was necessary to defuse the tense situation before him.[29]

The march only made it about ten blocks before it fell into disorder. The police followed the group and shot flares skyward so that they could clearly observe the situation; they then began shooting what sounded like automatic weapons but was actually many service revolvers going off in quick succession. The young people following the three men scattered into the night as quickly as they could. Farmer said to an officer, "What's the matter, can't you see what we're trying to do?" The policeman asked him if he had heard the bottles crashing. He replied he "hadn't heard a single bottle" until they began shooting, though Farmer conceded that people very well may have been throwing bottles but that he was unable to hear them from his position at the front of the march. The officer advised Farmer to tell "those people" to stop throwing bricks and bottles.[30]

Once what he referred to as his "Pied Piper effort" had failed, James Farmer was convinced that there was nothing more he could do to stop what was going on in the streets. The police would make it impossible, working against him or whomever would be pursuing similar efforts. All that was left to do was take care of the casualties, so he went back to 125th Street, gave armbands to CORE members, in an effort to mark them as noncombatants, and sent them out with stretchers to collect the wounded. The CORE office became a triage center, with several nurses on duty. They transported the severely injured to Harlem Hospital. Farmer carried the lessons he learned that night into 1965, refusing to go to Watts when fighting and looting broke out there, later reflecting that even Dr. King was unable to prevent or remediate the conflagration in Los Angeles.[31]

Just before midnight on July 20, policemen charged a group of "shouting youths" at 125th Street and Eighth Avenue. As the police clubbed their way into the young people, they unsurprisingly elicited a hail of bottles, bricks, and garbage. Police injured at least five in that fracas, all of whom received treatment at the CORE office up the street. Shortly after midnight, police arrested eight African American teenagers accused of "shoving and punching passengers" on a subway train they boarded at 125th Street.[32]

Sometime after midnight, the police reported a consistent barrage of bricks and rocks from the rooftops of buildings on Eighth Avenue between 130th and 131st Streets. While some of the many bars in Harlem selectively admitted customers that night, a number of others in the area decided that opening for business was more potential trouble than it was worth. Sam's West Side Bar and Grill, located on that block of Eighth Avenue, was open for business, though it would have done better to keep its doors shut. Multiple squad cars of police officers converged on the block to provide backup for their compatriots on the receiving end of the bricks. After allegedly witnessing two Black men smash a grocery store's windows and flee across the street into Sam's when spotted, the police went after the men, only to be met by a locked door. Police broke down the door and began attacking people inside and smashing up furniture in their pursuit of the men. The bartender contended that he had shut the bar down when someone smashed the windows in the supermarket and had locked the door, thinking it would keep him and his patrons safe. Instead, he said the police ignored the grocery store and came for his business.[33]

The process of forcibly entering and closing Sam's proved to be difficult: many patrons strongly resisted the policemen's violence, perceiving no reason for it. Police entering the bar later reported that those inside met them with punches and shoves, which they returned. Some officers fired into the establishment, through the windows, from the street, and smashed out the rest of the glass with their batons. At least six patrons, all African American, were seriously injured, all bleeding from the head. A journalist described seeing one man slumped against the wall, bleeding heavily from a gash in his head into his hat, which was filled to the brim, upside down on the floor. Two men suffered concussions, and one had multiple broken bones, versus one officer with a cut on his hand and another who sprained his thumb. When that reporter tried interviewing the NYPD lieutenant in charge—who was involved in perpetrating some of the violence himself—the officer refused to answer questions or give his name.[34]

The police succeeded in ejecting a mass of angry and agitated people, many likely in some state of intoxication, out onto the street in the midst of a third night of disorder. Not only had they all either been attacked or witnesses to the violence, but they now stood outside the devastated bar in the presence of their attackers, unable to legally defend themselves or pursue any kind of justice. Unsurprisingly, many of them were not eager to return to their apartments and instead remained in front of the bar, not just willing to battle with police but also voicing their intent to do so. Bayard Rustin came when he got word of the event and tried to calm the crowd. Once again, his calls for peace were shouted down, with one man loudly denouncing him as an unwanted "liberal." Upon surveying the aftermath of the raid on Sam's, Rustin's perspective changed. "My God," he said. "I didn't realize it was really like this. I don't blame the people for booing me. I wasn't aware the police actually treated people this way." Rustin soon left to go to the Thirty-Second Precinct, hoping to talk to the commander on duty, in an effort to do whatever he could do to try to reduce the violence in the streets.[35]

If we are to take Rustin at his word, this man who had called New York City home since 1937, had been incarcerated in federal prison for two years and local jails numerous times, beaten viciously by police as early as 1942, spent several weeks on a chain gang in North Carolina in 1949, had witnessed the same infamous scenes of attack dogs and firehoses used against children in Birmingham, Alabama, the summer before the uprisings, as well as many other similar but less publicized episodes, was quite familiar with state violence. Still, what he saw in the streets of Harlem in July 1964 appears to have shocked him. Rustin, while his skin color made him a target, did enjoy the privileges of traveling the country, effectively for a living, often out of the city for weeks and months at a time. Though he was not of the public stature of Malcolm X or James Farmer, Rustin did have powerful connections with civil rights figures, especially A. Philip Randolph locally and Dr. King nationally, that would have served to distinguish him from other Black New Yorkers and offered at least some protection from the worst of the NYPD's excesses. He also had not grown up in Harlem, nor did the city's crushing segregation confine him there, so he could not fully appreciate all the experiences that came with living almost all of one's life there. But the people in the neighborhood knew.[36]

Tensions had grown so high outside Sam's by this time that the officers called in the Tactical Patrol Force. Its members exited their three buses and physically dispersed the crowd with military precision. At least five hundred police officers attempted to keep people anywhere but in the streets of Harlem that night, again cracking the air with their bursts of gunfire time after time. Overall, at least twenty people were arrested; seventeen had to be hospitalized, including three police officers.[37] CORE reported having treated forty-five citizens for injuries at its headquarters.[38] Police shot two African American men, both twenty-eight years old, standing on the corner of Lenox Avenue and 118th Street in Harlem, with "stray bullets." One man was "grazed on the back"; the other "suffered a wound of the right hip."[39] At some point during the night, a person or people fired bullets into CORE's office, empty at the time. CORE maintained police did it out of spite.[40]

Meanwhile, sentiments favorable toward the outbreak in Harlem were rising in Bedford-Stuyvesant on the night of July 20. An untimely late-night CORE rally at the intersection of Fulton Street and Nostrand Avenue demanding justice for James Powell quickly spun out of control. Despite CORE's pleas to the crowd, most of those gathered had no interest in returning to their homes when the rally ended at 12:30 AM and began chanting "Killer cops" at the twenty officers watching them. A group of about one hundred demonstrators marched in a six-block square and returned to the intersection another four hundred strong. Black nationalist street speakers of no particular affiliation began giving speeches to the much larger crowd until about 1:30 in the morning, at which point the demonstrations ended for the evening. People on

Figure 8.3 NYPD officers inspect a torched police car on Herkimer Street and Nostrand Avenue in Bedford-Stuyvesant.

Source: Library of Congress, Prints and Photographs Division, NYWT&S Collection, LC-USZ62-137002.

the street then began throwing bottles at the police, which brought forty reinforcements and rapidly increasing violence and disorder. People in the crowd, which now numbered upward of one thousand, broke the windows of about thirty stores, looted some, and burned out a police car. By 2:30 in the morning, when the area had calmed for the night, police had arrested at least thirty people there and listed one as injured. They fired no shots.[41]

City officials and civil rights activists had been worried about unrest in Bedford-Stuyvesant for some time.[42] The disgraceful conditions among the area's African American residents were well-known and only worsening. On the first night of the uprisings in Harlem, there was an unrelated incident in the streets across the river in Brooklyn, but the city's papers covered it in conjunction with news of the turmoil. In Brownsville, the section of Brooklyn that abuts Bedford-Stuyvesant on its southeastern corner, police reported a "running, five-hour battle" between groups of Black men and Puerto Rican men. It ended with the arrest of seven men on gun charges, including possession of rifles and shotguns, and a dozen injuries, with two men shot. An eighteen-year-old Puerto Rican man had acid thrown in his face. This was a particularly vicious manifestation of the competition for economic and spatial resources between the two groups occupying the lowest rungs of New York's social, economic, and political ladders. Massive Puerto Rican migration into the city over the previous two decades had led to escalating tensions and resentment, as Puerto Ricans and African Americans often had to live in adjoining neighborhoods and contend for the same jobs. In response to the violence and fearful it could lead to full-scale uprisings, the Brooklyn headquarters of the NYPD announced it would be taking "extraordinary" unidentified precautions to prevent such a situation.[43] On this day, Bedford-Stuyvesant had not exploded, as feared, though city leaders may not have realized it. What would come tomorrow would be far worse.

9
Day Four: Tuesday, July 21

After three nights of spreading unrest in the largest city in the country, President Johnson directed the Federal Bureau of Investigation to probe the uprisings. With his job up to voters in three and a half months, Johnson had to appear vigilant, especially given Republican candidate Barry Goldwater's attacks on Johnson for not taking the issue of "security from domestic violence" seriously enough. Also wary of what a prolonged "race riot" would do to his ability to continue to pass civil rights legislation, Johnson felt he needed to try to foreclose his conservative opponents' opportunities to use what was happening in Harlem and Bedford-Stuyvesant as a demonstration of where more civil rights legislation would lead. His aides had been sending memos around the White House since the day after James Powell's death, making statements like "a great deal of the Negro leadership simply does not understand the political facts of life.... They are not sophisticated enough to understand the theory of the backlash." By Monday morning, Johnson's staff warned him that on-the-fence white voters would want to know why he had not responded to these uprisings, after being forceful in Mississippi and Georgia. Worried these voters would see unrest as unrest and not make distinctions between uprisings in the urban North and the spectacular denial of basic rights in the South, presidential aides urged him to take a strong stand on what was happening in New York.[1]

Johnson issued a press statement that day informing the public that his primary concerns with what was happening in New York were "the preservation of law and order and the right of our citizens to respect for their property and to be safe in their person" in the city they call home. Echoing Barry Goldwater's statements of just a few days earlier, the president declared, "In the preservation of law and order there can be no compromise—just as there can be no compromise in securing equal and exact justice for all Americans." Johnson was making clear his commitment to guaranteeing the rights of all citizens and ensuring equal protection under the law, full equality before the law, and safety both from violence and looting in Harlem and from grandstanding, bigoted southern sheriffs, mayors, and governors.[2]

Half a decade later, out of office, Johnson recounted his thoughts on this epoch of urban upheaval to Doris Kearns, a former aide. The former president expressed deep sympathy with those who had taken to the streets. Reflecting on what he and his administration had accomplished for its African American citizens and past the point of needing to win votes, Johnson seemed to believe that when all the celebratory packaging was stripped from the War on Poverty, Civil Rights Act, and Voting Rights Act, among other accomplishments, he simply had not delivered very much. "God knows how little we've really moved on this issue, despite all the fanfare. As I see it," he told Kearns, "I've moved the Negro from D+ to C–. He's still nowhere. He knows it. And that's why he's out in the streets. Hell, I'd be there too. . . . We'll never know how high a price we paid for the unkindness and injustice we've inflicted on people." But back in 1964, there was an election in under four months, and whatever he believed at the time, Johnson needed to show that he would not stand for or with those engaged in disorder, keeping "people who've worked hard every day to save up for a week's vacation or a new store and they look around and think they see their tax dollars going to finance a bunch of ungrateful rioters" in mind.[3]

Eager to display his commitment to both law and order, Johnson initially took up FBI Director J. Edgar Hoover on his willingness to helm the probe into New York's upheaval personally. He advised Hoover to tell city officials "that I have directed you to investigate the possibility of law violations and to get me a full report, just as you have in Mississippi and Georgia," though the situations were in no way comparable. Robert F. Kennedy, the attorney general and Hoover's boss, at least in name, was extremely displeased when got wind of this arrangement. Hoover was a living law enforcement legend, being the only director the FBI had ever had since its organization in 1935, and he had fashioned a reputation as a man who combated gangsters, communists, radicals, and, as would later become clear, just about anyone else who aroused suspicion or could pose a threat to his power, from civil rights leaders to presidents. Expressing concern that Hoover's involvement would bring unnecessary attention to the city and what was happening there, as well as irritate city leaders, with whom the administration had good working relationships, Kennedy urged LBJ to reconsider. Johnson did.[4] Instead, the president instructed Hoover to reach out to NYPD

Commissioner Murphy and Governor Rockefeller of New York to "offer them our complete cooperation" in discovering "who was responsible for doing what" and determining whether federal laws had been violated.[5] Johnson told Hoover he was getting "floods of wires and telegrams," with messages like "I'm a working girl. I'm afraid to leave my house. I feel the Negro revolution will reach Queens. Please send troops immediately to Harlem."[6]

In the same conversation, Johnson suggested to Hoover that "maybe you can put a quietus on that Muslim X and all that stuff," presumably referring crudely to Malcolm X.[7] While the civil rights movement had plenty of opponents and enemies, not the least of whom was Hoover, Malcolm represented to many Americans, especially white people, the sinister, threatening, and violent alternative to the nonviolent and integrationist civil rights movement. Even though Malcolm had left the Nation of Islam months earlier, it made no difference. Men like Johnson and Hoover saw him and his followers as threats that must be obstructed and suppressed at every turn. Recommending that Hoover silence anyone is a frightening prospect and not something to be taken lightly, given the FBI's extensive interference in all facets of the Black Freedom Struggle. As James Farmer said, but for different reasons, Malcolm was fortunate to be out of the country when this was all happening.

As Farmer attests, contrary to what many people would have expected, the Nation of Islam's adherents, known as Black Muslims, were "among the first people to get out there and say 'Now, that's idiocy. You don't start a war you can't win'" when the uprisings broke out in Harlem.[8] What Farmer witnessed, coupled with Claude Brown's description of the Nation, indicates that its members very likely helped reduce the amount of violence in the streets of Harlem during these nights of rage and chaos. In Brown's telling, the NOI "was closer to most Harlemites than any of the other organizations, much closer than the NAACP or the Urban League." They had a credibility that mainstream organizations did not because far from being social and cultural elites talking down to the working classes and those on the periphery of society, many of the men in the group had come from the community. These were men who had robbed people, gotten drunk on the corner, and shot up in doorways but had reformed themselves and now burned with desire to uplift the Black masses, eschewing all vices and exuding discipline. They knew Harlem, could relate to the dispossessed, and could speak with authority.[9]

For its part, the Nation of Islam disparaged the looting and violence in Harlem and Bedford-Stuyvesant, exclaiming on the front page of its newspaper, *Muhammad Speaks*, "THIS WOULD NOT HAPPEN!" in very large type, over a picture of police beating a man in Harlem during the unrest. The caption read, "This would not happen in Harlem or anywhere in black America under the leadership of The Honorable Elijah Muhammad, Messenger of Allah, the only black leader in America with the Divine solution to the critical problem of [the] American Negro."[10]

Inside the paper, Abdul Basit Naeem, a Pakistani immigrant residing in Bedford-Stuyvesant and publisher of his own periodical, expounded at length upon the idea that "had the vast majority of Harlemites and 'black Brooklynites' been Muslims—or followers of the Honorable Elijah Muhammad—there would have been . . . no rioting or cause for tension, violence and lawlessness in New York City." Naeem supported his conclusion with three arguments. First, Muslims and members of the Nation of Islam are opposed to violence in all incarnations, save for self-defense and protection of honor and property. Next, those in the Nation are relatively well-off and self-sufficient; even if they were in need, they would never violate their high moral character to steal and rob, and certainly not from liquor stores. Finally, if people had listened to Elijah Muhammad all along, then they would not be waiting on help from white politicians and pursuing the empty dream of integration; instead, they would focus on building up Black business and engaging earnestly in securing voluntary, chosen racial separation from white people. Naeem was certain that if African Americans finally began listening to Elijah Muhammad, "in due time Allah will turn Harlem, Bedford-Stuyvesant and all the black 'ghettos' of this continent into veritable Gardens of Paradise."[11]

The president called Acting Mayor Screvane the morning of July 21 to communicate his personal "willingness to cooperate in every way possible to help him in this time of agony." Johnson, demonstrating his belief in positive government action, which would become the cornerstone of his Great Society, asserted federal cooperation included "help in correcting the evil social conditions that breed despair and disorder." He had not considered sending in federal troops or marshals so far. Officials at the Department of Justice stated no federal laws had been broken as far as they knew, so they would not become further involved at this time. They explained it was standard for the FBI to investigate serious, recurring episodes of disorder.[12] The number of agents assigned to this case was confidentially put as high as two hundred, showing a tremendous fear of the unknown destructive power of Black neighborhoods.[13]

Johnson was undoubtedly aware of the international implications of the unrest in Harlem and Bedford-Stuyvesant. The United States had been under increasing pressure since the end of World War II to address flagrant racism throughout the country. America presented itself as the model of democracy and freedom to the rest of the world, especially countries emerging from colonialism, that is, newly liberated states within which the United States feared the spread of communism. As the Cold War between America and the Soviet Union escalated, so too did communist propaganda attacks exposing the hypocrisy of American race relations. Soviet newspapers and many other communist and left-radical organs in other countries ran countless stories of lynchings, racist beatings, segregation, violence, and other measures of racial discrimination. Many other newspapers across the globe covered these stories too, albeit in a less sensational way. The president and his advisers knew that every day these disturbances featured in the world's newspapers was one day too many. They had to act, get the uprisings extinguished, and appear to be doing something to remediate the circumstances that had led to such an unbecoming episode.

By Monday, papers throughout Europe were running front-page stories on the uprisings. Many of the headlines were exclamatory and dismal—"Mob March, Blood and Ruin!"; "In Harlem, the Devil Is Loose"; "A Cancer Called Harlem"; and "Night of Terror in the Negro Quarter of New York." And those were from papers that were not communist affiliated. Communist media ran headlines like "Harlem in State of Siege—Police Continue Repression Against Negroes" and "Bloody Street Slaughter in Harlem." Britain's *Guardian* asserted that Senator Goldwater's "extremism" bore heavy responsibility for the conflagration. The *London Daily Sketch* printed a series of "pictures to show the ticking time-bomb that is America now." The Soviet Tass news agency charged: "The authorities refuse to punish those responsible for the bloody events." Austria's communist *Arbeiter Zeitung* bluntly stated: "The conflict between colored and white is becoming a more serious problem. It is possible that problem will replace the East-West conflict. Considering the poverty of many Negroes amidst an affluent society it is not surprising that there are young Negroes who hate their white fellow citizens and support such organizations as the Black Muslims."

The Soviet press provided the most acerbic condemnation of American race relations and police behavior. Under the headline "Harlem Drenched in Blood," an *Izvestia* reporter wrote: "The truncheons of the swaggering New York policemen failed to keep the Negroes off the streets. The streets of Harlem were full of people and I saw that every one of those faces was a mask of hatred of the police. The Negro masses do not, as before, listen to the sermons of the advocates of non-violence." Like the *Guardian*, *Izvestia* also heaped a portion of the blame on the Goldwater campaign, writing that African Americans saw his run for office as "a counterattack by the racists." The foreign press was not alone in believing that Goldwater and what was then the far right had direct or indirect responsibility for these events.[14]

This press was bad news for Johnson and the Democrats. While Goldwater was already successfully taking aim at liberals for what he articulated as their permissive approach to social issues, he suddenly had urban disorder in one of the northern Democrats' seats of power as ammunition. With the election a few months away, Johnson and his allies were desperate to get the uprisings under control, out of the press, and forgotten. Many African American leaders shared that desire, seeing Goldwater as the worst possible option. Expecting a severe regression of civil rights under a potential Goldwater administration, Whitney Young, Martin Luther King Jr., Roy Wilkins, and A. Philip Randolph issued a united call for a national moratorium on all demonstrations until after the election. Wilkins believed that civil rights protests resulting in violence, regardless of who was responsible, essentially became "Goldwater rallies." James Farmer and John Lewis, chairman of the Student Nonviolent Coordinating Committee, both rejected the moratorium on the grounds that Black people had no other legitimate tools and that since the Urban League and NAACP did not use such tactics, their strategies would not have to change. Milton Galamison, a school boycott leader, declared the irrelevance of the establishment men to the northern cause, saying, "The people in the streets throwing bottles won't listen to these leaders anymore." Malcolm X, with his characteristic biting critique, took another path to deriding the four national leaders, saying they "have sold themselves out and become campaign managers in the Negro community for Lyndon Johnson."[15]

James Farmer, again demonstrating his faith in state action, applauded FBI involvement and encouraged as lengthy an investigation as permissible. Reacting to the news, Farmer said, "The FBI should launch a full and thorough investigation of all of the circumstances surrounding these terrible incidents. There has been provocation and brutal behavior by the police—by all the circumstances we mean both the bottle throwing and the billy swinging."[16]

Speaking to reporters in City Hall, Screvane expressed his gratitude to President Johnson, as well as his hopes and expectations for what the federal investigation would find. Confident that the groups holding rallies were receiving money from various individuals, though he left it unclear as to why small, often impromptu political rallies needed funding, Screvane was optimistic that the FBI could determine who these donors were. He believed that people at these rallies should be investigated for criminal conduct related to allegedly making "very inflammatory . . . anti-American . . . and seditious statements."[17]

Beyond laying blame, Screvane spent the better part of the day successfully avoiding a group of about thirty-five African American civil rights activists from Harlem, led by Isaiah Robinson, chairman of the Harlem Parents Committee, which had been picketing City Hall since 5 AM. They sought a meeting with him to discuss the uprisings, their causes, and what the city needed to do to address the issues at hand. After waiting for twelve hours, five of them, including Robinson, entered the building and refused to leave at its 5 PM closing time. They were then arrested for obstructing free movement in the hub of city government and "thereby endangering the safety of the people."[18]

When he exited the Iberia Airlines plane that afternoon into the sticky July air of New York City, Mayor Wagner resumed his role as chief elected official. After stepping to the tarmac at John F. Kennedy International Airport at 4:04 PM, Wagner gave a brief press conference, declaring his "deep faith in Commissioner Murphy and the ability of the Police Department to contain the situation." He then met with the highest-ranking city officials for close to an hour and departed for Gracie Mansion. There he convened a meeting with ten aides who briefed him in detail on the past three nights' events. They then collectively considered how to best implement Screvane's five-point program from the day before. After two and a half hours, at about 9 PM, the meeting ended, and Wagner went to bed, saying that he had been up since 2 AM.[19] Outside, the temperature was still 77, with matching humidity.

Civil rights demonstrators picketed NYPD headquarters, City Hall, Governor Rockefeller's city residence, and several police stations. At 240 Centre Street in Lower Manhattan, the NYPD's headquarters, an interracial group encountered a mob of 250 or so angry white teenage counterdemonstrators, throwing rotten eggs at them as well as a slew of insults, ranging from "Goldwater for president!" to "You nigger-loving bastards go home!" Police attempted to keep them away from the civil rights demonstrators, fearing more violence. The white teens resisted the police, throwing eggs at them as well. Policemen on the scene pushed them back but did not attempt to disperse or arrest any of them. When the civil rights picketers at police headquarters ended their protest at 11 PM, the counterdemonstrators were still there. The white teens followed them to the subway station, heckling and insulting them all the way, despite a police escort for the civil rights demonstrators. The police did not interfere with the white teenagers.[20]

Despite the previous night's chaos in Bedford-Stuyvesant, city leaders seemed to anticipate a tapering off of such activity or at least wanted to give off the public appearance of believing it to be so. Police officers, for the first time since Saturday, were no longer working twelve-hour emergency shifts, instead returning to their standard eight-hour workdays. Deputy Commissioner Walter Arm, head of community relations, told the press that conditions in Harlem were "slowly returning to normal."[21] However, a group of some three dozen African American community leaders in Bedford-Stuyvesant told the police that they did not believe that they, as a group or as individual leaders, could serve any effective purpose as a restraint on the explosive forces in the streets that had presented themselves the previous night.[22]

The Fourth Night: Fighting on Two Fronts

After another relatively quiet day, with the exception of two African American teenage boys arrested for attempting to remove banjos from a smashed pawnshop window at 8:30 in the morning, Harlem resumed its uprisings the night of July 21. Police again closed off the streets and awaited the fourth night of upheaval. The night saw more looting, more bottle throwing, more running, more window smashing, and more clashes with police. Until midnight, the temperature stayed in the upper seventies, while the humidity climbed into the eighties. As the humidity escalated, so too did the action in the streets. Shortly after the sun went down, two police officers caught two Black men who were allegedly in the process of looting a clothing store on Lenox Avenue between 111th and 112th Streets. A crowd of Harlemites surrounded the police, intent on freeing the two men. Police responded by firing their guns and calling reinforcements, who scattered the mob.[23] A group of African American teenagers marched back and forth along several blocks of 125th Street with "WANTED FOR MURDER—GILLIGAN THE COP" posters.[24]

The looting on this night was more scattered than previous nights, when it had been fairly centralized around a few main blocks. It could be that police were guarding those areas more intently than before, or perhaps the attractive businesses in that part of Central Harlem had already been emptied. Police claimed people in the streets this night were moving in groups of between ten and thirty, mostly composed of teenagers, with a few adults. At 118th Street, 150 police chased looters who had set upon a dry-cleaning establishment on the corner of Lenox. As soon as that crowd dissipated, another formed two blocks down at 116th and Lenox and began the same process at another cleaners. Then at

122nd Street, a short distance off of Lenox, looters formed a human chain to extract clothing from a shop more efficiently. The roving expropriators were emblematic of the frustrations the police had been experiencing since Saturday night—they could break up a crowd fairly easily and generally could dispel a group of looters without much trouble, but many of the people involved would just move to a new location where there were no police or wait for the police to leave and then resume their activities.[25]

In the midst of this, Mayor Wagner took an unannounced one-hour visit to Harlem at 11 PM, accompanied by Commissioner Murphy. Not retiring for the evening at 9 PM as he had earlier told his aides, the mayor toured Central Harlem up and down from West 110th to 135th Streets, from Central Park North to Harlem Hospital, and across Lenox, Seventh, and Eighth Avenues. Along the way, he reported "boarded-up windows," "itinerant gangs," and "some of the debris of battle," along with people fearfully looking out of their windows at streets where teenagers with helmets and walkie-talkies roamed, whom he termed "the loose gun powder of our day."[26] Following his tour, Wagner voiced his conviction "that the overwhelming majority of those who live in the Harlem community neither participated in nor appreciated the violence and disorder." After all, according to the mayor, "Of all groups in America, Negroes have the most to gain from law and order." To demonstrate this, he pointed to such landmark events in the civil rights movement as the 1954 Supreme Court decision in *Brown v. Board of Education* and the two-week-old Civil Rights Act, as well as the city's laws prohibiting housing discrimination.[27]

Bedford-Stuyvesant on this night was much more chaotic than it had been the night before. Around 9 PM, a Black street speaker was addressing a crowd of about two hundred at the corner of Fulton Street and Nostrand Avenue. As he spoke, someone smashed a drugstore window. People immediately ran, to which the speaker responded, "No! No! That's what the man wants you to do. . . . He wants you to riot so he can shoot you down!" People generally heeded his warning, if only briefly, slowly returning to the corner. As they did so, the "WANTED FOR MURDER—GILLIGAN, THE COP" flyers began appearing.[28] Police then charged the crowd, swinging nightsticks with abandon. This became a template for the night—police perceiving provocation or danger and then charging and beating whomever was closest.[29]

Near 9:30, the police had begun nonviolently dispersing a crowd that was circulating a rumor that a policeman had shot a young boy. One of a group of teenagers in the crowd threw a bottle at the police and ran. The police either did not realize or did not care who threw it and responded by firing their guns at a roof where they saw flashlights. The flashlights belonged to two police officers who were trying to tell the officers on the ground where the group of teenagers had gone.[30]

According to Inspector Walter Clarke of the NYPD, the fury of upheaval began in earnest a few hours later, when a person or people set off firecrackers at the intersection of Fulton Street and Arlington Place, a side street between Nostrand and Bedford Avenues. Apparently, both police and people milling about on the streets thought the sounds were gunfire. People ran for cover, and police ran to stop their flight. Predictably, fighting ensued. Police then began firing crowd-control shots. Things quickly spiraled out of control, with officers on the scene calling for reinforcements four times by 11 PM. Crowds estimated at one thousand roamed a sixteen-block area around the same epicenter as the night before, the intersection of Fulton and Nostrand, fighting police, smashing windows, and looting. The NYPD directed the Transit Authority to close two subway stations in the vicinity at 10:45 PM. By midnight, the one hundred police fighting the mobs had spent their ammunition and had to call for an emergency supply, with one officer having fired 150 rounds.[31]

The battle continued for over twelve hours, until 10 AM. Altogether, two hundred NYPD officers, helmeted and guns drawn, struggled to clear the streets. A police chaplain who was witness to the events described Tuesday night's actions as "much more serious" than what had been taking place in Harlem. A sergeant verified this when he described the night as "pure, undiluted hell."[32] Certainly some of the serious nature of that night lies at the feet of the NYPD and the Tactical Patrol Force, in particular. Jim O'Neil, a former TPF officer, recalls that he and his colleagues began rhythmically banging their axe handles on the floor of their department bus en route to Bedford-Stuyvesant, chanting "'Kill, kill, kill' again and again, over and over, louder and louder, like a deadly mantra." O'Neil claims three TPF squads fired three hundred bullets in under two minutes, many of them into buildings. And the TPF officers helped make hell on those streets, with "axe handles flailing and rioters falling."[33] Another TPF officer describes a sergeant commanding his officers to "Get those niggers!" Whether they needed the encouragement or not, officers did as he said, behaving more wildly and with less restraint than they had in Harlem, shouting "Go on, you bastards, run" and "I'm tired of you damn n——s" while beating whomever they could get their hands on.[34] After ten minutes of combat, "The street and sidewalks were covered with bodies, some unconscious, and some writhing in pain, bleeding and moaning." The police had subdued the crowds.[35]

The damage was evident in the bright midmorning light. Forty stores within a few blocks of Fulton and Nostrand had been looted. Along just one block of Fulton Street, between Bedford and Nostrand Avenues, twenty stores suffered smashed windows. Two hundred windows were broken out overall. Police described the extensive looting as "organized by hoodlums . . . who had taken advantage of emotions stirred up by the events in Harlem and the previous night's outburst" in Bedford-Stuyvesant. The alleged organizers had been "former runners in the illicit policy numbers racket" as young men who had become involved in more serious criminal activity as adults. Police arrested more than fifty, mostly for burglary or assaulting an officer. One teenager was arrested for hurling a Molotov cocktail at a gathering of police. Police shot and critically wounded two men, one of whom, twenty-three, police said leapt at an officer when caught looting and was shot in the stomach. The second man, thirty-six, stood accused of hitting a policeman in the chest with a can of vegetables; the officer then shot him in the abdomen.[36]

The willingness of some residents in Harlem and Bedford-Stuyvesant to continue battling the police and looting commercial establishments only increased the distress higher up the political ranks. The day had already begun with President Johnson deeply concerned, particularly for what these events communicated about his administration's goals and his leadership, as well as his chances to get elected. Johnson and the head of the FBI, J. Edgar Hoover, were in direct contact with the acting mayor of the city, upping the pressure on local officials to prevent further unrest. Again, they failed. While there was some light fighting in Brooklyn the night before, following the CORE rally, Bedford-Stuyvesant exploded late on July 21. The fourth night demonstrated that people in Harlem and Bedford-Stuyvesant still had a lot of fight in them.

10
Day Five: Wednesday, July 22

Wednesday, another day of people frantically organizing meetings to prevent another night of tumult, saw many demands but few concessions. The disorder had now stretched for four nights and crossed the East River into Brooklyn. There was no reasonable expectation this night would be any different; in fact, it might be worse. Could the chaos spread into Brownsville? Crown Heights? It was impossible to say. Following four nights of turmoil, the mayor gave a live speech, broadcast on radio and television, stressing the need for "law and order." What he offered the people of the city was nothing new, but he dressed it in progressive rhetoric. It was more of the same from the man who had cultivated the skills of appearing to be concerned and then appearing to act. The turmoil did not spread. In fact, it significantly diminished in Harlem. However, Bedford-Stuyvesant experienced intense fighting and looting, despite activists' efforts to prevent it.

In Washington, DC, Adam Clayton Powell Jr., the Democratic congressman from Harlem, gave a press conference on the upheaval. Powell presented a list of steps the city should take that would put an end to the unrest "before the sun goes down tonight." First and paramount was to establish a civilian review board, staffed by civilians, to hear complaints against the police. Following that, the NYPD should transfer one of the city's three Black police captains to the Twenty-Eighth Precinct on West 123rd Street in Central Harlem, suspend Lieutenant Gilligan, cease assigning rookie officers to Harlem, and prohibit the use of live ammunition in future disturbances. On this final point, the congressman remarked, "What has happened in Harlem is without precedent in the history of any police department in any city, including the Deep South. New York City ought to hang its head in shame."[1]

Also on Wednesday, numerous organizations throughout the city began voicing support for civilian review board reform. The New York Federation of Reformed Synagogues and New York chapter of the American Jewish Committee both agreed with the need to change how the city addressed alleged police misconduct, as did a group of fifteen Harlem clergy, headed by the Reverend Eugene Callender, who also decried the "unnecessary use of gunfire" and police violence in general during the disorder thus far.[2] The mayor's Committee of Religious Leaders, representing 7,500 Jewish, Protestant, and Catholic clergy, also asked the mayor to form a new review board. The community empowerment agency HARYOU-ACT, now under the control of Congressman Powell, demanded an all-civilian review board.[3]

James Farmer revealed that provocateurs had been making deceptive phone calls in his name to civil rights activists throughout the city yesterday, pushing them to hold demonstrations in volatile areas. Farmer stated that he was not opposed to demonstrations "outside the ghettos," but as he had stated earlier in his appearance at Mount Morris Ascension Presbyterian Church on Sunday, it would be foolish for Black people to take to the streets and fight the police—they could only lose. As for CORE, the organization he headed, its workers were still patrolling the streets as peacekeepers, trying to get people off of the streets—and when that failed, as witnesses to violent events and first-aid providers in their aftermath.[4]

That afternoon, Brooklyn Borough President Abe Stark held a conference at Brooklyn Borough Hall with sixty Black representatives from Bedford-Stuyvesant. Expressing that he was "deeply concerned about what effect this rioting will have on the nationwide progress of the civil rights movement," Stark wanted to try to develop solutions first hand. At the meeting's conclusion, the participants decided on four key courses of action both to end the uprisings and prevent them from recurring. First, local clergy and public officials should have access to a sound truck to make appeals for calm. Next, radio stations with significant teenage audiences should regularly broadcast public service announcements over the next several days urging their listenership to stay off the streets. Third, all participants agreed that they and their respective organizations, including Brooklyn CORE and the Brooklyn Urban League, would not hold demonstrations or mass meetings for an indefinite period. Finally, the group put in a collective request to Mayor Wagner for increased police presence, a civilian review board, a larger proportion of African American police officers in the community, and a pledge from the mayor that he would make legitimate efforts to address issues among youth that had created the conditions for the disorder, especially high unemployment, drug use, and a lack of engaging activities in the neighborhood.[5]

At 6:45 PM, with the temperature slowly falling to 76 degrees and the humidity rapidly climbing past 80 percent, Mayor Wagner delivered a speech aired on television and radio addressing the uprisings. Speaking live from a studio in Liederkranz Hall at 111 East Fifty-Eighth Street in Manhattan, the main thrust of his speech was a more compassionately packaged version of much of what Senator Goldwater had been promoting on the campaign trail—law and order. Confidently stating that "law and order are the Negroes' best friend," Wagner declared, "Without law and order Negro and civil rights progress would be set back half a century." By the mayor's estimation, what was happening in Harlem and Bedford-Stuyvesant was "mob rule," which "is the way of the Ku Klux Klan and the night riders and the lynch mobs." He went on to assure the city that "individuals or groups of hoodlums, rowdies, trouble-makers bent on destruction, theft or incitement to riot, drawn as they have been from all parts of the city, will be brought to a halt, and the guilty will be punished to the full extent of the law." Altogether, he used the term "law and order" at least nine times in the first few minutes of his twenty-three-minute speech.[6]

Following this segment of his address, the mayor strove to placate civil rights activists and the city's African American population in general with a series of announcements on the actions he would direct city officials to take. Starting this portion of his speech with "two firm convictions," Wagner declared his "complete confidence in Police Commissioner Murphy," who was adamantly opposed to any permutation of incorporating civilians into the Civilian Complaint Review Board, an all-police entity tasked with investigating citizens' complaints against NYPD officers, deciding the validity of them, and passing on recommendations for discipline to the commissioner, who retained full authority over all such matters. In a bit of rhetorical acrobatics, the mayor tried to convince proponents of civilian review that such a system already existed, since "the ultimate authority and responsibility for the police force rests in civilian hands—the Mayor himself." This was his second firm conviction. Accordingly, he promised that not only would Deputy Mayor Edward Cavanagh personally review "every case in charges involving alleged police brutality brought before the police board" but also that the mayor would begin accepting complaints of police brutality in his office and "that all such cases of complaints will be acted upon promptly."[7]

Curiously, he did allow that some police officers in the city, without indicating he believed that number to be small, were racist—"the prejudices which they always had and have retained despite the best training and indoctrination"—and were bound to "act as the individuals they are," particularly "in times of stress and danger." Referencing his opposition to civilian review reform, Mayor Wagner took the time to "emphasize that, in taking any of the steps we are taking, we are not bowing or surrendering to pressure. We will not be browbeaten by prophets of despair, or by peddlers of hate, or by those who thrive on continued frustration." The mayor concluded by appealing to every resident of New York City to "give me your hand and help in this critical situation."[8]

The mayor's speech gave little ground to civil rights activists' demands. Of the nine dicta he listed as points of action, the first two promised a restoration of law and order and swift retribution against all lawbreaking civilians. Beyond his assurances of heightened attention to complaints of police brutality, Wagner mostly rephrased City Council President Screvane's words from Monday about recruiting police from communities of color and bettering relations between the city, especially the police, and Black and Brown neighborhoods. The only new directive he mentioned was a vague and noncommittal plan to have Screvane, in cooperation with the Poverty Operations Board and the Poverty Council, both brand-new city antipoverty agencies, "step up these programs which will involve and engage the unemployed young people of our city in constructive counseling, training and work." The mayor provided the caveat that "some of these programs, of course, depend upon federal funds, which have not yet been made available."[9] The only potentially meaningful action the city would be taking at this time was contingent. In the end, Wagner's speech offered little new or of substance to the African American citizens of his city, and it is unlikely to have convinced anyone that change was at hand.

At 9 PM, with the temperature holding steady at 75 degrees and the humidity hovering around 82 percent, an interracial group of CORE demonstrators picketed NYPD headquarters for the second night running. White counterdemonstrators returned to meet them, though this time they were not primarily teenagers and were considerably more violent. As many as five hundred white people from Little Italy, a block away, came out to heckle, lambast, and attack the picketers. As the CORE members walked quietly with signs reading "Jim Crow must go," "Freedom now," and "Gilligan must go," they endured a two-hour long collective tirade, including "Communists go home!"; "Go back to Harlem!"; "White trash go home!"; "Niggers must go!"; and "N——s go home!" Entire families participated in the verbal assault, including young children, just as they did in cities throughout the country, wherever white people feared Black progress. An old white man who claimed to be a lifetime resident of the neighborhood told a reporter, "They come down here and disturb us. They're an outside element. They ought to go home." His statement was similar to what many southern white people said about civil rights activists, but here the activists were being called outsiders in their own city.[10]

When they did go home at 11 PM, two-thirds of the white mob attempted to prevent them from doing so. Despite the protection of eight police cars and seventy-five policemen on foot, this group of two hundred white people, mostly teenage boys, threw bottles, eggs, and firecrackers at the picketers and police en route to the Spring Street stop of the Lexington Avenue subway line. Police counterattacked with nightsticks, swinging wildly at the white teenagers, after having already pushed them back one block as a precautionary measure at 10:30. One of the bottle throwers managed to strike a CORE picketer on the head as she made her way down the subway steps, and one policeman was hit in the eye with broken glass. Both required hospitalization. The two-block trip from headquarters to the subway station, normally a four-minute walk, took fifteen minutes, with the white teenagers attacking the entire way.[11] One teenage Italian-American boy refused an African American officer's order to move, threatening him with "Hit me, nigger, hit me and you're dead." A number of policemen dealt with the boy, who then screamed, "The n—— cop hit me! An Italian cop can hit me, but not a n——!"[12]

The Fifth Night: Harlem Ebbs, Brooklyn Gushes

In Central Harlem, steel-helmeted police, in the smallest number since the uprisings began, were again at the ready all day, anticipating conflict in the streets for the fifth consecutive night. Instead, there was only sporadic trouble in scattered pockets throughout the neighborhood. At 129th Street and Fifth Avenue, during the day, a policeman was hit in the hand with a bottle. Later on, there were a few arrests and some looting. Police shot two men in separate incidents involving looting. They said one man, twenty-three years old, tried to run from a dry-cleaning establishment. He was shot in the stomach and critically injured. The other man, forty-six, supposedly charged a policeman when he was discovered leaving a liquor store with two bottles of alcohol and was shot in the leg. A sizeable group of African American teens gathered on 125th Street between Seventh and Eighth Avenues. They were reported to be "shouting and yelling and apparently looking for trouble" but quickly split up when upward of thirty police cars suddenly appeared. The largest incident took place at Lenox Avenue and

127th Street, when fifteen or so people broke through plywood covering smashed-out windows and looted a grocery store.[13]

Most notable this night was the arrest of an African American teenage boy who was handing out flyers with the headline "Bulletin No. 1, July 1964. Harlem Freedom Fighters: How to Make a Molotov Cocktail" and illustrated instructions on how to do just that. By 10:30 PM, with the temperature the same it had been two hours earlier, the streets were nearly devoid of anyone, save for police, one of whom described the evening as "quieter than a normal Wednesday night in Harlem."[14] Bedford-Stuyvesant, however, was in the throes of chaos.

Between 6 PM and midnight, people in the neighborhood called in sixty-two false alarms to the fire department, contributing to a general atmosphere of bedlam, with fire trucks constantly racing through the streets, sirens blaring. Meanwhile, members of the Brooklyn NAACP handed out leaflets on the corner of Nostrand Avenue and Fulton Street reading:

> Cool it, Baby. The message has been delivered.... We have been screaming for jobs, decent schools, clean houses, etc. for years.... Some folks just wouldn't listen.... We've been telling them that all hell was liable to break loose.... Today, everybody is listening with big ears.... The message has been delivered. Now it is time to let it sink in; violent demonstrations and looting hurt our cause. Folks like Senator Goldwater, Governor Wallace of Alabama, the John Birchers and extremists are fixing to do us up, and if we don't play it smart we'll give them the excuse they've been looking for.[15]

The leaflet is noteworthy for the recognition it provides of the uprisings' blunt effectiveness. While discouraging a continuation of such behavior and declaring it only has negative effects on civil rights efforts, part of the local NAACP's appeal is for people to stop looting and fighting the police because they have already made their point. Most importantly, according to the flier, those in power were now listening after years of ignoring civil rights organizations only because people took to the streets as a destructive force.

At a midnight meeting of an emergency umbrella organization composed of virtually every pro-Black group in Harlem, from the Urban League and the NAACP to the Nation of Islam and United African Nationalist Movement, the participants collectively declared that Wagner's response was wholly insufficient. Exceptional times created a degree of unity, though always tenuous, among organizations that otherwise sniped at one another in the press and had serious differences in beliefs. Tonight though, they came together in the common interest of Black advancement. They drew up new demands, which they sent in a telegram to the mayor's office. It stated that Commissioner Murphy, Deputy Commissioner Arm, and the inspector commanding the police in Harlem all must be fired. By the end of the three-hour meeting, the representatives had also decided to send a five-person committee to the next day's HARYOU meeting to learn how to best gain access to the mayor and others in City Hall.[16]

James Farmer, not present at the meeting, sent a message to city leaders through the press:

> Wagner did not go far enough. He should have condemned Powell's killing, Gilligan's action. He should have given us an independent civilian review board. Something concrete has to be done. We cannot restrain the people of Harlem without something concrete from the Mayor. We have to have a leadership conference with the Mayor and all Harlem leaders to prevent further violence and rioting.

Reverend Hildebrand concurred, despairing that "there was nothing new in Wagner's statement. There's no condemnation of Powell's killing, nothing. There's no longer any need to deny police brutality. It exists—just as plain as the news pictures from Harlem. There must be a civilian review board."[17]

After Tuesday night's prolonged chaos, police had been preparing for a serious battle in Brooklyn. Officers occupied nearly every corner throughout the area that had seen trouble the previous night. They set up a mobile command unit on the corner of Macon Street and Nostrand, one block north of Fulton Street. There, along with their communications truck, they massed police in cars and on foot. They also stationed anywhere between twenty and forty officers on horseback, the first time in years that mounted police had appeared in Bedford-Stuyvesant.[18]

A sound truck, as requested earlier in the day, crawled through the streets of Bedford-Stuyvesant, broadcasting its occupants' pleas for peace and an end to the tumult. "Ladies and gentlemen, will you please return to your homes. Help our community. Help us make Bedford-Stuyvesant a safe place again. Please do not destroy our community anymore. Please get off the streets," they beseeched anyone within earshot. Locals appreciated neither the message nor the tone coming from the truck. One middle-aged African American woman shouted, "Shit, man. These are our streets. You fools, you go home." Demonstrators held signs written hastily on whatever they could find, with one reading "WE GOING TO FIGHT UNTIL LT COP THAT KILLED THE NEGRO BOY IS BEHIND BARS."[19]

Other residents were hostile to the truck in different ways, especially after an NAACP official provided a defense of "the patrolman on the beat." At 9:30 PM, some of those patrolmen on the beat had to rescue the truck when a particularly opposed group of young African American residents began rocking the truck back and forth, trying to push it over. This came in response to the speaker's assurance that "Mayor Wagner and the city will see that Jimmy Powell and his family get a square deal." Many African American youth in New York, as well as most any other city, had grown up to have a complete lack of faith in the police department. In such an agitated state, about the last thing they wanted to hear was praise—especially praise from other Black people—for the police, who treated them as subjects at best. And as just about anyone could tell by looking around, Mayor Wagner did not seem to have done much for them thus far. Why would tomorrow be any different? After the crowd had been dispersed, police ordered the truck to leave the area and not return.[20]

This sound truck, like the others, had no calming effect on the crowds. To the contrary, people in the streets became more inflamed and began protesting the trucks and the organizations they represented. As Bayard Rustin explained few days later about those he encountered night after night on the streets of Harlem:

> They are not organized. Most of them, who were on those streets making trouble, are not in CORE, not in N-double-A [NAACP], not in any of the established groups. They are isolated, they are deprived. They are the ones who live in these rat-infested houses. They are the ones who have no jobs. And the problem is not that the NAACP and CORE have lost leadership—they never had it with these people. These are the unorganized and they have no one to speak for them.

Cleveland Robinson supported this analysis, relating that through his years as a labor organizer and experiences on the City Commission on Human Rights, he had seen that, by 1964, "The young people have no place to go, no place to turn. They are jobless and the Negroes are hopeless and they are desperate and they are becoming leaderless because nothing that we say now seems to matter. They see no hope." People like Rustin and Robinson were voicing the frustration of those who had long been in the movement, pushed hard, but were able to deliver so little, running into the wall of white liberalism over and over. No matter how they tried or what they tried, they could not produce much in the way of tangible gains. They also were bearing witness to the increasing marginalization of the civil rights movement at the local and national levels, almost certainly unaware that the 1963 March on Washington had been the peak of the national, interracial, pacifist movement. In the July uprisings, Rustin "found a great number of people who are not black nationalists or Muslims were in fact talking very much like them" and predicted "the problem that we face is that there will be an increase in black nationalism because it is the expression of the deep alienation." That is exactly what happened over the next several years, though "problem" is subjective.[21]

Twenty minutes after the sound truck incident, police began firing at the corner of Franklin Avenue and Fulton Street in an effort to break up a rowdy crowd. This signaled the beginning of the furor in the streets of Bedford-Stuyvesant that would take hold for at least the next two hours. Groups of

Figure 10.1 Bayard Rustin, left, and Cleveland Robinson talk at 170 West 130th Street in Harlem, the national headquarters for the 1963 March on Washington for Jobs and Freedom.

Source: Library of Congress, Prints and Photographs Division, NYWT&S Collection, LC-USZ62-133369.

mostly teens and young adults, generally male, waged another night of hit-and-run battle that kept police on the move and profoundly frustrated. Just as it had been in Harlem and last night in Bedford-Stuyvesant, as soon as the police managed to send a group of people running in different directions, another would form a block away where the police had not yet been or had just left. Shortly before midnight, a few female residents attacked a policeman on foot with their hands. He was saved when mounted police rode in with clubs swinging. Less than half an hour later, heavy, steady rain fell on the city and cleared many off the streets. The temperature was slowly slipping below 70 degrees, while the humidity was on its way to the ceiling. Bedford-Stuyvesant was quiet.[22]

Over the course of the night, those people making the uprising had broken at least two hundred store windows, some in the interest of looting but most as simply nihilism, in a ten-block area that radiated outward from the same epicenter as the two previous nights, Nostrand and Fulton. Police shot three men, arrested 122, and injured an untold number. Police said one of the gunshot victims was caught looting a dry-cleaning store, and another was accused of looting a check-cashing shop.[23]

At 3 AM, the NYPD raided Malcolm X's empty Organization of Afro-American Unity offices in the Hotel Theresa at 125th Street and Seventh Avenue while he was still in Egypt. They claimed to have seized, without giving reason, a loaded single-shot bolt-action rifle and 115 rounds of ammunition. Spokesmen for the police department noted that owning such a rifle and keeping such a quantity of ammunition was not a crime.[24]

Many in the city had long since grown weary of this unrest, and a fifth night only added to their sense of anxiety. Perhaps those residents of Harlem willing to engage in protest, fighting, and looting had also grown weary. This was not true of Bedford-Stuyvesant, though, and it was not clear when it would be. And the unidirectional, citizen-on-citizen violence that took place at NYPD headquarters did not receive nearly as much attention or condemnation from city leaders. The contempt that these residents of Little Italy felt for civil rights activists, Black and white, but especially Black, and the relative lack of concern elected officials demonstrated for it helps illustrate what was wrong in the city, as well as in America, and what sentiments led to the situation the city had faced the last five nights. Here were people demonstrating peaceably, orderly, and legally, yet neighborhood residents sought to extinguish their presence and message. They did not want to hear anything about inequality, discrimination, and injustice.

11
Day Six: Thursday, July 23

Thursday would prove to be a much cooler day in every way—from the weather to the action in the streets of Harlem and Brooklyn. The high temperature was an unseasonably cool 69 degrees. A steady breeze of around fifteen miles per hour kept up all day and into the night.

Deputy Mayor Cavanagh chose six men to serve as his staff in reviewing new complaints against the city's police. Along with the mayor's legislative assistant, Cavanagh drew five unnamed men—an investigator, two white lawyers, and two Black lawyers—from the city's Law Department, which is responsible for representing the city in all legal matters. They were to assist the deputy mayor in his new role, which he described as having two chief tasks. The first was to review the decisions of the Civilian Complaint Review Board. Then, he was "to make recommendations as to the form and procedure of the present board," meaning he would consult Mayor Wagner as to whether reforms should be made to the board, both in its composition and procedure. During an attempt to establish an independent review board through City Council legislation a few months earlier, Wagner made clear his opposition to reforming the board. Cavanagh's recommendations would be unlikely to sway Wagner.[1]

Deputy Police Commissioner Arm addressed the oft-repeated demand that a Black man be appointed to head at least one of Harlem's three police precincts. The NYPD had three African American captains in total—Lloyd Sealy, Eldridge Waith, and Arthur B. Hill. None of the three, according to Arm, was ready to head a precinct. Though they all had the requisite rank, none, he asserted, had enough experience to run a stationhouse. They would all need to continue working their respective details for an unspecified amount of time.[2]

Day Six: Thursday, July 23

Reverend Hildebrand, president of the New York NAACP and leader of Bethel AME, had enough criticism for those involved in the uprisings to go around. Excoriating the "reckless provocation of police officers" as responsible for escalating the intensity of the upheaval, Hildebrand chastised those Central Harlem and Bedford-Stuyvesant residents who veered from self-defense into property destruction and looting as harming "the cause of racial justice." Still, he seemed to find that regarding the shortest-term causes of the events, when one examined police behavior, there was an "urgent need to curb the reckless and panicky violence which characterized so much of the police activity during the disorders." As a result of their behavior, the reverend asserted, "there has been a loss of confidence in the police department from the commissioner down to the officer on the beat" throughout the city's African American neighborhoods. This would be an oft-repeated contention for the next two years, one that would help start another kind of racial battle.[3]

Back in Little Italy, last night's hatred flourished in the light of day, without the excuse of momentarily inflamed passions to explain it away. Italian-American residents spoke openly to a reporter about the CORE protests, race in general, and African Americans in particular. On Mulberry Street, a block away from 240 Centre Street, those gathered on stoops and stairwells made their feelings as clear as could be. A teenager proclaimed, "Niggers are no good," justifying that declaration with "Because they're black and I'm white." The teen's own family, given its religion, language, appearance, and culture, would not have been considered white just a few decades earlier. His friends piled on their contempt to the newsman: "You want your daughter to marry a n——?" "If you give 'em an inch they want a foot." "The way they've been treated in the South they should be treated all over." "We were getting along fine with the n——s until this thing happened." One attributed the protests to "n—— communists."[4]

These feelings were not limited to a group of impudent teenagers. Down the street, a man concluded that African Americans need to go "back to Africa" because "their whole basic argument is that they want to be white. And they never will." Among six women sitting on front steps, one opined, "The cops let them get away with everything. A white person doesn't have as much civil rights as a colored, now." Another agreed: "They've got more freedom than we have."[5]

Crude racism aside, these remarks get at a seemingly impossible divide. Many African Americans, in the city and elsewhere, recognized that the police treated them unfairly, both over- and underpolicing them and the neighborhoods in which they resided and exploiting these sections of the city for personal enrichment and to vent animosity. Even though it was still common for southern states to plainly deny Black people basic constitutional rights, such as access to the ballot, the children and grandchildren of European immigrants saw African Americans as having special privileges, more rights, and more freedom. It would have been hard for them to miss the marches, protests, and frequent violence against activists on television over the last few years or to ignore the intense political conflict over civil rights. Even in their city, African Americans and their allies had been demonstrating for decades, and lately more frequently, for access to quality schools, jobs, and housing.

This was just the point: people in Little Italy, and descendants of more recent European immigrants throughout the city and nation, especially the North, where many late-nineteenth- and early-twentieth-century European newcomers had settled, would have been quite aware of civil rights agitation and progress. Instead of recognizing that African Americans had faced profound exploitation and discrimination for centuries, far too many white people, including highly educated elites, wrote the protests off as the work of communists or entitled, unappreciative people. Both perspectives denied demonstrators and their aims any legitimacy. The critique frequently concluded with a recitation of the up-by-your-bootstraps tale: many immigrant groups had faced prejudice and exploitation throughout American history but had overcome those obstacles through hard work and quiet assimilation, not protest. Of course, Black people in America had been working hard for more than three centuries by 1964, but it had not done very much for them.

The greatest weakness of this criticism is that Black people in 1964 were not immigrants.[6] These were people whose ancestors had been here, involuntarily, alongside the English in Jamestown, the Dutch in New Amsterdam, and the Spanish in St. Augustine. Black people had been at the center of most significant developments in American history, from the Constitution to rock music. They were American through and through, but their skin color marked them as other, and law and structure and custom made sure to enforce their separation and subjugation. These old chains and traditions had carried through into 1964, but many white Americans refused to accept what was readily apparent, coming up with any number of explanations for why African Americans still lacked the rights, liberties, and opportunities that America was supposed to afford, with the addendum that they should keep waiting and be thankful for whatever they did have.

Such explanations were not limited to the uneducated, outwardly bigoted, or demagogic among the populace. For example, the Harvard political scientist Edward Banfield wrote in 1974 that "today the Negro's main disadvantage is the same as the Puerto Rican's and Mexican's.... Like earlier immigrants, the Negro has reason to expect that his children will have increases of opportunity even greater than his."[7] Charles Morris, a lawyer who held several positions in Mayor John Lindsay's administration, gave credence to the idea that African Americans are immigrants in transition. In *The Cost of Good Intentions*, his 1980 postmortem on Lindsay's progressivism, Morris writes, "Measured against the rate of progress of other immigrant groups, it could be argued that blacks were progressing about as fast as could be expected. Moreover, viewing blacks as urban immigrants is not all that unreasonable. The most massive black migrations Northward occurred only after World War II." Black people had been in New York since before it was New York, and any other "immigrant group" there since then had long moved out of liminal status. Yes, Black New Yorkers' numbers had grown rapidly after World War II, but half a million African Americans lived in the city in 1940, and they were already attending segregated schools, stuffed into Harlem, denied decent jobs, and largely living precarious existences.[8]

It is entirely unreasonable and, in fact, wrong to view Black New Yorkers, even southern migrants, as immigrants, because they did not come from another country. A more contemporary example is Leah Platt Boustan's study of Black workers, *Competition in the Promised Land: Black Migrants in Northern Cities and Labor Markets*, in which she writes, "After all, southern blacks were just the latest in a long line of migrants to settle in northern cities, following waves of Irish and German and then Italian, Polish, and Jewish arrivals from Europe."[9] These were people who were American to their core and if they had been allowed to maintain written knowledge of their ancestry could readily trace it back many decades, if not centuries, into colonial and early national America. They did not lack an understanding of American culture. They did not need to learn a new language. They did not have an exotic religion. Their dress was not peculiar. All that separated them was the artificial and enforced divide of race. In these various authors' perspectives, southernness is the primary marker of difference only when combined with Blackness. They do not apply the same analysis to southern white migrants, of whom there were many in America's northern and western cities in these same years. The meanings assigned to their appearance meant everything, and the ways white people acted on those meanings, not Black culture or their southern upbringings, are what kept Black people segregated and disadvantaged. European immigrants could change many things about themselves, but African Americans could not stop being Black over any amount of time, leaving them with no hope for progress apart from various forms of protest, which many white people then construed to be an expression of petulance, a lack of gratitude.[10]

For those Americans of older, Protestant, northern European lineage to accept the southern and eastern Europeans and their progenitors, the newcomers had to learn and practice, among other things, the ever-changing American system of race, which perpetually kept African Americans at the bottom of society. By the 1960s, many of these white ethnics—those who were only a few generations removed from Italy, Poland, Greece, and the Slavic nations, among other countries—had progressed and assimilated quite well into American society, with the days of flagrant animus toward them quickly receding into the background and increasingly better opportunities opening for future generations. They were moving away from competition with African Americans for low-prestige work and paltry wages.

However, the civil rights movement was making significant gains in the late 1950s and early 1960s, which raised the prospect of social, political, and economic progress for Black people. Were Black people less circumscribed and allowed better opportunities, they would pursue them in significant numbers. White people, especially those from the working and lower-middle classes, would find themselves once again in competition with upwardly mobile African Americans, which could lead to their children being in school with Black children and Black New Yorkers living in the neighborhoods where they wanted to live, whether Harlem or Little Italy. Many white people, and white ethnics in particular, who felt they had not yet fully realized the American dream, believed civil rights advances and demands for continued progress imperiled their racial and class identities. In their eyes, racial advancement was a zero-sum contest, and Black gains necessitated white losses. As Harlem CORE's Roy Innis, who would become the organization's national director in 1968, observed of Little Italy, "This community feels threatened. The people down here are not the most affluent in town and I think they feel threatened by the civil rights movement."[11] This status anxiety, the enduring fuel of America's racial problems, frequently manifested itself as hostility toward African Americans, especially those who were forthright in claiming rights.

A few hours after the residents of Mulberry Street spoke their minds, CORE was back on Centre Street with over 250 picketers. For the third consecutive night, they protested outside NYPD headquarters for Lieutenant Gilligan's prosecution and against police violence. Once again, white neighborhood residents, mostly Italian-American, came out to meet the group with violence and invective. Police kept the hundreds of angry white residents further away than they had the last two nights, hoping to prevent another night of assaults. Police arrested six teenage white boys for disorderly conduct after they drove past the CORE demonstrators and threw a cardboard sign at them reading "Get the smelly black bastards away from this block" with a hand-drawn representation of a Black man, apparently wearing a turban, with a dagger through his heart.[12]

When the picketers left at 11 PM, police walked them to different subway stations than the one they had been using the two prior nights, hoping to disrupt the patterns of the two previous nights. Still, white throngs gathered at intersections and attacked, throwing eggs, rocks, and garbage, sending a police inspector to the hospital after he was hit in the eye with a rock. Police again pushed the white mobs back to secure the demonstrators' safe passage to the subway, which they accomplished, thereby ending the racist violence.[13] Commissioner Murphy walked through the white crowds while this was happening, unrecognized for a time in his civilian clothes. After a few minutes, some realized who he was and began shouting at him for having the police protect the CORE people. After narrowly dodging a few eggs from the white mob, the commissioner told reporters, "Compared to what's been happening in Harlem, I don't consider this violence at all. There's a lot of talking and a lot of shouting, but no violence down here."[14]

Though his officers and the CORE demonstrators would likely disagree with his assessment of violence, no one could deny the surfeit of talking and shouting. One resident, Ernest Fiore, a graduate of Harvard Law, declared that the violence against the CORE picketers "wasn't really racial. No matter who was making that kind of noise would have been attacked. They should quit by 9 o'clock. We are a quiet community." One would imagine that the hundreds of residents screaming epithets in the streets night after night were considerably louder than the CORE picketers and that living next to the city's police headquarters would be less than idyllic. Al Santora, on the other hand, was adamant about the racial nature of the attacks. He proudly proclaimed, "I am a descendent of the man who discovered America [presumably Columbus]. What my people are, we have gotten by work, not by sit-ins, marches and unjust demands. I have more of a right to this government than those niggers do. This country belongs to the Indians, the Spanish and the Italians." Now shouting, Santora continued on about the living conditions of his neighborhood: "This is not a ghetto! This is a community. This is where you can walk the streets and not be mugged. This is where the streets are clean. The people themselves decide whether something is a community or a jungle. We'll fight for Goldwater. We'll fight in the streets and in the mountains." Frank Brunetto, an electrical engineer, had little more than pure hate to offer: "I came here tonight to watch the cannibals. I lived with them savages for nine years in a housing project. I know. I'm for Social Security, I'm for Medicare, I'm for unions, but damn it, I'm gonna vote for Goldwater to show the politicians we're sick and tired of the cannibals." A young man from the neighborhood standing nearby interjected that Goldwater was an "extremist." A crowd shouted him down and began chanting "Goldwater for President!"[15] This is the essence of the much-vaunted "white backlash," but it was there all along.

What this hostility toward Black people in general, demands for rights more specifically, and protests in particular missed was that activists were engaged in a broad effort to uplift the entire nation, not just Black people, and certainly not to disadvantage white people. While its effects disproportionately ensnared African Americans and other people of color, poverty cut across racial lines. Many white workers also suffered from automation and capital flight. Various iterations of the movement had been trying to make this clear for a very long time, as Cleveland Robinson explained:

What the Negro in the Harlems are fighting for is what's good for all of America, the working people of America. . . . All you have to do is to look at the statistics nationwide, when it comes to unemployment, when it comes to people who are living in poverty, when it comes to those who are not covered by state and or federal minimum wages, when it comes to those who are getting inadequate educations. We have been emphasizing percentages to show to the extent to which Negroes have been deprived, but masses of whites are being deprived also. And I believe that, in too many instances, what the Negroes fight is not being understood in the white community. And it's being understood as Negro versus white. Negroes want and must have white support, especially from the white working people all over the nation. And we want what's good for America.[16]

While this assessment by no means included all components of the struggle for Black rights, freedom, and liberation, it did in 1964 represent the positions of the mainstream organizations so many white people despised, such as CORE, the NAACP, the Southern Christian Leadership Conference, and the Student Nonviolent Coordinating Committee. Whether one looks at the federal government's abortive War on Poverty or the SCLC's shattered Poor People's

Campaign, a critical mass of progressives recognized that both Black and white Americans faced substantial, though unequal, challenges in employment and education and were being left behind.[17]

The Sixth Night: Harlem Rests, Brooklyn Sputters

For the first time since Saturday, there were no reported disturbances out of the ordinary in the streets of Central Harlem. No sizeable crowds formed, and no one looted, smashed windows, marched, or engaged in running battles with the police.

Some people in Bedford-Stuyvesant, though, still had not had their fill of such activities, and others sensed this. As darkness fell, with a temperature of 65 degrees, an NAACP sound truck once more slowly made its way through the streets of the neighborhood, with the by-now usual exhortations to stay off the streets blaring from the roof. Just as the night before, the crew in the truck initially met with some friendly reception but quickly had to leave the area to avoid a potentially explosive situation. Some residents made their feelings toward the NAACP's efforts visually apparent, carrying signs reading such things as "We Want NAACP to Stay Out of This," "We will fight now and pray later," and "Murphy's cops are youth killers." After about an hour of the organization's sermon of peace, people on the street, mostly teens, escalated their taunts to the point that NAACP staff felt it was no longer safe for them or the vehicle to remain in Bedford-Stuyvesant. In addition to the NAACP, as many as forty African American clergy walked and drove the streets of Bedford-Stuyvesant that night, pleading, reasoning, and arguing with people to stop smashing, looting, and fighting the police. Meanwhile, large numbers of helmeted police patrolled anxiously, backed up by twenty-two officers on horseback.[18]

The first hint that the upheaval might resume came when someone broke a drugstore window at Lewis and Gates Avenues, about a mile northeast of Nostrand and Fulton. When a white newspaper photographer took a picture of the looting from his car, his flash gave him away. Some people involved in the looting immediately turned on him, throwing bottles, cans, and a brick, which shattered his windshield. By the time police had come, ready for battle, no one was in sight, and the display merchandise in the window was gone. Similar situations took place throughout the night, like a skipping record that never makes it past the first few grooves. Police fired a handful of shots to break up crowds they found threatening and only engaged in relatively minor scuffles with people on the streets, ultimately arresting nineteen and injuring eight, though the actual numbers of the injured surely were higher and likely surpassed the number of arrests, given the NYPD's penchant for street justice during this episode. There was neither major looting nor prolonged fighting. Another condition that separated this night from the previous three was that instead of a localized area of action, tonight's geography of turmoil stretched twenty blocks north to the edge of Williamsburg, ten blocks east, twenty blocks south into Crown Heights, and ten blocks west, nearly crossing into Prospect Heights. On one of the two prior nights, such a spread would have been disastrous, but given the continually incipient nature of the night's happenings, it was comparatively an inconvenience.[19]

The Toll

Over the course of six nights, from Saturday, July 18, to Thursday, July 23, the police department estimated it had spent $1.5 million to handle the uprisings, 90 percent of which went to overtime costs. Ammunition, vehicle repairs, and medical bills comprised the rest.[20] The official NYPD assessment of destruction in Harlem was: one dead; eighty-five citizens injured; thirty-eight police injured; 202 arrested; and 122 damaged, vandalized, or looted businesses. In Bedford-Stuyvesant, where citizens rose up for four nights, from Monday, July 20, through Thursday, July 23, there were no reported deaths; ten injured civilians; twelve injured police officers; 302 arrested; and 556 damaged, vandalized, or looted businesses, with most of those numbers coming from Tuesday and Wednesday nights. The recorded injury count for citizens includes only those requiring hospitalization, but of course there were many more, given how quickly and frequently groups of officers became human tornados of nightsticks.[21]

According to at least two police sources, more than one civilian died in the unrest. One account claims the police killed an unknown number of people and disposed of their bodies: "It [the shooting of the man allegedly throwing bricks from a Harlem rooftop] would turn out to be the only death officially listed as occurring during the riots. The rash of floaters pulled out of the waters surrounding Manhattan, in the weeks following the end of the riots, was obviously a very large coincidence."[22] While the killing and dumping of bodies is possible, the fact that civil rights groups and activists do not seem to have picked up on a significant number of Black bodies being pulled out of the water, during a time when they would have been supremely focused on police violence and misconduct, makes this scenario unlikely. Another source notes a rumor circulated among NYPD officers in the weeks after the disturbances that bodies kept appearing in the lake in Central Park, a variation of the same story. Again, there is no corroboration provided, nor is there any in the historical record. In a less sensational and more credible account, a retired officer states definitively, "I know there was more than one dead. I saw more than that killed with my own eyes."[23]

The fact is that we will probably never know if there was only one fatality. What we do know is that there was a great deal of violence, and while some police acted with restraint, others did not. During and after the events of July 1964, many activists and Harlem residents continued to characterize the police as capricious and unnecessarily violent, citing the chaos in the streets as putting on display the treatment the NYPD provided daily. Critics attributed the violence and disrespect they saw in the NYPD to racial animus, the fact that a mostly white NYPD was patrolling a mostly Black neighborhood.

Bayard Rustin had a personal relationship with Harlem, its citizens, and its law enforcement, knowing "many police officers in Harlem by name and many more by sight and reputation." When assessing his experiences on the streets during the uprisings, he concluded, "One of the saddest aspects of those nights was the fact that many police officers who are among the better-behaved, reacted with the greatest fear and consequently with the most brutal conduct." This observation was neither hypothetical nor reached through hearsay. During the unrest, Rustin came upon a white officer he knew who had once turned over a juvenile shoplifter to him, with Rustin promising to bring the boy home and tell his father what he had done. Rustin now saw the officer "mercilessly" beating a woman to the pavement. When he implored the officer to stop, he did, only to turn his wrath on one of the leading proponents of nonviolence in the nation.[24]

NYPD spokespeople and defenders of the police denied officers perpetrated any unnecessary or unjustified violence, but one white officer who was there reflected decades later and concluded that this lack of restraint during the disturbances was at least born partly out of racial hostility. He describes among his fellow officers and him "a deep sea of racism and bitterness, poison and untamed cruelty in our souls. It was a boiling cauldron, and it didn't take a whole lot to push it over into the streets, onto the rooftops, or into the alleyways of Harlem on that night in July of 1964."[25]

Gangs were notably absent from the ferment, especially in Bedford-Stuyvesant, where there were more than twenty active at the time. Most of the looting occurred in sections of the neighborhood that had no organized gangs.

The noninvolvement of gangs was largely thanks to the work of two Youth Board supervisors, Eddie Allen and Frank Chandler, the latter of whom was Black, and the eleven who worked under them. Once the uprisings began in Harlem, the Youth Board workers met with the various gang leaders and had long conversations with them on the utility of looting and fighting police, eventually managing to convince them it would be counterproductive. The Youth Board staff also worked with the parents of gang members, many of whom contributed by hosting small all-night gatherings at their homes at which gang members could eat and play cards. Allen and Chandler also kept the Youth Board center at 129 Patchen Avenue in Bedford-Stuyvesant, a bit over a mile northeast of Fulton and Nostrand, open every night until at least 1 AM.[26]

Many in the city, from the police to those in city government to private citizens, anticipated a revival of chaos, violence, and destruction over the weekend. The anxiety, already palpable on Thursday, had substantially increased by Friday. While there would be much to come in terms of social and political wrangling, the "Harlem Riot" was over. No resurgence ever came, a fact that had little to do with the NYPD ensuring that its Harlem and Bedford-Stuyvesant precincts were "stacked" with officers or clergy of all faiths pleading all weekend for a restoration of "moral and spiritual stability."[27] The unrest had run its course. People did not have the energy to maintain such an intense collective level of activity indefinitely. Many people are more willing to take part in the earlier stages of a protracted eruption of this kind, as it is new and perhaps invigorating and exciting. The novelty quickly fades in the face of serious violence, leaving fewer people participating night by night, as the probability of escaping unharmed decreases.

Then there was the practical fact, especially in Bedford-Stuyvesant, that many stores had already been damaged or looted. For the property destruction to continue, it would have had to spread into other neighborhoods; this is fundamentally different than one committing such acts in the familiar streets of one's own neighborhood. Far fewer people would have been willing to join a roving band of plunderers ravaging the city, facing unfavorable odds in neighborhoods outwardly hostile toward them.

Conclusion

New York's July upheaval shines a light on conservatism, racism, and hostility to civil rights in the city, especially within its white ethnic populations. For three nights in a row, Italian-American residents from Little Italy, the neighborhood surrounding police headquarters, came out to attack nonviolent interracial demonstrators protesting police brutality. The neighborhood residents believed the CORE demonstrators to be part of a larger movement to extract undeserved economic gains from various levels of government. Locals frequently recalled how they and their families had come to a new country with nothing and worked hard to earn their positions in society, never resorting to protest. They articulated that civil rights activity was a front for laziness, greed, and lawlessness. Many white ethnic New Yorkers neither identified nor sympathized with Black residents. As the civil rights movement became more assertive, white ethnic hostility became more prominent, especially in the numerous Italian-American enclaves of Brooklyn and Queens. People who had previously supported liberal Democratic candidates in significant numbers moved to the right, favoring the presidential candidates Barry Goldwater and arch-segregationist Alabama Governor George Wallace. White ethnic hostility toward Black New Yorkers continued to escalate through the 1960s, with the 1966 civilian review board referendum and 1968 Ocean Hill–Brownsville school decentralization controversy as points that both showed and increased this hostility.

When the disorder moved south into Bedford-Stuyvesant, the chaos in the streets there showed more clearly than in Central Harlem the lack of effective Black political and social leadership in the city. Bedford-Stuyvesant did not have the history of leadership and organization that Harlem did. Black people of all backgrounds and ideologies had been competing for relevance in Central Harlem for most of the century, with the neighborhood being majority Black since the 1920s. Bedford-Stuyvesant differed in that it did not become predominantly Black until the 1950s.[28] Not only did this much younger community not yet have the time for organic grassroots leadership to develop by 1964, but the Black population also grew very quickly during the postwar period, making attempts at organization difficult to manage. Certainly, the neighborhood had civil rights activists, with Reverend Milton Galamison and Brooklyn CORE the most prominent, but Harlem was Black New York's political center.

Bedford-Stuyvesant saw far more property damage than Harlem. Many residents had already been displaced from other parts of the city, shoehorned into a place very much not of their choosing, increasing their latent resentment and sense of alienation. There were also more arrests, and the intensity of fighting between citizens and the police was greater. Street rallies regularly turned into looting and fighting. People like James Farmer and Bayard Rustin, who walked the streets of Harlem night after night during the tumult, never visited Bedford-Stuyvesant, and there was no one of their stature or ability to produce the same results, however limited they may have been. As for the civil rights activists who did, residents were more hostile toward them than were the people in the streets of Central Harlem. No people or organizations had enough authority in Bedford-Stuyvesant to channel residents' energies in other directions. Looting and destruction would probably have been worse in Harlem without the power of men such as James Farmer and Edward Mills Davis, who validated outraged citizens' anger but urged them away from destruction in the heat of the upheaval.

Finally, we see why civilian review board reform became so prominent an issue. Civil liberties and civil rights activists had been building a campaign favoring an independent review board for a few years, but the recent defeat of City Council legislation a month before the uprisings left the campaign seemingly moribund. The conflict with the police that characterized the disorder gave the issue new life. The police were not the primary cause of the disorder, but they were both a contributing factor and the source of ignition, and their behavior likely kept the unrest going for a longer period than it might have otherwise. Many Black New Yorkers felt contempt for the police well before 1964, for a combination of arrests, rude behavior, inadequate policing, graft, and violence. These feelings of resentment fused with intolerable residential, educational, and economic conditions to create a potent social explosive. Gilligan shooting Powell was also the last in a recent string of police shootings of African American and Puerto Rican New Yorkers. Powell's death incensed many Black New Yorkers, but it was not until the police met a demonstration seeking Gilligan's arrest with further brutality that the disturbances began. The police explained their violence during the upheaval as necessary in a time of catastrophe. Many residents and civil rights activists accused the police of using force well beyond what was necessary to defend themselves or control a situation, and indeed, the rapid, sustained employment of live ammunition was a breach of crowd-control protocol. While city officials denied these accusations, quite a few citizens and organizations felt police behavior during the unrest made review board reform more necessary than it ever had been.

12
After

I, personally, do not have any hope that the events of the last week will make any difference. Personally, I think what will happen is that law and order will again prevail, particularly in terms of containing the restless natives, keeping them within the confines of their ghetto. And once things return to normal, they will return to normal completely. In this return to normal will be the normal state of affairs of deteriorated housing, rat infestations, countless violations in the tenements of this community, the drab, dirty ugliness will continue, the horrible schools will continue, and the City of New York will continue to be lucky playing Russian Roulette with this explosive, volatile situation of Harlem.

–KENNETH CLARK

What followed in the weeks and months after the uprisings is as notable for its mundanity as anything else. Attention quickly faded locally, regionally, and nationally, and the Wagner administration was more than happy to move on. Eventually, three more summers of chaos in the nation's cities would lead to President Johnson's appointment of the Kerner Commission to study the roots of the seemingly endless urban upheaval. But in 1964, apart from a brief FBI investigation, there were no official attempts to understand what had happened in Harlem and Bedford-Stuyvesant. The mayor made a few promises, the police department moved some men around the city, but not much else happened. The city prosecuted those it had arrested, with the legal process drawing little attention, as most of the cases were for looting and disorderly conduct. Neither the state nor the police department prosecuted Lieutenant Gilligan, the man whose shots led to the uprisings.

Cleaning Up

In the days to follow, business owners in Central Harlem and Bedford-Stuyvesant assessed their losses. At the end of September, two months after the uprisings ended, thirty-eight shop owners from the two neighborhoods had filed claims totaling hundreds of thousands of dollars against the city for negligence, using a disputed Civil War–era state law.[1] By early October, insurers had already paid out more than $750,000 to businesspeople in both neighborhoods. An industry spokesman stressed the number would continue to climb as insurance companies processed more claims.[2] Given the types of policies business owners had purchased, many were not covered by insurance and closed for good. In February 1965, 125th Street in Central Harlem, the neighborhood's main commercial artery, had twenty-six vacant stores along a nine-block stretch. One year earlier, there were four vacancies.[3]

The city faced at least two personal-injury claims related to the disorder. Two African American women from Harlem filed lawsuits of $500,000 each against the city, alleging police had shot them. One, Mrs. Barbara Barksdale, was the woman James Farmer said he witnessed a police officer shoot when she requested help finding a cab. Barksdale said the bullet struck her in the left hip and exited her left buttock, leaving her with permanent injuries. The other, Mrs. Minnie Dwight, a forty-six-year-old bookbinding-machine operator, accused an unknown officer of shooting her in the back just after midnight on Tuesday, July 21. Dwight said the shooting left her with constant flashes of pain through her back.[4]

In the weeks after the uprisings, courts began processing the hundreds of people the NYPD had arrested. Many of the arrestees were in their twenties; others ranged from teenagers to men and women in their late forties. According to Kenneth Clark, those who participated actively in the unrest "were, in general, not the lowest class of Harlem residents—not primarily looters and semicriminals—but marginal Negroes who were upwardly mobile, demanding a higher status than their families had."[5] Most charges involved some combination of disorderly conduct, assault, and burglary. Some arrestees had their charges dropped or were acquitted, but most could not afford lawyers and were convicted, serving from thirty to ninety days, depending on such factors as prior records and severity of the alleged offense. Because most defendants lacked money, they also were unable to appeal their convictions, meaning their sentences stuck.[6] However, arrests were not limited to the days of turmoil. Through March 1965, the district attorney arrested at intervals several people for refusing to cooperate with a grand jury investigating William Epton.[7]

William Epton's trial, by far, was the most prominent court case to come from the uprisings. Epton, a Harlem native, head of the Harlem Defense Council, and a leader of the Maoist Progressive Labor Movement, was arrested July 25, 1964, and charged under a turn-of-the-century law with "criminal anarchy" and "conspiracy to overthrow the Government of the State of New York" for speeches he had made during the uprisings. After many delays, having the criminal anarchy charge dropped in favor of "advocacy" of criminal anarchy and being rearrested in court, Epton's trial began in October 1965. The prosecution presented a recording an undercover officer had made, which it said was of Epton speaking during the disturbances, asserting, "We're going to have to kill a lot of cops, a lot of the judges, and we'll have to go against their army." He was found guilty of all counts on December 20 of that year, immediately jailed, and sentenced to one year on January 27, 1966. Epton became the first person convicted under the criminal anarchy statute since the Red Scare of 1919, when authorities overreacted to two spates of bombings and persecuted communists, socialists, and anarchists. Despite appealing to the U.S. Supreme Court, Epton's conviction stood, and he served one year at the city's Riker's Island jail.[8]

In one of the Wagner administration's few positive responses to pleas from civil rights groups regarding the uprisings, Commissioner Murphy transferred more than fifty Black police to Harlem in the month after the disorder. Residents and community leaders had long demanded a somewhat more representational police force, but Commissioner Stephen P. Kennedy, an ardent reformer and stickler for what he perceived to be fairness, refused to make any assignments based on race, even to reduce obvious tensions.[9] Michael J. Murphy, the man who replaced him in 1961, did not hold the same reservations, but it took the exigencies the uprisings created for him to change NYPD policy and take action. Reacting to demands Black leaders placed before him during the upheaval, Murphy moved forty-five patrol officers, five sergeants, and three lieutenants to several precincts that covered Harlem.[10]

Perhaps most noteworthy and visibly, Murphy appointed Captain Lloyd Sealy, a Black man whose parents had emigrated from Barbados before his birth, to be in charge of the Twenty-Eighth Precinct, where the uprisings had begun. Sealy grew up in Brooklyn, where he still lived in 1964, and had joined the force in 1942. This appointment made Sealy the only Black man heading a precinct and only the second to have done so. Captain Sealy, who held bachelors and law degrees, had wanted to operate the Twenty-Eighth for some time. He replaced a Polish-American officer who was moved up into the position of deputy inspector. Sealy now oversaw about 370 men, 80 percent, or about three hundred, of whom were white.[11]

Residents, community leaders, and officers seemed to receive the new commander well, with Harlemites lining up to shake his hand on his first night on the job. One of them, a plumber, said Sealy "was needed here. I think the change will make a lot of difference. There's a lot of people waiting for a responsible person to talk to." Even a white officer under his command felt "it was about time" a Black man ran the precinct, believing "we need more Negro precinct commanders and some Puerto Ricans too."[12] While Captain Sealy may have made a difference in how members of the community saw and interacted with the police, he does not seem to have had much impact on the corruption officers practiced. The years between 1964 and 1966 were ones of great acceleration for the heroin trade in New York, as well as the department's involvement with it. The Twenty-Eighth Precinct had long been a hotbed of corruption, a condition that worsened substantially after 1964. To say that Sealy, a man who came up from the beat over decades, was ignorant of what was taking place in his precinct is implausible. The best-case scenario is that he was one of the many commanders the Knapp Commission found to be aware of the situation but unwilling to act, or perhaps unable, with higher forces constraining him.

Mayor Wagner tried burnishing his civil rights credentials when he invited Dr. Martin Luther King Jr. to meet with him for several days at the end of July. With the recent uprisings as the pretext for Dr. King's invitation, the mayor was hoping to appear proactive on civil rights matters. Instead, he succeeded in further alienating local leaders who could not understand what King could tell the mayor about Black New Yorkers that they could not. While King described their meetings as "frank, fruitful, and amicable," he found what New York's civil rights leaders had known for years: their discussions ended with not one formal agreement or concession from the mayor. King characterized Commissioner Murphy as "utterly unresponsive to either the demands or the aspirations of the Negro people." Continuing to describe his frustration with the commissioner, Dr. King said, "He is intransigent and has little understanding of the urgency of the situation. If he had, he would have suspended Lieutenant Gilligan at once, and would not have obstructed establishment of a public review board to investigate charges of police brutality."[13]

Gilligan

Lieutenant Gilligan was never arrested or suspended. A grand jury began meeting on July 21 and concluded without exonerating him on him September 1, 1964, after meeting for fifteen days, hearing from forty-five witnesses, including schoolchildren and the lieutenant, and taking 1,600 pages of testimony. The witnesses agreed that the apartment superintendent, Patrick Lynch, hosed down some of the boys; that they chased him into his building; and that James Powell had a knife, but they split on whether he menaced Gilligan with it. The twenty-three-member grand jury, which included two Black jurors, would have needed twelve votes for an indictment, but all twenty-three moved to find the lieutenant not culpable of criminal homicide.[14]

State law provided several justifications for Powell's death. The district attorney wrote that Gilligan was entitled to "shoot without retreating, however, if it was reasonable to believe at the moment of the attack that retreat was impossible or would have increased the danger. This is so even if, upon subsequent reflection, it appears that such belief was mistaken, and there was an opportunity to retreat without increasing the danger." What mattered, then, was the officer's claimed perception, not the reality, of the situation. Understanding that people, especially police officers, are sometimes forced to make quick decisions under high-stress conditions is important, as is acknowledging that those decisions may not always be the best ones. However, those choices can lead to unnecessary death and injury, with no one legally responsible. In the worst case, such a policy opens the door for officers to be able to claim dishonestly after the fact they felt there was no option but to use deadly force and not have to worry about any legal consequences. Furthermore, regulations concerning police violence justified homicide "in attempting lawfully to apprehend a person for a crime actually committed, when the circumstances are such that one would have reasonable cause for believing that the crime was a felony and that deadly force is necessary to apprehend the suspect. Assault with a knife, and assaulting a police officer with intent to resist lawful arrest, are felonies." The grand jury found that Gilligan met all of these conditions in trying to stop and arrest Powell, who it said was in the process of committing several felonies.[15]

Figure 12.1 "Has Giligan [sic] Been Cleared of the murder of James Powell" flier, 1963–1964.

Source: Arnie Goldwag Brooklyn Congress of Racial Equality (CORE) collection, ARC.002, Brooklyn Historical Society.

One of the Black jurors, George S. Schuyler, was a man of some renown by 1964. He had worked for A. Philip Randolph and Chandler Owen's *The Messenger* magazine in the earlier part of the century and had associated himself with Marcus Garvey's Universal Negro Improvement Association. He wrote for the Black-owned *Pittsburgh Courier* for decades and worked as the NAACP's business manager. In the 1940s, Schuyler abandoned civil rights advocacy and over the rest of his life grew increasingly conservative, publicly attacking his former colleagues, as well as King and W. E. B. Du Bois. He wrote for the John Birch Society's periodical, supported Barry Goldwater for president, and ran for Adam Clayton Powell's congressional seat as a candidate for the Conservative Party in 1964. When Schuyler declared of his jury service, "I did the right thing, and so did the rest of the jury," his political beliefs were so far out of step with those of almost all African Americans that it would have been difficult for anyone concerned with the fairness of the grand jury process to trust his judgment.[16]

Throughout the investigation and after, Lieutenant Gilligan's whereabouts had been a secret. The department had hidden him away, perhaps on Long Island with his in-laws. On sick leave for months after his encounter with young Powell, department policy required him to remain at home. When reporters went looking for him at his Stuyvesant Town apartment after the grand jury cleared him, none of his neighbors had seen Gilligan or his family in weeks, and the name on their mailbox had changed. Neither the department nor the building manager would comment on where he had been.[17] Near the end of September, the NYPD announced the lieutenant's hand injury had healed but that he would remain on sick leave for an old back problem he had aggravated when shooting Powell; he was still not to be found at home.[18] Gilligan returned to a desk job on November 12, a few days after the three-member, all-NYPD Civilian Complaint Review Board cleared him of wrongdoing.[19] However, the department moved him to a different, unnamed precinct, once Brooklyn CORE announced its intent to picket the Ninety-Second Precinct in Williamsburg.[20] After a few years, the department forced Gilligan to retire. Apparently, his back injury never healed, and he was again out on sick leave for most of 1967. In January 1968, the NYPD announced he would retire in three months, after collecting his accrued sick pay. He would receive a yearly pension of $8,484.75, which was three-quarters of his salary at his retirement, as well as the seventy-seven dollars in military disability payments he received every month, related to his time as a Marine in World War II and Korea.[21]

Between his return to the force and his retirement, Gilligan filed millions of dollars in slander and libel lawsuits against a host of individuals and organizations, including Dr. King, James Farmer, William Epton, Jesse Gray, the Harlem Progressive Movement, the Harlem Defense Council, CORE, and the Tri-Line Offset Company, which was alleged to have printed the "WANTED FOR MURDER—GILLIGAN THE COP" posters. Gilligan sued King for allegedly characterizing Powell's death as one in which "Murder has been committed. The shooting of James Powell by Lieutenant Gilligan was murder." He sued Farmer for demanding that "Gilligan must be arrested and charged with murder" and for falsely telling the press that Gilligan had been admitted to a mental hospital after he shot Powell. The rest of the suits all revolved around the wanted poster circulated in Harlem and its employment of the term "murder."[22]

The lieutenant retained Roy M. Cohn as his lawyer, famous for his work as Senator Joseph McCarthy's attack dog during the Army-McCarthy hearings of 1954. This man who had made a name for himself destroying people's lives by labeling them as communists, gay, or both was now actively seeking the financial ruin of national and local civil rights leaders and organizations. Conducting himself as the conservative partisan that he was, Cohn continued suing Dr. King even after his assassination. Gilligan, a man who had served the department with distinction since 1947, defined his career, and life, by shooting James Powell, whether it was justified or not. He would forever be Thomas Gilligan, the lieutenant who shot that boy and whose actions led to the July 1964 uprisings. No matter how many lawsuits he filed or whether he won or lost them, none of that could ever be erased or reversed.[23]

Finding the Communists

Speaking to the press on July 21, Paul Screvane, City Council president and acting mayor while Wagner was out of the country, declared that "fringe groups, including the Communist Party," were intentionally inciting the chaos in the streets, though he offered no evidence, only supposition. He told reporters that "I don't think there's any question about" the party's responsibility and that the uprisings had been "agitated by and sponsored by and participated in by the fringe groups in the community."[24] Screvane was not the only one. At Lyndon Johnson's direction, J. Edgar Hoover called Governor Rockefeller to let him know FBI agents would be investigating. They also discussed who was likely behind the uprisings.[25] Both were certain communists were active in inciting people to rise up, but

Rockefeller also had a second suspect: extreme conservatives. He told Hoover that Goldwater acolytes had personally and repeatedly predicted racial unrest in the state, almost threateningly; Hoover promised the governor he would follow that lead, but nothing came of it.[26]

Screvane's assumption of communist involvement as an article of faith was fairly common, at least among white people of various political persuasions, from the president of the United States, to the governor of New York State, to the director of the FBI, to police officials. Lez Edmond, the African American activist, journalist, and academic, described an encounter he witnessed outside Harlem's Twenty-Eighth Precinct late into the night during the initial upheaval in the streets. Inspector Thomas Pendergast, in charge of the precinct for the night, declared to an unnamed Black nationalist, "Listen, you and I both know who's doing all this. It's the commies." The other man responded, "Inspector Pendergast, for Christ's sake, these children wouldn't know Marx or Lenin if they were to come back from the tombs and walk down the streets of Harlem right this minute." Or, as Cleveland Robinson put it, "I believe the communists to be found in Harlem are as real as hens' teeth. Either you are an FBI agent or you are a crazy fool to be a communist today."[27]

What that man was conveying to the inspector was that the people of Harlem did not need communists, or anyone else, to evoke rage and hostility in them. One of Harlem's "most respected educational leaders" saw the uprisings as an indigenous, organic movement, "the expression of a frustration of a people who have been denied any consideration for more than 300 years. I don't see how any person with any intelligence could think or expect anything but this, and I marvel that there's been so little violence coming from the black community."[28] While most residents may not have been willing to fight the police and loot and burn businesses, descriptions of seething resentment and displeasure in Harlem abound. The alienation and hostility so many Harlemites felt came from the daily indignities that discrimination and segregation imparted, not the teachings of an ideologue, foreign or local. It was easy for white politicians, bureaucrats, officials, and others to blame someone other than themselves. In the same way that white southerners attributed civil rights movements to "outside agitators," northern white people did the same, with communism the ubiquitous malevolent force. An unnamed civil rights leader described labeling Black resistance as communist in this way:

> I think that this is an insult to the Negro community. The implication behind such a remark is that Negroes don't have sense enough to holler when they're

hurt.... I think the American people need to realize that the communists are not segregating the schools, the communists have not heaped the Negroes in these ghettoes, and that it's an evasion of the issue to try to point to some unpopular and extraneous political force instead of actually grappling with the problem.[29]

It was a convenient way for local white people and national and northern politicians to deny culpability for what was right in front of their eyes, allowing them to maintain the lie of the good North, where the only discrimination that took place was at the individual level and all segregation was voluntary or accidental.

James Baldwin had discredited this line of thinking in 1961. He understood the power dynamics at play, the reasons for attributing Black resistance and resentment to communism, and what it said about the North, the nation, and the abilities of African Americans. Baldwin saw the tendency to blame outsiders as heaping more extensive indignities and insults upon Black people. For him, believing in communist influence in matters of civil rights was to suggest that Black people in America are generally happy and thus that only agents employing subversive foreign ideologies could push them into action. Following the logic further, even if some element of the African American population were displeased, those people would be unable to take action through their own will, needing someone else to tell them what to do.[30]

Communists in the city publicly responded to Deputy Mayor Screvane's charges that communist groups had incited the unrest. On July 22, Robert Thompson and William L. Patterson, spokesmen for the New York District Communist Party, declared the party's firm disapproval of "violence as a means of eliminating ghetto life." They characterized these allegations as "Mr. Screvane's big lie," one they saw as an effort to "hide the hell of ghetto life" and "an incitement to a police force that cannot but reflect the racist policies of an administration callous to the democratic demands of its Negro citizens." The Progressive Labor Movement, headed in Harlem by William Epton, wearily lamented blaming "outside agitators" as "the oldest trick in the book." The primary goal of this tactic, according to the group's spokesperson, is "to divide the people of Harlem against themselves."[31]

Mississippi's senator James O. Eastland, a crude racist and one of the most powerful men in the U.S. Senate, spoke on the Senate floor about the ongoing unrest. He was adamant that "evidence of Communist participation and leadership in civil rights demonstrations is being brought into the open." Eastland's form of proof was recalling that Jesse Gray had pleaded the Fifth

Amendment when forced to appear before the House Un-American Activities Committee in 1960. Dr. King, addressing a rally later in the day in Eastland's home state, laughed off his charges: "There are as many Communists in this freedom movement as there are Eskimos in Florida."[32]

None of these denials stopped the *New York Daily News* from publishing a sensationalist, disgraceful article in the midst of the uprisings, the title of which directed readers to "Blame Hate Groups, Red & White, for Harlem Terror." As the flaming-hot lede exclaimed, "Professional, well-financed agitators by the hundreds, representing both the extreme left and extreme right, are whipping up the violence in Harlem and Bedford-Stuyvesant—and the legitimate responsible civil rights organizations have lost control, The News established last night." According to the three reporters who co-wrote the article, dozens of NYPD detectives worked with the FBI to uncover communists controlling "1,000 young fanatics dedicated to violence" in the city. And as "one high source disclosed, both the Commies and extreme southern right wingers have been supporting the Black Muslims because they are the most violent muscle unit." In this version of Harlem, communists could count on a regular paycheck, showing up to Lewis Michaux's National Memorial African Bookstore every Friday at 4 PM to get paid, which probably made the invented position of "professional agitator" quite alluring to some readers. Attempting to prove the outside nature of the agitation, the reporters claimed, "one policeman reported, he and other cops—white and Negro—were insulted by youngsters 'who didn't even speak New York English. They obviously had been brought up from the South.'" These young people, if real, probably had indeed been brought up from the South—by their parents, just like many thousands of other Harlem residents. The article's authors were either unaware of the extent of Black migration or discarded it for narrative convenience. That day's *Daily News* made its way to President Johnson's desk, who found the article noteworthy enough to read several paragraphs over the phone to J. Edgar Hoover, urging him to pick up a copy.[33]

All of this talk of communism, and the ease with which authorities and others in the public threw such allegations, reflected both a fear and a desire to suppress dissent and protest. In 1964, labeling a group, movement, or individual as communist was still an effective way to marginalize, discredit, and silence. While the McCarthy show trials were long over, the Cold War was not. Vietnam was heating up, though it was a tiny conflict compared to what it would be in a year. Castro's forces had taken over Cuba just a few years earlier, Korea was divided, a wall had gone up through the middle of Berlin three years ago, and the Cuban Missile Crisis was not even two years prior. Scholars such as Martha Biondi and Mary Dudziak have thoroughly demonstrated the impact the Cold War and the harassment and persecution of active, former, and suspected communists had on the civil rights movement's organizations, goals, and theoretical framework. Anticommunism hit the New York City civil rights movement particularly hard, given the decades of communist agitation in the city and the strong presence of the Communist Party in Harlem in the 1930s and 1940s, as Mark Naison has shown.[34]

This all served to delegitimize the very legitimate struggles African Americans and their allies waged against various forms of segregation, discrimination, and abuse. The same is true of baseless suspicions that conservative extremists had at least some hand in fomenting the uprisings, which Johnson and Rockefeller harbored. Tendencies to deny that northern Black people could have profound grievances and that they possessed the agency to act upon them as they saw fit conferred a greater power upon communism than actually existed. It provided one more vector to exacerbate America's collective paranoia. As though arms races, space races, and proxy wars were not enough, respected people in positions of power in all regions of the country were telling the white public that communists were riling up African Americans and pushing them into the streets to create civil unrest and destabilize the country, painting Black people as witless dupes.

In reality, despite what politicians and police said, the FBI determined that neither communists nor any other organized group had any meaningful involvement with the uprisings in New York, or Philadelphia, or New Jersey, or anywhere else that summer. In its report on the summer upheaval, released in late September, the FBI wrote, "The evidence indicates that aside from the actions of minor organizations or irresponsible individuals there was no systematic planning or organization of any of the city riots." The report noted that some who had participated in meetings during the chaos in Harlem, such as Bill Epton, William Patterson, and Jesse Gray, had various past and present affiliations with communist and socialist organizations but characterized them as outliers who attempted to inflame tensions as individuals. "The facts developed," the FBI found, "lead to the clear conclusion that there is no discernible pattern of organization of the riots from city to city."[35]

The report's authors cited social and economic conditions as having far greater import in 1964's urban conflict than any individuals or organizations. They recognized "that many of these areas are characterized by miserable living conditions, houses that are badly maintained, many of them rat infested and filthy. Drunkenness, narcotics peddling, prostitution, idleness, frustration, poverty and lack of opportunity are part of the atmosphere many people in these districts breathe."[36] Here, the FBI would agree with ordinary Harlem and Bedford-Stuyvesant residents and with Kenneth Clark, James Farmer, Dr. King,

Whitney Young, Roy Wilkins, and a virtually endless list of others. The nation's premier law enforcement professionals had found that there were more obvious and apparent causes of the disturbances. Their director, J. Edgar Hoover, would have been quite pleased to have discovered meaningful communist activity in these events, as it would have provided further cover for his agency to undermine and neutralize civil rights organizations. Instead, his agents could find no evidence and so were forced to conclude that participants saw only the red of rage and blood. Despite the report's clear language, politicians and social critics continued piling on accusations of communism.

It worked. According to a November 1965 Gallup poll, 51 percent of white Americans believed communists were extensively involved in civil rights protests, while 27 percent suspected "at least some" involvement. Three years after the upheaval in Harlem and Bedford-Stuyvesant, 71 percent of white people in America believed that the continual disturbances in Black neighborhoods throughout the nation's cities were "organized efforts."[37]

Jobs

Mayor Wagner made considerable promises of assistance for Black youth in the aftermath of the uprisings. Like many of his promises, they grabbed headlines and sounded impressive, but, in the end, little came of them. On July 25, Wagner pledged he would provide $223,000 to Bedford-Stuyvesant Youth in Action, a community agency designed to fight poverty and related maladies in the heavily disinvested neighborhood. Wagner characterized the grant as allowing YIA "to probe the basic causes of youth delinquency and the housing, health, employment, social welfare, recreation and other conditions affecting the residents of Bedford-Stuyvesant." The year was 1964, and Wagner had been in office since 1955. That Bedford-Stuyvesant had deep social and economic problems was not a recent discovery. Anyone who knew what Bedford-Stuyvesant was would have been aware of these basic truths for years. These problems had only worsened during Wagner's tenure, but his language suggested that this was a sudden revelation in the wake of upheaval. Indeed, the mayor said, the city "must take effective and comprehensive action to relieve the basic causes of poverty, unemployment and other ills which trigger violence and lawlessness." There had been plenty of opportunity to do just that in the last ten years.[38]

A few days later, the Wagner administration announced a new effort to employ up to twenty thousand young people at dozens of city agencies. The scheme was directed at those between the ages of sixteen and twenty-one with no or few recognized job skills. The previous week's events gave the recruiting drive a certain gravity, with the city's welfare commissioner telling nearly one hundred high-ranking officials from municipal departments: "This program must succeed, or we can look forward to something more awful and more terrible than anything we have seen so far." Wagner ordered all those at the meeting to move the matter of targeted hiring to the "top priority of all your programs and undertakings." Each agency had until August 15, about two weeks, to come up with a plan to find positions for young people who may have "difficulty in conforming to the rules," for example, those who are consistently late and refuse to follow supervisors' directives.[39]

Finally, on July 31, the mayor gave an address in which he promised immediate hiring in a variety of areas, both temporary and permanent. To deal with the problem of unemployed high-school dropouts, Wagner would order five city departments to hire a total of one thousand young people for the rest of the summer, at a rate of $1.50 an hour, fifty cents more than the federal minimum wage for workers in such fields. It was not clear how this would effectively help anyone who had dropped out of high school, given that these people would not be resuming their educations at the end of the month and would once again be out of work. Local 32-B of the Building Service Employees International Union would begin training another three hundred young people, mostly men, for permanent positions in building maintenance. The city would train up to two hundred youths in traffic equipment maintenance; assist in opening a job training and placement center in South Jamaica, Queens; and work to recruit racial and ethnic minorities onto the police force.[40]

By the end of August, when Wagner had said the city would have hired at least a thousand marginalized young people, it had not even come close to achieving this modest goal. The Reverend Dr. Eugene Callender, writing for the Citywide Coordinating Committee, an organization of fifty clergymen who ministered in Harlem and Bedford-Stuyvesant, derided the program as a "cruel hoax" that had delivered "a handful of jobs for show and publicity purposes." The city had only accounted for two hundred hires, including twenty-six who picked weeds for the Highways Department. The ministers claimed they had referred large numbers of young people to city agencies for these jobs, many of whom returned with similar accounts of being told no positions were available.[41]

These men of the cloth had begun their own hiring program in response to the uprisings, raising $112,000 to employ 630 teenagers, also paying $1.50 an hour, to perform maintenance work on churches and community centers, as well as engaging in voter registration. Their money had run out by the end of August, and they had encouraged the city to take it over, but City Council President Paul Screvane, in charge of municipal antipoverty efforts, had "lost" the paperwork the clergy gave him and could not find the time to meet with them. The group suggested the city as a whole and young people in Harlem and Bedford-Stuyvesant in particular would be better off "if Mr. Screvane were to spend his time hunting for money instead of for witches."[42]

In Bedford-Stuyvesant, residents received nothing from Wagner's promises. The city created no new jobs there. There were no emergency programs to address alienation and rage. Instead, the mayor focused some attention on Harlem, a neighborhood with established political and media voices, and all but ignored Bedford-Stuyvesant, a far-less-organized area, full of new arrivals, its borders ever-expanding. Those whose businesses were damaged on Fulton Street left their windows boarded up. By the beginning of 1965, pavement where a once-vacant lot stood was the only visible progress in the neighborhood.[43]

Conclusion

In a criticism remarkable for its consistency and for the diversity of those making it over the years, Callender opined, "It is quite obvious that the Mayor, who acts only when he is backed to the wall, announced his job program as a sop to the Negro community following the rioting, but now that things have cooled off so has his enthusiasm for the job program." Time and again, Wagner responded to crises with bold promises and declarations. Time and again, he failed to follow through. Time and again, it seemed these were tactics that he used to look responsive but ultimately do little, correctly anticipating that some new event would supplant the current exigency in short order. Wagner approached educational segregation, capital flight, job discrimination, residential segregation, and police corruption in the same way. He had done it once more, in what was the most immediate crisis he had confronted in all his years holding political office. The mayor decided effectively to take no action on the destructive power people in Harlem and Bedford-Stuyvesant had wielded in July 1964, and it was thanks to good luck and the hard work of community leaders and activists that similar events did not take place while he was in office for the next year and a half. The city's streets stayed comparatively calm in spite of him, not because of him.[44]

13

Reforming the Civilian Complaint Review Board

Civilian oversight of the police was the most persistently demanded policy change across the city in the aftermath of the uprisings. Wagner and his allies had consistently defeated City Council legislation seeking to implement such practices, but the election of 1965 offered a new opportunity. John V. Lindsay, the city's forty-three-year-old progressive Republican congressman from the Upper East Side, had committed to civilian oversight of the police in his first speech as a mayoral candidate. He won a three-way race and pursued the implementation of his pledge once he took office on January 1, 1966.[1]

The board he created in May of that year—four civilians and three police officials—drew intense opposition from the Patrolmen's Benevolent Association, the labor union representing the NYPD rank and file, and from conservative allies in politics and business. They launched immediate legal challenges and collected tens of thousands of signatures from New Yorkers to secure a ballot question in November on banning civilians from any oversight role of the police. It also generated little enthusiasm from civil rights and civil liberties organizations, who generally found Lindsay's new board to be the weakest possible manifestation of such an entity. In the face of intense, organized opposition to civilian participation in reviewing citizens' complaints, these groups found themselves in the position of having to fight to keep something many of them viewed as too much of a compromise solution. Amid the escalating conflict, the board went to work, unsure of its fate but preparing as though it were a permanent fixture, with members doing their best to ignore the deafening discord around them.

Executive Action

Since the Civilian Complaint Review Board's creation in 1953, neither the police department nor its rank and file ever favored or embraced the panel. It was born out of corruption and turpitude, a reluctantly established entity intended to mollify critics of police hostility and brutality, after the public discovered the NYPD had made a secret deal with Department of Justice officials to shield itself from federal civil rights investigations. With such a background, it was unlikely the board would ever fully serve its stated purpose, as the CCRB was an entirely internal operation, and the organization that ran it was opposed to its robust functioning. Over the next decade, civil liberties and civil rights groups pressured the police department and city to operate the board in more independent and transparent ways, but they largely refused.[2]

Following the uprisings, one of the activists' major demands was to appoint esteemed New Yorkers unconnected to the police department to the CCRB. Before July 1966, the CCRB operated without civilian input. Three deputy NYPD commissioners would receive and decide complaints civilians had filed against the police. The members would then pass on recommendations regarding potential corrective action against accused officers to the police commissioner, who had complete and final say over the outcome. The results were closed to public and often not communicated to the complainant. Those who favored a civilian review board but were unhappy with this iteration saw the situation as one of the police investigating themselves, which many consistently referred to as a "whitewash." They did not believe that the body would operate objectively but that the police would tend to look out for one another and dismiss complaints, regardless of validity. To counter this perceived lack of neutrality, proponents of reforming the review board demanded either adding a plurality of civilians to the existing board or abolishing it and creating a new board that operated independently of the NYPD, whose members would report to another city official. Lindsay chose the first option, which he hoped would produce a workable compromise.

On May 2, 1966, despite two threatened lawsuits, the mayor announced the creation of the new Civilian Complaint Review Board via Commissioner Howard Leary's General Order No. 14. Lindsay had hired Leary away from the Philadelphia Police Department, which he had been running for the past three years, coexisting with that city's all-civilian oversight body, the Police Advisory Board. Leary immediately embarked on a "top-to-bottom" reorganization of the NYPD, promoting Lloyd Sealy from captain to assistant chief inspector, skipping two ranks, as well as moving Sanford Garelik, a Jewish man, to chief inspector, the highest rank a uniformed officer can achieve. This was seen as finally destroying the "Irish mafia," as the NYPD had long been known, given the disproportionate representation of Irish-Americans across its ranks.[3]

The mayor was careful to speak of the board exclusively in a positive light, wishing to have it seen as a means to generate respect and trust between officers and the communities they policed. As a study his campaign had commissioned the previous November advised, "Solid citizen support is essential to all phases of public safety. Without information and cooperation, the police are thrown back on their own relatively limited resources. With public support and confidence, they become the active force in a city-wide fight against crime." Lindsay argued the board would "protect police officers from malicious or baseless accusations," as complaints would now only appear in an officer's permanent record if the commissioner found them substantiated. The mayor assured New Yorkers that the board "will lead to better communication and understanding between the police, and the people, particularly those people in deprived areas where crime is most prevalent and police protection is most valued." He spoke highly of the city's police, praising and thanking them for their service and dedication.[4]

Following his initial remarks, the mayor revealed the eleven-member selection committee responsible for nominating the four civilians to the review board. Lindsay named as chairman Herbert Brownell, President Eisenhower's attorney general and well known for his relatively strong progressive stances on civil rights. He had played a large role in drafting the Civil Rights Act of 1957 and in guiding the president's action in the Little Rock school integration crisis. The selection committee had a list of 130 people, about a dozen of whom were women, to whittle down to eight, with Lindsay selecting four from it.[5]

Dissatisfaction

Though long expected, Lindsay's announcement sent shockwaves throughout the city. It came against a backdrop of surging complaints against police, numbering 186 in the first three months of the year, potentially putting the department on track to receive seven hundred by the end of the year, versus the 324 from all of 1965. It seemed the review board issue was now timelier than ever. Groups on either side of the mayor immediately criticized Lindsay's board. The NYCLU issued a press release the same day, accusing Lindsay of staying "on the safe side." The statement contended "only a completely independent board will be a fully effective deterrent to police abuse of authority" and announced the NYCLU's intent to "continue to press for a completely independent review board with an independent investigative staff," unlike Lindsay and Leary's board, which would use only police officers to investigate complaints. The organization articulated independence as necessary because as its lawyers had seen in the "great many cases" it had handled before the CCRB "all too often, witnesses to incidents of police abuse disappear or become forgetful when they discover they must describe the events they have seen to police investigators." The NAACP was also critical, with its national general counsel Robert Carter citing "serious inadequacies" that would do little to remediate the "suspicion and hostility" the city's Black and Puerto Rican communities felt toward the police. A local NAACP head referred to the mayor's plan as "dressing up the same old system," with the organization's state president voicing a similar opinion.[6]

The PBA and its allies went on the attack, with John J. Cassese, the organization's president since 1959, pronouncing, "You won't satisfy these people until you get all Negroes and Puerto Ricans on the board and every policeman who goes in front of it is found guilty." The *Daily News* went further, professing the board would be "infested sooner or later with cop-haters, professional liberals, representatives of pressure groups and the like, to the great detriment of the police force." Cassese told of how he was "sick and tired of giving in to minority groups with their whims and their gripes and shouting," threatening mass resignations from the NYPD in response to the modified board. Cassese said he and the PBA "consider the Mayor's proposal improper, illegal and undesirable." The PBA seized upon the legality aspect of its criticisms and pursued this course for the next six months. The PBA had already petitioned New York State's Supreme Court to prevent the mayor from implementing the board, contending the plan violated a line in the city charter dictating the policing commissioner is to have "cognizance and control" of all matters regarding the NYPD. Though the PBA lost this suit, Lindsay had good reason to worry, for police lawsuits had recently hamstrung review boards in Rochester, NY, and Philadelphia, forcing them to halt all activities.[7]

Cassese and the PBA's opposition to the board was a change from five years earlier, when they had campaigned for a law that would have created a civilian-led committee to oversee the commissioner's disciplinary actions against his officers. That was in 1959, when the NYPD rank and file were increasingly at odds with their commissioner, Stephen Kennedy, a man who had risen through the ranks to become the leader of the force in 1955 yet who so thoroughly rejected the PBA's labor militancy that he tore up his membership card on television in 1960. In response, the organization expelled him. Kennedy, an ultimately failed anticorruption crusader, fired, demoted, and transferred hundreds of officers throughout his tenure. The commissioner dismissed men found to be working second jobs and refused to grant his officers the ability to file grievances with an external body, insisting the PBA was not a union. By 1961, labor relations had become so toxic in the department that officers staged a work slowdown and forced his resignation. Kennedy's replacement, Michael Murphy, was not a reformer, nor was he particularly compelled to pursue corruption. He was more willing to tolerate and work with the PBA, so the organization saw no need to

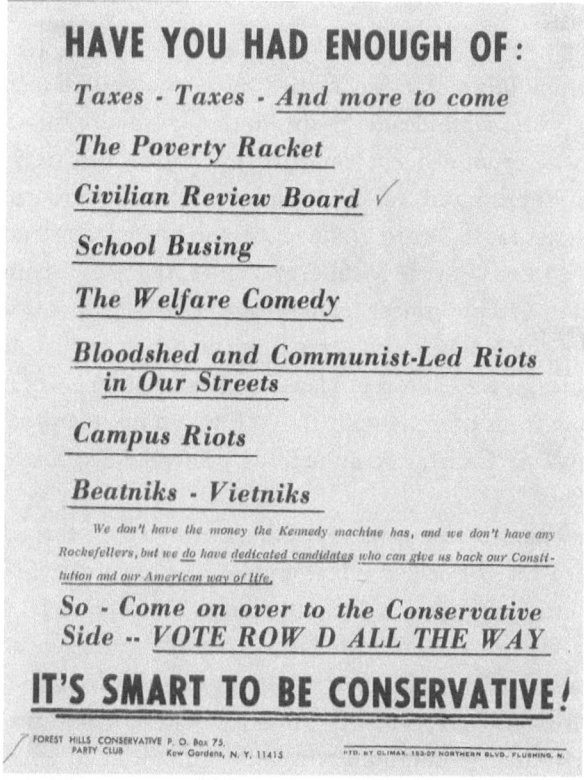

Figure 13.1 Promotional material from the Forest Hills Conservative Party Club.

Source: Algernon D. Black Papers, Rare Book and Manuscript Library, Columbia University Library.

bring in an outsider to supervise him. Its opposition to civilian oversight was situational, not born of a rigid objection on principle.[8]

On July 7, the PBA delivered 51,852 signatures to the city clerk's desk as part of the process of making eliminating and banning Lindsay's board a ballot initiative in November. The Conservative Party's leader, William F. Buckley Jr., brought a separate bundle of 40,383 signatures. Both had the same goal—to prohibit anyone who was not an NYPD employee from serving on a review board, thereby disposing of not just this review board but of blocking in perpetuity any civilian involvement. Lindsay and the network of organizations and individuals opposing the PBA knew this was coming but underestimated how much support the anti–review board forces had in the city.[9]

The New Board

Four days later, on July 11, Lindsay named the civilian board members. Algernon Black, the white senior leader of the humanist New York Society for Ethical Culture, was appointed chairman of the panel. The sixty-five-year-old Black, born to English and Russian immigrant parents, grew up in an integrated Harlem, on 100th Street; graduated magna cum laude from Harvard in 1923; and had worked with the NYSEC ever since, rising to become the head of the organization. Deeply concerned with social justice, he was vice president and director of the NAACP and served on the boards of the ACLU and the Citizens Committee for Children. Black received written encouragement and congratulations from officials with the White House, Planned Parenthood, the state's Supreme Court, and numerous professionals, academics, clergy, and labor leaders.[10]

Lindsay also named Thomas R. Farrell, a thirty-seven-year-old white Army vet and lawyer who had helped integrate middle-class areas of the Bronx and served as president of the Bronx Catholic Interracial Council; Dr. Walter Isaiah Murray, a fifty-five-year-old African American professor of education at Brooklyn College, raised in the Midwest and with a doctorate from the University of Chicago; and Manuel Diaz Jr., a forty-three-year-old Puerto Rican World War II veteran, former chief of community affairs at the anti–juvenile delinquency organization Mobilization for Youth, and current executive director of the Puerto Rican Community Development Project, with a master's degree in social work from Columbia University. Commissioner Leary, responsible for choosing the three NYPD members, selected the African American former U.S. assistant district attorney Franklin Thomas, the thirty-two-year-old Brooklyn-born deputy commissioner in charge of the department's legal matters; Edward McCabe, fifty-seven, a white twenty-five-year veteran of the FBI currently overseeing the department's division of licenses; and Deputy Inspector Pearse Meagher, a forty-seven-year-old white officer who had joined the force in June 1941. McCabe was reappointed to the board after serving on the all-police board under Commissioner Murphy. At this gathering, Chief Inspector Garelik spoke of the "enormous benefits" the board would offer both the department and community. Few NYPD officers shared his sentiments.[11]

As with Lindsay's nomination of the selection committee two months earlier, his critics attacked immediately. PBA President Cassese hurriedly announced a press conference in which, banging his fist on the podium before him, he assessed the members as "so pro–civil rights and so Lindsay-thinking" that "Lindsay went out of his way to get these four." As A. Philip Randolph later pointed out, the U.S. Constitution is pro–civil rights. Cassese's comments "stunned" the editorial board of the *New York Post*, which asked, "Should it be 'anti–civil rights?'" Roy Innis, the Harlem CORE chairman, was dissatisfied with Lindsay's selections, arguing that none of the men was in "close enough touch with the minority groups in the ghetto areas. I don't think they have suffered to the same degree the indignities of individuals in the ghetto." Innis found them to be lacking in life experience, regardless of skin color, saying he "would have preferred to see some representation from the ghetto, to see people on the board who work there, live there, are in active contact with the realities of the ghetto. After all, police brutality affects ghetto residents more than anyone else." Such criticism, no matter from whom, would soon be low on Lindsay's list of problems.[12]

Resistance

While Cassese spoke at the Warwick Hotel, a much more dangerous storm was brewing in the adjoining room, where Rodney Ettman was convening the initial gathering of the Independent Citizens Committee Against Civilian Review Boards. With the former NYPD commissioner Michael Murphy as its honorary chairman and several state senators as members, the committee was neither independent nor composed of average citizens. Ettman was a wallpaper manufacturer from Woodmere, a town on Long Island about twenty miles southeast of Manhattan. He had gathered thirty or so businessmen "to actively oppose civilian review of individual police action in New York City and where else it may be proposed" to "free the policeman from all these encumbrances." The maker of vertical adornments saw those gathered in the Sussex Room, including himself, as "captains of industry." Or at least, Ettman said, "That's what I'd like to think they are." The men vowed to raise half a million dollars to wage an "educational campaign" to destroy Lindsay's board and prevent anything like it in the future. This was in addition to the $1.5 million the PBA had pledged to spend, essentially the contents of its treasury. Lindsay met with Cassese and Norman Frank, a Madison Avenue advertising executive who had been working as the PBA's public relations consultant for several years, two days later. He told Cassese and Frank "if anything happened in New York—if there was a blow-up—they would be responsible." The mayor felt preemptively blaming them for something similar to what had happened in Harlem and Bedford-Stuyvesant two years earlier left them "a little floored" but was not sure if it had much effect.[13]

It took supporters of independent review, the people and organizations who now found themselves compelled to defend a board toward which they were ambivalent or worse, nearly a month to marshal an organization in response. On August 4, the Federated Associations for Impartial Review, or FAIR, announced its formation, with money from the American Civil Liberties Union. Initially composed of the New York Civil Liberties Union, the Citizens Union, the Liberal Party, CORE, the Union of American Hebrew Congregations, the Guardians Association, the Anti-Defamation League of B'nai Brith, the Catholic Interracial Council, and forty other groups, including both the Young Republican and Democratic Clubs, NYCLU Executive Director Aryeh Neier predicted it would have seventy-five member organizations within a month. Speaking for the group, Neier said, "We are taking the position that legal action is unpredictable and we feel we must organize our efforts at this time." FAIR estimated it would need at least $500,000 to preserve the board; its opposition had been planning a coordinated media assault for weeks and committed to spend up to $2 million on it. Review board members, in agreement with Lindsay, decided to not participate in the campaign in any way. They declined all invitations for speaking engagements and requests for interviews, believing "it is not in the public interest" that they "engage in political controversy or attempt to justify the existence of the Board or the appointments to it."[14]

Functioning

In the meantime, the new Civilian Complaint Review Board had gone to work with little fanfare, operating at 201 Park Avenue South, near Seventeenth Street. This was not in a police station but instead the office the previous commissioner had opened to take complaints. The civilian board members spent time observing departmental trials, consulting with police officials, and getting to know how the department worked, a process they would continue throughout their service. The board now had a staff of secretaries and a full-time executive director, Harold Baer Jr., a former assistant U.S. attorney, who was to oversee operations and serve as the connection between the commissioner and the board. Bernard Jackson, an African American former police officer, assistant U.S. district attorney, president of the Bronx NAACP, and area director of the regional office of the Office of Economic Opportunity, was appointed assistant director. The office was accepting complaints, starting July 1, at the rate of about three per day, which groups such as the Legal Aid Society, City Commission on Human Rights, ACLU, NAACP, Urban League, and CORE could file on a person's behalf. Algernon Black, the chairman, spoke of board members developing a relationship of "respect and understanding," never splitting into police and civilian factions.[15]

Once the board received a complaint, one of its more than two dozen NYPD investigators, who investigated only these complaints, would get to work, speaking with the complainant, the officer or officers, and any witnesses. Previously, the accused officer's supervising officer would be responsible for the investigation, creating, at a minimum, the appearance of a conflict of interest. But under the new board, those investigators would then send reports to the executive or assistant director, who would read them and forward them in groups of twenty to board members to study in advance of the next weekly meeting. After discussion, the board could file them as unsubstantiated, which they often did, meaning there was not enough evidence, no witnesses, or the complaints were unfounded. Conciliation was a new feature of the board, a decision in which members viewed complainants as feeling having been wronged but ignorant of the law and police regulations. In that situation, representatives from the board would explain to the complainant why she or he was wrong and why the officer had not committed any real transgressions, aside from, at worst, a breach of etiquette. Once a case went to conciliation, it was concluded, and the complaint could not be pursued further. If the board decided the officer had violated a policy but not to the extent that a reprimand was warranted, the officer would be judged to need "instructions," meaning one of the two complaint supervisors working for the board, an NYPD inspector and deputy inspector, would speak to the officer about his behavior.[16]

When the board determined the officer had seriously transgressed, such as sticking his gun in a double-parked milkman's ribs while drunk; dragging a twelve-year-old boy who had not paid for his bus ride by the hair for a block and a half; drinking alcohol with, molesting, and taking "suggestive" pictures of underage girls while off duty; or shoving his neighbor through a plate-glass door, then it would recommend charges, meaning that board members, always

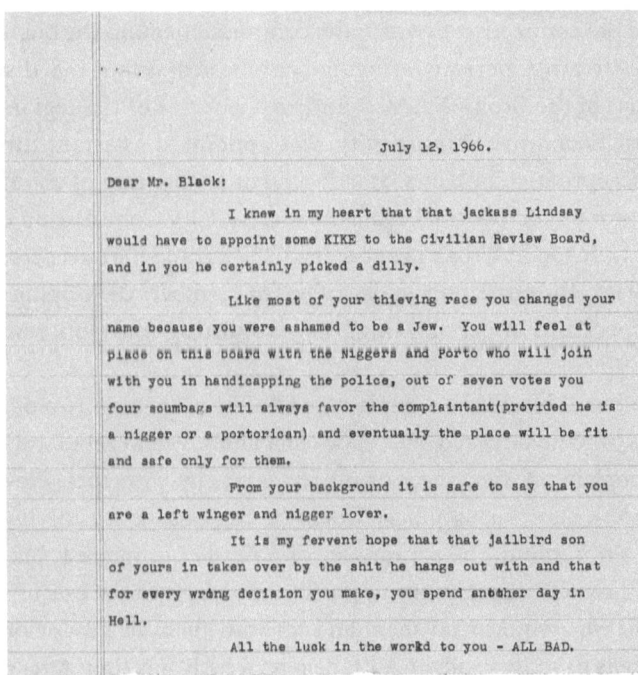

Figure 13.2 An example of the hate mail members of the new Civilian Complaint Review Board received.

Source: Algernon D. Black Papers, Rare Book and Manuscript Library, Columbia University Library.

unanimously, advised the commissioner to hold a departmental trial for the officer in question. The commissioner would decide if a trial were appropriate. The board's recommendation of charges was the only instance in which an officer who was the subject of a civilian complaint would have that complaint noted in his personnel file. Before July 1, all complaints, regardless of validity or outcome, went into an officer's file, potentially derailing aspirations for higher rank. Along the way, if there were major evidence-based discrepancies between the two sides while investigating, the board could request a confidential hearing and subpoena witnesses to better determine what had happened. Board members neither conducted nor attended the hearing, with a professional hearing officer in charge, forwarding a transcript to the board to use in making its determination. At no point would the board ever meet with accused officers or preside over them in a hearing or trial. As for Cassese's charges the board would find every officer who went before it "guilty," there was no such thing as "guilty" for the board, since it had no involvement with either civil or criminal courts, serving solely as an advisory panel for the commissioner, who had no obligation to do anything with the board's recommendations.[17]

Board members were receiving other kinds of complaints; they had endured threats and abuse ever since their names had been made public. The white members had received phone calls, letters, and in-person verbal assaults from late-night visitors calling them "nigger lovers." Dr. Murray, the lone African American civilian member, changed his phone number after someone called his home and yelled "n——!" into his wife's ear. Black received an anonymous letter, dated July 12, in which the writer "knew in my heart that that jackass Lindsay would have to appoint some KIKE to the Civilian Review Board. . . . Like most of your thieving race you changed your name because you were ashamed to be a Jew. You will feel at place on this board with the N——s and Porto who will join you in handicapping the police." A number of others, who included their names, wrote to Black, deriding him as a communist and subversive.[18]

Conclusion

Just the act of reconfiguring the CCRB evoked considerable hostility from the rank and file of the police department, their political allies, and ordinary white New Yorkers. Their concerns were not rooted in the board's practices or its record, as it had not had the time to produce either. The police commissioner and his top deputies could express support for it all they wanted and vouch for the board members' fairness, but they would never sway their opposition, as their differences were not about procedure. What the PBA and those on its side were so against was the notion of civilians having any involvement whatsoever in oversight of the police—even if that oversight had no authority, no punitive powers, no interaction with accused officers, and no legal powers beyond subpoenaing witnesses. The board had a one-civilian majority, and most of the rest of its staff were NYPD officers. And while opponents of the board rendered the civilian members as cartoonish, liberal bogeymen, in reality, very few people had known who Algernon Black was beforehand. Virtually no members of the general public—or the NYPD, for that matter—knew the other three. The overwhelming majority of NYPD officers and their union leadership wished to remain an isolated island, ostensibly serving the public but answering solely to their own.

The challenges to the reconfigured CCRB would soon prove to be serious and powerful, if that were not already evident. Anti–review board forces were marshaling allies, resources, and strategy in ways that FAIR was not. Here, we can see early indications of the power, resolve, and political skills of the PBA, which had been a recognized bargaining unit for only a few years. By May, Lindsay had already been through serious labor strife, handling and losing badly a transit workers' strike that began on his first day in office, but he may not have been prepared for how ferocious the officers' union was prepared to be in order to keep civilians out of police business entirely.

14
A Referendum

Mayor Lindsay's modification of the CCRB elicited a wave of opposition from the Patrolmen's Benevolent Association and conservative groups, which joined forces and won a subsequent referendum prohibiting civilians from serving on the review board. Police authorities, officers, and their allies had long opposed civilian involvement in police affairs, but the level to which they resisted these renewed demands, both individually and as an organized group, was unprecedented. Other cities had established analogous review panels in the early 1960s, but it was only in New York, this liberal city, that we see such an intense level of police resistance to the idea. The police went on a well-financed campaign offensive, which precipitated a marked deterioration of race relations in the city. The PBA's victory at the polls represents a police department, in opposition to its leadership no less, wielding an unprecedented level of political power.

The 1966 referendum marked the end of the city's civil rights coalition among African Americans and white allies, particularly Jewish New Yorkers. While many residents felt review board reform was necessary, Black New Yorkers especially believed so. Black community leaders and residents argued that civilian participation in the review of complaints against police would help curb the types of police behavior about which they had long complained, namely, brutality, discourtesy, and apathy toward street crime in Black neighborhoods. Consequently, those against review board reform framed it as a civil rights issue, one that would disproportionately benefit Black citizens—even though white people filed most of the complaints. Substantial numbers of white New Yorkers believed any change to the city's system of reviewing complaints against its police officers would be giving in to unjust demands from civil rights activists, a movement toward which these white citizens were no longer sympathetic, if they ever had been. With both pro- and anti-review board forces presenting complaint reform as a matter of civil rights, even though at its core it was not, many of the city's white voters cast their ballots as if the referendum were on the notion of civil rights itself.

White voters, especially white ethnics, overwhelmingly chose to eliminate civilians from the board.[1] The board's ultimate defeat after years of hard work was a bitter rebuke to the coalition favoring civilian oversight. Civil rights activists and many Black New Yorkers took the loss particularly hard, feeling they had not asked for much in desiring their public servants to have a slight measure of accountability to the citizenry. The PBA's refusal to compromise on complaint reform and its racially charged campaign contributed to an increase in resentment between the city's Black communities and the police. White voters' overwhelming support for the PBA pushed many Black activists and citizens in the city to feel that relying on white people for support, which had often been tenuous, was no longer desirable. The racial acrimony the review board referendum fostered convinced significant numbers of Black New Yorkers they would have to look inward to secure freedom and equality. Black Power ideologies began to emerge nationally during the referendum campaign, giving a name to the self-reliance and self-determination many Black New Yorkers had already practiced. As a result, the city quickly became a hotbed of Black Power activism. Less than two years after the referendum, the Ocean Hill–Brownsville school decentralization struggle showed the progress of this inward turn and how white New Yorkers reacted to it.

Campaigning

By mid-September 1966, Mayor Lindsay was declaring, "We are on the upswing, we have a fighting chance" to keep the review board. The Guardians Association, representing the 1,360 Black NYPD officers, came out against the PBA's position and pledged to fight to keep the hybrid CCRB. James Meredith, the man who integrated the University of Mississippi with the protection of the federal government in 1962, and who in June had been shot during his one-man March Against Fear in Mississippi, appeared at a pro–review board rally on September 13. Lindsay felt energized by the heavyweights who had recently signed on as co-chairs of FAIR—Herbert Brownell, the former attorney general; Bronx Borough President Herman Badillo; the civil rights giant A. Philip Randolph;

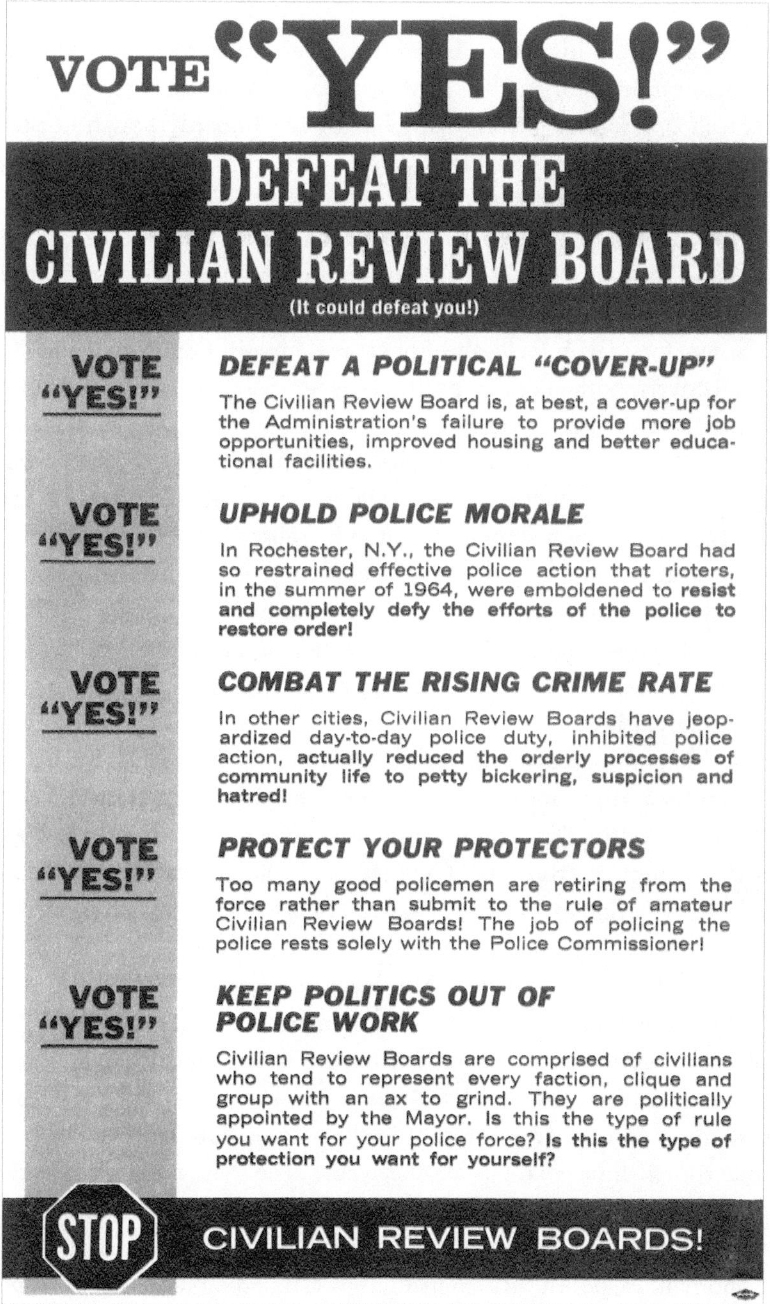

VOTE "YES!"

DEFEAT THE CIVILIAN REVIEW BOARD
(It could defeat you!)

VOTE "YES!"

DEFEAT A POLITICAL "COVER-UP"
The Civilian Review Board is, at best, a cover-up for the Administration's failure to provide more job opportunities, improved housing and better educational facilities.

VOTE "YES!"

UPHOLD POLICE MORALE
In Rochester, N.Y., the Civilian Review Board had so restrained effective police action that rioters, in the summer of 1964, were emboldened to resist and completely defy the efforts of the police to restore order!

VOTE "YES!"

COMBAT THE RISING CRIME RATE
In other cities, Civilian Review Boards have jeopardized day-to-day police duty, inhibited police action, actually reduced the orderly processes of community life to petty bickering, suspicion and hatred!

VOTE "YES!"

PROTECT YOUR PROTECTORS
Too many good policemen are retiring from the force rather than submit to the rule of amateur Civilian Review Boards! The job of policing the police rests solely with the Police Commissioner!

VOTE "YES!"

KEEP POLITICS OUT OF POLICE WORK
Civilian Review Boards are comprised of civilians who tend to represent every faction, clique and group with an ax to grind. They are politically appointed by the Mayor. Is this the type of rule you want for your police force? Is this the type of protection you want for yourself?

STOP CIVILIAN REVIEW BOARDS!

Figure 14.1 Anti–review board campaign material from the Independent Citizens Committee Against Civilian Review Boards.

Source: John Vliet Lindsay Papers (MS 592), Manuscripts and Archives, Yale University Library.

Morris Abram, from his review board selection committee; and Theodore W. Kheel, a labor moderator and one of Mayor Wagner's closest advisers. All major candidates for the state's governorship were now on board, though Rockefeller refused to campaign for the issue, citing it as strictly one of local importance. Donald D. Shack, vice chairman of the NYCLU, went before the Republican State Committee, contending, "This referendum, while it will only confront the citizens of New York City on the ballot, has not only state-wide significance but national significance," likening it to the "problems in the Deep South." The state's two U.S. senators, Jacob Javits and Robert F. Kennedy, Republican and Democrat, respectively, both accepted positions as honorary co-chairs and vowed to support the board however they could.[2]

Norman Frank, the PBA's public relations man, biblically portrayed the senators' support as "the story of David and Goliath.... The Goliaths are gathering, but David will reign supreme because he represents the people and a just cause." The PBA announced it intended to secure 370 billboards, open twenty storefronts, and employ thousands of door-to-door campaigners to defeat the review board. It now counted the anti-integration organization Parents and Taxpayers, the American Legion, the Brooklyn Bar Association, and American Nazi groups as allies.[3]

As the referendum moved closer, the PBA and its allies stepped up their emotional appeals and groundless accusations. An ICCACRB pamphlet claimed with no evidence that "too many good policemen are retiring from the force rather than submit to the rule of amateur Civilian Review Boards!" Cassese warned voters, "I don't think you'll have a Police Department after one year of such a board" and that "if we don't do something now and take care of this situation, maybe there'll be nobody left in this great city of ours." He also claimed that "Communism and Communists are somewhat mixed in this fight. If they are not in the forefront, they are making hay while the sun shines.... If we wind up with a review board we will have done Russia a great service." America's global nemesis "should send a medal to the City of New York and say, 'thank you for accomplishing what I haven't been able to do these many years.'" He was not alone in his beliefs, with other police organizations and various far-right individuals and groups supporting his claim.[4]

An anonymous, poorly written flier falsely claimed Lindsay's civilian appointees were secretly communists conspiring to ruin the police department. It labeled Algernon Black as "affiliated with sixty-two communist and subversive organizations." Manuel Diaz, as head of Mobilization for Youth, presided over a "hotbed of communists." Thomas Farrell's guilt came through his association with the Anti-Defamation League, which was "probably the largest and most efficient private gestapo in the world today," employing what was likely a deliberately inflammatory term for a group whose mission is to combat anti-Semitism and prejudice. As for Walter Isaiah Murray, the flier wrongly named him head of the new review board and proved his allegiance to Marx, Lenin, and Stalin through his membership on the board of the NAACP.[5]

Other publications that smeared those in favor of the new board as communists contained more verbose expansions of the same ideas and claims, including commonly referring to Algernon Black by his Russian, Jewish, immigrant mother's maiden name, Bellchowsky. None of them explained what would have been a much wider conspiracy, given that Herbert Brownell Jr., the man who helped convince Dwight Eisenhower to run for president and served as his first attorney general, had interviewed and approved each member of the new board, personally phoning Black to invite him to meet with the selection panel Brownell chaired.[6]

In the weeks leading up to the referendum, the Independent Citizens Committee Against Civilian Review Boards published a number of full-page ads in the sympathetic *Daily News*. One featured a white woman, in curlers, looking anxiously out a window, with the caption, "All mothers wait up at night! We can't take chances . . . not with our children!" The text of the ad used crime statistics to inspire fear in voters, claiming once again that the new review board would suddenly render the police unwilling to do their jobs. An October appeal employed a photograph of a policeman with one hand tied behind his back. Another attacked the Philadelphia review board, with alleged statements from members of the board and policemen in the city indicating it was nothing but an opportunity for criminals to harm the police. A separate but related ad featured a photograph of a cash register amid debris on a sidewalk, purporting to show "the aftermath of a riot in city that *had* a civilian review board," with the content blaming the Philadelphia board for, at a minimum, the severity of the uprisings there. What the ads did not note, nor did anyone else citing Philadelphia as an example of how destructive review boards are to police work, was that the city's police force had the best clearance rate of the nation's ten largest cities, solving crimes at a higher rate than their counterparts in New York, Los Angeles, and Chicago, all while having an all-civilian board since 1958. Though crime had risen nationally by 8 percent across the nation in the first half of 1966, it had fallen by more than 5 percent in Philadelphia.[7]

Its most memorable campaign visual, which appeared on September 26, depicted a young white woman emerging from a subway entrance, alone on a

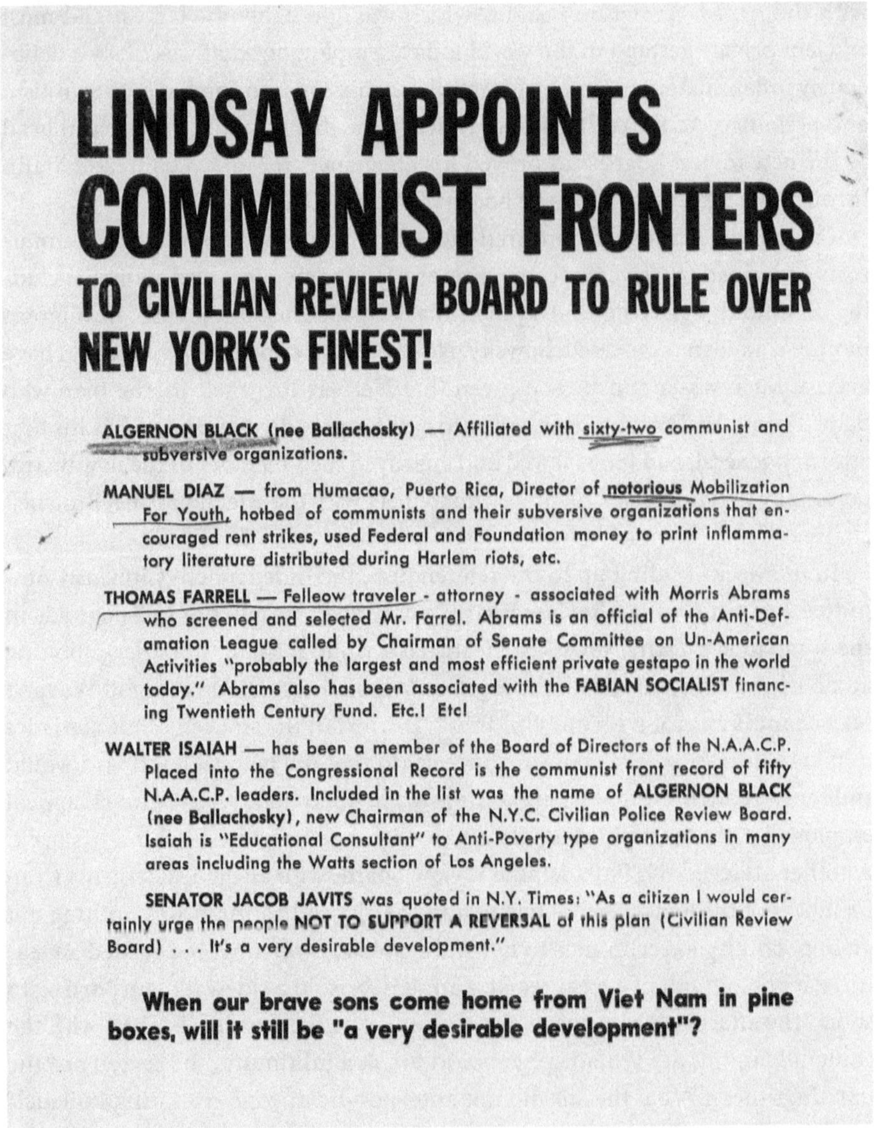

LINDSAY APPOINTS COMMUNIST FRONTERS
TO CIVILIAN REVIEW BOARD TO RULE OVER NEW YORK'S FINEST!

ALGERNON BLACK (nee Ballachosky) — Affiliated with sixty-two communist and subversive organizations.

MANUEL DIAZ — from Humacao, Puerto Rica, Director of notorious Mobilization For Youth, hotbed of communists and their subversive organizations that encouraged rent strikes, used Federal and Foundation money to print inflammatory literature distributed during Harlem riots, etc.

THOMAS FARRELL — Felleow traveler - attorney - associated with Morris Abrams who screened and selected Mr. Farrel. Abrams is an official of the Anti-Defamation League called by Chairman of Senate Committee on Un-American Activities "probably the largest and most efficient private gestapo in the world today." Abrams also has been associated with the FABIAN SOCIALIST financing Twentieth Century Fund. Etc.! Etc!

WALTER ISAIAH — has been a member of the Board of Directors of the N.A.A.C.P. Placed into the Congressional Record is the communist front record of fifty N.A.A.C.P. leaders. Included in the list was the name of ALGERNON BLACK (nee Ballachosky), new Chairman of the N.Y.C. Civilian Police Review Board. Isaiah is "Educational Consultant" to Anti-Poverty type organizations in many areas including the Watts section of Los Angeles.

SENATOR JACOB JAVITS was quoted in N.Y. Times: "As a citizen I would certainly urge the people NOT TO SUPPORT A REVERSAL of this plan (Civilian Review Board) . . . It's a very desirable development."

When our brave sons come home from Viet Nam in pine boxes, will it still be "a very desirable development"?

Figure 14.2 Propaganda and lies.

Source: Algernon D. Black Papers, Rare Book and Manuscript Library, Columbia University Library.

dark street. The caption read, "The Civilian Review Board must be stopped! Her life ... your life ... may depend on it. Send your contribution today!" The ICCACRB told the public:

> This is your fight against the spread of crime in the streets. . . . Only the policeman stands between your family and the continuous threat of the hooligan, the addict and the criminal. . . . A police officer constantly puts his life on the line for you. He must not hesitate. . . . In this time of explosive violence and increasing disregard for law and order, our Police Department must be given the authority to act effectively to safeguard the entire community. . . . With a Civilian Review Board, it may be the police officer who hesitates, not the criminal.

Lindsay characterized the ad as "an attempt to incite racial tensions."[8]

Roy Wilkins, executive director of the NAACP, vilified ICCACRB's message as "the slimiest kind of racism." Speaking at length, he asserted this type of media assault was "calculated to arouse fear and counteraction among white people. It calls upon them to rescue the poor, lonely, frightened, about-to-be-attacked white girl." For him, this was evidence that "the people who have organized the fight against the review board have organized a sly and dirty campaign against New York's Negro citizens." The ICCACRB was relying on the nascent rhetoric around "law and order" that politicians were using to speak about race in ways that people would understand while avoiding overt discussions of race. Wilkins saw this in the campaign image, stating, "All along, the opponents of the review board have talked about 'minority groups' and how about the review board is to be a protection for these minorities. They have talked, publicly and privately, about 'minorities and crime.'" The moderate NAACP leader accused the PBA of campaigning "on a sewer level," saying their campaign "spreads fear. It spreads racial suspicion and hate. It arouses passions. It splits the city." Wilkins brought his statement to a finish by harkening back to the days when justice was a rope from a tree, frustrated that the PBA had deliberately aroused "the dogs of racial hatred, mixing with that already deadly concoction the blood-pumping ingredient of 'protecting white womanhood.'" To the end, Cassese, Frank, and their advertising man, Arthur Fischer, all denied racial prejudice or animus played any part in what they were doing. As they told it, there was no racial message, just crime versus law and order, right versus wrong, good versus evil.[9]

The columnist Jimmy Breslin, already well known for his article on the gravedigger at President Kennedy's funeral, lamented the comingling of public service with politics and the ways that the PBA was attempting to achieve its ends, as well as the ends themselves. Writing for the *New York Post* in 1966, Breslin said the city's police, whom he called "my people," would become his enemies should they win, "because nobody who carries a gun can be allowed to have the power, even the hint of the power, that this referendum will give them." He saw Cassese and Frank as clearly appealing to racial prejudice, the former crudely and the latter with more subtlety, having "taken the policemen and played on their fears and prejudices and brought them into the business of voting." When they won, as he predicted they would, November 1966 would be "the month the white backlash becomes a fact."[10]

PBA ads would not be the extent of racism in the campaign, and certainly not the crudest. The National Renaissance Party, a neo-Nazi organization headquartered in an apartment on West Ninetieth Street, called for a "mass outdoor rally of white patriots to defend our New York police against a red-sponsored 'civilian review board.' Don't let Jews and Negroes smash the white man's last line of defense against the planned black revolution in New York City." The flier, using the Tannenberg font, one of the Nazi Party's official typefaces, promoted the "America First rally" in Yorkville, the same neighborhood where James Powell had been killed. On August 5, at Eighty-Fourth and Second, two blocks away from where the pro-Nazi German American Bund had been headquartered in the late 1930s and early 1940s, members and followers were called to protest the hybrid review board and fictitious forced busing of white students to Harlem. The party's logo, at the top of the flier, resembled the Nazi Party's Reichsadler emblem, with two swords crossed behind a stylized eagle and a single lightning-bolt-style *s*, reminiscent of the Nazi Party's SS organization, most directly involved with carrying out the Holocaust, over its chest. An issue of the *National Renaissance Bulletin* printed around the same time featured a drawing of two simian caricatures of Black men zealously knifing a white woman, while a forlorn white policeman stands by, his hands in irons labeled "civilian review board." Below several paragraphs of racist paranoia and hatred, the party wrote out the message the drawing communicated: "WHITE PEOPLE! UNITE AND FIGHT BACK! PROTECT OUR WOMEN!" The blood was definitely pumping. This organization said what the PBA meant but could not communicate explicitly.[11]

Then, as today, extremist politics played a role in mainstream politics. Such organizations may have had small memberships, but their import and meaning goes beyond their numbers. They allow for the vicarious expression of feelings that society has deemed distasteful, drawing silent supporters who believe they cannot join for social reasons. One need not subscribe to everything the National Renaissance Party believed to agree with its ideas about

MASS OUTDOOR RALLY OF WHITE PATRIOTS TO DEFEND OUR NEW YORK POLICE AGAINST A RED-SPONSORED "CIVILIAN REVIEW BOARD"!

DON'T LET ORGANIZED JEWS AND NEGROES SMASH THE WHITE MAN'S LAST LINE OF DEFENSE AGAINST THE PLANNED BLACK REVOLUTION IN NEW YORK CITY!

James H. Madole, dynamic leader of the National Renaissance Party, who recently appeared on the ALAN BURKE SHOW (Channel 5 TV) has been smeared by the enemies of Western Civilization as a "Neo-Nazi", "a notorious hatemonger and anti-Semite", "a super patriot", and even as "THE ANTI-CHRIST" by a Columbia University student newspaper. Madole has spoken to as many as 5000 people at a single Yorkville rally and been railroaded into prison by conniving politicians WHO SEEK TO PERMANENTLY SILENCE ANY VOICE RAISED IN BEHALF OF THE RIGHTS OF WHITE TAXPAYERS BY FAIR MEANS OR FOUL! WHY DO HOWLING JEWISH FANATICS ALWAYS TRY TO DROWN OUT MADOLE'S WORDS. YOU CAN LEARN FOR YOURSELF. MADOLE WILL SPEAK IN YORKVILLE TO EXPRESS OPPOSITION TO MAYOR LINDSAY'S PLAN TO PLACE "CIVIL RIOTS" LEADERS IN CONTROL OF YOUR NEW YORK CITY POLICE FORCE!

TIME AND PLACE OF RALLY:

This outdoor mass rally will take place on FRIDAY EVENING, AUGUST 5TH, (BETWEEN 7:30 P:M & 9:30 P:M), ON THE SOUTHWEST CORNER OF 84TH STREET & SECOND AVENUE MEETINGS WILL TAKE PLACE EVERY FRIDAY EVENING, AFTER AUGUST 5TH, AT THE SAME TIME AND LOCATION UNTIL FURTHER NOTICE. Speakers will be James H. Madole, Director of the NRP; Robert Burros, Orange County Chairman of the NRP; and Edward Cassidy, Party Secretary.

SOME VITAL ISSUES TO BE DISCUSSED ON AUGUST 5TH:

1. The NRP opposes the plan devised by Red Jewish intellectuals to forcibly bus your White kids from Yorkville into the crime-ridden slums of Harlem to attend broken down schools without proper sanitary facilities while the illegitimate human refuse of the Black ghettos are poured into beautiful, modern schools in Yorkville PAID FOR BY WHITE TAXPAYERS! Lindsay sends his children to strictly segregated PRIVATE SCHOOLS but unfortunate low income Whites risk their childrens' lives SO THAT LINDSAY CAN GAIN BLACK VOTES. We also object to low income White families in Yorkville being forced into racially-integrated CITY HOUSING PROJECTS so that luxury apartments can be erected for wealthy Jews and the political prostitutes that serve them.

2. The NRP opposes the plan, which originated in the Communist Party platform of 1935, calling for a "CIVILIAN REVIEW BOARD" dominated by racial minorities with the highest crime rate in the USA. Lindsay has chosen the Russian Jew, Algernon Black, a former official of the left-wing WORKERS DEFENSE LEAGUE and a leader in the NAACP, TO HEAD THIS IMPARTIAL BOARD. EVERY SINGLE MEMBER OF LINDSAY'S PROPOSED BOARD HAS BEEN CONNECTED WITH LEFT-WING "CIVIL RIOTS" AGITATION. We might as well place Al Capone and John Dillinger in charge of police

COME TO 84th STREET AND SECOND AVENUE IN YORKVILLE ON FRIDAY EVENING, AUGUST 5TH, AT 7:30 P:M (AND EACH FRIDAY THEREAFTER). Bring every White patriot with you to hear Madole. LETS FIGHT BLACK POWER WITH MILITANT WHITE POWER. Write for sample literature or send contributions to back up your White fighters to:

National Renaissance Party, Box 10, 127 West 83rd Street, New York 24, NY

Figure 14.3 Neo-Nazi rally in Yorkville against the new CCRB on August 5, 1966.

Source: Algernon D. Black Papers, Rare Book and Manuscript Library, Columbia University Library.

Figure 14.4 "News" from the National Renaissance Party, a far-right, white supremacist organization headquartered in New York City.

Source: Algernon D. Black Papers, Rare Book and Manuscript Library, Columbia University Library.

race, which did not look that different from what many white New Yorkers believed. The organization as a whole, and its public persona, may have been extreme, but to many white Americans, not all of its ideas were. As much as people like William F. Buckley Jr. might sniff and chuckle when others pointed out the support of such organizations, the PBA and its more mainstream allies spent far more time attacking those who favored keeping the new board than they did denouncing fascism enthusiasts who supported them. The PBA and the far right utilized much of the same rhetoric and imagery, specifically communism, race, and gender, with the extremist groups' lack of a tether allowing them to be as blunt as they wished.

Review board proponents responded by stepping up their efforts. The mayor gave an address in which he described the battle to keep his board intact as "perhaps the most important fight I have ever seen." Lindsay said he was "appalled to discover, after passage of many civil rights bills, that many of the wonderful liberals are slightly doctrinaire, it appears. . . . History has seen before established liberals not smart enough to see the importance of crucial fights. The result is that we are set back for many years." Commissioner Leary went on the offensive against the PBA, putting himself in an awkward position. Taking aim at the anti–review board campaign's major claim, Leary said, "The suggestion has been made . . . that the existence of a civilian review board reduces the effectiveness of the police and thereby threatens the safety of the people of New York," and then flatly stated, "This suggestion is totally without foundation." As commissioner, Leary could point out in September, "The review board has been in operation now for some three months. During that time there has been absolutely no discernible rise in crime, nor has there been any discernible reduction in arrests." All sixteen local branches of the NAACP in the city united to coordinate a campaign in favor of the board, committing to "hold meetings, distribute literature, make door to door contacts, utilize sound trucks and conduct a consistent educational campaign until Election Day, November 8."[12]

With only a month to go, Lindsay campaigned to such an extent that it superseded his other priorities and duties. The mayor was now spending nine hours a day, from 3 PM until midnight, on the streets doing walking tours for the board. He was often met with hostile shouts: "Go back to City Hall," "Why do you always kowtow to the colored?," and "Talk in Bedford-Stuyvesant," are just a few. Lindsay gave a Sunday morning address on October 16, at St. George's Episcopal Church, on Sixteenth Street at Stuyvesant Square. Rector Edward O. Miller, the church's spiritual leader, began by arguing there is no conflict between religion and politics, saying, "Everything is political. . . . You can't really be alive today as a religious person without constantly confronting the political." He then listed the church's heritage of outspoken righteousness on such issues as slavery, labor disputes, a woman's right to birth control, and pacifism during World War II, asking his congregation, "Was that politics or religion?" Miller implored his congregation to support the board: "The policeman, with screeching sirens, flashing red lights, handcuffs hanging from his belt, visible bullets and a gun, and the right to force one in humiliation apart from family and friends into a stationhouse about which horrible stories have been told, often seems the most frightening, visible omnipresent threat to the liberty of those who have no one to speak for them."[13]

The mayor followed and thanked the rector and congregation for allowing him to speak, expressing his belief that the review board was a moral issue. Lindsay then explained how the board functioned, pointing out it had been

Figure 14.5 Mayor John Lindsay speaks at St. George's Cathedral in support of his reformed Civilian Complaint Review Board on October 16, 1966, three weeks before the referendum.

Source: Algernon D. Black Papers, Rare Book and Manuscript Library, Columbia University Library.

accepting complaints, the "vast majority" from white New Yorkers; making investigations; and holding hearings since July. The new CCRB, finding 89 percent of all complaints either lacked evidence or were the results of misunderstandings, had been deciding a higher proportion of the remainder in favor of the police than its predecessor had, giving Lindsay the opportunity to describe it as "the best protection and shield that a police officer could possibly have." In conclusion, Mayor Lindsay averred that the proposed charter amendment's wording would "virtually cut off your elected political leadership from any voice at all in the administration and performance control of our 28,000-man police force." If the anti–review board forces were successful, Lindsay warned, people would look back years later and query, "How in heaven's name did we permit this to happen?" The answer, said the mayor, would be that "fear set in."[14]

The various groups trying to save Lindsay's board were holding rallies and speaking engagements at a furious rate, trying to drum up support for the board however they could. Chief Inspector Garelik and Assistant Chief Inspector Sealy spoke at these rallies, along with the chairman of the city's Commission on Human Rights, William H. Booth; Senator Kennedy; Mayor Lindsay; and many others. Booth led several voter registration–themed marches through places like Bedford-Stuyvesant and Corona, Queens, as part of a concerted effort to get Puerto Rican and African American New Yorkers to register to vote. On Saturday, October 22, Lindsay appeared at five separate rallies between 4:15 PM and 5:35 PM, from Seventy-Second Street up to 110th Street, with such figures as Congressman William Ryan; Councilman Theodore Weiss, who had introduced CCRB reform legislation in 1964; and several state senators and assemblymen. Senator Kennedy declared the board a national issue: "The eyes of the country are focused on New York." Should the board go down, "it will have a major effect throughout the country and will set back the cause of civil rights and progressive government."[15]

During this intensive campaigning, review board advocates were picking up additional supporters, such as the National Maritime Union and small civic and neighborhood organizations. Eighty-six Catholic priests from Brooklyn and Queens signed a statement declaring their support for the board, proffering, "The idea that the Civilian Complaint Review Board would make a policeman choose to disregard his professional oath as an officer of the law is an insult to his integrity." Larger allies were still signing on as well, including the United Federation of Teachers and nine groups representing a total of 1.5 million Jews. The same week, lawyers for one of Roy Wilkins's nephews, a fifteen-year-old boy from the Washington Heights section of Upper Manhattan, filed a $250,000 lawsuit against the NYPD for allegedly beating and kicking him while handcuffed in a police station, throwing him down stairs, and having him forcibly committed to Bellevue Hospital's psychiatric ward, where he was bound to a wheelchair.[16]

Meanwhile, the PBA was conducting a truck tour with "go-go girls" dancing on the back to convince people to vote for their amendment. Spending several hours traveling through various sections of Brooklyn on October 23, the vehicle featured a combination of dancing women, Jewish folk songs, and speakers denouncing Mayor Lindsay. PBA President Cassese told a group of people, "It's a shame that with a stroke of the pen the mayor of the City of New York would nullify your police protection." One campaign worker tried in vain to explain to an elderly man in a mixture of English and Yiddish that a vote of "yes" meant "no" on the review board. When the man was still confused, the worker declared, "It's that Lindsay," blaming the mayor for the confusing vote the PBA had intentionally set up, in which voting affirmatively meant you were against the board. When a young woman favoring the board asked Cassese for "facts and figures" to support his claims, she was denounced as a communist and was asked, "Comrade, where's your hammer and sickle?" One day earlier, police had arrested a National Maritime Union official driving a pro–review board sound truck in the Bronx, claiming he had no permit, a charge the driver disputed.[17]

The ICCACRB, with the PBA's support, continued with its media blitz. Cole Fischer Rogow, Inc., a minor advertising agency, curated a series of advertisements. One minute-long commercial featured Michael Murphy, the former police commissioner, and Cassese speaking directly to the audience. Another was the film version of its earlier print advertisement featuring the lone white woman emerging from the subway onto a darkened street. There was a third focusing on the aftermath of an urban uprising. There was also a series of ten-second spots with comments from New Yorkers "concerned with safety in the streets." The campaign's final television spot showed "hoodlum types (12 or 15) from the waist down, flashes of chains, tipping over ashcans, a gun for a second and a switchblade for a second. Not threatening any person, just a threat to the community." This was from the company's president, Arthur A. Fischer. Thirty advertising agencies and people involved with the industry took out a large advertisement in the *New York Times* excoriating Cole Fischer Rogow for producing the ad, with one executive declaring, "This type of advertising has no business in the profession, if we are to be a profession." FAIR, on the other hand, printed dry pamphlets using statistics such as the number of complaints dismissed and the fact that three policemen sat on the panel to explain why the review board was not destroying the city's police.[18]

If you knew the facts you'd vote NO to save the Civilian Review Board

Here are THE FACTS:

1. **NEW YORK CITY HAS A CIVILIAN REVIEW BOARD AND IT WORKS:** The new civilian review board has been in operation since July and functioned smoothly and effectively throughout this past summer.

2. **FAIR AND EQUAL TREATMENT:** The Civilian Review Board guarantees fair and equal treatment for all New Yorkers—citizen and police officers alike. Under the present Civilian Review Board complaints are reviewed by an impartial board of four distinguished civilians and three top cops. This is the review board we are fighting to keep.

3. **BETTER UNDERSTANDING:** In cities across the nation, the cry of "police brutality" has been used to stir discontent and divisiveness and to exploit the tension of the ghettos. But this summer, New York City's new Civilian Review Board played a significant role in bringing unprecedented understanding between members of the Police Department and people of the ghetto and clearly demonstrated that there is no longer any reason for anyone to take his grievances to the streets since the new Board guarantees a fair hearing to all.

4. **REDUCE CRIME AND IMPROVE PROTECTION:** This is precisely what happened in Philadelphia. Eight years ago, advocates of good government created a Civilian Review Board in Philadelphia. Today, Philadelphia has the lowest crime rate and the best rate of solving crimes of any major city in the United States. It has made the policeman's job easier and improved police protection.

5. **THE POLICE COMMISSIONER HAS FINAL AUTHORITY:** Under the new Civilian Review Board, only the Police Commissioner can prefer charges against a member of the Police force; only the Commissioner can order a Department Trial; only the Police Commissioner has the authority to pass judgment on a member of the force; and only the Commissioner can place the charges on the Police officer's record.

6. **BROADEST SUPPORT IN HISTORY:** Among the thousands of distinguished New Yorkers and prominent civic organizations supporting the retention of the new Civilian Review Board are Senators Javits and Kennedy, Mayor Lindsay, Council President Frank D. O'Connor, Governor Rockefeller, Franklin D. Roosevelt, Jr., Borough Presidents Herman Badillo and Percy Sutton, Morris Abram, Herbert Brownell, Theodore Kheel, A. Philip Randolph, The Association of the Bar of the City of New York, The Catholic Interracial Council, The Citizens Union, The City Club, The American Jewish Congress, The Protestant Council of New York, the ADA, CDV, The World Journal Tribune, New York Times and New York Post.

7. **WHO IS AGAINST IT?** The Conservative Party, the John Birch Society, and the PBA.

These are all the FACTS we need to know! How About You?

Vote NO on the PBA Proposition
Vote NO on the Conservative Party Proposition

Don't Let Them Destroy the Civilian Review Board!

FAIR, Federated Associations for Impartial Review • The Governor Clinton Hotel 371 Seventh Avenue, NYC

Figure 14.6 Factual campaign literature in favor of keeping the Civilian Complaint Review Board, from Federated Associations for Impartial Review, 1966.

Source: Algernon D. Black Papers, Rare Book and Manuscript Library, Columbia University Library.

Sinister Motive?

Less than two weeks before voters were to decide the issue, legal analysts pronounced the discovery of a "sleeper clause" within the PBA's amendment that posed a potential threat to basic democratic rights. While there had been two separate questions scheduled to be on the ballot, one from the PBA and another from the Conservative Party, the Conservative Party had its initiative removed so that voters would not have to vote on two similar amendments. The part of the PBA's measure in question read, "Neither the Mayor, the Police Commissioner, nor any other officer of the City of New York shall have the power to authorize any person, agency, board or group to receive, to investigate, to hear or to require or to recommend action upon, civilian complaints against members of the Department." The Association of the Bar of the City of New York, taking the unusual step of giving a public position on an issue, claimed the language could "virtually insulate the Police Department" from city investigations into matters that were wholly unrelated to civilian review, such as bribery, corruption, and other assorted illegal activities in which police had historically taken part.[19]

The association believed that, if implemented, the proposed alteration of the city charter provided the NYPD with the power to prevent most of the rest of the city government from investigating it and its officers. This referendum, then, could hamstring the mayor, the City Commission on Human Rights, the City Council, and the commissioner of investigation, who had jurisdiction over all city departments, rendering the department exempt from official municipal scrutiny. The potential limits on power would be "wholly contrary to our fundamental governmental principle of checks and balances." In its findings on the review board and upcoming referendum, the group wrote:

> The proposal could constitute a substantial restructuring of investigative powers and virtually insulate the Police Department alone among city agencies, from scrutiny by other official bodies. Such privileged status for any agency, and especially one which exercises such vital powers over the public's daily activities, is wholly contrary to our fundamental governmental principle of checks and balances.

Samuel I. Rosenman, the organization's former president and counsel to presidents Franklin Roosevelt and Harry Truman, warned "some aspects of the secret police methods of past and present totalitarian governments" were possible outcomes.[20]

Arnold Fraiman, the commissioner of investigation, agreed, declaring the PBA was "asking the voter to build a wall of immunity around the police of New York—to grant them what is accorded no law enforcement body in the country, not even the F.B.I. or the C.I.A." Senator Kennedy expounded upon the last part of Fraiman's point, speaking of his experiences as U.S. attorney general and working extensively with the civilian leadership of the Department of Defense. As Lindsay viewed the recent development, "We are no longer talking about complaints of brutality and discourtesy. We are speaking of the entire breadth of citizen grievances, including graft and corruption." The normally composed mayor, already stirred, became even more emotional as he attested, "It is time for those who oppose the Civilian Review Board to decide whether they are nonetheless willing to go all the way—whether they are willing to let the Police Department of this city become a law unto itself." The PBA, for its part, emphatically denied it had any such intentions, claiming it was only interested in wiping out the review board.[21] The discovery of this alleged sleeper clause did not wake up enough voters.

Defeat

For all the effort those struggling to keep Lindsay's board intact exerted, they lost by a landslide on November 8. The hybrid Civilian Complaint Review Board was destroyed, 1,307,738 votes to 768,492, a difference of nearly 540,000. Only in Manhattan did voters choose to keep the board, 234,485 to 168,391. It was a bloodbath in every other borough, with individuals going against the board by two to one or more. In Staten Island, it was nearly five to one. While some of the many voting districts within each county of the city voted for the board's continuation, the rest of the districts in each borough overwhelmed them. Lindsay, with the defeat weighing heavily upon him, gave a midnight press conference at Gracie Mansion, where he cited "emotion, misunderstanding and fear" as responsible for the board's death. When questioned as to whether the decision was a rebuke of his leadership, he could only muster, "I don't know. I have no idea at all. It's irrelevant."[22]

Norman Frank characterized the victory as "a mandate to create and pursue a meaningful program for the furtherance of understanding between the community and the police." Frank said those who believed in either an independent review board or one of the hybrid versions should move on and "join hands in a citywide effort to promote cooperation and understanding at all levels." He vowed the PBA would "devote the same energy and fervor" it expended in its campaign against the board to "restore the confidence of minority groups" in the NYPD. It is unclear that anyone, including Frank, believed what he was saying. Cassese, as he explained in his victory speech at the Sheraton-Atlantic at Broadway and Thirty-Fourth, saw "eight million winners," referring to the number of New Yorkers, declaring, "Thank God we saved this city." Effusive, he also claimed to have saved the nation and quoted Abraham Lincoln twice, including the last line of the Gettysburg Address, in which Lincoln proclaims that government of, by, and for the people will not perish from the earth. Outside, someone stole attendees' fur coats from the coat check room.[23]

As a *New York Times* headline crudely stated the next day, "Board's Defeat Elates Police, Saddens Negroes." New York's African American voters had supported the board overwhelmingly, as had Puerto Rican voters. The article described "Bitter laughter, deep hurt, cynical shrugs, forebodings of violence," and "a feeling that once again the white man had turned his back on the black man" as sentiments widely held in places like Harlem and Bedford-Stuyvesant. Dozens of Black NYPD officers, working with the NAACP, including William Johnson, the Guardians Association president, would soon sue the PBA for spending their dues payments in a manner that the plaintiffs characterized as illegal. Johnson said the PBA had "taken the money of Negro and Puerto Rican policemen and engaged themselves in a racist and divisive campaign." By the end of the year, they had conditionally agreed to withdraw their suit, after Theodore Kheel had offered to arbitrate the dispute.[24]

The board was dead, and the city had no recourse. Two weeks later, Commissioner Howard Leary appointed a new all-police board, including two holdovers from Lindsay's board, Franklin Thomas and Edward McCabe. The other three were white men. The previous executive director, Harold Baer Jr., stayed on as well. Leary also appointed forty-five police officers, ranging in rank from those walking a beat to Assistant Chief Inspector Sealy, to fifteen advisory panels charged with reviewing reports and making recommendations to the renewed all-police board.[25]

For their last gathering, Algernon Black hosted all of his former board colleagues for dinner at his apartment on West Seventy-First Street the night after the election.[26]

Conclusion

Lindsay and FAIR had had little chance of victory. Though they received the editorial support of the *New York Amsterdam News, New York Times, New York Post, New York World Herald Tribune,* several radio stations, and every television station in the city that commented on the board, it did little for them. The top of the police department—Leary, Garelik, Sealy—gave public defenses of and support for the board. Leary was from Philadelphia, but the other two were career NYPD men who had worked their way up from the beat, veterans with decades of experience. Garelik told an interviewer on the radio station WMCA that the board would protect officers, citing the high percentage of complaints

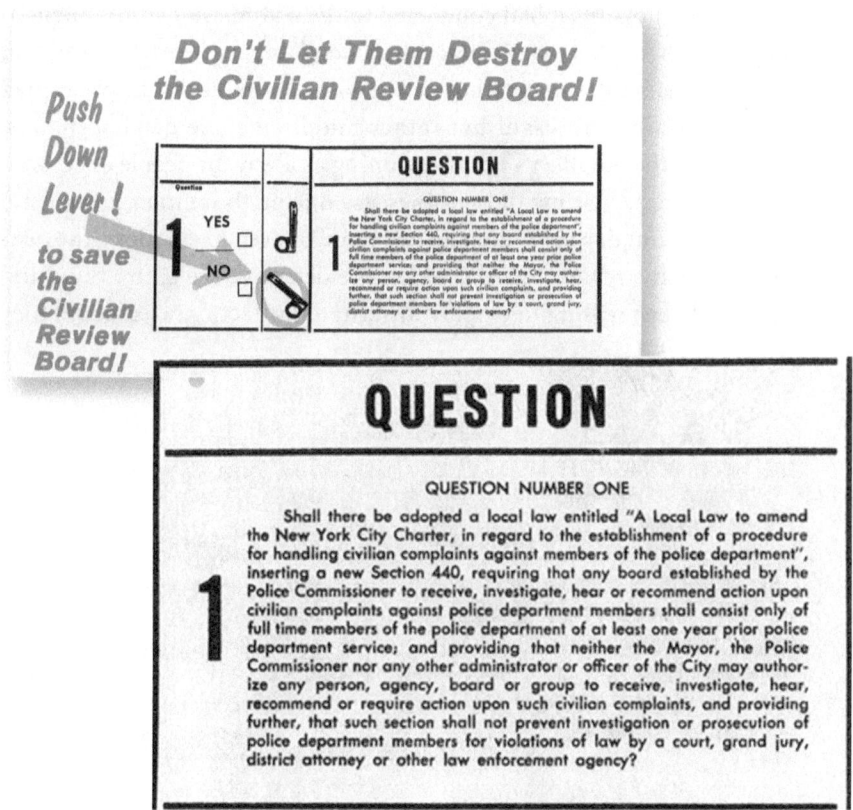

Figure 14.7 Part of FAIR's guide to voting in the referendum.

Source: John Vliet Lindsay Papers (MS 592), Manuscripts and Archives, Yale University Library.

determined to be unsubstantiated or minor, and provide "the community with a safety valve for its real or imagined grievances against the police."[27]

The PBA and Independent Citizens Committee Against Civilian Review Boards outspent them by a huge margin, started their campaign earlier, had a more focused message, and were willing to engage in emotional appeals to fear and racism. They were much more coordinated and never wasted time with infighting. FAIR, however, was a motley coalition of groups that had often only uneasily gotten along in the past, if they had interacted at all. Most of the groups in FAIR were fighting for something in which they did not even really believe. They wanted an independent board, but political realities forced them to struggle for Lindsay's board or end up with nothing at all.

FAIR's campaign was mostly based in logic, facts, and rationale. It argued that in its four months of operation, the board had only seen fit to forward four cases out of 193 complaints it had completed to the commissioner for potential departmental trial. It noted that 60 percent of complainants were white and that the bulk of complainants, since it began operation, were not from places like Harlem and Bedford-Stuyvesant but rather middle-income neighborhoods, which meant that the board was not functioning as a way for people of color to lash out at the police.[28] Crime did not increase during those months, nor did arrests go down.[29] But dry facts often do not stand up well to emotion. The people trying to save the review board were on the defensive the entire time, and even if they had been willing to employ unscrupulous tactics, what could they

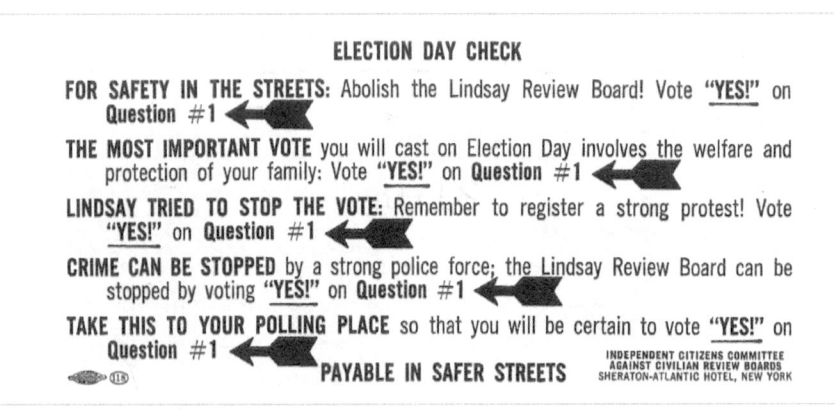

Figure 14.8 Part of the ICCACRB's guide to voting in the referendum, framed in much more sensational terms.

Source: John Vliet Lindsay Papers (MS 592), Manuscripts and Archives, Yale University Library.

have really done, attacked the police and told people they should fear arbitrary violence? Such a strategy would only have helped the PBA because it would have provided justification for the PBA's slander of "cop-haters" as comprising the bulk of the board's supporters. FAIR did veer into replicating PBA/ICCACRB tactics with its "Do New Yorkers Want a Police State?" flier, featuring a photograph of white policemen on one side and on the other expounding upon the notion that "This Hidden 'Sleeper Clause' Could Turn New York Into a Police State." In general, FAIR and its allies went to pains to praise the NYPD, speaking of the great majority of officers as doing their jobs and doing them well but citing the board as necessary to investigate objectively the few problematic individuals sure to emerge in a force of more than 27,000.[30]

What were those who voted against the board, many of whom were working-class outer-borough white people, voting for in their minds? The police and law and order, as well as perceived class solidarity with the police. What were they voting against? Crime; communism; "cop-haters"; "minority groups with their whims and their gripes and shouting"; liberalism; Mayor Lindsay, Senator Kennedy, and Senator Javits, all of whom were men of rather substantial means; CORE; the NAACP; Jews; and so on. Many saw Algernon Black, a man of Jewish descent who had devoted his life to social justice and progressive causes, as the embodiment of much of what they feared. Mayor Wagner recognized Black in 1963 with an award for "distinguished citizenship," declaring he had "demonstrated in the area of youth work, civil rights, religion and civic-mindedness, the moral, intellectual and community-minded qualities of a selfless and inspired leader and earned thereby, through 40 years of devoted service, the appreciation and gratitude of the people of New York." Apparently not all of them.[31]

As for those casting their ballots to preserve Lindsay's panel? They were voting for civil rights, progress, civil liberties, good government, and fairness. They were voting against police excess, racism, and conservatism. But those voting to abolish the board had more compelling motivations, and there were many more of them.

As Aryeh Neier of the NYCLU opined in the aftermath, "When the concept of race or civil rights attaches to a referendum, it cannot win." While civilian review was a matter relevant to civil rights, it was much more centrally related to civil liberties. However, both sides made the referendum about civil rights, and it is true that most civil rights measures have come into effect without voter approval. If the Civil Rights Act of 1964 or the Voting Rights Act were left up to the electorate, they would not have become law when they did. Those opposed to the review board tirelessly connected its existence to the advancement of the civil rights movement, which they portrayed negatively. FAIR and Lindsay also said the board was a civil rights issue. Though they meant it in a positive way and saw the continued progress of the liberal, interracial African American civil rights movement as good, they failed to understand that they were confirming the PBA's accusations. FAIR could point out that white New Yorkers filed most complaints, the bulk were dismissed, and then less than 3 percent of those left were found against the officer in question, but this truth did not make much of an impression on opposed voters. By 1966, many white voters had come to view the civil rights movement negatively.[32]

Once African Americans won full legal equality and a restoration of their constitutional rights with the Voting Rights Act in 1965, many white people, even those who had previously considered themselves supporters of the civil rights movement, saw no need for continued civil rights agitation, much less Black Power. Many northern urban white residents conceived of racial inequality as a contest in which resources were available in fixed quantities, so Black victory meant white loss. They viewed struggles for housing, education, and economic opportunities as attempts to take from them, and this perspective was certainly prominent in New York City, as Jonathan Rieder shows in his study of the Canarsie section of Brooklyn. These residents were not sympathetic to the fact that African Americans had historically been denied access to the same economic and social structures that had allowed so many European immigrant groups to achieve class mobility. Seeing liberals as lacking the ability and commitment to sufficiently address inequality, many Black New Yorkers took increasingly militant approaches to obtain economic justice and security. Following the November 1966 referendum, racial hostility and resentment in the city would intensify for decades.

EPILOGUE
Insufficient Funds

We are not now helping the American people deal with the real questions because we don't want to debate the hard things. We don't want to face the profound economic problems in the face of all the nation which are here. We do not want to face the revolutionary concept of tearing down ghettoes because it's costly and it requires a political movement to do it.

—BAYARD RUSTIN

Americans tend to like a history that is progressive. We prefer one that is always getting better, in which we right past wrongs. Sometimes we stumble, but always in the service of moving forward. And this view of history is sometimes true—slavery ended, women can vote, and same-sex marriage is the law of the land. These were monumental accomplishments. But if something is only sometimes true, it is not really true, and it is not accurate. These victories came through great struggle, not because people in power suddenly realized that what was happening was wrong. Examining any one of these achievements quickly reveals serious problems with this triumphal version of history, perhaps none more so than slavery.

Slavery did not simply end, and it certainly did not end because we as a country agreed it was immoral. The enslaved had always resisted bondage, and a fervent, radical abolitionist movement grew in the three decades before the Civil War. Most white Americans never supported any action or policy to end slavery. The federal government finally destroyed the institution after a group of states provoked and fought a war to secure its perpetual growth and expansion, as well as to destroy the country. Before the Civil War, slavery had not been on its way out, either. The numbers of the enslaved grew enormously over the course of the first half of the nineteenth century, and were likely to continue to do so, reaching just under four million by 1860. Slavery had expanded westward, with rancorous debates about its spread emerging with each new piece of territory purchased, seized, or conquered. And for many white people, not just in the South, the end of slavery was something to be feared, not welcomed.

The abolition of slavery made America a better, more just place. But as A. Philip Randolph pointed out, the country had little appetite to integrate freedpeople into society. Reconstruction followed the Civil War, and while rife with problems, it was a time of great promise for African Americans. The nation had an opportunity to reset its relationship with race but rather quickly decided not to. For a precious few years, Black men voted and held office in remarkable numbers. But after about a decade, the federal government abandoned Reconstruction, leaving African Americans at the mercy of the individual southern states. Jim Crow, wholesale disfranchisement, lynching, and widespread forced and coerced labor ensued, to no one's surprise. Though things got better when slavery ended and while the federal government was willing to actively pass and enforce Reconstruction laws, policies, and constitutional amendments, afterward they fell off a cliff—and stayed at the bottom for decades. In the middle of the twentieth century, activists finally compelled the various branches of the federal government to muster the political will to enforce the rights that Reconstruction had afforded; this was not fully accomplished until 1965, with the passage of the since-dismantled Voting Rights Act. It is not possible to look at the last 150 or so years of American history and honestly see an upward trajectory for those descended from enslaved people.[1]

New problems have emerged along the way, problems we have created, marking definite regression. Climate change and the Great Pacific Garbage Patch are transnational scourges, recent contributions from industrialization and technology. Such situations have gotten worse with time, and they will continue to do so unless people in power decide these things are worth fixing. In America, opioid abuse and addiction seem to have no limits. When I was in primary and secondary school, getting shot in class never occurred to me. Now active-shooter drills are part of the curriculum. Mass shootings happen in houses of worship, grocery stores, and shopping malls, yet there is insufficient political will to do anything substantive about this problem. In 1964, there were about two hundred thousand Americans incarcerated, a figure that stayed flat for the next decade; today, the number is 2.3 million, made up overwhelmingly of people who are poor, Black, Brown, or some combination. Sometimes, things get worse.

In New York City in the 1950s and 1960s, almost everything was getting worse for African Americans. Some were pulling away into the middle class and beyond, moving into all-white suburbs or heavily white parts of Manhattan, but most were not. They instead saw schools get more segregated, employment less stable, and housing more separate and unequal. Racial inequality grew, despite the many civil rights victories the national movement was winning at the federal level. The national movement tended to focus on the South, where discrimination was blatant and explicit. Activists had a much harder time dealing with the subtler but no less damaging manifestations of racism in the North and West. Racism's effects were everywhere, but its perpetrators were nowhere to be found. Despite decades of organizing, voting, petitioning, demonstrating, pleading, sitting in, boycotting, and suing, nothing seemed to work. African Americans and their allies were unable to prevent their fortunes from declining, even though those running the city said they were on their side. People got tired of this. They left the South, they followed the rules, they worked hard, they sent their kids to school, but they got nowhere. Over time, many of them were getting less than nowhere and saw their children facing an even worse future. What else could be done?

Whether your reverend of reference is Dr. King or Theodore Parker, the idea that the moral arc of the universe is long yet bends toward justice is a popular one. It can indeed bend toward justice, but it needs to be bent with great force. Dr. King knew this better than anyone. Ending slavery involved roughly 750,000 dead soldiers, as well as some undetermined number of dead civilians, the physical annihilation of vast amounts of southern property and infrastructure, and billions of dollars spent. The full force of the federal government, including multiple conscriptions, was necessary to destroy the nation's peculiar institution. This was not a gradual bending toward justice; it was using all available means to push the arc aside and render some measure of justice immediately. While the Civil War did not begin as a war to end slavery, it became one, and was successful, but at an enormous cost.

I can understand Dr. King using the concept as a movement-building tool, a phrase that could help keep morale high, but it has long outlived that purpose, winding up sewn into a rug in the Obama White House. I can also understand wanting to stay hopeful during dark days and trying to give other people something they can hold. Ultimately, the moral arc of the universe bends whichever way the people in charge decide it will, and this is far too often away from justice.

The people in charge also can be replaced, persuaded, and pushed, but the people choosing them have to want justice, have to choose them because they are at least open to pursuing justice, and have to be willing to keep the pressure on. They also have to be able to vote, at a minimum.

Learning

The events I discuss in this book are over fifty years old. How far has the moral arc bent since then? Not far enough, unfortunately.

> Some of the best public elementary schools in New York City are in Community School District 3, on Manhattan's West Side. At those schools, the vast majority of children pass the annual state tests, gifted and talented programs buzz with activity, and special programs attract promising young musicians or families who want a progressive approach to education. But none of those schools are in Harlem.
>
> In District 3's Harlem schools, there are no gifted and talented programs. Of the six elementary schools there where students take the state tests, only one comes close to the citywide passing rates of 38 percent in reading and 36 percent in math. At one school, only 6 percent of third- through eighth-grade students passed the most recent math tests . . .
>
> Unlike in many parts of the city, in District 3—which runs from 59th Street to 122nd Street along Manhattan's western flank, then takes a dogleg into Harlem—people from different races and socioeconomic levels often live near one another. The district's schools, however, are sharply divided by race and income, and diverge just as sharply in their levels of academic achievement.
>
> Nowhere is that tale of two districts clearer than in Harlem.[2]

This is from a *New York Times* article published in January 2017. It could have been from January 1964. The mayor at the time, Bill de Blasio, had criticized previous mayoral administrations, going back decades, for not having done enough to address school segregation, though he preferred to not use the terms "segregation" and "integration" in public. He also blamed housing segregation for much of the educational apartheid students experience, just as so many of his predecessors and their appointees did, into the Wagner years.[3] His first schools chancellor, Carmen Fariña, saw school segregation as a problem of branding; that is, that schools were doing an ineffective job in selling themselves to parents across racial, ethnic, and class lines. Later in her tenure, she cited school segregation as a priority, but one for which local districts would have to devise solutions.[4] Her replacement, Richard Carranza, saw educational segregation as a major problem and assumed office with a new plan to combat racial inequality in the schools. After three years, he resigned in February 2021, with segregation almost completely unchanged.[5] Nearly sixty years after a major grassroots campaign to force the city to desegregate its schools, officials were still just planning to do so, as they were then.

In 1965, Kenneth Clark estimated that without the city making sincere efforts to reduce segregation in its schools, the public school population in 1980 would be three-quarters Black and Puerto Rican, and closer to 90 percent in Manhattan.[6] Forty years after his predicted future, he was still close, though his racial and ethnic proportions did not capture today's ethnic and racial diversity. Clark could not have foreseen the large numbers of immigrants soon to come from throughout the world, especially Asia, who would arrive as a result of the Immigration and Nationality Act of 1965, which eliminated the old quota system that kept people throughout Asia out of the United States.

For the 2019–2020 school year, the city's Department of Education reported that its schools were 40.6 percent Hispanic, 24.9 percent Black, 16.3 percent Asian, 15.1 percent white, and 3.1 percent classified outside of those groups. And in Manhattan, public school students were 44.2 percent Hispanic, 22.7 percent Black, 17 percent white, 11.8 percent Asian, and 4.3 percent students who identify otherwise. Across the city, 72.6 percent of public school students were living in poverty.[7] Despite this great diversity, the city has operated the most segregated school system in the country for years.[8] In 2014, 85 percent of Black students and 75 percent of Latinx students attended schools that were less than 10 percent white, whether they were zoned by neighborhood or not.[9] The city's eight specialized public high schools, to which students are admitted by exceptional performance on one examination, which can only be taken twice, are highly segregated, with its most selective, Stuyvesant High School, offering ten spots out of 760 to Black students for the 2020–2021 school year. Offers to Black students had been declining, from thirteen in the 2017–2018 school year, ten the next year, and seven for 2019–2020. Black and Latinx students make up just 11 percent of the eight testing schools' student bodies. Attending one of the eight testing high schools has a much greater impact on a college application than having graduated from one of the other more than five hundred public high schools in the city. Such is the reality of America, particularly in the North and West—diversity and segregation go hand in hand.[10]

Living

Residential segregation is an enduring problem in much of America and especially in New York City. While measures of segregation have fallen over the decades, the city's metrics of separation are significantly higher than the national average. New York is one of the most diverse cities in the nation but also one of the most segregated. More than 80 percent of Black or white New Yorkers would have to move to achieve an equal racial distribution in the city. This number, known as the dissimilarity index, is twenty points above the country's mean. The Hispanic-white figure is around 65 percent, while the Asian-white number is about 50 percent.[11] This segregation continues to have profound effects on life outcomes, starting with education and health, as Black and Latinx neighborhoods tend to be closer to sources of pollution, such as waste-disposal sites. Students in these areas still overwhelmingly receive inferior educations from the very start of schooling, putting them at increasing disadvantage as they move from primary to middle to secondary school.

Working

In early 2020, the Black unemployment rate nationally was lower than it had ever been, at 5.8 percent, but was still nearly twice the white unemployment rate, just as it was in the 1960s.[12] Unemployment rates in the city for Black workers were more than twice those of their white counterparts, with Black men unemployed 2.5 times the rate of white men. American workers' wages were increasing, including those of Black workers, but a substantial wage gap persisted. While the margins had narrowed, the Black-white wage gap once again widened after 2000. In 2020, Black workers across all classes and industries were earning less than their white counterparts than in 1979. In New York City, median wages in 2016 were $74,288 for white men, $60,724 for white women, $45,076 for Black men, and $42,431 for Black women.[13] On the whole, Black male workers in America were earning wages 31 percent lower than white men's; Black women's were

19 percent lower than white women's. When controlling for factors such as education, experience, and geography, Black men earned 22 percent less than white men. Black women earned 34 percent less than white men and about 12 percent less than white women and Black men. While college graduates earned more than those without bachelor's degrees, Black and white workers who finished college saw a greater pay disparity than they had forty years earlier—about 18 percent. Among the highest-paid workers, the gap was 34.7 percent.[14]

When factored out, these disparities mean that Black families were earning just over $57 to every $100 the average white family brought in and had $5 in wealth for every $100 that same white family owned.[15] These financial divides create experiential, educational, and emotional gaps for Black children, who have to grow up in a society in which their likelihood of living in a family that does as well as a comparably educated and employed white family is low because of structural factors beyond their or their parents' control. While social mobility is low in America in general, it is particularly so for African Americans. Throughout America, the parts of the country that offer white children the least likelihood for economic advancement still create better results than the places that offer the best opportunities for Black children.[16] One of the most tragic outcomes of racism and poverty is that Black babies have the least chance of any in New York City to even grow up, with an infant mortality rate three times that of white babies.[17]

And then COVID-19 hit. Black people in New York, just like in the rest of the country, were among the worst affected in every way. Their infection rates in New York City have been about the same as those of white city dwellers, but the Black death rate after nearly a year of the pandemic was about 1.8 times that of white New Yorkers. Nationally, Black people have died at a rate about 1.4 times that of white Americans.[18] In the first six months of 2020, Black life expectancy decreased by 2.7 years, compared to 0.8 for white people, a direct outcome of the pandemic.[19] African Americans are much more likely to carry several of the conditions—especially diabetes and high blood pressure—that aggravate an infection and greatly increase the likelihood of death. They also are more likely to be uninsured or underinsured and to have had negative interactions with medical professionals, resulting in medical care being something to avoid unless necessary. In this pandemic, such delays have often meant that the care came too late.[20]

While many Black workers, because of our country's structural racism and austere social policies, had no choice but to keep showing up for their newly minted "essential" and often low-wage jobs, risking infection, others—especially in food, transportation, hospitality, and retail—lost their jobs quickly. In May 2020, the Black unemployment rate hit 16.8 percent, matching a more-than-two-decade peak from March 2010, which had been the highest since January 1984.[21] Sadly, only recessions have narrowed Black-white unemployment gaps in modern history, and that is again true here. A month earlier, the Black unemployment rate was 16.7 percent, compared to 14.2 percent for white workers, but white people started to pull away in May, dropping their rate to 12.4 percent. By March 2021, the Black unemployment rate was 9.6 percent, against 5.4 percent for white people.[22]

Policing

The NYPD is still the largest municipal police force in the country, with about 36,000 officers. It is far more racially and ethnically diverse today—51 percent white, 27 percent Hispanic, 15 percent Black, 7 percent Asian, and less than 1 percent Native American. Far more women serve than fifty years ago, but their proportion is still small, at only 17 percent. One major difference is that for decades women have been able to serve in every role on the force, though they have not yet done so.[23]

The NYPD is also far less corrupt. Gone are the days when carrying bags of cash back to the stationhouse to be divvied up among all was standard practice. Precincts no longer deal heroin. The allegations of institutionalized corruption that do surface from time to time involve officers claiming they work under arrest and ticket quotas, which the state outlawed in 2010. The department and mayor have denied that such requirements exist, though evidence seems to indicate that at least some commanders have continued to use them in practice.[24]

The CCRB became 50 percent civilian in 1987, and Mayor David Dinkins succeeded in making it all civilian in 1993. The PBA was still unhappy about proposed changes to oversight and protested, most notably in its ten-thousand-strong vulgar and violent demonstration at a September 1992 City Council hearing on the bill, but it was an abortive effort, and this time, the union lost. Since Dinkins's alterations, the Civilian Complaint Review Board has been composed of thirteen civilians. The City Council selects one person from each borough, and the mayor selects five people, including the chair. None of these people can have worked in law enforcement. The police commissioner chooses three, who will have law enforcement backgrounds. The board is the largest such agency in the country, with dozens of investigators and a substantial budget. It accepts thousands of complaints a year, dismisses most of them outright, and substantiates about 10 percent. The CCRB still just makes recommendations to the commissioner, who has full authority to do as he wishes with the information. Most of the time, the commissioner, regardless of who is occupying the post, does very little, even when complaints are substantiated. He doles out lenient official reprimands and punishments, allowing the board to claim a higher number of accepted recommendations to the commissioner than ever before, appearing to increase its effectiveness.[25] The police still do their jobs.

Violent crime in the city, by most measures, had been consistently falling to new all-time lows, though the pandemic and the various calamities it unleashed have contributed to sharp increases in shootings. There were nearly half as many murders in 2019 as there were in 1963: 318 versus 563; this number jumped to 447 in 2020. Reports of rapes have decreased, but hate crimes have increased, especially against people of East Asian heritage.[26] This general reduction in crime had proceeded for almost thirty years, despite the city drastically reducing its use of stop-and-frisk, a practice to which the state granted imprimatur with a 1965 law.[27] For decades, the police practiced the on-street search of anyone who aroused an officer's suspicion; "furtive movements" or simply being in a location with a high crime rate was enough to arouse said suspicion. Consent is not a concern, because the person being searched has no right to refuse. In the first decade or so of the twenty-first century, the use of stop-and-frisk escalated sharply. Mayor Michael Bloomberg, a strong proponent of the practice, took office in 2002, and that year officers stopped and frisked 97,296 people. The figures surged to 313,523 in 2004 and to a peak of 685,724 in 2011.[28]

In 2014, the de Blasio administration, with the aid of a federal lawsuit that its predecessor's administration lost, overhauled stop-and-frisk: now officers needed to have strong suspicion of criminal activity. From 2002 through the first half of 2018, 90 percent of those who officers detained were Black or Latinx, though the city is about 45 percent white. Ninety percent were released, having been found not to be engaging in or possessing anything illegal. Put another way, every year the NYPD was stopping and frisking tens to hundreds of thousands of people who were doing nothing illegal. Nearly two decades after Bloomberg took office, the department was searching thousands of people a year, in the low five figures, the large majority of whom would not be arrested.[29] There is no evidence the practice measurably reduces crime, certainly none to justify the humiliation it perpetrates and resentment it engenders.

The police still kill people, intentionally and otherwise, in New York and all across the country, though there is no official national count of how many. Over the past decade, NYPD officers have shot and killed a varying number of people a year, ranging from about a dozen down to perhaps as few as two in 2019, though data are frustratingly hard to acquire. Nationally, best estimates indicate that the police have shot and killed about a thousand people a year in the last few years, with Black people comprising at least one-quarter of the total, though they make up only about 13 percent of the U.S. population. Latinx people average at least 15 percent of those the police shoot and kill, closer to their proportion of the population, which is about 18 percent. White people seem to be underrepresented in these figures, accounting for around 45 percent of police shooting deaths but making up 60 percent of Americans. For now, it is impossible to say how much higher any of these percentages really is, given the lack of any official reporting or data collection; there also is a number of those shot and killed whose race is unknown.[30] Of course, the police kill people by other means, such as choking, shocking, running them over with their cars, beating, and so on, and there is no accurate count of those deaths. It is not clear when or how this will end, given how aggressive and militarized policing has become, combined with the centuries-old conscious and unconscious belief in this country that Black men are inherently criminal and dangerous.

In 1964, the name of James Powell resonated around the city, regardless of one's interest in civil rights. Today, his name has been forgotten. In New York, people know Ramarley Graham and Akai Gurley, and many may remember Ousmane Zongo, Tim Stansbury, and Amadou Diallo. In recent years, many Americans would recognize names like Oscar Grant, Trayvon Martin, Eric Garner, Mike Brown, and Freddie Gray. While revising this book, the list has continued to grow—Laquan McDonald, Tamir Rice, Walter Scott, Sandra Bland, Nathaniel Pickett II, Alton Sterling, Philando Castile, Terence Crutcher, Stephon Clark, Antwon Rose, Botham Jean, Atatiana Jefferson, Breonna Taylor, Daniel Prude. There are many others. George Floyd. *George Floyd.* Overall, these victims and their families still do not have a reasonable expectation of justice. Many officers are either not charged, are acquitted, or are convicted of lesser crimes and receive much lighter sentences than other people would.

Many of the recent cases have attracted attention because of video evidence from police body and dashboard cameras and, especially, from the only tool that has really managed to exert effective leverage: the smartphone. Even then, the odds have merely been improved. Many of us have seen the footage of Eric Garner struggling to breathe—we've seen it far more than we care to. We have seen how and why he died—but the outcome? One fired officer and a $5.9 million payment to his family, more than five years later. Video forced the state of Georgia to reclassify Ahmaud Arbery's lynching at the hands of vigilantes, one of whom was former law enforcement, from justified to murder. The last five humiliating, dehumanizing, agonizing minutes of George Floyd's life will live on forever, with people able to watch a white police officer slowly, deliberately starve him of oxygen with a knee pressed into the back of his neck for nine minutes and twenty-nine seconds, well after he was dead. The smartphone helps document what happened—but, equally important, it counters police lies, such as that Walter Scott had taken his killer's Taser and the officer feared for his life, when in reality Scott was running away, unarmed, and was shot in the back, or that Floyd was resisting and just happened to experience medical distress.[31]

Ferguson burned, Baltimore burned. People paid attention, though the attention did not lead to much in the way of short-term progressive change. Minneapolis burned, and then hundreds of thousands of Americans, in a diverse coalition, demonstrably tired of the systemic murder of Black people, have gone out into the streets of every state and colony—Puerto Rico, Guam, the U.S. Virgin Islands, Samoa, and the Northern Mariana Islands—beginning in May 2020. People across the world, from Brazil and Mexico to England and Italy to Korea and Japan to Australia and New Zealand, demonstrated for their lives and in support of the struggle in America. They are adamantly determined to get white people to accept that Black lives matter; force them to confront all the ways that these lives have been written off, exploited, and discarded for centuries; and dismantle the persistent structural barriers that govern race. What was just one more snuffed Black life in America is now a global matter, giving rise to the most widespread and sustained protests in history. Politicians and pundits speak of the summer of 2020 as a "racial reckoning," but it remains to be seen what will come of it or why it will be different this time.

Things can get better, but we have to try. A critical mass of Americans tried during Reconstruction, and life for African Americans improved vastly and improbably. There were still massive strides to be made, but if you had told anyone in 1860 that in ten years slavery would be over, that the formerly enslaved would become citizens, and that the adult men among them could vote, no one, whether pro-, anti-, or indifferent to slavery, would have believed you. Black people were owning property, running businesses, serving in Congress and state legislatures, holding hundreds and hundreds of local and state offices, and going to public schools. That any of this continued for a period of years was only possible because activists, voters, and politicians forced the federal government to protect these abilities. Once it stopped, once voters walked away from Reconstruction, once politicians lost the political will, Reconstruction died a slow death over the late nineteenth century, because it was not possible for African Americans and their allies to resist ex-Confederates and neo-Confederate state and local governments on their own. We stopped trying. Hopefully, future historians will be able to write of 2020 as a year when American racial inequality began to change in substantial ways, but it will only happen if we make it.

Notes

Introduction

1. For a complete treatment of federally sponsored housing segregation, see Richard Rothstein, *The Color of Law: A Forgotten History of How Our Government Segregated America* (New York: Norton, 2017).
2. See Martha Biondi, *To Stand and Fight: The Struggle for Civil Rights in Postwar New York City* (Cambridge, MA: Harvard University Press, 2003), for a comprehensive assessment of civil rights in the city during the forties and fifties.
3. Senator Wagner was instrumental in writing the Social Security Act and sponsored the National Labor Relations Act, also known as the Wagner Act, which guaranteed private sector workers' rights to unionize, bargain collectively, and strike.
4. The SNCC's Freedom Summer was a campaign to register voters in the most repressive state in the nation, provide an education to students suffering from legal segregation, and build a new Democratic Party in the state to challenge the long-standing white supremacist organization at the Democratic National Convention in Atlantic City at the end of the summer. Within days of the campaign's initiation in June, three young activists went "missing," and their bodies were dug up six weeks later.
5. Kenneth B. Clark, *Dark Ghetto: Dilemmas of Social Power* (New York: Harper & Row, 1967), 15.
6. Max Lerner, "The Negro American and His City," in *The Conscience of the City*, ed. Martin Meyerson (New York: G. Braziller, 1970), 348.
7. *Harlem: Test for the North*, WNBC, July 26, 1964.
8. Lyndon B. Johnson, "Statement by the President Upon Making Public an FBI Report on the Recent Urban Riots," American Presidency Project, ed. Gerhard Peters and John T. Woolley, University of California, Santa Barbara, https://presidency.ucsb.edu/node/242721.
9. In May 1968, the Black local school board, headed by the unit administrator Rhody McCoy, dismissed nineteen white and mostly Jewish teachers from their district for poor performance. They were not fired but instead were to be reassigned elsewhere in the city.

In response, the city's teachers union launched a series of strikes that dragged on for months, both revealing and creating fissures in the much-vaunted Black and Jewish alliance that would result in its substantial degradation. The strikes also accelerated the process of Jewish people in the city becoming more accepted among other white New Yorkers. The city's large white middle-class population broadly backed the teachers and generally saw the issue as a racial attack on their fellow white people, which inevitably meant they would choose the side on which they perceived their best interests to be. This made an issue that was at its core about education and community power into one about Black and white. See Jerald Podair, *The Strike That Changed New York: Blacks, Whites, and the Ocean Hill–Brownsville Crisis* (New Haven, CT: Yale University Press, 2002); and Jerald Podair, "The Ocean Hill–Brownsville Crisis: New York's *Antigone*," unpublished conference paper, Gotham History Festival, October 2001, New York City.

10. Craig Steven Wilder, *A Covenant with Color: Race and Social Power in Brooklyn* (New York: Columbia University Press, 2000), 220.
11. Matthew Countryman, *Up South: Civil Rights and Black Power in Philadelphia* (Philadelphia: University of Pennsylvania Press, 2006), 7. While the only date one can put on the emergence of Black Power as a brand of activism is Stokely Carmichael's June 16, 1966, speech in Greenwood, Mississippi, Black Power was not an ideology Carmichael invented, nor was the phrase new. Black Power drew on long-standing traditions of Black self-help, Black nationalism, and Black self-defense. In 1954, the celebrated African American author Richard Wright had published an account of his time journeying through the Gold Coast, soon to become Ghana, entitled *Black Power*. Adam Clayton Powell Jr. had used the phrase in at least one speech, a commencement address at Howard University, that predates Carmichael's employment of it by several weeks. It is clear that many of the beliefs and practices that would soon come to comprise Black Power were alive in Central Harlem in 1964 and had been for decades, from the separatism of Marcus Garvey and the Nation of Islam to the self-defense of Malcolm X and Black mothers' demanding community control of local schools.
12. Black Power cannot be understood apart from the civil rights movement, just as the two cannot be understood to be the same movement. Black Power was only able to emerge through its relationships to the civil rights movement and by identifying itself against integrationist goals. As Timothy Tyson argues through the life story of the Monroe, North Carolina, NAACP leader Robert F. Williams, "'the civil rights movement' and 'the Black Power movement' emerged from the same soil, confronted the same predicaments, and reflected the same quest for African American freedom." Timothy B. Tyson, *Radio Free Dixie: Robert F. Williams and the Roots of Black Power* (Chapel Hill: University of North Carolina Press, 1999), 3. Peniel Joseph writes, "Civil rights and Black Power, while occupying distinct branches, share roots in the same historical family tree." Peniel E. Joseph, *The Black Power Movement: Rethinking the Civil Rights–Black Power Era* (New York: Routledge, 2006), 4. When Stokely Carmichael gave his famous Black Power speech in Greenwood, Mississippi, and declared he was not going to jail anymore, he wasn't angry just about being arrested, nor was he angry just with police violence. Carmichael was fed up with Black marginalization in political, economic, and social realms. He felt that groups like the SCLC and NAACP did not have the necessary goals or tactics to win freedom for Black

Americans, nor did they desire to win it quickly. Still, even Dr. King believed Black people should seek collective political and economic power as a group to secure equality. Tactically, the major differences between Black Power and integrationist ideologies were separatism versus inclusion, disciplined nonviolence as a principle versus nonviolence as one of many tools, and the speed at which freedom should be pursued. As Peniel Joseph points out, Black Power emerged out of frustrations with the mainstream civil rights movement. Peniel E. Joseph, "Black Liberation Without Apology: Rethinking the Black Power Movement," *Black Scholar* 31, no. 3 (2001): 2–19. Militants were also frustrated with the American state's failure to respond adequately to Black people's needs and demands. It is important to remember that many Black power activists came out of integrationist organizations like the Student Nonviolent Coordinating Committee and CORE. For these activists, it was their experiences in life and in their work that pushed them to militant positions. It is impossible to separate Black Power from civil rights.

13. Jonathan Rieder, *Canarsie: The Jews and Italians of Brooklyn Against Liberalism* (Cambridge, MA: Harvard University Press, 1985); Jim Sleeper, *The Closest of Strangers: Liberalism and the Politics of Race in New York* (New York: Norton, 1990); Frederick F. Siegel, *The Future Once Happened Here: New York, D.C., L.A., and the Fate of America's Big Cities* (New York: Free Press, 1997), 9; Kenneth D. Durr, *Behind the Backlash: White Working-Class Politics in Baltimore, 1940–1980* (Chapel Hill: University of North Carolina Press, 2003).

14. Paul Chevigny, *Police Power: Police Abuses in New York City* (New York: Pantheon, 1969); Marilynn S. Johnson, *Street Justice: A History of Police Violence in New York City* (Boston: Beacon, 2003); Clarence Taylor, *Fight the Power: African Americans and the Long History of Police Brutality in New York City* (New York: New York University Press, 2019).

1. Living

1. Andrew Beveridge, "An Affluent, White Harlem?," *Gotham Gazette*, August 27, 2008, https://www.gothamgazette.com/index.php/demographics/4062-an-affluent-white-harlem; Andrew Beveridge, "Gotham's Shifting Population," *Gotham Gazette*, September 2, 2008, https://www.gothamgazette.com/index.php/city/4077-harlems-shifting-population. By 1990, Central Harlem's population had declined more than 57 percent, to a low of just over one hundred thousand. Six hundred and seventy-two of them were white, according to the U.S. Census that year; Sam Roberts, "No Longer Majority Black, Harlem Is in Transition," *New York Times*, January 6, 2010; Andrew Small, "The Gentrification of Gotham," *City Lab*, April 28, 2017, https://www.citylab.com/life/2017/04/the-gentrification-of-gotham/524694/; "NYC-Manhattan Community District 10—Central Harlem PUMA, NY," *Census Reporter*, https://www.censusreporter.org/profiles/79500US3603803-nyc-manhattan-community-district-10-central-harlem-puma-ny/. As of this writing, Central Harlem is about 15 percent white; "NYC-Brooklyn Community District 3—Bedford-Stuyvesant PUMA, NY," *Census Reporter*, https://www.censusreporter.org/profiles/79500US3604003-nyc-brooklyn-community-district-3-bedford-stuyvesant-puma-ny/.

2. HARYOU, *Youth in the Ghetto: A Study of the Consequences of Powerlessness and a Blueprint for Change* (New York: Harlem Youth Opportunities Unlimited, 1964), 97; Craig Steven Wilder, *A Covenant with Color: Race and Social Power in Brooklyn* (New York: Columbia University Press, 2000), 206; U.S. Census Bureau, *Race, 1960*, socialexplorer.com/tables/C1960TractDS/R12571507; U.S. Census Bureau, *Race, 1970*, socialexplorer.com/tables/C1970/R11923477; U.S. Census Bureau, *Race, 1980*, socialexplorer.com/tables/C1980/R11923493; U.S. Census Bureau, *Race, 1990*, socialexplorer.com/tables/C1990/R11923494; U.S. Census Bureau, *Race, 2000*, www.socialexplorer.com/tables/C2000/R11923496. Prepared by Social Explorer.
3. Wayne Phillips, "3-Man Authority to Guide Housing Urged on Mayor," *New York Times*, March 10, 1960; Richard Plunz, *A History of Housing in New York City: Dwelling Type and Social Change in the American Metropolis* (New York: Columbia University Press, 1990), 268, 274. The city refused to include commercial space, which would have had the effect of reducing social isolation and alienation, at the bottoms of these public housing towers, as it wished to remain out of competition with private builders; Fred J. Cook and Gene Gleason, "The Shame of New York," *The Nation*, October 31, 1959, 277.
4. Letter from Rev. W. Eugene Houston, Chairman of the Central Harlem Housing Committee, Welfare and Health Council of New York, to Robert Olnick, March 7, 1955, Harlem Neighborhoods Association records, 1941–1978, Sc MG #364, Box 3, Folder "CHCCP Housing Committee—1955 to 1958," Manuscripts, Archives and Rare Books Division, Schomburg Center for Research in Black Culture, New York Public Library, hereafter referred to as SCRBC; "Tenants in Harlem Allege Ouster Plot," *New York Times*, February 2, 1955. Lenox Terrace still stands as a luxury rental complex, located across from the New York Public Library's Schomburg Center for Research in Black Culture, and the Olnick Organization still operates the 1,700 apartments. The first buildings were finished in 1958.
5. Carl J. Pelleck and John T. O'Grady, "Sick of Housing Alibis, Harlem Group Cracks Down," *New York Post*, January 26, 1955.
6. Joseph Kahn and Ted Poston, "Harlem Tenants Shiver Without Heat as City Departments Refuse to Act," *New York Post*, February 6, 1955.
7. Pelleck and O'Grady, "Sick of Housing Alibis, Harlem Group Cracks Down."
8. Senator Wagner was instrumental in writing the Social Security Act and sponsored the National Labor Relations Act, also known as the Wagner Act, which guaranteed private sector workers' rights to unionize, bargain collectively, and strike.
9. Barry Gottehrer, *New York City in Crisis: A Study in Depth of Urban Sickness* (New York: McKay, 1965), 16. Cook and Gleason, "The Shame of New York," 276.
10. Letter from Harris L. Present, Chairman of the City Wide Committee on Housing Relocation Problems, to Mayor Wagner, February 14, 1955, Harlem Neighborhoods Association records, 1941–1978, Sc MG #364, Box 3, Folder "CHCCP Housing Committee—1955 to 1958," SCRBC. Olnick was not removed from the project. He went on to become a major developer, building high-rise apartment buildings in New York, New Jersey, Connecticut, and Florida and garden apartments in several Southern California locations.
11. Letter from Rev. W. Eugene Houston, Chairman of the Central Harlem Housing Committee, Welfare and Health Council of New York, to Robert Olnick, February 24, 1955,

Harlem Neighborhoods Association records, 1941–1978, Sc MG #364, Box 3, Folder "CHCCP Housing Committee—1955 to 1958," SCRBC.
12. Letter from Rev. W. Eugene Houston, Chairman of the Central Harlem Housing Committee, Welfare and Health Council of New York, to Mayor Wagner, February 24, 1955, Harlem Neighborhoods Association records, 1941–1978, Sc MG #364, Box 3, Folder "CHCCP Housing Committee—1955 to 1958," SCRBC; Letter from Robert C. Weaver to Rev. W. Eugene Houston, Chairman of the Central Harlem Housing Committee, Welfare and Health Council of New York, April 21, 1955, Harlem Neighborhoods Association records, 1941–1978, Sc MG #364, Box 3, Folder "CHCCP Housing Committee—1955 to 1958," SCRBC.
13. "Pays Fine Rather Than Live in Home," *New York Amsterdam News*, February 12, 1955.
14. Central Harlem Council for Community Planning of Welfare and Health Council of New York City, Summary of Minutes of Housing Committee Meeting, November 15, 1956, Harlem Neighborhoods Association records, 1941–1978, Sc MG #364, Box 1, Folder "Central Harlem Council Board of Directors 1955," SCRBC; "Moses to 'Get Tough' on Developers," *New York Amsterdam News*, April 16, 1955.
15. Martha Biondi, *To Stand and Fight: The Struggle for Civil Rights in Postwar New York City* (Cambridge, MA: Harvard University Press, 2003), 123.
16. Gottehrer, *New York City in Crisis*, 103.
17. Letter from Rev. W. Eugene Houston and Mrs. Mildred B. Fischer, September 20, 1955, Harlem Neighborhoods Association records, 1941–1978, Sc MG #364, Box 1, Folder "Central Harlem Council Board of Directors 1955," SCRBC; Cook and Gleason, "The Shame of New York," 287.
18. Gottehrer, *New York City in Crisis*, 103–8; Robert A. Caro, *The Power Broker: Robert Moses and the Fall of New York* (New York: Knopf, 1974), 20.
19. Biondi, *To Stand and Fight*, 234. This survey excludes the Riverton Houses, an intentionally all-Black middle-class complex in Harlem that the Metropolitan Life Insurance Company began building in 1944 in an effort to silence critics of the ardently white Stuyvesant Town further downtown.
20. "Statement of the State Rent Administrator on Relocation of Tenants Displaced by Private Demolition for Residential Building," Harlem Neighborhoods Association records, 1941–1978, Sc MG #364, Box 1, Folder "Central Harlem Council Board of Directors 1955," SCRBC.
21. "SLUM CLEARANCE OR PEOPLE CLEARANCE? (Fact Sheet on 'Title I' Urban Redevelopment)," June 1955, Harlem Neighborhoods Association records, 1941–1978, Sc MG #364, Box 1, Folder "Central Harlem Council Board of Directors 1955," SCRBC. Criticism of how cities, with federal backing, carried out urban renewal crossed ideological lines. The conservative political scientist Edward Banfield declared in 1974: "The injury to the poor inflicted by renewal has not been offset by benefits to them in the form of public housing (that is, housing owned by public bodies and rented by them to families deemed eligible on income and other grounds)." Banfield saw urban renewal as "mainly for the advantage of the well-off—indeed, of the rich." Edward C. Banfield, *The Unheavenly City Revisited* (Boston: Little, Brown, 1974), 16, 17.
22. Cook and Gleason, "The Shame of New York," 286–91.

23. Cook and Gleason, "The Shame of New York," 286–92.
24. HARYOU, *Youth in the Ghetto*, 99, 116. Nine percent of Central Harlem's population in 1964 was classified as either "foreign born" or "of foreign parentage"; Alphonso Pinkney and Roger R. Woock, *Poverty and Politics in Harlem: Report on Project Uplift 1965* (New Haven, CT: College & University Press, 1970), 28.
25. HARYOU, *Youth in the Ghetto*, 101–5. While some people may appreciate old housing and view it positively, these were not buildings that had been well maintained or restored.
26. Fred Halstead, Anthony Aviles, and Don Charles, *Harlem Stirs* (New York: Marzani & Munsell, 1966), 27, 62.
27. "District Health Administration—Central Harlem—Quarterly Report—October, November and December 1954," Harlem Neighborhoods Association records, 1941–1978, Sc MG #364, Box 1, Folder "Central Harlem Council Board of Directors 1955," SCRBC.
28. Pinkney and Woock, *Poverty and Politics in Harlem*, 32, 33. Harlem had 130 doctors in 1964, or one for every 1,790 people. The World Health Organization currently recommends 2.5 doctors per thousand people. Harlem had 0.56. The infant mortality rate was 49.5 per one thousand births in Harlem, and 27.3 for the city. Central Harlem also had a rate of sexually transmitted infections six times that of the city, claiming one-fifth of all reported cases in those under twenty-one years of age. In a time when it was not uncommon for Americans to contract tuberculosis, one-quarter of Manhattanites infected lived in Central Harlem, which had only one-tenth of the island's populace. The neighborhood also had one-third of those who died from it. In the early 1960s, TB deaths in America numbered in the high four figures. They currently hover around five hundred, about a 95 percent decline, though the country's population has increased about 70 percent between then and now. Only suicide rates in Central Harlem were lower than the citywide average. But the admission rate to state mental health facilities was three times that of the city as a whole, with 38.5 per 10,000 Central Harlem residents versus thirteen per 10,000 New Yorkers. Kenneth B. Clark, *Dark Ghetto: Dilemmas of Social Power* (New York: Harper & Row, 1967), 81–83.
29. Biondi, *To Stand and Fight*, 115; Pinkney and Woock, *Poverty and Politics in Harlem*, 38.
30. Jack Newfield, *Robert Kennedy: A Memoir* (New York: New American Library, 1988), 88.
31. Randolph left Harlem in 1968 for a cooperative apartment complex the International Ladies' Garment Workers' Union sponsored in the Chelsea section of Manhattan, at Ninth Avenue and Twenty-Seventh Street. This is the same complex, Penn South, in which Bayard Rustin had lived since it opened in 1962. Both men would live there until their deaths, Randolph in 1979 and Rustin in 1987. Paul Delaney, "A. Philip Randolph Is Dead; Pioneer in Rights and Labor," *New York Times*, May 17, 1979.
32. Newfield, *Robert Kennedy*, 87.
33. For the Brooklyn CORE story, see Brian Purnell, *Fighting Jim Crow in the County of Kings: The Congress of Racial Equality in Brooklyn* (Lexington: University Press of Kentucky, 2013).
34. Gray also organized the sardonic "World's Worst Fair" on 117th Street in Central Harlem, protesting the city's $24 million expenditure on the 1964–1965 World's Fair in Queens and the fair's one-sided representation of life in New York. Gray's fair opened May 30, 1964, about a month after the World's Fair, and featured sidewalk exhibits of photographs portraying ramshackle apartments' interiors, as well as an appearance by boxing legend

Joe Louis. Its slogan was "We Don't Need a World's Fair—We Need a Fair World." "Rally to Protest Housing Is Held on Harlem Block," *New York Times*, May 31, 1964. Gray continued working as a housing activist, forming the National Tenants Organization. He ran for several offices, including for city council, for Adam Clayton Powell's seat in the House of Representatives, and successfully for state assemblyman in 1972, serving one two-year term (1973–1974).

35. Halstead, Aviles, and Charles, *Harlem Stirs*, 50.
36. McCandlish Phillips, "Harlem Tenants Open Rent Strike," *New York Times*, September 28, 1963.
37. Lawrence O'Kane, "City Hall Crowds Disrupt Hearing on Rent Control," *New York Times*, January 24, 1964; "Governor Assails Wagner on Slums." Rent strikers' demonstrations included a simultaneous picket of the 28th Precinct in Harlem and police headquarters downtown on February 8, 1964. The Community Council on Housing accompanied the demonstrations with copies of the following leaflet: "The police department in Harlem is here to protect the slumlords, not the tenants. These facts clearly show why: 1) When the slumlords are guilty of no heat, no hot water, and the rats biting our children, the police department does nothing. This goes on year in and year out. 2) When tenants are being robbed, or when apartments are broken into, where are the police? Somewhere drunk? In some woman's apartment? In a garage asleep? Collecting graft and payoffs from prostitutes? Payoffs from number men or dope peddlers? But when it is time to illegally evict a tenant for a slumlord, the *whole* police department acts with great speed." Rent strikers saw a complex picture of who was responsible for maintaining the city's slums. Halstead, Aviles, and Charles, *Harlem Stirs*, 99.
38. Halstead, Aviles, and Charles, *Harlem Stirs*, 101; Mark Naison, *White Boy: A Memoir* (Philadelphia: Temple University Press, 2002), 40–42; Thomas J. Sugrue, *Sweet Land of Liberty: The Forgotten Struggle for Civil Rights in the North* (New York: Random House, 2008), 402–6; George Breitman, ed., *Malcolm X Speaks* (New York: Grove, 1990), 89.
39. Halstead, Aviles, and Charles, *Harlem Stirs*, 64.
40. Community Council of Greater New York, *Brooklyn Communities: Population Characteristics and Neighborhood Social Resources* (New York: Bureau of Community Statistical Services, Research Dept., 1959), 98; Brian Purnell, "A Movement Grows in Brooklyn: The Brooklyn Chapter of the Congress of Racial Equality (CORE) and the Northern Civil Rights Movement During the Early 1960s," PhD diss., New York University, Graduate School of Arts and Science, 2006, 22.
41. Newfield, *Robert Kennedy*, 90. Newfield, an eyewitness to the process commonly called white flight, writes, "I remember how one frightened white family two blocks away from me—on Hart Street—became a neighborhood legend by simply walking out of their home one day, leaving all their furniture behind, and never returning."
42. Pratt Institute, *Stuyvesant Heights: A Good Neighborhood in Need of Help* (Brooklyn: Community Education Program, Planning Dept., Pratt Institute, 1965), 23. Residents surveyed indicated that bars should be closed, that there were too many bars in the area, and that the prevalence and easy availability of alcohol promoted teenage drinking.
43. Eliot Asinof, *People vs. Blutcher: Black Men and White Law in Bedford-Stuyvesant* (New York: Viking, 1970), 30.

44. Eric C. Schneider, *Vampires, Dragons, and Egyptian Kings: Youth Gangs in Postwar New York* (Princeton, NJ: Princeton University Press, 1999), 43.
45. Mary H. Manoni, *Bedford-Stuyvesant: The Anatomy of a Central City Community* (New York: Quadrangle, 1973), 4. Bedford-Stuyvesant had an owner-occupancy rate of 15 percent, lower than that of the borough and the city but higher than Central Harlem and Brownsville.
46. Community Council of Greater New York, *Brooklyn Communities*, 98.
47. Pratt Institute, *Stuyvesant Heights*, 1, 15. 22.1 percent of all dwellings contained more than 1.01 person per room in 1964, versus 20 percent in Central Harlem, 12.9 percent in Brooklyn, and 12.3 percent in the city.
48. Asinof, *People vs. Blutcher*, 30.
49. Wilder, *A Covenant with Color*, 210.
50. Schneider, *Vampires, Dragons, and Egyptian Kings*, 45.
51. Gottehrer, *New York City in Crisis*, 196.
52. Halstead, Aviles, and Charles, *Harlem Stirs*, 17.
53. Schneider, *Vampires, Dragons, and Egyptian Kings*, 45. He writes, "While only about 13 percent of the city's population in 1950 was Puerto Rican or African American, these groups comprised 37 percent of the displaced."
54. Urban League of Greater New York press release, March 22, 1956, Harlem Neighborhoods Association records, 1941–1978, Sc MG #364, Box 2, Folder "Central Harlem Council Board of Directors 1956," SCRBC.
55. Gottehrer, *New York City in Crisis*, 123, 124. The eight Clear and Present Dangers were: "contagious diseases which create a hazard for other tenants; past or present engagement in illegal occupations; evidence that an individual is prone to violence; confirmed drug addiction; rape or sexual deviation; grossly unacceptable housekeeping; record of unreasonable disturbance of neighbors or destruction of property; and other evidence of behavior which endangers life, safety, or morals." The twenty-two Conditions Indicative of Potential Problems were: "alcoholism; use of narcotics; record of anti-social behavior; membership in a violent teenage gang; record of poor rent payment or eviction for nonpayment; highly irregular work history; frequent separations of husband and wife; husband or wife under 18 years of age; placement of children; out-of-wedlock children; common-law relationship where there is no impediment to marriage; presence of one or more children who are not the offspring of the applicant; family with minor children which does not include both parents; lack of parental control; mental illness which required hospitalization; unusually frequent changes in place of residence; poor housekeeping standards, including lack of furniture; elderly persons whose ability to care for themselves on the premises is questionable; apparent mental retardation; obnoxious conduct during process of application; and recent discharge from service with other than honorable discharge."
56. Deborah Wallace and Rodrick Wallace, *A Plague on Your Houses: How New York Was Burned Down and Public Health Crumbled* (London: Verso, 1998), 14–16. The Title I projects intended for middle-class inhabitation were generally more than 99 percent white.
57. Banfield, *The Unheavenly City Revisited*, 16. As Arnold Hirsch notes regarding those who have labeled the Housing Act of 1949 as a failure or an example of distorted implementation, the legislation "merely did what it was intended to do. If anything was distorted, it

was the judgment of those who attributed goals to the program that were not contemplated by the powers directing it." Arnold Hirsch, *Making the Second Ghetto: Race and Housing in Chicago, 1940–1960* (Cambridge: Cambridge University Press, 1983), 272.
58. Nicholas D. Bloom, *Public Housing That Worked: New York in the Twentieth Century* (Philadelphia: University of Pennsylvania Press, 2008). Bloom views the city's public housing in a positive light for not falling into "welfare housing." While it is true that public housing in New York City afforded a higher standard of living to residents than most other cities did, huge numbers of people, the most needy, were deliberately excluded and left to plummet through gaping holes in the safety net. D. Bradford Hunt, *Blueprint for Disaster: The Unraveling of Chicago Public Housing* (Chicago: University of Chicago Press, 2009). New York's public housing program differed greatly from Chicago's. The New York City Housing Authority was run like a business, there was little room to build massive housing projects in New York, and the NYCHA performed a detailed screening of its applicants, rejecting most.
59. Gottehrer, *New York City in Crisis*, 16.
60. "Text of Wagner Talk Outlining 9-Point Slum Drive," *New York Times*, December 23, 1959.
61. Gottehrer, *New York City in Crisis*, 16, 108; Charles G. Bennett, "Mayor Demands Housing Action," *New York Times*, September 27, 1961; R. W. Apple Jr., "Governor Assails Wagner on Slums," *New York Times*, January 24, 1964. The city, after years of effort, had pushed the state legislature to pass the Receivership Law in June 1962, allowing the city to assume ownership of the properties and take whatever remediation was deemed necessary. By early 1964, the city had considered 275 buildings for this action but had only taken over fifteen; Rockefeller stated that "there is a lack of enforcement of existing laws both in the building code and in sanitary conditions." The commissioner of the Department of Buildings, Harold Birns, responded that "code enforcement in New York City today is more intensive and has expanded more than at any other time in the city's history." "City to Unify Drive to End Housing Bias," *New York Times*, September 23, 1963; "Listing of Buildings with 50 Violations or More as of Nov. 1," *New York Times*, January 24, 1964. The winning building had 230 pending violations, with two runners-up tied at 212. Woody Klein, *Let in the Sun* (New York: Macmillan, 1964), 235, 236.
62. Kenneth Clark, *The Negro Protest: James Baldwin, Malcolm X, Martin Luther King Talk with Kenneth B. Clark* (Boston: Beacon, 1963), 5. Baldwin was born in Harlem in 1924 and was raised at 131st Street and Seventh Avenue. In the early 1950s, the New York City Housing Authority's Saint Nicholas Houses replaced his childhood home, along with everything else on the four blocks between 127th and 131st Streets. It is worth noting Baldwin's "growing up" took place during the Great Depression.

2. Working

1. Eric C. Schneider, *Vampires, Dragons, and Egyptian Kings: Youth Gangs in Postwar New York* (Princeton, NJ: Princeton University Press, 1999), 33. 1.1 million Black people called New York City home in 1960.
2. Martha Biondi, *To Stand and Fight: The Struggle for Civil Rights in Postwar New York City* (Cambridge, MA: Harvard University Press, 2003), 12. In 1940, 64 percent of Black women

and 40 percent of Black men in New York worked these jobs. Those figures had declined to 36 percent and 23 percent by 1947. *Equal Employment Opportunity: Hearings Before the Subcommittee on Employment and Manpower of the Committee on Labor and Public Welfare, United States Senate, Eighty-eighth Congress, First Session, on S. 773, S. 1210, S. 1211, and S. 1937, Bills Relating to Equal Employment Opportunities*, July 24, 25, 26, 29, 31, August 2, 20, 1963 (Washington: US Government Printing Office, 1963-1964), 377.
3. Biondi, *To Stand and Fight*, 21-22.
4. Charles C. Killingsworth, "Negroes in a Changing Labor Market," in *Employment, Race, and Poverty*, ed. Arthur M. Ross and Herbert Hill (New York: Harcourt, Brace & World, 1967), 50, 59-61. In the South, the ratio was 1.7 for both women and men. Between then and as of this writing, the Black unemployment rate has always been at least 66 percent higher than that of white people, and usually double. In the Midwest, Black unemployment rates were 2.8 times higher for men, 2.6 for women, and in the West, 2.3 for men and 1.8 for women. *Nation's Manpower Revolution: Hearings before the Subcommittee on Employment and Manpower of the Committee on Labor and Public Welfare, United States Senate, Eighty-eighth Congress, First Session, Relating to the Training and Utilization of the Manpower Sources of the Nation*, 1963 (Washington: US Government Printing Office, 1963-1964), 1092.
5. Vivian W. Henderson, "Regions, Race, and Jobs," in *Employment, Race, and Poverty*, ed. Arthur M. Ross and Herbert Hill (New York: Harcourt, Brace & World, 1967), 89, 91, 92.
6. Killingsworth, "Negroes in a Changing Labor Market," 69.
7. Leah P. Boustan, *Competition in the Promised Land: Black Migrants in Northern Cities and Labor Markets* (Princeton, NJ: Princeton University Press, 2017), 66-68; *Equal Employment Opportunity*, 328.
8. Herbert Hill, "Twenty Years of State Fair Employment Practices Commissions: A Critical Analysis with Recommendations," *Buffalo Law Review* 14, no. 22 (1964): 22.
9. *Equal Employment Opportunity*, 377.
10. Killingsworth, "Negroes in a Changing Labor Market," 52.
11. *Equal Employment Opportunity*, 324, 378. Only in Florida and Washington, DC, did the income gap shrink, and it stayed the same in New Jersey and Oklahoma.
12. Henderson, "Regions, Race, and Jobs," 246, 250.
13. Hill, "Twenty Years of State Fair Employment Practices Commissions," 22.
14. *Equal Employment Opportunity*, 321, 375.
15. T. J. English, *The Savage City: Race, Murder, and a Generation on the Edge* (New York: William Morrow, 2012), ii, iii.
16. Henderson, "Regions, Race, and Jobs," 86-88.
17. Milton Friedman and Rose D. Friedman, *Capitalism and Freedom* (Chicago: University of Chicago, 1962), 108-9. According to Friedman, "It is a striking historical fact that the development of capitalism has been accompanied by a major reduction in the extent to which particular religious, racial, or social groups have operated under special handicaps in respect of their economic activities; have, as the saying goes, been discriminated against." He also believed the American dedication to private property to be so strong that even white supremacy and its practitioners in the post–Civil War South refused to deny African Americans the right to own land. In fact, white southerners did attempt to

prevent Black people from owning land, both in law and custom. Beyond that, it simply was not necessary when the institution of sharecropping set in, taking care of the issue without the unpleasantness of crudely discriminatory laws. Nathan Glazer, *Affirmative Discrimination: Ethnic Inequality and Public Policy* (New York: Basic Books, 1975).

18. Kenneth Clark, "Sex, Status, and Underemployment of the Negro Male," in *Employment, Race, and Poverty*, ed. Arthur M. Ross and Herbert Hill (New York: Harcourt, Brace & World, 1967), 141.
19. *Equal Employment Opportunity*, 325.
20. Kenneth B. Clark, *Dark Ghetto: Dilemmas of Social Power* (New York: Harper & Row, 1967), 35.
21. *Equal Employment Opportunity*, 325.
22. Henderson, "Regions, Race, and Jobs," 93.
23. Clark, "Sex, Status, and Underemployment of the Negro Male," 139; *Nation's Manpower Revolution*, 325. The U.S. Department of Labor anticipated in 1957 that by 1970 the nation would need 42 percent more professional and technical workers, 24 percent more service personnel, 22 percent more skilled workers, 18 percent more semiskilled workers, and fewer unskilled workers than it had in 1960. Put another way, the Department of Labor expected the need for unskilled work to decrease, which would lead to higher unemployment among the people in that sector, either because they lack skills or have skills they are not permitted to utilize, barring retraining and further education.
24. Clark, *Dark Ghetto*, 35.
25. Clark, "Sex, Status, and Underemployment of the Negro Male," 139.
26. Henderson, "Regions, Race, and Jobs," 93.
27. Joshua Benjamin Freeman, *Working-Class New York: Life and Labor Since World War II* (New York: New Press, 2000), 8, 143, 168.
28. Paul H. Norgren, "Fair Employment Practice Laws: Experience, Effects, Prospects," in *Employment, Race, and Poverty*, ed. Arthur M. Ross and Herbert Hill (New York: Harcourt, Brace & World, 1967), 556.
29. Clark, *Dark Ghetto*, 35. The median income for the city was $5,103. Freeman, *Working-Class New York*, 181; Alphonso Pinkney and Roger R. Woock, *Poverty and Politics in Harlem: Report on Project Uplift 1965* (New Haven, CT: College & University Press, 1970), 31.
30. Biondi, *To Stand and Fight*, 270.
31. Eliot Asinof, *People vs. Blutcher: Black Men and White Law in Bedford-Stuyvesant* (New York: Viking, 1970), 30.
32. Clark, *Dark Ghetto*, 27–29, 36. The stagnating/declining trades were transportation, manufacturing, communication and utilities, and wholesale and retail employment.
33. Arthur M. Ross, "The Negro in the American Economy," in *Employment, Race, and Poverty*, ed. Arthur M. Ross and Herbert Hill (New York: Harcourt, Brace & World, 1967), 19.
34. Clark, "Sex, Status, and Underemployment of the Negro Male," 141.
35. Martin Meyerson, "Urban Policy: Reforming Reform," in *The Conscience of the City*, ed. Martin Meyerson (New York: G. Braziller, 1970), 365.
36. James Baldwin, *The Price of the Ticket: Collected Nonfiction, 1948–1985* (New York: St. Martin's/Marek, 1985), 328. Originally, this was from an address Baldwin gave to an audience of educators in October 1963. The *Saturday Review* published it two months later.

37. Schneider, *Vampires, Dragons, and Egyptian Kings*, 31, 44; Barry Gottehrer, *New York City in Crisis: A Study in Depth of Urban Sickness* (New York: McKay, 1965), 92–95. New Jersey was offering construction costs up to $1.75 less per square foot than in parts of New York, taxes nearly half that of the city, and cheaper land.
38. Gottehrer, *New York City in Crisis*, 94–101. Companies were able to obtain second mortgages up to 30 percent of their first through a city and state partnership. The city used half of the department's budget in 1964–1965 to promote tourism.
39. Freeman, *Working-Class New York*, 150.
40. John V. Lindsay, *The City* (New York: New American Library, 1970), 80.
41. Biondi, *To Stand and Fight*, 20, 269. An official investigation found the state employment service was doing this in 1959. Freeman, *Working-Class New York*, 68; Hill, "Twenty Years of State Fair Employment Practices Commissions," 52.
42. Hill, "Twenty Years of State Fair Employment Practices Commissions," 39–55.
43. Hill, "Twenty Years of State Fair Employment Practices Commissions," 54–56.
44. Hill, "Twenty Years of State Fair Employment Practices Commissions," 34.
45. Hill, "Twenty Years of State Fair Employment Practices Commissions," 66; "Concern in New City Told to Rehire Negro Plumber," *New York Times*, February 24, 1964.
46. Hill, "Twenty Years of State Fair Employment Practices Commissions," 34, 62–66. The journeyman's test, a thorough written exam, was essential for a worker in a skilled construction trade, in this case plumbing, to move on from being an apprentice. Journeyman status certifies the individual is competent, well trained, and has plenty of experience. It allows for independent work, higher wages, and the eventual opportunity to become a master in one's field.
47. Hill, "Twenty Years of State Fair Employment Practices Commissions," 66–68; Sydney H. Schanberg, "State Says Union Barred Negroes for Last 76 Years," *New York Times*, March 5, 1964; Sydney H. Schanberg, "Union Is Ordered to Open Its Rolls," *New York Times*, March 24, 1964. The local admitted two cohorts of forty apprentices per year, who would train for four years, on the job and in the classroom, until they were able to pass the journeyman's exam, at which point they would begin earning $5.25 an hour for a thirty-five hour workweek, giving them a base salary of $9,555 a year, which is about $80,000 in 2020. Apprentices started at $2.09 an hour and worked up to $4.18 before reaching journeyman status. Even the starting rate provided annual earnings of $3,822, before overtime, which already put them ahead of half of Harlem families. This was a good wage for the young men, required to be between the ages of eighteen and twenty-three, who were admitted as apprentices. This is what Black workers were missing out on and part of what kept them so much poorer. Sydney H. Schanberg, "N.A.A.C.P. Attacks Union in Bias Case," *New York Times*, March 7, 1964; "Penalty for Bias in Union Sought," *New York Times*, April 4, 1964. Local 28 appealed the decision in court but settled in August, agreeing to accept all of the SCHR's provisions. This decision does not seem to have done much to remedy Local 28's issues, as it settled a discrimination case in 2015 with the U.S. Equal Employment Opportunity Commission, originally filed in 1971 (yes, forty-four years earlier), for nearly $13 million. This case documents the ways that Local 28 went through with admitting people of color to the union but then proceeded to discriminate against them in work assignments, costing the "journeypersons," as the EEOC refers to them, significant wages

over time. There was an earlier settlement, as part of the same case, for more than $6 million. Part of the 2015 settlement was to "equalize work opportunities for non-white and white union members." The legacies of racism and discrimination continue for a very long time, even when brought into the open. U.S. EEOC, "Sheet Metal Union Agrees to Pay an Estimated $12 Million in Partial Settlement of Race Bias Lawsuit," http://eeoc.gov/eeoc/newsroom/release/4-2-15.cfm.
48. David H. Golland, *Constructing Affirmative Action: The Struggle for Equal Employment Opportunity* (Lexington: University Press of Kentucky, 2011), 36.
49. Brian Purnell, *Fighting Jim Crow in the County of Kings: The Congress of Racial Equality in Brooklyn* (Lexington: University Press of Kentucky, 2013), 216–17.
50. Purnell, *Fighting Jim Crow in the County of Kings*, 218–45.
51. Charles R. Morris, *The Cost of Good Intentions: New York City and the Liberal Experiment, 1960–1975* (New York: Norton, 1980), 213. Morris was an assistant budget director and then in charge of welfare and medical programs during the second term of John Lindsay's administration. He argues that "the view that the low socio-economic status of blacks demonstrated not only past discrimination but continued oppression was, for the most part, simply wrong."

3. Union Work

1. Joshua Benjamin Freeman, *Working-Class New York: Life and Labor Since World War II* (New York: New Press, 2000), 101.
2. Paul Frymer, *Black and Blue: African Americans, the Labor Movement, and the Decline of the Democratic Party* (Princeton, NJ: Princeton University Press, 2008), 1, 24–32.
3. Freeman, *Working-Class New York*, 99–102.
4. Charles R. Morris, *The Cost of Good Intentions: New York City and the Liberal Experiment, 1960–1975* (New York: Norton, 1980), 87–91. While this all gave the appearance of reciprocal harmony between the city and those who worked for it, Wagner was not interested in simply rolling over for municipal workers and letting them dictate the terms of their employment to the city. For the first few years, these unions were tiny and specific to those performing a particular role, allowed to negotiate only over wages, with each subset of workers having to essentially ask Wagner directly for permission. Through this process, he hoped to keep unions small, weak, yet loyal, which would be the best case for him, as it would allow him to continue building his reputation as a champion of the working class but alleviate some of his opponents' worst concerns, particularly those of the fiscal variety. By the end of his third term, in 1965, it had all gotten out from under Wagner's thumb, and labor had outmaneuvered him. The unions got bigger and more aggressive, unwilling to have a paternalistic relationship with the mayor. Wagner's negotiators backed down repeatedly, first to welfare caseworkers and supervisors, then to building inspectors, trash collectors, firemen, and police. Each fed off the others' victories, which had a cyclical effect. In building a new political base he hoped to keep indebted to him, Wagner's creation attacked and haunted him within only a few years. He lost control, and he knew it.

5. John E. Hutchinson, "The AFL-CIO and the Negro," in *Employment, Race, and Poverty*, ed. Arthur M. Ross and Herbert Hill (New York: Harcourt, Brace & World, 1967), 404. The three Black senators, Cory Booker, Kamala Harris, and Tim Scott, introduced antilynching legislation anew in 2018, which passed unanimously. The House declined to take it up but passed its own Emmett Till Antilynching Act in February 2020, by a vote of 410–4. In the Senate, Rand Paul objected to the bill, claiming it "would cheapen the meaning of lynching by defining it so broadly as to include a minor bruise or abrasion." Mitch McConnell, the Senate majority leader, insisted the bill go up for unanimous consent rather than a roll call vote. As Senator Paul did not drop his objection and Leader McConnell did not allow debate and a vote, the bill died with the conclusion of the 116th Congress, on January 3, 2021. Nicholas Fando, "Frustration and Fury as Paul Holds Up Anti-Lynching Bill in Senate," *New York Times*, June 6, 2020.
6. Hutchinson, "The AFL-CIO and the Negro," 403, 413; Frymer, *Black and Blue*, 59; John D. Pomfret, "A.F.L.-C.I.O. Aloof on Capital March," *New York Times*, August 14, 1963.
7. Hutchinson, "The AFL-CIO and the Negro," 406. Carey was also a committed anticommunist who was instrumental in having his former union, the United Electrical, Radio and Machine Workers of America, thrown out of the CIO in 1949 for its allegedly red leadership. It was in actuality a progressive/leftist union, but at that time many people did not bother to make such a distinction. He then became president of the union the CIO chartered as a replacement, the International Union of Electrical, Radio and Machine Workers.
8. David H. Golland, *Constructing Affirmative Action: The Struggle for Equal Employment Opportunity* (Lexington: University Press of Kentucky, 2011), 66.
9. Golland, *Constructing Affirmative Action*, 67.
10. Golland, *Constructing Affirmative Action*, 17, 68–69.
11. Frymer, *Black and Blue*, 1, 30–34. Once the provision went into force, legal bills and losses quickly piled up for unions that continued to violate the new law. With this remade federal approach to racial discrimination, and with affirmative action policies in hand, the Departments of Labor and Justice also began moving in real ways against unions and contractors who clung to the old ways. Within fifteen years, one in four Black workers would be a dues-paying member of the labor movement, a situation that would have seemed an unrealistic goal only twenty years earlier.
12. Kenneth B. Clark, *Dark Ghetto: Dilemmas of Social Power* (New York: Harper & Row, 1967), 43; Freeman, *Working-Class New York*, 45.
13. Herbert Hill, "Twenty Years of State Fair Employment Practices Commissions: A Critical Analysis with Recommendations," *Buffalo Law Review* 14, no. 22 (1964): 35; Herbert Hill, "The Untold Story," *The Crisis*, November 1962, 513–21.
14. Clark, *Dark Ghetto*, 44, 45.
15. Freeman, *Working-Class New York*, 167. On a top-ten list of office space built, this amount of square footage was more than twice the combined total the next nine cities constructed during the same time.
16. Brian Purnell, *Fighting Jim Crow in the County of Kings: The Congress of Racial Equality in Brooklyn* (Lexington: University Press of Kentucky, 2013), 212; Golland, *Constructing Affirmative Action*, 38.

17. Joseph Lelyveld, "Building Unions Facing New Civil Rights Protests," *New York Times*, May 27, 1964.
18. Purnell, *Fighting Jim Crow in the County of Kings*, 212–15.
19. Joseph Lelyveld, "Lomax Says Chaos Looms in Negro Drive for Rights," *New York Times*, April 13, 1964.
20. Frymer, *Black and Blue*, 60.
21. Sydney H. Schanberg, "Plumbers' Dispute May Halt Project," *New York Times*, May 6, 1964; A. H. Raskin, "Labor and Civil Rights," *New York Times*, May 20, 1964.
22. Sydney H. Schanberg, "City Rights Panel Balked on Walkout of Plumbers," *New York Times*, May 5, 1964; Raskin, "Labor and Civil Rights."
23. Schanberg, "Plumbers' Dispute May Halt Project."
24. Schanberg, "City Rights Panel Balked on Walkout of Plumbers."
25. Schanberg, "Plumbers' Dispute May Halt Project."
26. "Plumbers Stay off City Job in Bronx," *New York Times*, May 8, 1964; Sydney H. Schanberg, "President Enters Plumbers' Dispute," *New York Times*, May 9, 1964; Lelyveld, "Building Unions Facing New Civil Rights Protests."
27. A. H. Raskin, "Union Discrimination Is Hard to Erase," *New York Times*, May 10, 1964; Golland, *Constructing Affirmative Action*, 70; Gene Ruffini, *Harry Van Arsdale, Jr.: Labor's Champion* (London: Routledge, 2015), 118–20. Just a few years earlier, Local 3 had been a typical father-son union that shut out African Americans and Puerto Ricans from advancement. It accepted them, but they were mostly relegated to a low level of the union, earning the lowest wages and enduring the worst working conditions among members. The construction division of Local 3, which offered the best wages and conditions, was entirely white. Van Arsdale negotiated a five-hour workday, five days a week, for unionized construction electricians, with one hour of guaranteed overtime per day. Part of his negotiating strategy was to promise contractors a much larger supply of apprentices, who could do simple work that journeymen were currently doing, thereby reducing costs. He used this victory to deliberately recruit African American and Puerto Rican men into the apprentice ranks.
28. Frymer, *Black and Blue*, 68; Golland, *Constructing Affirmative Action*, 1.
29. Frymer, *Black and Blue*, 47–48. Parent unions might assert authority over a local in instances of corruption or insubordination but were unlikely to do so over racial discrimination, especially in this era.
30. Frymer, *Black and Blue*, 47.
31. Schanberg, "President Enters Plumbers' Dispute," 1.
32. Sydney H. Schanberg, "CORE Pickets Plumbers Union Office," *New York Times*, May 12, 1964.
33. Sydney H. Schanberg, "Pickets Blockade Plumbers' Office," *New York Times*, May 13, 1964; "Plumbers' Office Blockaded Again," *New York Times*, May 14, 1964.
34. Layhmond Robinson, "Rights Unit Ends Effort to Solve Plumber Dispute," *New York Times*, May 17, 1964; Sydney H. Schanberg, "Meany Supports Bronx Plumbers," *New York Times*, May 15, 1964.
35. Golland, *Constructing Affirmative Action*, 23–33.
36. Hutchinson, "The AFL-CIO and the Negro," 403–5.

37. Hutchinson, "The AFL-CIO and the Negro," 405–8; Golland, *Constructing Affirmative Action*, 33; Reminiscences of Kenneth Bancroft Clark (1985), 538, Columbia Center for Oral History Archives, Rare Book & Manuscript Library, Columbia University in the City of New York.
38. Martin Arnold, "3 to Be Coached on Plumber Test," *New York Times*, May 20, 1964.
39. Damon Stetson, "3 Negroes Pass Plumbers' Test," *New York Times*, August 7, 1964.
40. As Nancy Banks argues, those involved with resolving the dispute "were more concerned about taking credit for hammering out an agreement quickly than advancing the cause for racial justice or providing the four minority workers with a fair chance at union membership." Nancy Ann Banks, "The Last Bastion of Discrimination: The New York City Building Trades and the Struggle Over Affirmative Action, 1961–1976," PhD diss., Columbia University, 2006.
41. "Time for a Crackdown," *New York Times*, May 6, 1964.
42. Rochdale Village, in Jamaica, Queens, was intended to be an integrated cooperative, though the labor that built it was almost entirely white. About 10 percent of its residents were Black when it opened in 1963, but it quickly became majority Black, as white residents abandoned their new homes rather than live among Black people and all the fears they represented. Peter Eisenstadt, "Rochdale Village and the Rise and Fall of Integrated Housing in New York City," in *Civil Rights in New York City: From World War II to the Giuliani Era*, ed. Clarence Taylor (New York: Fordham University Press, 2011).
43. Clayton Knowles, "Wagner Says City Has Not Discussed Negro Preferment," *New York Times*, October 29, 1963; "Rights Unit Head Backs Job Stand," *New York Times*, November 18, 1963; Barry Gottehrer, "Urban Conditions: New York City," *Annals of the American Academy of Political and Social Science* 371 (1967). *Social Goals and Indicators for American Society* (May 1967), 1:143; Fred J. Cook and Gene Gleason, "The Shame of New York," *The Nation*, October 31, 1959, 275. The *Nation*'s contemporary account of Wagner's deliberate inaction is more biting than Gottehrer's, coming two years into Wagner's second term: "He never tires of citing his father's political homilies, as if they contained the essence of all political wisdom. If they did, there would be, of course, no argument; but, unfortunately, the sayings on which the Mayor seems to put the greatest stress are those that represent, at best, only negative virtues. A bit of the father's wisdom that the Mayor frequently cites is to the effect that often the best way to handle a problem is to do nothing; you'd be surprised, he says, how frequently today's crisis fades away tomorrow. 'When in doubt, don't,' the Mayor often quotes his father as having said. But the motto which the Mayor uses to justify inaction may have been better suited to the more deliberate role of legislator that his father filled than to the chief executive of a city whose crushing problems demand swift, vigorous and decisive action. These positive traits that New York so desperately needs are the very ones that are most lacking in its Mayor." In another account, Gottehrer, a former journalist with *Newsweek* and the *New York Herald Tribune*, wrote: "When a problem cropped up and exploded in the city's newspapers, Mayor Wagner followed a well-defined formula. First he would release an immediate and overblown statement of concern, and then he would call for the formation of a special committee, invariably headed by City Council President Paul Screvane or Deputy Mayor Edward Cavanagh. With few exceptions, these committees

whitewashed the problem, and since another crisis ordinarily erupted by the time the report had been completed, the recommendations of the committee would usually die unpublicized and ignored." Barry Gottehrer, *New York City in Crisis: A Study in Depth of Urban Sickness* (New York: McKay, 1965), 54.

4. Learning

1. Clarence Taylor, *Knocking at Our Own Door: Milton A. Galamison and the Struggle to Integrate New York City Schools*, Columbia History of Urban Life (New York: Columbia University Press, 1997), 54.
2. Taylor, *Knocking at Our Own Door*, 52.
3. "The PUBLIC and the SCHOOLS—Bulletin of the Public Education Association, March 1955," Harlem Neighborhoods Association records, 1941–1978, Sc MG #364, Box 1, Folder "Central Harlem Council Board of Directors 1955," SCRBC.
4. Gerald E. Markowitz and David Rosner, *Children, Race, and Power: Kenneth and Mamie Clark's Northside Center* (Charlottesville: University Press of Virginia, 1996), 93, 97.
5. "CENTRAL HARLEM COUNCIL FOR COMMUNITY PLANNING—*SUMMARY OF MINUTES* of Meeting of *BOARD OF DIRECTORS*," February 9, 1956, Harlem Neighborhoods Association records, 1941–1978, Sc MG #364, Box 2, Folder "Central Harlem Council Board of Directors 1956," SCRBC. The school was James Fenimore Cooper Junior High School 120, at 18 East 120th Street, renamed in 1976 for Dr. Louis T. Wright, the Black physician and civil rights activist. Luxury condos now occupy the site.
6. Taylor, *Knocking at Our Own Door*, 52.
7. Taylor, *Knocking at Our Own Door*, 54.
8. Urban League of Greater New York press release, November 10, 1955, Harlem Neighborhoods Association records, 1941–1978, Sc MG #364, Box 1, Folder "Central Harlem Council Board of Directors 1955," SCRBC.
9. John H. Bracey, August Meier, and Randolph Boehm, press release, February 27, 1957, Papers of the NAACP: Part 3: The Campaign for Educational Equality; Series D: Central Office Records, 1956–1965; Reel 6: Desegregation, Schools; Schools, New York (Bethesda, MD: University Publications of America, 1996).
10. Kenneth Clark, *Dark Ghetto: Dilemmas of Social Power* (New York: Harper & Row, 1967), 118.
11. Richard Severo, "Kenneth Clark, Who Helped End Segregation, Dies," *New York Times*, May 2, 2005. Kenneth and Mamie Phipps Clark had been conducting studies since the 1940s, asking African American children to play with Black and white dolls and identify various characteristics, such as which ones looked like them and which ones were "good," in order to demonstrate that segregation damaged Black children's self-image. The NAACP submitted the Clarks' findings as part of its evidence before the Supreme Court, which found the outcomes persuasive; *Harlem: Test for the North*, WNBC, July 26, 1964; Robert D. McFadden, "Basil A. Paterson, Whose Political Reach Touched Harlem and Beyond, Dies at 87," *New York Times*, April 14, 2014; Basil Paterson, "Negroes in City University," *New York Times*, February 1, 1964. Paterson was president of the Harlem NAACP, a state

senator, deputy mayor, New York's secretary of state, Democratic nominee for lieutenant governor in 1970, a labor mediator for decades after, and a powerful behind-the-scenes player in Democratic politics. He was also the father of future governor David Paterson. PS 123 Mahalia Jackson is on the site of PS 5 today, at 140th Street and Edgecombe Avenue. He also attended PS 139, which is now the New York City Housing Authority's PS 139 Senior Center, on 140th Street, between Adam Clayton Powell Jr. and Malcolm X Boulevards.

12. Ben Keppel, *The Work of Democracy: Ralph Bunche, Kenneth B. Clark, Lorraine Hansberry, and the Cultural Politics of Race* (Cambridge, MA: Harvard University Press, 1995), 17–20.
13. Markowitz and Rosner, *Children, Race, and Power*, 105–8.
14. Clark, *Dark Ghetto*, 115.
15. David Rogers, *110 Livingston Street: Politics and Bureaucracy in the New York City Schools* (New York: Random House, 1968), 15–16.
16. Alphonso Pinkney and Roger R. Woock, *Poverty and Politics in Harlem: Report on Project Uplift 1965* (New Haven, CT: College & University Press, 1970), 34. The nation's first charter school opened in 1992, in St. Paul, Minnesota. Clark, *Dark Ghetto*, 114.
17. "Desegregating the Public Schools of New York City: A Report Prepared for the Board of Education of the City of New York," 13, Papers of the NAACP: Part 3: The Campaign for Educational Equality; Series D: Central Office Records, 1956–1965; Reel 7: Desegregation, Schools; Desegregation NYC General 1964; Markowitz and Rosner, *Children, Race, and Power*, 105, 106.
18. Taylor, *Knocking at Our Own Door*, 52.
19. Barry Gottehrer, *New York City in Crisis: A Study in Depth of Urban Sickness* (New York: McKay, 1965), 5. PS 170 was located at 37 West 111th Street. Today it is PS 208, PS 185, and Harlem Link Charter.
20. Gottehrer, *New York City in Crisis*, 155. Critics would brand Shanker a racist for his leadership, militancy, and tactics in the rancorous Ocean Hill–Brownsville teachers' strike that began in 1968.
21. Clark, *Dark Ghetto*, 125.
22. PS 258, at 141 Macon Street, was closed for poor performance in 2010 and now houses PS K140, a special-needs school. Memo from June Shagaloff to Closter Current and Roy Wilkins, November 2, 1956; memo from June Shagaloff to Messrs. Carter, Current, Marshall, Moon, Morsell, and Wilkins, December 11, 1956; Minutes—Meeting of N.Y. Branch Presidents and Chairmen of Education Committees, November 21, 1956, all in Papers of the NAACP: Part 3: The Campaign for Educational Equality; Series D: Central Office Records, 1956–1965; Reel 6: Desegregation, Schools; Schools, New York.
23. Memo from Roy Wilkins to June Shagaloff, undated, but in response to her December 11 memo, Papers of the NAACP: Part 3: The Campaign for Educational Equality; Series D: Central Office Records, 1956–1965; Reel 6: Desegregation, Schools; Schools, New York.
24. Benjamin Fine, "Integration Plea Charges City Lag," *New York Times*, July 12, 1957.
25. "Parents Picket City Hall Over Delay in Integration," *New York Times*, September 20, 1957.
26. "Toward the Integration of Our Schools: Final Report of the Commission on Integration, Board of Education of the City of New York," Papers of the NAACP: Part 3: The

Campaign for Educational Equality; Series D: Central Office Records, 1956–1965; Reel 6: Desegregation, Schools; Schools, New York.

27. Markowitz and Rosner, *Children, Race, and Power*, 98, 99. Clark was chair of the subcommittee on Educational Standards and Curriculum.
28. Letter from Mrs. Carrie E. Haynes and Mrs. Ruby Sims to Mrs. Harriet Pickens, October 21, 1958, Harlem Neighborhoods Association records, 1941–1978, Sc MG #364, Box 2, Folder "CHCCP Board of Directors 1957 to 1958," SCRBC; "7 Negro Children Attend Tutoring," *New York Times*, September 12, 1958; "Harlem Action Barred," *New York Times*, September 18, 1958; "Pupils' Plea Denied," *New York Times*, September 25, 1958; "State Will Study 3 Harlem Schools," *New York Times*, October 30, 1958.
29. "6 Mothers Summoned," *New York Times*, November 12, 1958.
30. "4 Mothers Guilty in School Boycott," *New York Times*, December 4, 1958.
31. Leonard Buder, "2 Harlem Schools Called Inferior as Court Frees Two in Boycott," *New York Times*, December 16, 1958.
32. Warren Weaver Jr., "2 Bid State Study City School 'Bias,'" *New York Times*, January 28, 1959.
33. Adina Back sees parents' activism in Central Harlem as having a "measurable impact on the Board's general resistance to implementing substantive desegregation programs." The protests and boycotts had an impact on the board's rhetoric, but it is difficult to see the school board as taking action that helped more than a handful of the city's Black children. The people in charge of the school system often put the responsibility for desegregation on Black parents through implementing voluntary programs that were poorly advertised. As for mandatory transfers, school board officials either transferred only a few students or reversed course altogether, citing opposition from white parents. Adina Black, "Up South in New York: The 1950s School Desegregation Struggles," PhD diss., New York University, 1997, 308.
34. Letter from Roy Wilkins to Charles H. Silver, July 24, 1959, Papers of the NAACP: Part 3: The Campaign for Educational Equality; Series D: Central Office Records, 1956–1965; Reel 7: Desegregation, Schools; Schools, New York City and State, 1956–1965.
35. Taylor, *Knocking at Our Own Door*, 102–13.
36. Robert H. Terte, "30 Begin a Sit-in at School Board," *New York Times*, September 18, 1962. Robert H. Terte, "Students in Sit-in to Get Transfers," *New York Times*, September 19, 1962.
37. Brian Purnell, *Fighting Jim Crow in the County of Kings: The Congress of Racial Equality in Brooklyn* (Lexington: University Press of Kentucky, 2013), 180–94. PS 200 is still PS 200 but goes by PS 200 Benson, in Bath Beach. Leonard Buder, "3 Negro Students Get Police Escort: Parents Tell of Threat in Brooklyn Racial Dispute," *New York Times*, December 4, 1962. Later in 1963, Jerome and Elaine Bibuld would be convicted of disorderly conduct for their participation in CORE's protests at the Downstate Medical Center construction site. Mr. Bibuld paid a $150 fine; Mrs. Bibuld spent ten days in jail while pregnant, refusing to pay her fine. She also refused to submit to a vaginal examination during her intake into the Women's House of Detention, for which she was kept in solitary confinement. "Rights Protester Ends 10-Day Term," *New York Times*, January 24, 1964.
38. Purnell, *Fighting Jim Crow in the County of Kings*, 206. Park Slope today, while still overwhelmingly white, is a wealthy neighborhood again, as it was in the earlier part of the

twentieth century, with homes selling at an average price of more than one million dollars. And while PS 282 is much better off than it was in 1962, it is still a majority Black school, despite its location.
39. Harlem Parents Committee press release, undated, Harlem Neighborhoods Association records, 1941–1978, Sc MG #364, Box 6, Folder "HANA Committees—Harlem Parents Committee, June 1963–July 1963," SCRBC; "Why We March," Harlem Neighborhoods Association records, 1941–1978, Sc MG #364, Box 6, Folder "HANA Committees—Harlem Parents Committee, June 1963–July 1963," SCRBC.
40. "Questions and Answers," Harlem Neighborhoods Association records, 1941–1978, Sc MG #364, Box 6, Folder "HANA Committees—Harlem Parents Committee, August 1963–1965," SCRBC.
41. Consider that during this time, on July 17, 1963, a U.S. district court judge ordered the East Baton Rouge Parish School Board in Louisiana "to start desegregation this fall by advising all 12th grade students, regardless of race, that they may apply for transfer to any school of their choice." Nothing similar would ever take place in New York. "Baton Rouge Gets Order on Schools," *New York Times*, July 18, 1963.
42. "Statement of the National Association for the Advancement of Colored People, 13 New York City Branches, Before the Board of Education of the City of New York, January 6, 1964," Papers of the NAACP: Part 3: The Campaign for Educational Equality; Series D: Central Office Records, 1956–1965; Reel 7: Desegregation, Schools; Desegregation NYC General 1964.
43. Harlem Parents Committee press release, July 31, 1963, Harlem Neighborhoods Association records, 1941–1978, Sc MG #364, Box 6, Folder "HANA Committees—Harlem Parents Committee, June 1963–July 1963," SCRBC.
44. Taylor, *Knocking at Our Own Door*, 121–23.
45. Eric Marcus, "Bayard Rustin," *Making Gay History*, podcast, January 10, 2019, https://www.makinggayhistory.com/podcast/bayard-rustin. Rustin had been arrested in Pasadena, California, for sexual intimacy with one of two men in a car in 1953. He pleaded guilty to "lewd vagrancy," for which he served sixty days in jail and had to register with the Pasadena Police Department as a sex offender. Governor Gavin Newsom pardoned him in February 2020, thirty-three years after Rustin died. He had been a member of the Young Communist League in the late 1930s and early 1940s, quickly abandoning the party once it advocated support for the Soviet war effort, in favor of integrationist and pacifist organizations.
46. Taylor, *Knocking at Our Own Door*, 124–44; "Statement on the Establishment of the Harlem Freedom Schools," Harlem Neighborhoods Association records, 1941–1978, Sc MG #364, Box 6, Folder "HANA Committees—Harlem Parents Committee, August 1963–1965," SCRBC.
47. "Received by Hand from Stanley Lowel [sic]," September 5, 1963, Harlem Neighborhoods Association records, 1941–1978, Sc MG #364, Box 6, Folder "HANA Committees—Harlem Parents Committee, August 1963–1965," SCRBC.
48. "100 Years . . . What Is 'All Deliberate Speed?'" flier, November 29, 1963, Harlem Neighborhoods Association records, 1941–1978, Sc MG #364, Box 6, Folder "HANA Committees—Harlem Parents Committee, June 1963–July 1963," SCRBC.

49. Wallace S. Sayre and Herbert Kaufman, *Governing New York City: Politics in the Metropolis* (New York: Norton, 1965), 235–36.
50. Sayre and Kaufman, *Governing New York City*, 283. There were fourteen school boards in Manhattan, ten in the Bronx, twenty in Brooklyn, eight in Queens, and two in Staten Island. Clark, *Dark Ghetto*, 137.
51. "Boycott Jim Crow Schools" flier, Harlem Neighborhoods Association records, 1941–1978, Sc MG #364, Box 6, Folder "HANA Committees—Harlem Parents Committee, June 1963–July 1963," SCRBC.
52. "Statement of the Chairman, Mr. Robinson Delivered Before the Public Meeting Held with Dr. Calvin Gross, Superintendent of Schools, August 14, 1963, P.S. 108, Man. 108th Street and Madison Avenue, N.Y.C," Harlem Neighborhoods Association records, 1941–1978, Sc MG #364, Box 6, Folder "HANA Committees—Harlem Parents Committee, August 1963–1965," SCRBC.
53. Fred Halstead, Anthony Aviles, and Don Charles, *Harlem Stirs* (New York: Marzani & Munsell, 1966), 104. Significantly, between 100,000 and 150,000 of them were Puerto Rican. Galamison organized a second boycott for March 16. Despite less public support for the event, 268,000 students stayed home that day, 168,000 more than the daily absentee average.
54. Leonard Buder, "Boycott Cripples City Schools; Absences 360,000 Above Normal; Negroes and Puerto Ricans Unite," *New York Times*, February 4, 1964.
55. Taylor, *Knocking at Our Own Door*, 113.
56. Rogers, *110 Livingston Street*, 18, 24–34; Clark, *Dark Ghetto*, 115.
57. Peter Kihss, "New Group Fights Mass Pupil Shifts," *New York Times*, October 3, 1963.
58. Fred Powledge, "Oppose Shifting of Pupils: Demonstrators March at City Hall Against Board of Education's Integration Plan," *New York Times*, March 13, 1964.
59. Joseph Lelyveld, "Parents to Stage a Protest Today," *New York Times*, March 12, 1964.
60. Leonard Buder, "275,638 Pupils Stay Home in Integration Boycott; Total 175,000 Over Normal," *New York Times*, September 15, 1964. At one school in the Bensonhurst section of Brooklyn not involved with pairing, all 475 students stayed home. Thomas Buckley, "Absenteeism 100% at Unpaired School," *New York Times*, September 15, 1964; Leonard Buder, "School Boycott Eases on 2d Day; Gross Stays Firm," *New York Times*, September 16, 1964. White parents had far more faith in the will of the school system to address racial segregation. Their main fear, given how small the pairing program was, was that even though the schools their children attended were not paired, sooner or later the city would come for them. Most parents, when pressed, claimed they were simply opposed to the forced transfer of students.
61. HARYOU, *Youth in the Ghetto: A Study of the Consequences of Powerlessness and a Blueprint for Change* (New York: Harlem Youth Opportunities Unlimited, 1964), 231.
62. Halstead, Aviles, and Charles, *Harlem Stirs*, 14.
63. Pinkney and Woock, *Poverty and Politics in Harlem*, 35.
64. Brian Purnell, "A Movement Grows in Brooklyn: The Brooklyn Chapter of the Congress of Racial Equality (CORE) and the Northern Civil Rights Movement During the Early 1960s," PhD diss., New York University, Graduate School of Arts and Science, 2006, 23.

65. Milton Galamison, "Bedford-Stuyvesant—Land of Superlatives," in *Harlem, U.S.A.*, ed. John Henrik Clarke (New York: Collier, 1971), 205.
66. "Wilkins Calls for Firm School Program in NYC," April 17, 1964, Papers of the NAACP: Part 3: The Campaign for Educational Equality; Series D: Central Office Records, 1956–1965; Reel 7: Desegregation, Schools; Desegregation NYC General 1964.
67. "Desegregating the Public Schools of New York City: A Report Prepared for the Board of Education of the City of New York," 5–8, Papers of the NAACP; Markowitz and Rosner, *Children, Race, and Power*, 105, 106; Clark, *Dark Ghetto*, 114; "Wilkins Calls for Firm School Program in NYC," April 17, 1964, Papers of the NAACP: Part 3: The Campaign for Educational Equality; Series D: Central Office Records, 1956–1965; Reel 7: Desegregation, Schools; Desegregation NYC General 1964.

5. The New York City Police Department

1. United States, Tom Wicker, and Otto Kerner, *Report of the National Advisory Commission on Civil Disorders* (New York: Dutton, 1968), 321.
2. Paul Chevigny, *Edge of the Knife: Police Violence in the Americas* (New York: New Press, 1995); Paul Chevigny, *Police Power: Police Abuses in New York City* (New York: Pantheon, 1969); Marilynn S. Johnson, *Street Justice: A History of Police Violence in New York City* (Boston: Beacon, 2003); Clarence Taylor, *Fight the Power: African Americans and the Long History of Police Brutality in New York City* (New York: New York University Press, 2019).
3. Leonard Shecter, *On the Pad: The Underworld and Its Corrupt Police: Confessions of a Cop on the Take* (New York: Putnam, 1973), 85, 200, 201. Johnson describes the third degree as a "highly elastic term," which "encompassed a variety of questionable police interrogation practices including physical violence and torture, prolonged grilling, food and sleep deprivation, and psychological coercion." Such practices began falling out of favor in the 1930s, thanks to a combination of judicial decisions, reform-oriented police officials, and pressure from activists. They did not cease entirely and were once again accepted during America's War on Terror, reborn as "extraordinary rendition." Johnson, *Street Justice*, 122. The U.S. Supreme Court's 1966 decision in *Miranda v. Arizona* required police officers to inform arrestees of their rights to legal representation and against self-incrimination.
4. Shecter, *On the Pad*, 202.
5. T. J. English, *The Savage City: Race, Murder, and a Generation on the Edge* (New York: William Morrow, 2012), 74, 122.
6. Lez Edmond, "Harlem Diary—'The Long, Hot Summer,'" in *Reporting Civil Rights*, part 2: *American Journalism, 1963–1973* (New York: Library of America, 2003), 153–55; Layhmond Robinson, "Negroes' View of Plight Examined in Survey Here," *New York Times*, July 27, 1964; Pratt Institute, *Stuyvesant Heights: A Good Neighborhood in Need of Help* (Brooklyn: Community Education Program, Planning Dept., Pratt Institute, 1965), 22–25; Joseph P. Viteritti, *Police, Politics, and Pluralism in New York City: A Comparative Case Study* (Beverly Hills, CA: Sage, 1973), 13.
7. Arthur Niederhoffer, *Behind the Shield: The Police in Urban Society* (Garden City, NY: Doubleday, 1967), 61.

8. Martin Luther King Jr., "Beyond the Los Angeles Riots," *Saturday Review*, November 13, 1965.
9. Michael F. Armstrong, *They Wished They Were Honest: The Knapp Commission and New York City Police Corruption* (New York: Columbia University Press, 2012), 4.
10. The department's maximum authorized size was 26,726. Bernard Stengren, "4,700 Teenagers Take Police Tests for Trainee Posts," *New York Times*, March 22, 1964.
11. Bernard Stengren, "127 Women Take Sergeant's Test," *New York Times*, April 12, 1964. The test put them in line to be promoted to sergeant when openings arose. The list was supposed to rank candidates by their scores on the test. If promoted, new sergeants made $8,405 in 1964. The list was thrown out every four years, with 1965 being one of those years; anyone who wanted to get back on the list would need to retake the test. Richard Goldstein, "Gertrude Schimmel, 96, a Police Pioneer," *New York Times*, May 13, 2015.
12. Niederhoffer, *Behind the Shield*, 16, 17, 34–39. At the time, the NYPD's ranks were patrolman, sergeant, lieutenant, captain, deputy inspector, inspector, deputy chief inspector, assistant chief inspector, and chief inspector. Sergeant through captain required civil service exams. The commissioner appointed everyone above captain. Forty years earlier, police officers had come from the lower classes. During the Great Depression, a paucity of employment opportunities allowed the NYPD to be much more selective in its hiring, as many young men who would have sought out other professions were out of work. In 1940, more than half of new recruits had graduated college. The 1960s NYPD was predominantly Irish (close to 45 percent), followed by Italians (about 25 percent), Jews (around 10 percent), Germans (less than 10 percent), Poles (5 percent), and Greeks (a little more than 1 percent). Black men were about 5 percent, and Puerto Ricans numbered even fewer than women, at less than one-tenth of 1 percent. It was also 70 percent Catholic. Viteritti, *Police, Politics, and Pluralism in New York City*, 16.
13. Niederhoffer, *Behind the Shield*, 42–45. The Bureau of Labor Statistics' inflation calculator equates this starting salary to over $53,000 in 2021 dollars. http://data.bls.gov/cgi-bin/cpicalc.pl.
14. Armstrong, *They Wished They Were Honest*, 84.
15. Niederhoffer, *Behind the Shield*, 44–51.
16. John V. Lindsay, *The City* (New York: New American Library, 1970), 180, 181; Viteritti, *Police, Politics, and Pluralism in New York City*, 13.
17. Robert Leuci, *All the Centurions: A New York City Cop Remembers His Years on the Street, 1961–1981* (New York: William Morrow, 2004), 16, 17.
18. Armstrong, *They Wished They Were Honest*, 86.
19. Shecter, *On the Pad*, 176.
20. Shecter, *On the Pad*, 91–110.
21. *The Knapp Commission Report on Police Corruption*, 170–72. Six hundred dollars in the mid-1960s is over $5,000 in 2021, adjusted for inflation, a potentially ruinous amount of money for restaurants, which commonly operate on very thin margins.
22. Leuci, *All the Centurions*, 29, 30, 241; *The Knapp Commission Report on Police Corruption*, 2, 3, 66–68, 177; Armstrong, *They Wished They Were Honest*, 52; Shecter, *On the Pad*, 98, 119. Collecting kickbacks from tow truck drivers and undertakers for directing business their way and threatening business owners in heavily permitted industries such as

construction, dining, and liquor sales with significant fines if they did not pay up were other sources of illicit income officers derived from legal businesses.
23. *The Knapp Commission Report on Police Corruption*, 170–78.
24. Armstrong, *They Wished They Were Honest*, 36.
25. Fred J. Cook and Gene Gleason, "The Shame of New York," *The Nation*, October 31, 1959, 311, 312. All captains were men until 1971, when Commissioner Patrick Murphy promoted Gertrude Schimmel, one of the first female sergeants and lieutenants.
26. *The Knapp Commission Report on Police Corruption*, 2.
27. Armstrong, *They Wished They Were Honest*, 121. $250 adjusts to over two thousand dollars in 2021.
28. Shecter, *On the Pad*, 104, 158, 188.
29. Leuci, *All the Centurions*, 171; Armstrong, *They Wished They Were Honest*, 119.
30. Shecter, *On the Pad*, 158.
31. Shecter, *On the Pad*, 90.
32. Leuci, *All the Centurions*, 175, 176; *The Knapp Commission Report on Police Corruption*, 3, 97. Meade Esposito, head of the Kings County Democratic Committee from the late sixties to the early eighties, faced numerous credible allegations of corruption, including selling judgeships, throughout his career.
33. *The Knapp Commission Report on Police Corruption*, 3, 167, 168. In the mid-1960s, uniformed officers occupied virtually every position in a precinct, including clerical work, payroll, and answering the phones. The only civilians would have been maintenance staff. Five hundred dollars in the mid-1960s is equivalent to more than $4,200 in 2021. Shecter, *On the Pad*, 86.
34. Shecter, *On the Pad*, 91, 179–82.
35. Armstrong, *They Wished They Were Honest*, 86, 119. Logan lost his job when caught accepting a drug dealer's bribe in 1971. He became a cab driver and then resurfaced in 1992, when he was sentenced to prison for life for helping to run a nationwide LSD operation that used Grateful Dead shows as distribution points. Robert F. Howe, "Californian Charged with Heading National LSD Ring Tied to Va. Cases," *Washington Post*, May 6, 1993.
36. *The Knapp Commission Report on Police Corruption*, 180, 184, 185.
37. Shecter, *On the Pad*, 97; Leuci, *All the Centurions*, 36, 37.
38. *Knapp Commission Report on Police Corruption*, 78.
39. Kenneth Clark, *Dark Ghetto: Dilemmas of Social Power* (New York: Harper & Row, 1967), 29.
40. Claude Brown, *Manchild in the Promised Land* (New York: Macmillan, 1965), 182. In 1982, Grandmaster Flash and the Furious Five, from the South Bronx, illustrated that numbers was still relevant in "The Message": "You'll admire all the number-book takers." A decade later, Nas, from Queens, boasted "'Cause in the streets, I'm well known like the number man," in his 1992 debut single, "Halftime."
41. Leuci, *All the Centurions*, 104, 105.
42. *Knapp Commission Report on Police Corruption*, 61, 71.
43. Themis Chronopoulos, "Police Misconduct, Community Opposition, and Urban Governance in New York City, 1945–1965," *Journal of Urban History* 44, no. 4 (2015): 655; Jack Roth, "Police Found Lax in Harlem Gaming," *New York Times*, March 12, 1959. In the

mid-twentieth century century, the NYPD was composed of seven borough commands—Manhattan North, Manhattan South, Brooklyn North, Brooklyn South, Queens, Bronx, and Staten Island. Each of those was composed of several divisions, which in turn contained several precincts, for a total of seventeen divisions and seventy-four precincts.

44. Cook and Gleason, "The Shame of New York," 310.
45. Chronopoulos, "Police Misconduct, Community Opposition, and Urban Governance in New York City," 655; English, *The Savage City*, 123, 124; *Knapp Commission Report on Police Corruption*, 71.
46. Cook and Gleason, "The Shame of New York," 311.
47. *Knapp Commission Report on Police Corruption*, 1; Leuci, *All the Centurions*, 105.
48. Armstrong, *They Wished They Were Honest*, vii.
49. Shecter, *On the Pad*, 111–13.
50. Armstrong, *They Wished They Were Honest*, 184.
51. Leuci, *All the Centurions*, 105.
52. Armstrong, *They Wished They Were Honest*, 2; Leuci, *All the Centurions*, 105; *Knapp Commission Report on Police Corruption*, 72.
53. *Knapp Commission Report on Police Corruption*, 3, 4; Shecter, *On the Pad*, 95, 364; Armstrong, *They Wished They Were Honest*, 119, 121, 245.
54. Eric Schneider, *Smack: Heroin and the American City* (Philadelphia: University of Pennsylvania Press, 2008), 10, 44, 113.
55. Brown, *Manchild in the Promised Land*, 253, 406.
56. Shecter, *On the Pad*, 190, 191.
57. Armstrong, *They Wished They Were Honest*, 158.
58. *Knapp Commission Report on Police Corruption*, 67, 93, 99.
59. Schneider, *Smack*, 111, 112.
60. *Knapp Commission Report on Police Corruption*, 93, 96.
61. *Knapp Commission Report on Police Corruption*, 101.
62. Shecter, *On the Pad*, 191.
63. *Knapp Commission Report on Police Corruption*, 91, 92.
64. Schneider, *Smack*, 112. Three thousand dollars in the mid-1960s adjusts to about $25,000 in 2021.
65. Schneider, *Smack*, 112–14.
66. *Knapp Commission Report on Police Corruption*, 92.
67. Schneider, *Smack*, 116–18; Jim O'Neil and Mel Fazzino, *A Cop's Tale: NYPD: The Violent Years: A Detective's Firsthand Account of Murder and Mayhem* (Fort Lee, NJ: Barricade, 2009), 68.
68. *Knapp Commission Report on Police Corruption*, 2, 106, 107; Armstrong, *They Wished They Were Honest*, 140, 145.
69. Leuci, *All the Centurions*, 312, 313; Shecter, *On the Pad*, 189. Adjusting the $73 million for inflation, discounting the changing value of drugs, results in about $500 million in 2021. NYPD officers had likely allowed for, assisted, and promoted the sale of far more heroin and cocaine than that over the same period of time.
70. United States, *The Challenge of Crime in a Free Society: A Report* (Washington: U.S. GPO, 1967); Robert M. Fogelson, *Violence as Protest: A Study of Riots and Ghettos* (Garden City,

NY: Doubleday, 1971); Joshua Benjamin Freeman, *Working-Class New York: Life and Labor Since World War II* (New York: New Press, 2000); United States, Wicker, and Kerner, *Report of the National Advisory Commission on Civil Disorders*; Martha Biondi, *To Stand and Fight: The Struggle for Civil Rights in Postwar New York City* (Cambridge, MA: Harvard University Press, 2003); Johnson, *Street Justice*; Barry Gottehrer, *New York City in Crisis: A Study in Depth of Urban Sickness* (New York: McKay, 1965); Taylor, *Fight the Power*.

71. Shecter, *On the Pad*, 123, 200; English, *The Savage City*, 339. When Algernon Black, the newly appointed chair of the Civilian Complaint Review Board, toured the Twenty-Fifth Precinct in 1966, he described the jail cells as "worse than anything we had seen in the Middle Ages. But the occupants, most of them were semi-conscious or under alcohol or drugs, and most were in filthy rags." Algernon D. Black, "Civilian Complaint Review Board," 24, October 22, 1974, Algernon D. Black Papers, Box 26, Civilian Complaint Review Board—1, Rare Book and Manuscript Library, Columbia University Library.
72. Leuci, *All the Centurions*, 50.
73. Charles R. Morris, *The Cost of Good Intentions: New York City and the Liberal Experiment, 1960–1975* (New York: Norton, 1980), 95. A statute known as the Lyons Law required municipal workers to live in the city but was repealed in 1962. Many police had already been living outside the city before this, but the abolishment of this law led to an exodus.
74. Brown, *Manchild in the Promised Land*, 190.
75. Armstrong, *They Wished They Were Honest*, 86.
76. HARYOU, *Youth in the Ghetto: A Study of the Consequences of Powerlessness and a Blueprint for Change* (New York: Harlem Youth Opportunities Unlimited, 1964), 79, 135; Clark, *Dark Ghetto*, 174.
77. Brown, *Manchild in the Promised Land*, 191. Kenneth Clark assessed Powell as a fundamentally corrupt man, driven by money and power. Richard Severo, "Kenneth Clark, Who Helped End Segregation, Dies," *New York Times*, May 2, 2005.
78. A few years after *Dark Ghetto*, the social scientist David Boesel provided a framework for understanding segregated, disinvested neighborhoods as colonies, arguing that a place like Harlem "is not simply a repository for an aggregate of uprooted black people—unlike those sprawling shanty towns on the outskirts of cities in the Third World. Rather the ghetto represents a system of control presided over by white people, the main function of which has been to prevent the urban influx of blacks from disrupting established social, economic and political relations in white society." Such neighborhoods are "composed of a series of functionally reciprocal institutions run by whites, which provision and control the black residents. The cornerstone, a segregated housing market tightly controlled by white realtors, confines black people to a restricted area, providing a basis for—among other things—largely segregated and decidedly inferior schools, again run by whites." David Boesel, "An Analysis of the Ghetto Riots," in *Cities Under Siege: An Anatomy of the Ghetto Riots, 1964–1968*, ed. David Boesel and Peter H. Rossi (New York: Basic Books, 1971), 329.
79. Leuci, *All the Centurions*, 30, 174. Leuci claims he was living paycheck to paycheck on $18,000 a year in the late 1960s, or more than $135,000 adjusted for inflation in 2021. Shecter, *On the Pad*, 111, 207.

80. English, *The Savage City*, 346.
81. English, *The Savage City*, 124.
82. *Knapp Commission Report on Police Corruption*, 6, 7.
83. "Who Speaks for Harlem?," moderated by Edwin Newman, WNBC, July 26, 1964.
84. Brown, *Manchild in the Promised Land*, 190.

6. A Death and Protests

1. Gerald Horne argues that the "dramatic nature" of uprisings "grabs and holds attention and can motivate sweeping social reform.... Uprisings also can be inspirational.... The character and tactics of Watts 1965 were imitated in Newark, Detroit, and a host of other cities." I agree with him, but this argument should be applied to Harlem and Bedford-Stuyvesant in 1964. New York's uprisings were major news. Watts was but a larger conflagration. Gerald Horne, *Fire This Time: The Watts Uprising and the 1960s* (Charlottesville: University Press of Virginia, 1995), 41–42.
2. Whitney Young of the Urban League, Roy Wilkins of the National Association for the Advancement of Colored People, and James Farmer of the Congress of Racial Equality all called the New York area home. Only Martin Luther King Jr. of the Southern Christian Leadership Conference and John Lewis of the Student Nonviolent Coordinating Committee lived elsewhere, in Atlanta. Regardless of where they lived, none of these men had much influence in New York City, as they were all generally seen as dealing with southern issues. Even when accounting for the fact that Young, Wilkins, and Farmer may not have been present in the city often during the early 1960s, frequently away for various campaigns and engagements, their underwhelming influence in New York helps show the profound divides between the national organizations and the millions of African Americans living in the North in the early 1960s. A. Philip Randolph, who was among other things the head of the Brotherhood of Sleeping Car Porters, the organizer of 1941's March on Washington Movement, and both the originator and director of the 1963 March on Washington for Jobs and Freedom, lived in New York City for the better part of seven decades, as did Malcolm X for most of the last decade of his life.
3. Herb Goldstein and Edward Cumberbatch, "After a Boy's Funeral, a Rights Leader Weeps," *New York Post*, July 20, 1964. Though the city's neighborhood borders tend to be fluid over time, Manhattan's Yorkville section was recognized in 1964 as the area spanning the distance between Seventy-Second Street, East Harlem at Ninety-Sixth Street, Third Avenue, and the East River. Jack Newfield, *Robert Kennedy: A Memoir* (New York: New American Library, 1988), 90; T. J. English, *The Savage City: Race, Murder, and a Generation on the Edge* (New York: William Morrow, 2012), 5. Marchers could travel by one of thirteen reserved trains, more than nine hundred charter buses, or the countless cars and vans private citizens, organizations, and church groups employed to transport them.
4. Theodore Jones, "Negro Boy Killed; 300 Harass Police," *New York Times*, July 17, 1964.
5. Sue Reinert, "Near Riot—Student Slain by Policeman," *New York Herald Tribune*, July 17, 1964.
6. Theodore Jones, "Teen-age Parade Protests Killing," *New York Times*, July 18, 1964.

7. Jones, "Negro Boy Killed; 300 Harass Police."
8. Martin Arnold, "Police Board Absolves Gilligan in Slaying of Negro Teen-Ager," *New York Times*, November 7, 1964; Sue Reinert, "The Bitter Students . . . the Watchful Police," *New York Herald Tribune*, July 18, 1964.
9. Jones, "Negro Boy Killed; 300 Harass Police."
10. Arnold, "Police Board Absolves Gilligan in Slaying of Negro Teen-Ager." Theodore Jones, "Few Present as Boy Shot by Policeman Is Buried," *New York Times*, July 21, 1964.
11. Reinert, "Near Riot—Student Slain by Policeman."
12. Jones, "Teen-age Parade Protests Killing."
13. Jones, "Negro Boy Killed; 300 Harass Police."
14. Jones, "Teen-age Parade Protests Killing."
15. Jones, "Negro Boy Killed; 300 Harass Police."
16. Ralph Blumenfeld and Kenneth Gross, "City Probes Slaying of Boy, 15, by Cop," *New York Post*, July 17, 1964.
17. Reinert, "Near Riot—Student Slain by Policeman."
18. "New York: Unanimous Decision," *Time*, September 11, 1964.
19. Reinert, "The Bitter Students . . . the Watchful Police."
20. Jones, "Teen-age Parade Protests Killing."
21. Reinert, "The Bitter Students . . . the Watchful Police." In 1961, Gilligan shot a sixteen-year-old boy in front of Gilligan's house who he said had broken into a car. When Gilligan confronted him, the boy supposedly hit him in the hand with a fire-hose nozzle, breaking two fingers. Gilligan then shot him, but the boy "was not seriously injured." It would not be until 1967 that the NYPD would restrict the use of deadly force to either life-threatening situations or in the interest of taking violent felons into custody.
22. Blumenfeld and Gross, "City Probes Slaying of Boy, 15, by Cop."
23. "Why Not Suspend the Cop?" *New York Amsterdam News*, July 25, 1964.
24. "Text of F.B.I. Report to President on Summer Riots in 9 Cities Over Country," *New York Times*, September 27, 1964.
25. Jones, "Negro Boy Killed; 300 Harass Police."
26. Reinert, "Near Riot—Student Slain by Policeman."
27. Jones, "Negro Boy Killed; 300 Harass Police."
28. Reinert, "Near Riot—Student Slain by Policeman."
29. Reinert, "Near Riot—Student Slain by Policeman."
30. Jones, "Teen-age Parade Protests Killing."
31. "The Slain Boy: Neighborhood Views Conflict," *New York Post*, July 17, 1964.
32. Jones, "Negro Boy Killed; 300 Harass Police."
33. Reinert, "Near Riot—Student Slain by Policeman."
34. Jones, "Negro Boy Killed; 300 Harass Police."
35. Blumenfeld and Gross, "City Probes Slaying of Boy, 15, by Cop."
36. Reinert, "The Bitter Students . . . the Watchful Police."
37. Reinert, "The Bitter Students . . . the Watchful Police"; Jones, "Teen-Age Parade Protests Killing."
38. Reinert, "The Bitter Students . . . the Watchful Police."
39. Reinert, "The Bitter Students . . . the Watchful Police."

40. "Mother Hysterical at Boy's Bier," *New York Times*, July 19, 1964.
41. Paul L. Montgomery, "Night of Riots Began with Calm Rally," *New York Times*, July 20, 1964.
42. Paul Montgomery and Francis X. Clines, "Thousands Riot in Harlem Area; Scores Are Hurt," *New York Times*, July 19, 1964.
43. Montgomery, "Night of Riots Began with Calm Rally."
44. Montgomery and Clines, "Thousands Riot in Harlem Area; Scores Are Hurt."
45. Joseph Endler and James W. Sullivan, "Harlem Explodes: Negroes Battle Police," *New York Herald Tribune*, July 19, 1964.
46. Montgomery and Clines, "Thousands Riot in Harlem Area; Scores Are Hurt."
47. Montgomery, "Night of Riots Began with Calm Rally."
48. Montgomery, "Night of Riots Began with Calm Rally."
49. Montgomery, "Night of Riots Began with Calm Rally." Commissioner Stephen P. Kennedy established the TPF in 1959. A former officer recalls the initial plan was to call the organization Special Services, but with World War II fairly fresh in people's minds, the commissioner thought better of NYPD officers wearing lapel pins reading "SS." Robert Leuci, *All the Centurions: A New York City Cop Remembers His Years on the Street, 1961–1981* (New York: William Morrow, 2004), 45.
50. Montgomery and Clines, "Thousands Riot in Harlem Area; Scores Are Hurt." A former member of the TPF later made bold statements about how the group generally operated: "We took out our axe handles, which were longer, heavier, and better in a fight than our nightsticks—hey only dumb animals don't use tools. Fairness was not in our creed but winning on the street was. Instilling fear in the bad guys was what kept you and other cops alive and by extension the good citizens in your charge.... Officially we only carried department-issued nightsticks but unofficially, when it came to choice of weapons, the department always looked the other way for the TPF." Jim O'Neil and Mel Fazzino, *A Cop's Tale: NYPD: The Violent Years: A Detective's Firsthand Account of Murder and Mayhem* (Fort Lee, NJ: Barricade, 2009), 37. The Harlem Defense Council alleged that Inspector Pendergast's order was "Clear those niggers out of here." True or not, given the racism many NYPD officers exhibited, it was not hard to believe. "Police Terror in Harlem," Arnie Goldwag Brooklyn Congress of Racial Equality (CORE) collection, ARC.002, Box 3, Folder 5, Brooklyn Historical Society.
51. Ed James, "Harlem: By 2 Who Were There," *New York Post*, July 20, 1964.
52. James, "Harlem: By 2 Who Were There."
53. Montgomery, "Night of Riots Began with Calm Rally."
54. Montgomery, "Night of Riots Began with Calm Rally."
55. Francis X. Clines, "Policemen Exhaust Their Ammunition in All-Night Battle," *New York Times*, July 20, 1964.
56. O'Neil and Fazzino, *A Cop's Tale*, 44.
57. Montgomery, "Night of Riots Began with Calm Rally."
58. Bill Whitworth, "Tinderbox Harlem: Saturday Night and Sunday Morning," *New York Herald Tribune*, July 20, 1964.
59. Fred Ferretti and Martin G. Berck, "Tinderbox Harlem: New Outbursts Snap Uneasy Truce," *New York Herald Tribune*, July 20, 1964.

60. Montgomery and Clines, "Thousands Riot in Harlem Area; Scores Are Hurt."
61. Whitworth, "Tinderbox Harlem: Saturday Night and Sunday Morning."
62. Montgomery and Clines, "Thousands Riot in Harlem Area; Scores Are Hurt."
63. Whitworth, "Tinderbox Harlem: Saturday Night and Sunday Morning."
64. George Barner, "Three Violent Days," *New York Amsterdam News*, July 25, 1964.
65. Whitworth, "Tinderbox Harlem: Saturday Night and Sunday Morning."
66. Montgomery and Clines, "Thousands Riot in Harlem Area; Scores Are Hurt."
67. R. W. Apple Jr., "Police Defend the Use of Gunfire in Controlling Riots in Harlem," *New York Times*, July 21, 1964; Ted Poston and Ralph Blumenthal, "Riot Toll: 1 Killed, 119 Hurt," *New York Post*, July 20, 1964.
68. "Says Police Shot to Kill," *New York Times*, July 21, 1964.
69. James, "Harlem: By 2 Who Were There."
70. Clines, "Policemen Exhaust Their Ammunition in All-Night Battle."
71. Whitworth, "Tinderbox Harlem: Saturday Night and Sunday Morning."
72. Whitworth, "Tinderbox Harlem: Saturday Night and Sunday Morning."
73. Apple, "Violence Flares Again in Harlem; Restraint Urged."
74. Montgomery and Clines, "Thousands Riot in Harlem Area; Scores Are Hurt"; Ferretti and Berck, "Tinderbox Harlem: New Outbursts Snap Uneasy Truce."
75. Montgomery and Clines, "Thousands Riot in Harlem Area; Scores Are Hurt."
76. Leuci, *All the Centurions*, 63.
77. Apple, "Violence Flares Again in Harlem; Restraint Urged."
78. O'Neil and Fazzino, *A Cop's Tale*, 45.
79. Ferretti and Berck, "Tinderbox Harlem: New Outbursts Snap Uneasy Truce." An NYPD detective who claims to have been on the scene as a young officer at the time of Jenkins's shooting asserts the same inspector who headed the TPF rewarded Jenkins's shooter with sandwiches and beer. O'Neil and Fazzino, *A Cop's Tale*, 44.
80. Edward Cumberbatch, "Harlem: By 2 Who Were There," *New York Post*, July 20, 1964.
81. Poston and Blumenthal, "Riot Toll: 1 Killed, 119 Hurt."
82. "Another Look at 'Why the Harlem Riots?,'" *New York Amsterdam News*, August 1, 1964. Communists and radical labor organizers popularized "Cossack" earlier in the twentieth century as a derogatory term for the police, referencing the ethnic soldiers famous for their brutality while suppressing insurrection during the Russian revolution of 1905.
83. Ferretti and Berck, "Tinderbox Harlem: New Outbursts Snap Uneasy Truce."
84. Ferretti and Berck, "Tinderbox Harlem: New Outbursts Snap Uneasy Truce."
85. Apple, "Violence Flares Again in Harlem; Restraint Urged."
86. Paul Chevigny, *Police Power: Police Abuses in New York City* (New York: Pantheon, 1969), 141–43.
87. James, "Harlem: By 2 Who Were There."
88. Cumberbatch, "Harlem: By 2 Who Were There." James Farmer believes Malcolm X was fortunate to have been elsewhere at the time: "Malcolm, luckily for him, during the Harlem riot, was out of the country, that summer of 1964. . . . He was out of the country. Had he been in the country then, he would have had the awful dilemma of putting up or shutting up. He'd been talking violence and guys said, 'OK, here we are now, tell us what to do. Join us.' He couldn't have done it. Then he'd just have to keep quiet, or he would be

telling them to 'shit or get off the pot.'" Reminiscences of James Farmer (1979), 294, Columbia Center for Oral History Archives, Rare Book & Manuscript Library, Columbia University in the City of New York.
89. Apple, "Police Defend the Use of Gunfire in Controlling Riots in Harlem"; Reminiscences of James Farmer, 295.
90. Fred Powledge, "Screvane to Meet Rights Leaders," *New York Times*, July 20, 1964.
91. Edward Cumberbatch and Alfred T. Hendricks, "Woman Accuses Cop in Shooting," *New York Post*, July 21, 1964; "Harlem: Hatred in the Streets," *Newsweek*, August 3, 1964.
92. Clines, "Policemen Exhaust Their Ammunition in All-Night Battle."
93. Ferretti and Berck, "Tinderbox Harlem: New Outbursts Snap Uneasy Truce."
94. Amiri Baraka, *The Autobiography of LeRoi Jones* (New York: Freundlich, 1984), 192, 193.

7. Daybreak: Sunday, July 19

1. Paul Montgomery and Francis X. Clines, "Thousands Riot in Harlem Area; Scores Are Hurt," *New York Times*, July 19, 1964.
2. Francis X. Clines, "Policemen Exhaust Their Ammunition in All-Night Battle," *New York Times*, July 20, 1964.
3. "Behind the Harlem Riots—Two Views," *New York Herald Tribune*, July 20, 1964. Murphy claimed sixteen civilians were injured; newspaper headlines and articles refer to "scores."
4. Fred Ferretti and Martin G. Berck, "Tinderbox Harlem: New Outbursts Snap Uneasy Truce," *New York Herald Tribune*, July 20, 1964.
5. Ferretti and Berck, "Tinderbox Harlem: New Outbursts Snap Uneasy Truce."
6. Junius Griffin, "'Guerilla War' Urged in Harlem," *New York Times*, July 20, 1964. Jesse Gray, in a courtroom hearing a week later, testified that he was referring to the possible necessity of guerilla warfare in Mississippi, not New York. In his words, "I introduced the speakers at the meeting in Mount Morris Presbyterian Church and then I said that people in New York and Chicago were saying that guerilla warfare might be the only solution in Mississippi. To change the situation it might be necessary to shoot and kill. I told the audience, about 600 people, that I, too, felt that in Mississippi guerilla warfare might be the only solution, but I did not know what should be done in New York, did not know the solution." As for the one hundred Black revolutionaries, he attested, "I did call for 100 men to die for freedom if necessary—100 key people, each something like a platoon leader. They must be trained to organize because lack of organization was the weakness in Harlem. Each leader would get 100 others and we would have a well-trained force to protect us and to achieve our rights in housing, jobs, schools and against police brutality." Henry Beckett, "Jesse Gray Back on Stand," *New York Post*, July 29, 1964.
7. Griffin, "'Guerilla War' Urged in Harlem."
8. Griffin, "'Guerilla War' Urged in Harlem"; Ted Poston and Ralph Blumenthal, "Riot Toll: 1 Killed, 119 Hurt," *New York Post*, July 20, 1964.
9. Lez Edmond, "Harlem Diary—'The Long, Hot Summer,'" in *Reporting Civil Rights*, part 2: *American Journalism, 1963–1973* (New York: Library of America, 2003), 143.

10. Edmond, "Harlem Diary," 143.
11. Ferretti and Berck, "Tinderbox Harlem: New Outbursts Snap Uneasy Truce."
12. R. W. Apple Jr., "Violence Flares Again in Harlem; Restraint Urged," *New York Times*, July 20, 1964.
13. *Harlem: Test for the North*, WNBC, July 26, 1964. An extended portion of Farmer's comments, as captured on tape: "Fellow freedom fighters—my brothers, I think the time has come when people in Harlem have got to unite. We cannot afford this division and this warfare among ourselves. What I saw last night, I saw the cops who were united, and I saw black men and women running this way, that way, the other way, undecided which way they were going. I saw New York's night of Birmingham horror. A Negro woman walked up to the cops last night—I was there for five and a half hours walking the streets—the Negro woman walked up to the cops and said, 'Help me get a taxi so I can go home.' A policeman drew his revolver and shot her in the groin. She wound up in Harlem Hospital. Yes, CORE field secretary Lewis Smith helped her into an ambulance and took her to Harlem Hospital. [crowd noise] Now, hold it just a minute, now wait. Brothers, I share your anger. You have a right to be angry, but let me tell you the whole story, what was happening there. Do you know that the police went into a grocery store, the cops went into a grocery store and beat up people who were merely customers at the store? Nobody was throwing anything—men, women and children. We have the numbers, the badge numbers of those policemen. I saw police shooting into homes, tenement houses, and into the Theresa Hotel. Went into the Theresa Hotel and in two rooms, 806 and 808, there were bullet holes through the window, through the woodwork, and buried into the ceiling and the walls. Three bullet holes in one room and two bullet holes in another. While we are still here shouting down one another, disagreeing, we cannot get together. Mr. Charlie gets together." Given the nature of Farmer's claims, that this meeting was the day after the first night of upheaval, and the already highly inflamed sentiments of those in attendance, it is not surprising that some men were moved to immediately bring the fight to the police.
14. Ferretti and Berck, "Tinderbox Harlem: New Outbursts Snap Uneasy Truce."
15. Ferretti and Berck, "Tinderbox Harlem: New Outbursts Snap Uneasy Truce." Rustin's homosexuality was a likely factor in the degree of enmity he experienced during the disturbances.
16. *Harlem: Test for the North*.
17. Staughton Lynd, *Nonviolence in America: A Documentary History* (Indianapolis, IN: Bobbs-Merrill, 1966), 497.
18. Lynd, *Nonviolence in America*, 495–97.
19. Martin Luther King Jr., "Next Stop: The North," *Saturday Review*, November 13, 1965, 35.
20. Reminiscences of James Farmer (1979), 318, Columbia Center for Oral History Archives, Rare Book & Manuscript Library, Columbia University in the City of New York.
21. King, "Next Stop: The North," 33.
22. David Boesel, "An Analysis of the Ghetto Riots," in *Cities Under Siege: An Anatomy of the Ghetto Riots, 1964–1968*, ed. David Boesel and Peter H. Rossi (New York: Basic Books, 1971), 326.

23. Kenneth B. Clark, *Dark Ghetto: Dilemmas of Social Power* (New York: Harper & Row, 1967), 184.
24. Fred Powledge, "Screvane to Meet Rights Leaders," *New York Times*, July 20, 1964.
25. Apple, "Violence Flares Again in Harlem; Restraint Urged"; Theodore Jones, "Witnesses Praise Two Negro Officers in Harlem," *New York Times*, July 23, 1964.
26. "Another Look at 'Why the Harlem Riots?,'" *New York Amsterdam News*, August 1, 1964.
27. Apple, "Violence Flares Again in Harlem; Restraint Urged"; Jones, "Witnesses Praise Two Negro Officers in Harlem."
28. Ferretti and Berck, "Tinderbox Harlem: New Outbursts Snap Uneasy Truce."
29. Ferretti and Berck, "Tinderbox Harlem: New Outbursts Snap Uneasy Truce"; "Malcolm X Lays Harlem Riot to 'Scare Tactics' of Police," *New York Times*, July 21, 1964.
30. Herb Goldstein and Edward Cumberbatch, "After a Boy's Funeral, a Rights Leader Weeps," *New York Post*, July 20, 1964.
31. Apple, "Violence Flares Again in Harlem; Restraint Urged."
32. Apple, "Violence Flares Again in Harlem; Restraint Urged."
33. Ferretti and Berck, "Tinderbox Harlem: New Outbursts Snap Uneasy Truce."
34. Leonard Katz and Normand Poirier, "Crowd Awaits the Injured at the Hospital," *New York Post*, July 20, 1964.
35. Poston and Blumenthal, "Riot Toll: 1 Killed, 119 Hurt."
36. Poston and Blumenthal, "Riot Toll: 1 Killed, 119 Hurt"; Paul Hoffman, "A Second 15-Year-Old Is Shot," *New York Post*, July 20, 1964.
37. Katz and Poirier, "Crowd Awaits the Injured at the Hospital."
38. Apple, "Violence Flares Again in Harlem; Restraint Urged."
39. "'Casualty' List in Battle of Harlem," *New York Amsterdam News*, July 25, 1964.

8. Spreading Anxiety: Monday, July 20

1. Mayor Wagner told President Johnson on July 22 he believed that those citizens actively participating in the unrest "may want to go to the southeast Bronx, you see, and that sort of stretches our manpower a bit, but so far we're all right in that direction." "Lyndon Johnson and Robert Wagner on 22 July 1964," Conversation WH6407-12-4304, *Presidential Recordings Digital Edition, Lyndon B. Johnson: Civil Rights, Vietnam, and the War on Poverty*, ed. David G. Coleman, Kent B. Germany, Guian A. McKee, and Marc J. Selverstone (Charlottesville: University of Virginia Press, 2014–), https://www.prde.upress.virginia.edu/conversations/4000569.
2. Theodore Jones, "Few Present as Boy Shot by Policeman Is Buried," *New York Times*, July 21, 1964.
3. Jones, "Few Present as Boy Shot by Policeman Is Buried"; Sue Reinert, "Harsh Words, No Violence at Boy's Funeral," *New York Herald Tribune*, July 21, 1964.
4. Fred Powledge, "Screvane to Meet Rights Leaders," *New York Times*, July 20, 1964. The City Commission on Human Rights dates back, in various forms, to Mayor La Guardia's administration in 1944. Taking its current name in 1955, it was a frustrated agency

empowered only to deal with housing discrimination, and even then it could only take enforcement action after first obtaining a court order to do so. It was mainly an investigatory body and also held hearings. If someone came to it with a complaint regarding prejudice in the workplace, for example, the CCHR could take no action apart from referring the individual to the State Commission for Human Rights. This did not change until late 1965. Peter Kihss, "New Law Increases Powers of City Rights Board," *New York Times*, December 16, 1965.

5. Peter Kihss, "City to Increase Negro Policemen on Harlem Duty," *New York Times*, July 21, 1964.
6. Maurice C. Carroll and Edward J. Silberfarb, "Harlem Seethes for 3d Night; Mayor Summoned from Spain," *New York Herald Tribune*, July 21, 1964. A representative for the VA later denied this but did acknowledge that the lieutenant had been receiving and would continue to receive a $77 monthly disability check for an undisclosed condition related to his time in the service, $700 in 2021 dollars.
7. Kihss, "City to Increase Negro Policemen on Harlem Duty."
8. Kihss, "City to Increase Negro Policemen on Harlem Duty."
9. Kihss, "City to Increase Negro Policemen on Harlem Duty."
10. Carroll and Silberfarb, "Harlem Seethes for 3d Night; Mayor Summoned from Spain."
11. Kihss, "City to Increase Negro Policemen on Harlem Duty." Robinson was the first National Vice President of the Negro American Labor Council, which A. Philip Randolph formed in 1960, having experienced years of frustration in getting the AFL-CIO to take ending discrimination in and integrating organized labor seriously. Walter Reuther was the only major figure in organized labor to accept Randolph's invitation to address the NALC's founding convention. Reminiscences of Kenneth Bancroft Clark (1985), 540, Columbia Center for Oral History Archives, Rare Book & Manuscript Library, Columbia University in the City of New York.
12. Kihss, "City to Increase Negro Policemen on Harlem Duty."
13. "Violence Erupts for Third Night," *New York Times*, July 21, 1964; Carroll and Silberfarb, "Harlem Seethes for 3d Night; Mayor Summoned from Spain"; Peter Kihss, "Screvane Links Reds to Rioting," *New York Times*, July 22, 1964. The HDC/PLM office, combined with the neighboring building, 338, has been the home of the Harlem Church of Christ since 1984. To honor his contributions to Black life and freedom, the city gave Lenox Avenue a second official name in 1987: Malcolm X Boulevard.
14. R. W. Apple Jr., "Violence Flares Again in Harlem; Restraint Urged," *New York Times*, July 20, 1964.
15. Warren Berry, "Coast Police Asks Troops for Harlem," *New York Herald Tribune*, July 21, 1964.
16. Barbara Benson, "Why Harlem Negroes Riot," *New York Times*, July 22, 1964.
17. Claude Sitton, "Six Negroes Barred at Alabama School," *New York Times*, February 6, 1964; "Send Troops to Harlem, Alabama Mayor Urges," *New York Times*, July 22, 1964; "Alabama School Burns," *New York Times*, April 19, 1964.
18. Junius Griffin, "Harlem Businessmen Put Riot Losses at $50,000," *New York Times*, July 21, 1964.

19. Gay Talese, "Puerto Rican Peace Patrol Acts to Keep East Harlem Calm," *New York Times*, July 23, 1964.
20. Talese, "Puerto Rican Peace Patrol Acts to Keep East Harlem Calm," 13.
21. "Violence Erupts for Third Night."
22. "Violence Erupts for Third Night."
23. "Violence Erupts for Third Night."
24. Carroll and Silberfarb, "Harlem Seethes for 3d Night; Mayor Summoned from Spain."
25. "Violence Erupts for Third Night."
26. Carroll and Silberfarb, "Harlem Seethes for 3d Night; Mayor Summoned from Spain"; Ted Poston, "50 Injured in Harlem," *New York Post*, July 21, 1964.
27. Reminiscences of James Farmer (1979), 296, Columbia Center for Oral History Archives, Rare Book & Manuscript Library, Columbia University in the City of New York. Bayard Rustin attests to an incident of unprovoked violence against a white man during the uprisings in Harlem: "I saw a Negro churchwoman help to blockade a street to stop a white taxi driver. After her sons had beaten him almost to unconsciousness, she helped them to rob him, leaving him in great agony on the street." Staughton Lynd, *Nonviolence in America: A Documentary History* (Indianapolis, IN: Bobbs-Merrill, 1966), 496.
28. "Violence Erupts for Third Night."
29. "Violence Erupts for Third Night"; Carroll and Silberfarb, "Harlem Seethes for 3d Night; Mayor Summoned from Spain"; Reminiscences of James Farmer, 297, 298. Overton was a significant presence in the labor movement. He had long been a business agent with Local 338 of the Retail, Wholesale, and Department Store Employees Union in New York. He was also a national vice president of the Negro American Labor Council, succeeding Cleveland Robinson, who became president after Randolph retired in 1962.
30. Poston, "50 Injured in Harlem," 53; James Farmer, *Lay Bare the Heart: An Autobiography of the Civil Rights Movement* (New York: Arbor House, 1985), 282, 283; Reminisces of James Farmer, 298.
31. Reminisces of James Farmer, 299. He says of King's public address in Watts: "It was a good sermon and in calmer times it would have been effective. But in time of a riot, it was totally ineffective."
32. "Violence Erupts for Third Night."
33. "Violence Erupts for Third Night"; "Mobs Fight Police Again in Brooklyn and Harlem Area," *New York Times*, July 22, 1964; Lez Edmond, "Harlem Diary—'The Long, Hot Summer,'" in *Reporting Civil Rights*, part 2: *American Journalism, 1963–1973* (New York: Library of America, 2003), 147.
34. "Violence Erupts for Third Night"; Poston, "50 Injured in Harlem"; Edmond, "Harlem Diary," 148.
35. "Mobs Fight Police Again in Brooklyn and Harlem Area," *New York Times*, July 22, 1964; Poston, "50 Injured in Harlem." Poston's quote is "We don't want no liberal niggers here!"; Edmond, "Harlem Diary," 148.
36. John D'Emilio, *Lost Prophet: The Life and Times of Bayard Rustin* (New York: Free Press, 2003), 46–47, 174. Rustin refused to obey segregation laws on a 1942 bus trip from Louisville to Nashville, which resulted in Tennessee police beating him on the bus and at the

police station, along with a ceaseless torrent of racist verbal abuse. In 1949, Louisiana police "stood on him in the backseat of the car" and "knocked his teeth out" for being gay. This was a man who understood white violence, especially from the police, quite well.
37. "Violence Erupts for Third Night."
38. Poston, "50 Injured in Harlem."
39. "Mobs Fight Police Again in Brooklyn and Harlem Area."
40. Sue Reinert, "CORE's Harlem Office—Where the Wounded Talk," *New York Herald Tribune*, July 22, 1964; Maurice C. Carroll and Edward J. Silberfarb, "Wagner Takes Over in Riots; Johnson Orders FBI to City," *New York Herald Tribune*, July 22, 1964; "Mobs Fight Police Again in Brooklyn and Harlem Area."
41. "Violence Erupts for Third Night"; "Manhattan Rioting Crosses Bridges, Spreads to Brooklyn," *New York Amsterdam News*, July 25, 1964.
42. R. W. Apple Jr., "The Chief Policeman Talks About His Beat," *New York Times*, June 21, 1964.
43. Bill Whitworth, ". . . And in Brooklyn," *New York Herald Tribune*, July 20, 1964; "7 in Brownsville Seized in Battle," *New York Times*, July 20, 1964.

9. Day Four: Tuesday, July 21

1. Taylor Branch, *Pillar of Fire: America in the King Years, 1963-65* (New York: Simon & Schuster, 1998), 417, 418.
2. "Statement by President," *New York Times*, July 22, 1964. In his acceptance speech at the Republican National Convention in San Francisco on July 16, 1964, Goldwater spoke of a vision of his party in which it fights for "freedom—balanced so that liberty lacking order will not become the slavery of the prison cell; balanced so that liberty lacking order will not become the license of the mob and of the jungle." "We Republicans," in 1964, "seek a government that attends to its inherent responsibilities of maintaining a stable monetary and fiscal climate, encouraging a free and a competitive economy and enforcing law and order." And, in his most remembered line, "I would remind you that extremism in the defense of liberty is no vice. And let me remind you also that moderation in the pursuit of justice is no virtue." Moderation and compromise are interchangeable here.
3. Doris Kearns Goodwin, *Lyndon Johnson and the American Dream* (New York: St. Martin's Griffin, 1991), 305, 306. Kearns had not yet married at the time, thus the lack of the Goodwin surname in the text. The entire quotation is a baffling mix of sympathy for African Americans, paternalism, regional exceptionalism, and belief in the Lost Cause version of Reconstruction. Still, Johnson did seem to have to a real understanding of at least some aspects of contemporary Black life in America and how much more work there was to be done. His comment continues: "It was bad enough in the South—especially from the standpoint of education—but at least there the Negro knew he was really loved and cared for, which he never was in the North, where children live with rats and have no place to sleep and come from broken homes and get rejected from the Army. And then they look on TV and see all the promises of a rich country and they know that some movement is beginning to take place in their lives, so they begin to hope for a lot more. Hell,

when a person's released from jail or his parents, it is only natural that he takes advantage and turns to excess. Remember the Negroes in Reconstruction who got elected to Congress and then ran into the chamber with bare feet and white women. They were simply not prepared for their responsibility. And we weren't just enough or kind enough to help them prepare. So we lost a hundred years going backward. We'll never know how high a price we paid for the unkindness and injustice we've inflicted on people—the Negroes, Mexicans, and Jews—and everyone who really believes he has been discriminated against in any way is part of that great human price. And that cost exists where many people may not even think it does. No matter how well you may think you know a Negro, if you really know one, there'll come the time when you look at him and see how deep his bitterness is,"

4. Michael R. Beschloss, *Taking Charge: The Johnson White House Tapes, 1963–1964* (New York: Simon & Schuster, 1998), 461, 462. Hoover had also headed the FBI's predecessor, the Bureau of Investigation, for over a decade before its transformation into the FBI. Kennedy's issue was probably more than just not wanting to bring attention to what was happening in New York. He and Hoover had a terrible relationship, with Hoover holding a voluminous file on his late brother's various exploits, but their acrimony also involved other issues, including their approaches to dealing with crime. Hoover famously denied the existence of organized crime for years, for example. This rivalry and distaste for each other colored their every interaction and actions toward each other via third parties. Hoover's recent trip to Mississippi was related to the disappearance, torture, and murder of three civil rights workers, James Chaney, Michael Schwerner, and Andrew Goodman, in June. Their bodies would not be discovered until early August. This was the organized, planned murder of three young men who were working to secure basic constitutional rights, like voting, for African Americans in Mississippi because the federal government would not do it. While the sight of chaos and destruction in the streets of Harlem and Bedford-Stuyvesant was spectacular, the events were not planned, they were not a continuation of a centuries-long system of racist terror, and those in the streets directed very little violence toward civilians, reserving their rage almost entirely for the police. Johnson was making a false equivalence.
5. E. W. Kenworthy, "Johnson Orders Full F.B.I. Inquiry in Harlem Riots," *New York Times*, July 22, 1964.
6. Beschloss, *Taking Charge*, 462; "Lyndon Johnson, J. Edgar Hoover, and Lee White on 21 July 1964," Conversation WH6407-11-4295, *Presidential Recordings Digital Edition*, http://prde.upress.virginia.edu/conversations/4000564.
7. Beschloss, *Taking Charge*, 462.
8. Reminiscences of James Farmer (1979), 293, Columbia Center for Oral History Archives, Rare Book & Manuscript Library, Columbia University in the City of New York.
9. Claude Brown, *Manchild in the Promised Land* (New York: Macmillan, 1965), 336.
10. *Muhammad Speaks*, August 14, 1964.
11. Abdul Basit Naeem, "No Riots, No Lawlessness If Harlem Heed Council [sic] of Muhammad," *Muhammad Speaks*, August 14, 1964. Naeem published the magazine *Moslem World & the U.S.A.* every two months for a period in the mid-1950s. He was quite supportive of the NOI and worked steadfastly to introduce Elijah Muhammad and Malcolm X to

orthodox Muslims. This is all the more noteworthy for the fact that the Nation of Islam took practices and beliefs of Islam and merged them with novel creations of its mysterious founder, W. D. Fard, and Elijah Muhammad, his successor, to make a distinctive religion that was geared toward African Americans. It was not a version of Islam that Muslims would have recognized or accepted as their own. When Malcolm X left the Nation, he adopted Sunni Islam as his faith.

12. Kenworthy, "Johnson Orders Full F.B.I. Inquiry in Harlem Riots."
13. Peter Kihss, "Wagner Asserts Disorders Harm Negroes' Cause," *New York Times*, July 23, 1964.
14. "Harlem Riots Make Headlines in Europe," *New York Herald Tribune*, July 22, 1964.
15. R. W. Apple Jr., "Negro Leaders Split Over Call to Curtail Drive," *New York Times*, July 31, 1964; Jon Margolis. *The Last Innocent Year: America in 1964: The Beginning of the "Sixties"* (New York: Perennial, 2000), 280.
16. "President's Warning," *New York Herald Tribune*, July 22, 1964.
17. Peter Kihss, "Screvane Links Reds to Rioting," *New York Times*, July 22, 1964.
18. Kihss, "Screvane Links Reds to Rioting."
19. Maurice C. Carroll and Edward J. Silberfarb, "Wagner Takes Over in Riots; Johnson Orders FBI to City," *New York Herald Tribune*, July 22, 1964.
20. Carroll and Silberfarb, "Wagner Takes over in Riots; Johnson Orders FBI to City."
21. Kihss, "Screvane Links Reds to Rioting."
22. "Brooklyn Riots Continue, Police Shoot 2 as Looters," *New York Times*, July 23, 1964.
23. "Mobs Fight Police Again in Brooklyn and Harlem Area," *New York Times*, July 22, 1964.
24. Carroll and Silberfarb, "Wagner Takes Over in Riots; Johnson Orders FBI to City."
25. Carroll and Silberfarb, "Wagner Takes Over in Riots; Johnson Orders FBI to City."
26. "Mobs Fight Police Again in Brooklyn and Harlem Area."
27. Kihss, "Wagner Asserts Disorders Harm Negroes' Cause."
28. Carroll and Silberfarb, "Wagner Takes Over in Riots; Johnson Orders FBI to City."
29. Alfred T. Hendricks, "Looters on Brooklyn Rampage," *New York Post*, July 22, 1964.
30. Hendricks, "Looters on Brooklyn Rampage."
31. "Mobs Fight Police Again in Brooklyn and Harlem Area"; "Manhattan Rioting Crosses Bridges, Spreads to Brooklyn," *New York Amsterdam News*, July 25, 1964.
32. "Mobs Fight Police Again in Brooklyn and Harlem Area."
33. Jim O'Neil and Mel Fazzino, *A Cop's Tale: NYPD: The Violent Years: A Detective's Firsthand Account of Murder and Mayhem* (Fort Lee, NJ: Barricade, 2009), 48–49.
34. T. J. English, *The Savage City: Race, Murder, and a Generation on the Edge* (New York: William Morrow, 2012), 76.
35. O'Neil and Fazzino, *A Cop's Tale*, 49.
36. "Mobs Fight Police Again in Brooklyn and Harlem Area"; "Brooklyn Riots Continue, Police Shoot 2 as Looters."

10. Day Five: Wednesday, July 22

1. Warren Weaver Jr., "Powell Says Riots Can End If Mayor Meets 5 Demands," *New York Times*, July 23, 1964.

2. Peter Kihss, "Wagner Asserts Disorders Harm Negroes' Cause," *New York Times*, July 23, 1964.
3. "To End Riots . . . ," *New York Herald Tribune*, July 23, 1964.
4. Robert W. White and Fred C. Shapiro, "The Protest," *New York Herald Tribune*, July 23, 1964.
5. "Brooklyn Riots Continue, Police Shoot 2 as Looters," *New York Times*, July 23, 1964.
6. "Text of Wagner's Radio-TV Appeal for Restoration of Law and Order in City," *New York Times*, July 23, 1964. Goldwater used the phrase "law and order" once in his speech at the RNC.
7. "Text of Wagner's Radio-TV Appeal for Restoration of Law and Order in City."
8. "Text of Wagner's Radio-TV Appeal for Restoration of Law and Order in City."
9. "Text of Wagner's Radio-TV Appeal for Restoration of Law and Order in City."
10. "White Youths Clash with CORE Pickets," *New York Times*, July 23, 1964.
11. "White Youths Clash with CORE Pickets."
12. Kenneth Gross, "Whites Stone CORE Pickets," *New York Post*, July 23, 1964.
13. "Brooklyn Riots Continue, Police Shoot 2 as Looters"; White and Shapiro, "The Protest." Dry-cleaning businesses were popular targets during the disturbances. They likely represented easy and poorly secured targets. While your neighbors' used clothing may not have been an ideal prize, it filled the need to acquire upon which some were acting during these events.
14. "Relative Calm Is Restored to Riot-Torn Areas Here," *New York Times*, July 24, 1964.
15. "Brooklyn Riots Continue, Police Shoot 2 as Looters"; White and Shapiro, "The Protest."
16. Ralph Blumenfeld, "Negroes to Mayor: 'Not Enough,'" *New York Post*, July 23, 1964.
17. Blumenfeld, "Negroes to Mayor: 'Not Enough.'"
18. "Brooklyn Riots Continue, Police Shoot 2 as Looters"; White and Shapiro, "The Protest."
19. "Brooklyn Riots Continue, Police Shoot 2 as Looters"; Jack Newfield, *Robert Kennedy: A Memoir* (New York: New American Library, 1988), 91.
20. White and Shapiro, "The Protest"; Alfred T. Hendricks and Edward Cumberbatch, "More Looting in Brooklyn; Harlem Quiet," *New York Post*, July 23, 1964.
21. "Who Speaks for Harlem?," moderated by Edwin Newman, WNBC, July 26, 1964. Rustin, a fervent integrationist, saw Black nationalism in all its incarnations as a negative development in response to intransigent white racism. He believed Black separatism, whether voluntary or forced, would indefinitely prolong racial inequality.
22. White and Shapiro, "The Protest"; "Brooklyn Riots Continue, Police Shoot 2 as Looters."
23. "Brooklyn Riots Continue, Police Shoot 2 as Looters"; "Relative Calm Is Restored to Riot-Torn Areas Here."
24. Peter Kihss, "Cavanagh Picks 6 to Aid His Review of Police Cases," *New York Times*, July 24, 1964.

11. Day Six: Thursday, July 23

1. Peter Kihss, "Cavanagh Picks 6 to Aid His Review of Police Cases," *New York Times*, July 24, 1964.

2. Kihss, "Cavanagh Picks 6 to Aid His Review of Police Cases."
3. Kihss, "Cavanagh Picks 6 to Aid His Review of Police Cases."
4. Fred Powledge, "Mulberry Street Is Angered Over CORE Pickets," *New York Times*, July 24, 1964. The paper published these quotes in 1964 as transcribed, with no censorship.
5. Powledge, "Mulberry Street Is Angered Over CORE Pickets."
6. Given America's restrictive immigration laws, beginning in 1924 and continuing through 1965, the federal government allowed very few Africans entry into the United States. The Afro-Caribbean population rose and fell over time but had been in a lull for over a decade at this point. Spanish-speaking people of African descent from the Caribbean and living in America, who would have been mostly Puerto Ricans in 1964, were generally treated as distinct from Black people whose ancestors had been in the country for generations and mostly descended from enslaved people.
7. Edward C. Banfield, *The Unheavenly City Revisited* (Boston: Little, Brown, 1974), 78.
8. Charles R. Morris, *The Cost of Good Intentions: New York City and the Liberal Experiment, 1960–1975* (New York: Norton, 1980), 78–80. This all relies on assumptions and a willingness to ignore basic facts of American history and economic realities. For example, Morris views the average Black man moving north as doing well for himself, because the North paid higher wages, neglecting that it had significantly higher costs of living, and that it would be difficult to find many Black men in Harlem or Bedford-Stuyvesant in 1964 who were satisfied with their economic situations: "One important alternative view of Northern [sic] blacks—as modern immigrants—casts black problems in quite a different perspective than the paradigm that underlay, for instance, the original conceptions of the antipoverty program. Measured against the rate of progress of other immigrant groups, it could be argued that blacks were progressing about as fast as could be expected. Moreover, viewing blacks as urban immigrants is not all that unreasonable. The most massive black migrations Northward [sic] occurred only after World War II, and while it is not possible to allocate birth rates precisely among native and immigrant blacks, it is entirely plausible that the majority of blacks in New York City are post-1940 immigrants or their children. The black migrations were driven by the same economic impulses that motivated most other new arrivals. To civil rights leaders the Northern [sic] slums may have been the failure of a dream, but to blacks emigrating from the shantytowns of the South, they represented substantial advancement. A man who earned the median Southern [sic] black income in 1960 and emigrated North [sic] to earn the median Northern [sic] black income in 1970 would have seen his income more than triple." Morris goes on to hold up West Indians as model immigrants unafraid of Protestant values like hard work and thrift, inferring that African Americans have much to learn from them: "It has long been documented, for example, that West Indians, with their intense devotion to hard work, thrift, and economic self-improvement, fare much better on the mainland than do American blacks, although both are presumably subject to the same discriminatory barriers, both were enslaved about the same time from the same parts of Africa, and the West Indian system of slavery was, if anything, even more degrading than that in America."
9. Leah P. Boustan, *Competition in the Promised Land: Black Migrants in Northern Cities and Labor Markets* (Princeton, NJ: Princeton University Press, 2017), 3.

10. James Gregory's work on southern migration in the middle of the twentieth century examines race and culture, pertaining to both Black and white southern migrants, and does not single out Black southerners as some exotic other who should be understood as foreigners. James Gregory, *The Southern Diaspora: How the Great Migrations of Black and White Southerners Transformed America* (Chapel Hill: University of North Carolina Press, 2005).
11. Robert C. White and Fred C. Shapiro, "Violence Subsides on 6th Night; Police Brace for Weekend," *New York Herald Tribune*, July 24, 1964.
12. "Relative Calm Is Restored to Riot-Torn Areas Here," *New York Times*, July 24, 1964.
13. White and Shapiro, "Violence Subsides on 6th Night; Police Brace for Weekend"; "Relative Calm Is Restored to Riot-Torn Areas Here."
14. "Relative Calm Is Restored to Riot-Torn Areas Here."
15. "Behind Little Italy's Riot: Pride—and Prejudice," *New York Post*, July 26, 1964. Santora was demonstrating a common attitude from white people toward Black people, especially those pressing for equal rights and opportunity. This perspective completely ignores the work that enslaved Africans and African Americans did in physically constructing America and serving as a foundation for its economy, in the North and South as well as during the century after the Civil War, during which African Americans were legally and openly denied constitutional rights. Santora was speaking on a day, one of thousands, when many Black southerners were denied the right to vote and Black northerners were gerrymandered into electoral weakness. Racists were still harassing, attacking, and killing civil rights workers in the South. No European immigrant groups, at any time, were ever subjected to anything approximating this treatment. And what he also leaves out, either by way of ignorance or intent, is that Italians, just like Germans and the Irish, gained acceptance into white society through a number of avenues, including demonstrating their individual and collective contempt for African Americans, the lowest rung on the American racial ladder. Columbus never visited the American mainland.
16. "Who Speaks for Harlem?," moderated by Edwin Newman, WNBC, July 26, 1964.
17. America had recently "discovered" poverty, through the publication of Michael Harrington's *The Other America* in 1962. The War on Poverty made great promises that faced hard political realities, but the growing war in Vietnam devoured its funding. Dr. King had been building an interracial campaign in 1967 and 1968 to demand that the government implement and fund an economic bill of rights to address widespread poverty in America, with a planned caravan to DC, where demonstrators would live in a tent city on the National Mall. His murder in April threw the events into disarray, and the campaign suffered greatly. The tent city lasted a month before police cleared it out with tear gas and arrests.
18. White and Shapiro, "Violence Subsides on 6th Night; Police Brace for Weekend"; "Relative Calm Is Restored to Riot-Torn Areas Here."
19. White and Shapiro, "Violence Subsides on 6th Night; Police Brace for Weekend"; "Relative Calm Is Restored to Riot-Torn Areas Here." As Jim O'Neil, the TPF officer, tells it: "We spent the next two days, six TPF cops to a radio car, riding around and stopping whenever we spotted looters. We would get out of the car, kick the shit out of them, get back into the car, and move on." Jim O'Neil and Mel Fazzino, *A Cop's Tale: NYPD: The*

Violent Years: A Detective's Firsthand Account of Murder and Mayhem (Fort Lee, NJ: Barricade, 2009), 50.
20. Emanuel Perlmutter, "Police Costs in Riots Put at $1.5 Million," *New York Times*, July 26, 1964.
21. Kihss, "Cavanagh Picks 6 to Aid His Review of Police Cases"; "The Week's Riot Toll," *New York Post*, July 26, 1964.
22. O'Neil and Fazzino, *A Cop's Tale*, 44.
23. T. J. English, *The Savage City: Race, Murder, and a Generation on the Edge* (New York: William Morrow, 2012), 76–77.
24. Staughton Lynd, *Nonviolence in America: A Documentary History* (Indianapolis, IN: Bobbs-Merrill, 1966), 496.
25. Robert Leuci, *All the Centurions: A New York City Cop Remembers His Years on the Street, 1961–1981* (New York: William Morrow, 2004), 63.
26. Alfonso Narvaez, "Why Gangs Shunned the Riots," *New York Post*, July 26, 1964.
27. Kihss, "Cavanagh Picks 6 to Aid His Review of Police Cases"; White and Shapiro, "Violence Subsides on 6th Night; Police Brace for Weekend."
28. Brian Purnell, "A Movement Grows in Brooklyn: The Brooklyn Chapter of the Congress of Racial Equality (CORE) and the Northern Civil Rights Movement During the Early 1960s," PhD diss., New York University, Graduate School of Arts and Science, 2006, 21, 22.

12. After

1. "Riot Claims Against NYC in Millions," *New York Amsterdam News*, September 26, 1964; Charles G. Bennett, "24 Claims Filed Here Over Riots," *New York Times*, September 1, 1964.
2. "Assess Riot Losses in Harlem, Brooklyn," *New York Amsterdam News*, October 10, 1964.
3. Peter Kihss, "Harlem Planner Urges More City Aid," *New York Times*, February 12, 1965.
4. Sara Slack, "Woman Shot In Riot Sues for $500,000," *New York Amsterdam News*, August 1, 1964; George Barner, "Riot Victims Seek Million $ Damages," *New York Amsterdam News*, January 30, 1965. The outcomes of their claims are unknown.
5. Kenneth B. Clark, *Dark Ghetto: Dilemmas of Social Power* (New York: Harper & Row, 1967), 15.
6. Les Matthews, "What Happened to Those Arrested During the Riot," *New York Amsterdam News*, August 22, 1964.
7. "Four Are Arrested on Contempt Charge," *New York Amsterdam News*, October 31, 1964; "One Negro in Contempt in Riot," *New York Amsterdam News*, March 13, 1965.
8. William Epton, *We Accuse: Bill Epton Speaks to the Court* (Brooklyn: Progressive Labor Party, 1966); Douglas Martin, "William Epton, 70, Is Dead; Tested Free-Speech Limits," *New York Times*, February 3, 2002.
9. Themis Chronopoulos, "Police Misconduct, Community Opposition, and Urban Governance in New York City, 1945–1965," *Journal of Urban History* 44, no. 4 (2015): 655.
10. "45 New Patrolmen, 5 Sgts., 3 Lieutenants," *New York Amsterdam News*, August 22, 1964.

11. Peter Kerr, "Lloyd G. Sealy Is Dead at 69; Held High Posts with Police," *New York Times*, January 5, 1985. Commissioner Kennedy appointed the first, George Redding, to command Bedford-Stuyvesant's Eightieth Precinct in 1956. Redding was the city's Black first for several ranks, from captain through deputy chief inspector; he died three years before Sealy's promotion.
12. Martin Arnold, "Murphy Appoints a Negro to Head Harlem Precinct," *New York Times*, August 15, 1964. Sealy was promoted two years later to assistant chief inspector and retired in 1969. He taught at John Jay College of Criminal Justice until his death, suffering a heart attack in the classroom in 1985.
13. Philip Benjamin, "Dr. King Confers with Mayor on City and U.S. Rights Issues," *New York Times*, July 28, 1964; R. W. Apple Jr., "Negro Leaders Split Over Call to Curtail Drive," *New York Times*, July 31, 1964; R. W. Apple Jr., "Wagner Rejects Demands for Civilian Police Board," *New York Times*, August 1, 1964.
14. Jack Roth, "Gilligan Cleared by Grand Jurors in Killing of Boy," *New York Times*, September 2, 1964.
15. "Text of Report by District Attorney on Investigation Into Gilligan Case," *New York Times*, September 2, 1964.
16. Robert Alden, "All of Jury Agreed to Absolve Gilligan," *New York Times*, September 4, 1964.
17. Charles Grutzner, "Gilligan's Leave Is Still in Force," *New York Times*, September 2, 1964.
18. Walter Carlson, "Gilligan May Get Surgery on Back," *New York Times*, September 25, 1964.
19. Douglas Robinson, "Gilligan Will End Leave Tomorrow," *New York Times*, November 11, 1964; Martin Arnold, "Police Board Absolves Gilligan in Slaying of Negro Teen-Ager," *New York Times*, November 7, 1964.
20. Douglas Robinson, "Gilligan Shifted to Avoid Pickets," *New York Times*, November 12, 1964.
21. "Gilligan Retiring from City Police," *New York Times*, January 22, 1968. Gilligan's pension was the equivalent of nearly $65,000 in early 2021.
22. Robert E. Tomasson, "Gilligan Is Suing King and Farmer," *New York Times*, May 27, 1965. It is not clear when, where, or even if King made such a statement. "Lieut. Gilligan Sues Dr. King for Million," *New York Times*, July 15, 1965; Robert E. Tomasson, "Gilligan Upheld on Right to Sue Those Who Called Him a Killer," *New York Times*, April 26, 1968. What, if anything, came of the lawsuits is unclear. In April 1968, Gilligan was still in appellate court, determining if his suits could go forward. The court ruled they could, and he was suing Dr. King after he had been assassinated. However, Farmer won a motion to be dropped from the suit, as there was no evidence of his involvement. Gilligan v. King, 48 Misc.2d 212, 264 N.Y.S.2d 309 (N.Y. Sup. Ct. 1965).
23. Richard Pearson, "Roy Cohn, Controversial Lawyer and McCarthy Aide, Dies at 59," *Washington Post*, August 3, 1986. Cohn went on to be, among other things, a counselor for members of the mafia and an actively corrupt political operative, ultimately disbarred for a number of grave improprieties, including failing to repay a hundred-thousand-dollar loan and attempting to force a wealthy, dying man to change his will so that Cohn was a beneficiary.
24. Peter Kihss, "Screvane Links Reds to Rioting," *New York Times*, July 22, 1964.

25. Michael R. Beschloss, *Taking Charge: The Johnson White House Tapes, 1963–1964* (New York: Simon & Schuster, 1998), 462; Lyndon B. Johnson, "Statement by the President on the Riots in New York City," in *The American Presidency Project*, ed. Gerhard Peters and John T. Woolley, http://presidency.ucsb.edu/node/238962; "Lyndon Johnson, J. Edgar Hoover, George Reedy, and Lee White on 21 July 1964," Conversation WH6407-11-4291, 4292, *Presidential Recordings Digital Edition*, http://prde.upress.virginia.edu/conversations/4000562.

26. Taylor Branch, *Pillar of Fire: America in the King Years, 1963–65* (New York: Simon & Schuster, 1998), 418. President Johnson also suspected right-wing extremist involvement, hoping someone could "make the other people stop and think a little bit, particularly the Negroes, before they become the tools of some of these right-wing cranks." He speculated that the supremely wealthy Texas petroleum baron and Republican donor Haroldson Lafayette Hunt Jr. was funding the disorder. "Lyndon Johnson and Robert Wagner on 22 July 1964," Conversation WH6407-12-4304, *Presidential Recordings Digital Edition*, http://prde.upress.virginia.edu/conversations/4000569; "Lyndon Johnson, Walter Heller, and George Reedy on 23 July 1964," Conversation WH6407-12-4314, 4315, http://prde.upress.virginia.edu/conversations/4002673. When Johnson asked Deputy Attorney General Nicholas Katzenbach on July 25 about far-right involvement, he told the president, "There's just been some speculation and rumors, and not even very good rumors."

27. Lez Edmond, "Harlem Diary—'The Long, Hot Summer,'" in *Reporting Civil Rights*, part 2: *American Journalism, 1963–1973* (New York: Library of America, 2003), 141; "Who Speaks for Harlem?," moderated by Edwin Newman, WNBC, July 26, 1964. Johnson told Hoover while discussing the tumult in Harlem, "I think the Communists are in charge of it."

28. Edmond, "Harlem Diary," 148–50.

29. *Harlem: Test for the North*, WNBC, July 26, 1964.

30. James Baldwin, *Nobody Knows My Name: More Notes of a Native Son* (New York: Dial, 1961), 74. "What I find appalling—and really dangerous—is the American assumption that the Negro is so contented with his lot here that only the cynical agents of a foreign power can rouse him to protest. It is a notion which contains a gratuitous insult, implying, as it does, that Negroes can make no move unless they are manipulated. It forcibly suggests that the Southern attitude toward the Negro is also, essentially, the national attitude. When the South has trouble with its Negroes—when the Negroes refuse to remain in their 'place'—it blames 'outside' agitators and 'Northern interference.' When the nation has trouble with the Northern Negro, it blames the Kremlin. And this, by no means incidentally, is a very dangerous thing to do. We thus give credit to the Communists for attitudes and victories which are not theirs. We make of them the champions of the oppressed, and they could not, of course, be more delighted."

31. Peter Kihss, "Wagner Asserts Disturbances Harm Negroes' Cause," *New York Times*, July 23, 1964. Thompson was white; Patterson was African American.

32. Bill Whitworth, "Rights Chiefs Deny Reds Incited Riots," *New York Herald Tribune*, July 23, 1964. In the 1950s, the SCLC, NAACP, and other organizations had engaged in rigorous programs of expelling communists and cutting ties with anyone whose

political affiliations were suspicious. Bayard Rustin's interest in communism as a young man was one reason he stayed mostly behind the scenes of organizing.

33. Jack Mallon, William Federici, and Henry Lee, "Blame Hate Groups, Red & White, for Harlem Terror," *New York Daily News*, July 22, 1964; "Lyndon Johnson and J. Edgar Hoover on 22 July 1964," Conversation WH6407-12-4305, *Presidential Recordings Digital Edition*, http://prde.upress.virginia.edu/conversations/4000570.
34. Martha Biondi, *To Stand and Fight: The Struggle for Civil Rights in Postwar New York City* (Cambridge, MA: Harvard University Press, 2003); Mary L. Dudziak, *Cold War Civil Rights: Race and the Image of American Democracy* (Princeton, NJ: Princeton University Press, 2000); Mark Naison, *Communists in Harlem During the Depression* (New York: Grove, 1985).
35. "Text of F.B.I. Report to President on Summer Riots in 9 Cities Over Country," *New York Times*, September 27, 1964.
36. "Text of F.B.I. Report to President on Summer Riots in 9 Cities Over Country."
37. Bettye Eidson, "White Public Opinion in an Age of Disorder," in *Cities Under Siege: An Anatomy of the Ghetto Riots, 1964–1968*, ed. David Boesel and Peter H. Rossi (New York: Basic Books, 1971), 394, 395.
38. Charles G. Bennett, "Brooklyn Antipoverty Program Is Set," *New York Times*, July 26, 1964.
39. Charles G. Bennett, "City Begins Drive for 20,000 Jobs," *New York Times*, July 30, 1964.
40. "Text of Wagner's Statement on Harlem," *New York Times*, August 1, 1964. $1.50 an hour is about $12 an hour in early 2019.
41. Paul L. Montgomery, "Ministers Assail City on Job 'Hoax,'" *New York Times*, August 29, 1964.
42. Montgomery, "Ministers Assail City on Job 'Hoax.'"
43. Jack Newfield, *Robert Kennedy: A Memoir* (New York: New American Library, 1988), 91.
44. Montgomery, "Ministers Assail City on Job 'Hoax.'"

13. Reforming the Civilian Complaint Review Board

1. The Democratic-majority City Council sat on a review board bill for more than a year and a half, declining to vote on it, in deference to their leader, Mayor Wagner. Theodore Weiss, a reform Democrat from the Upper West Side, introduced a bill in April 1964 that would have created a nine-member, all-civilian panel. His fellow reform Democrat and future mayor, Ed Koch, helped draft it. Ruth Cowan, "The New York City Civilian Review Board Referendum of November 1966: A Case Study of Mass Politics," PhD diss., New York University, 1970, 117; "Read and Remember How Council Voted," *New York Amsterdam News*, July 3, 1965. Lindsay defeated the Conservative Party candidate William F. Buckley and the Democrat Abraham Beame. John V. Lindsay for Mayor Campaign Press Center News Release, May 21, 1965, American Civil Liberties Union Records, The Roger Baldwin Years, Box 1082, Folder 19, Public Policy Papers, Department of Rare Books and Special Collections, Princeton University Library.

2. In July 1952, NYPD Commissioner George Monaghan dispatched some deputies to make an arrangement in which civil rights violations filed with the U.S. Department of Justice against city officers would be turned over to the NYPD for self-investigation. In the course of his struggle to maintain the arrangements among the many federal authorities who were unaware of such a deal, Monaghan informed the head of the local FBI office that federal civil rights legislation was only "for that section of the country south of the Mason-Dixon line." When the attorney general discovered in January 1953 what his subordinates had done, he annulled the agreement, which soon became public and resulted in congressional hearings in a matter of weeks. No one at the NYPD would be punished or fired over this, but Monaghan had to give his critics something in order to relieve pressure on both himself and the department. On May 22, the commissioner established the Civilian Complaint Review Board to receive and adjudicate citizens' complaints against officers, something for which civil liberties and rights groups had pressed for several years. Cowan, "The New York City Civilian Review Board Referendum of November 1966," 60; "Brutality Charges Against City Police Under U.S. Inquiry," *New York Times*, February 17, 1953; Luther A. Huston, "F.B.I. Agents Depict Rebuff by Monaghan," *New York Times*, March 6, 1953; Charles Grutzner, "Monaghan Denies Police-F.B.I. Deal to Hide Brutality," *New York Times*, February 18, 1953; Charles Grutzner, "Halley Urges City Sift 'Deal' on F.B.I.; Mayor Disagrees," *New York Times*, February 19, 1953; Charles Grutzner, "Monaghan Ouster Sought Over 'Deal' in Brutality Cases," *New York Times*, February 20, 1953.

3. Leary had been with the PPD since 1940, rising through the ranks to become deputy commissioner several years before the city's Police Advisory Board went into effect. Leary had also been in charge of the PPD in August 1964, when it responded to the three-night uprising there. He had prohibited officers from serving on horseback, pulling their guns, and using fire hoses and dogs. Altogether, of all the responding officers, one fired one shot over three nights. Still, two citizens died, and more than three hundred each were wounded and arrested. Lenora E. Berson, *Case Study of a Riot: The Philadelphia Story* (New York: Institute of Human Relations Press, American Jewish Committee, 1966), 15–20, 52; Michael T. Kaufman, "Police Shake-up Begun by Leary; Top Aide Chosen," *New York Times*, February 26, 1966; Woody Klein, *Lindsay's Promise: The Dream That Failed: A Personal Account* (New York: Macmillan, 1970), 140.

4. Eric Pace, "Suit Threatened on Police Board," *New York Times*, February 15, 1966; "Suit Threatened on Police Board," *New York Times*, April 28, 1966; *Report to Mayor-Elect John V. Lindsay* (New York: The Task Force, 1965), 15; "Text of Statements and Preamble of Order on Police Board," *New York Times*, May 3, 1966; General Orders No. 14: Amendments to the Rule and Procedures, Civilian Complaints—Revised Procedures, May 17, 1966, ACLU Records, The Roger Baldwin Years, Box 1083, Folder 2; "Mayor John V. Lindsay's TV Report on the Civilian Review Board with Police Commissioner Howard R. Leary," May 2, 1966, John Vliet Lindsay Papers (MS 592), Manuscripts and Archives, Yale University Library, Box 60, Folder "Civilian Review Board—TV Report."

5. "Review Board Is In," *New York Amsterdam News*, May 7, 1966; "Where Do You Stand on the Civilian Review Board?," 1966, Algernon D. Black Papers, Box 26, Civilian Complaint Review Board—2; John Corry, "The Man of That Board," *New York Times Magazine*,

November 6, 1966; Civilian Complaint Review Board, May 10, 1966, Lindsay Papers, Box 366, Folder "Mayor's Screening Committee." The committee also featured the Reverend Donald S. Harrington, a white Unitarian minister who presided over the interracial Community Church of New York; William H. Booth, an African American lawyer and chairman of the New York City Commission on Human Rights; Morris B. Abram, a Jewish civil rights attorney and president of the American Jewish Committee; Sandy F. Ray, minister of the Cornerstone Baptist Church in Brooklyn and lifelong friend of Martin Luther King Sr. and family; Dr. C. B. Powell, the African American editor and publisher of the *New York Amsterdam News*; and several other lawyers, the dean of Fordham University School of Law, and a white teacher and former United Federation of Teachers vice president. Kenneth Clark and Whitman Knapp, a future federal judge and head of the commission bearing his name that would investigate police corruption, were notable finalists.

6. Martin Gansberg, "Complaints Rise on Police Action," *New York Times*, April 7, 1966; NYCLU News Release, May 17, 1966, ACLU Records, Box 1083, Folder 2; "Review Board Is In"; "Memorandum: Re: Civilian Complaint Review Board Reorganization," March 15, 1966, Lindsay Papers, Box 367, Folder "Civilian Review Board—1966." Some component of Lindsay's team had suggested shared responsibility between NYPD and civilian investigators, working in teams. "Working Paper—Civilian Review Board," March 14, 1966, Lindsay Papers, Box 367, Folder "Civilian Review Board—1966."

7. Eric Pace, "Booth Condemns Cassese Remark," *New York Times*, May 19, 1966; "NAACP Assails PBA Review Board Stand," *New York Amsterdam News*, May 21, 1966; Roy Wilkins, "Advice to Mr. Cassese," *New York Amsterdam News*, May 28, 1966; "Mayor Gets Police Board Nominations," *New York Times*, May 29, 1966; "A Promise Kept," *New York Amsterdam News*, July 16, 1966; Jackie Robinson, "Civilian Review Board Fight," *New York Amsterdam News*, July 16, 1966. Rochester's board had only been in operation since March 26, 1963. It was composed of nine civilians and had no disciplinary powers. It received fourteen complaints that year. Letter from Ross Guglielmino to Arnold Hoffman, June 17, 1964, Lindsay Papers, Box 374, Folder "Rochester—Police Advisory Board." Cassese believed, regarding African Americans, that "for 100 years these people were entitled to their rights and for 100 years they didn't receive them to a degree, although up north I know that we were doing pretty good because we worked with them and we associated with them and we got along with them." Newsmakers broadcast transcript, WCBS, 7, Lindsay Papers.

8. Arthur Niederhoffer, *Behind the Shield: The Police in Urban Society* (Garden City, NY: Doubleday, 1967), 176; Themis Chronopoulos, "Police Misconduct, Community Opposition, and Urban Governance in New York City, 1945–1965," *Journal of Urban History* 44, no. 4 (2015): 657; Charles R. Morris, *The Cost of Good Intentions: New York City and the Liberal Experiment, 1960–1975* (New York: Norton, 1980), 19. Wagner had the power to recognize the PBA as a union but hewed to his policy of staying out of municipal agencies' affairs to preserve his own image, instead choosing to allow the relationship between Kennedy and his men to fully collapse.

9. Klein, *Lindsay's Promise*, 199–201; "Group Drops Anti Review Board Drive," *New York Amsterdam News*, July 16, 1966; Conservative Party Petition, undated, ACLU Records, Box 1083, Folder 2.

10. Algernon D. Black Papers, Box 26, Civilian Complaint Review Board—1; Algernon D. Black, "New York City—Civilian Complaint Review Board/1966," 6, Algernon D. Black Papers, Box 26, Civilian Complaint Review Board—2; Algernon D. Black, "Civilian Complaint Review Board," 1-11, October 22, 1974, Algernon D. Black Papers, Box 26, Civilian Complaint Review Board—1.
11. Emanuel Perlmutter, "Lindsay to Name 4 Civilians Today for Police Board," *New York Times*, July 11, 1966; "And the Six Other Members," *New York Times*, July 12, 1966; "Civilian Bd. Named; Mayor Keeps Word," *New York Amsterdam News*, July 16, 1966; Bernard Weinraub, "New Police Board Has Two Negroes and Puerto Rican," *New York Times*, July 12, 1966; John H. Bracey, August Meier, and Randolph Boehm, "Majority Report of a Special Subcommittee to Study the Feasibility of Creating an Independent Civilian Complaint Review Board," Papers of the NAACP: Part 22, Branch Department General Administrative File Civilian Review Board—New York Reports 1965. (Bethesda, MD: University Publications of America, 1996); "Biographies—The Seven Board Members," Lindsay Papers, Box 242, Folder "Civilian Review Board Clippings"; "Profile—Manuel Diaz, ACSW," Lindsay Papers, Box 367, Folder "Personnel Screening Commission, 1966–1971."
12. Weinraub, "New Police Board Has Two Negroes and Puerto Rican"; A. Philip Randolph, "A Fight We Cannot Lose," *New York Amsterdam News*, August 6, 1966; "Reviewing the Review Board," *New York Post*, July 12, 1966.
13. Weinraub, "New Police Board Has Two Negroes and Puerto Rican"; "New Group Fights Police Review Unit," *New York Times*, August 2, 1966; Klein, *Lindsay's Promise*, 202; David Burnham, "Frank, Denying Impropriety, Quits P.B.A. Post," *New York Times*, June 7, 1969. People contributed money from out of state to defeat the board, including the Chicago Police Association, that city's equivalent of the PBA. Algernon D. Black, "New York City—Civilian Complaint Review Board/1966," 4, Algernon D. Black Papers, Box 26, Civilian Complaint Review Board—2. Norman Frank ran for the Democratic nomination for mayor of New York City in 1969 but does not appear to have made it to the primary.
14. Bernard Weinraub, "Ruling Due Today on Review Board," *New York Times*, August 5, 1966; Paul Hofmann, "Negro Policeman Criticizes P.B.A," *New York Times*, August 29, 1966; "FAIR Steering Committee Meeting," 1–2, August 5, 1966, Algernon D. Black Papers, Box 26, Civilian Complaint Review Board—2; "American Civil Liberties Union Bulletin # 2278," October 24, 1964, Algernon D. Black Papers, Box 26, Civilian Complaint Review Board—2. David Dinkins, who as mayor would work with the City Council to create an all-civilian board in 1993, served on FAIR's campaign committee. Letter from Algernon D. Black to the Honorable John V. Lindsay, October 5, 1966, Algernon D. Black Papers, Box 26, Civilian Complaint Review Board—4; "Members of F.A.I.R," Lindsay Papers, Box 242, Folder "Civilian Review Board Clippings."
15. Bernard Weinraub, "Civilian Police Review Board Gets Off to Smooth Start Here," *New York Times*, July 16, 1966. Vincent Broderick, commissioner when Lindsay took office, had tried to quiet critics the previous year by opening in a commercial space an office solely dedicated to taking complaints. He reasoned that its staff, in civilian clothes, and the physical separation from any police precinct would remove the barrier that many observers believed prevented more people from filing complaints, which was having to enter a police precinct and interact with uniformed officers. "Statement of Police Commissioner

Vincent L. Broderick Before the Committee on City Affairs, of the City Council, June 29, 1965," NYPD press release, Lindsay Papers, Box 367, Folder "Police—Civilian Review Board"; Bernard Weinraub, "Now Civilians Share the Beat," *New York Times*, August 21, 1966; "Review Bd. Member Reports Threats," *New York Amsterdam News*, August 20, 1966; "Ex-Cop Asst. Head of Review Board," *New York Amsterdam News*, September 3, 1966; Algernon Black, *The People and the Police* (New York: McGraw-Hill, 1968), 82, 87, 102, 221. During the four months the hybrid board functioned, CORE, the newspaper *El Diario*, the NYCLU, the NAACP Legal Defense and Education Fund, the Student Nonviolent Coordinating Committee, the Brownsville Community Center, the City Commission on Human Rights, and District Attorney's Office all submitted complaints. Orientation Program for Civilian Members of the Civilian Complaint Review Board, Lindsay Papers, Box 366, Folder "The Board."
16. "Report of Operations for the Civilian Complaint Review Board," January 23, 1967, Lindsay Papers, Box 367, Folder "Civilian Review Board—1966 Annual Report."
17. "Report of Operations for the Civilian Complaint Review Board," Lindsay Papers; "The New Review Procedure," Lindsay Papers, Box 371, Folder "Literature—Police Review Board, 1966"; "The Barry Gray Show—Interview with Inspector Garelik," October 24, 1966, Lindsay Papers, Box 374, Folder "Statements—Police Civilian Review Board." The board determined that all four incidents occurred beyond a reasonable doubt. "Allegations Where Charges Were Recommended by the Board," Lindsay Papers, Box 367, Folder "Civilian Review Board—1966 Annual Report." Departmental trials were and are completely separate from criminal and civil proceedings, having no ramifications beyond internal NYPD matters.
18. "Review Bd. Member Reports Threats," *New York Amsterdam News*, August 20, 1966; Letter to Algernon Black, July 12, 1966, Algernon D. Black Papers, Box 26, Civilian Complaint Review Board—3; Letter from R. J. Ritter to Algernon Black, August 4, 1966, Algernon D. Black Papers, Box 26, Civilian Complaint Review Board—3; Letter from James A. McFarland to Algernon Black, July 23, 1966, Algernon D. Black Papers, Box 26, Civilian Complaint Review Board—3; Letter from Jane Lindstrom to Algernon Black, Algernon D. Black Papers, Box 26, Civilian Complaint Review Board—3.

14. A Referendum

1. African American New Yorkers voted 5 to 1 in favor of the board, and Puerto Rican New Yorkers voted nearly 3 to 1. White people of Italian and Irish backgrounds voted against it in larger numbers and greater proportions. Jews voted 55 percent to 45 percent in favor of abolishing the board.
2. "Statement of Donald D. Shack, Vice Chairman New York Civil Liberties Union Before the Platform Advisory Committee of the New York State Republican State Committee," August 22, 1966, American Civil Liberties Union Records, Box 1083, Folder 2; "FAIR Wins Backing, Works to Win Ballot," *Civil Liberties in New York*, October 1966, ACLU Records, Box 491, Folder 1; "Review Bd. Drive Kicked Off Uptown," *New York Amsterdam News*, October 8, 1966; Woody Klein, *Lindsay's Promise: The Dream That Failed: A Personal*

Account (New York: Macmillan, 1970), 222; Bernard Weinraub, "2 Senators Back Mayor on Police," *New York Times*, August 25, 1966; "Guardians Still Back Review Bd," *New York Amsterdam News*, September 3, 1966; Bernard Weinraub, "Brownell to Fight for Police Board," *New York Times*, September 13, 1966; Bernard Weinraub, "P.B.A. Plans Door-to-Door Fight Against Review," *New York Times*, September 26, 1966; Thomas A. Johnson, "Negro Policemen Split with P.B.A," *New York Times*, October 4, 1966; "How Do *You* Feel About the Civilian Review Board?," Algernon D. Black Papers, Box 26, Civilian Complaint Review Board—2; FAIR press release, September 14, 1966, Lindsay Papers, Box 242, Folder "Civilian Review Board Clippings."

3. Thomas R. Brooks, "25,000 Police Against the Review Board," *New York Times Magazine*, October 16, 1966, 36–37, 124–33.
4. "If You Want a Safer New York . . . ," Lindsay Papers, Box 369, Folder "Literature, Police Review Board, 1966"; WINS editorial, "Civilian Review Board—#2," July 12–13, 1966, Lindsay Papers, Box 369, Folder "Editorials"; Klein, *Lindsay's Promise*, 228; "Police Head Likens Review Board Backers to Hitler and Mussolini," *Herald-News*, August 31, 1966. The presidents of the national and New Jersey Fraternal Order of Police both agreed and publicly asserted communists were behind review board campaigns; Newsmakers broadcast transcript, WCBS, 10, Lindsay Papers.
5. "Lindsay Appoints Communist Fronters to Civilian Review Board to Rule Over New York's Finest!," Algernon D. Black Papers, Box 26, Civilian Complaint Review Board—3.
6. "Our Police! And Civilian Review Boards," Bronx American Opinion Reading Room, Algernon D. Black Papers, Box 26, Civilian Complaint Review Board—3. According to this newsletter, "The establishment of Review Boards to intimidate our police, that front line of defense, has now been given A-1 priority by the Communist Party, U.S.A." "Police Review Board: Voters to Get Last Word," *Counterattack*, October 7, 1966, Algernon D. Black Papers, Box 26, Civilian Complaint Review Board—3. This publication cited Algernon Black's involvement with a tribute to the intellectual giant W. E. B. Du Bois as proof of his communism. And it cited review boards as "a major step toward the legalization of chaos and anarchy, forerunners of Communist conquest." Pete Hamill, a columnist for the *New York Post*, labeled Cassese "Super Whitey," the "mild-mannered former traffic cop . . . who will hold off the Reds, protect the morality of the community, and save us all from our drift into socialism and communism." Referring to Cassese's proclamation that communists were behind the new board and fighting to protect it, Hamill sardonically imagined a scene in Moscow: "Cassese has finally discovered what all the Russian experts in the last 35 years never could find out: what Joe Stalin and his band of thugs were doing in the Kremlin. They were sitting around saying things like, 'Hey, I got an idea for knocking out religion in New York and breaking the spirit and creating confusion in the Police Dept. Let's ply our wares for a . . . *civilian review board!*' Can't you hear the huzzahs in the room before Stalin calls in his cops and has everyone in the joint shot?" Pete Hamill, "Super Whitey," *New York Post*, October 1, 1966.
7. ICCACRB newspaper advertisements, Algernon D. Black Papers, Box 26, Civilian Complaint Review Board—3; "Myths About the Review Board," 1, 4, Lindsay Papers, Box 242, Folder "Civilian Review Board Clippings"; "Review Board Battle Page," *New York Daily News*, October 27, 1966.

8. Klein, *Lindsay's Promise*, 228; Brooks, "25,000 Police Against the Review Board," 37.
9. Roy Wilkins, "Sly Campaign Against Negroes," *New York Amsterdam News*, October 15, 1966; Dick Schaap, "Police Celebrate," *New York World Journal Tribune*, November 9, 1966, Algernon D. Black Papers, Box 26, Civilian Complaint Review Board—4.
10. Jimmy Breslin, "My People, My Enemies," *New York Post*, [November 1966], Algernon D. Black Papers, Box 26, Civilian Complaint Review Board—4.
11. "America First Rally in Yorkville!," Algernon D. Black Papers, Box 26, Civilian Complaint Review Board—3; "National Renaissance Bulletin," Algernon D. Black Papers, Box 26, Civilian Complaint Review Board—3.
12. Klein, *Lindsay's Promise*, 232; Sidney E. Zion, "Civilian Review Board," *New York Times*, September 11, 1966; Bernard Weinraub, "Leary Assails P.B.A. Accusations," *New York Times*, September 28, 1966; "NAACP Branches Map Review Board Fight," *New York Amsterdam News*, September 24, 1966.
13. Klein, *Lindsay's Promise*, 250; Bernard Weinraub, "Mayor Starts Sidewalk Tours for Review Board," *New York Times*, October 5, 1966; Bernard Weinraub, "Poll Favors Foes of Review Board," *New York Times*, October 14, 1966; "The Police Department's Civilian Complaint Review Board: Addresses Presented at a Special Civic Service on Sunday Morning, October 16, 1966," October 16, 1966, ACLU Records, Box 1082, Folder 19.
14. "The Police Department's Civilian Complaint Review Board: Addresses Presented at a Special Civic Service on Sunday Morning, October 16, 1966." During its four-month period of work, only two out of 146 cases were not settled unanimously by the seven-member board. Algernon D. Black, interview by William H. Booth, 89.3 WYNC FM, October 1, 1968. Most complaints came in person or by phone, with male complainants outnumbering females two to one, and unjustified use of violence the subject of half of complaints. More than half of complainants were white people filing grievances against white police officers. Algernon Black, *The People and the Police* (New York: McGraw-Hill, 1968), 100, 101.
15. "Your Crucial Vote," *New York Amsterdam News*, October 1, 1966; "Booth Will Lead Voter March Sat," *New York Amsterdam News*, October 8, 1966; Klein, *Lindsay's Promise*, 254; Bernard Weinraub, "City Police Board Called U.S. Issue," *New York Times*, October 13, 1966.
16. "Coney Island Group Backs Review Bd," *New York Amsterdam News*, October 8, 1966; Malcolm Nash, "NMU Winding Up; Backs Review Bd," *New York Amsterdam News*, October 8, 1966; "S. Ozone Pk. Assn. Campaigns for Bd," *New York Amsterdam News*, October 15, 1966; George Barner, "Youth Files $250,000 Suit in Police Brutality," *New York Amsterdam News*, October 22, 1966.
17. "Brooklyn Areas Toured by P.B.A," *New York Times*, October 24, 1966; Maurice Carroll, "Police Halt Sound Truck Backing Review Board," *New York Times*, October 23, 1966.
18. Philip H. Dougherty, "Advertising: Civilian Review Board Fight," *New York Times*, October 18, 1966; Philip H. Dougherty, "Advertising: Review Board Foes Criticized," *New York Times*, November 8, 1966; Richard L. Gilbert, *I Was a Mad Man: A Madison Avenue Memoir* (New York: Diversion, 2013). Cole, Fischer, Rogow sued the thirty agencies for libel. The suit was dismissed in February 1968. Cole Fischer Rogow, Inc. v. Carl Ally, Inc., 288 N.Y.S.2d 556, 29 A.D.2d 423 (N.Y. App. Div. 1968). A federal court convicted Marvin R.

14. A Referendum

Cole and Arthur A. Fischer as individuals, and their company as an entity, of tax evasion in 1971, sentencing Cole to one year and Fischer to three months in prison, along with a total of $60,000 in fines, spread across the men and the company they had recently dissolved; "2 Sentenced Here for Evading Taxes," *New York Times*, December 10, 1971.

19. Bernard Weinraub, "Review Board Backers Accused of 'Smear' Tactics," *New York Times*, October 25, 1966.
20. Sidney E. Zion, "'Sleeper Issue' on Police Referendum Wakes Up," *New York Times*, October 30, 1966; Association of the Bar of the City of New York, "Report on the Referendum Question Concerning the New York City Civilian Review Board," 1966, 5–7.
21. "Court Limits Vote on Police Board to P.B.A. Proposal," *New York Times*, October 27, 1966; Bernard Weinraub, "Bar Sees Scrutiny of Police Barred If the P.B.A. Wins," *New York Times*, October 29, 1966; "NYCLU Spearheads FAIR Campaign in Fight for Life of Civilian Review Board," *Civil Liberties in New York*, September 1966, ACLU Records, Box 491, Folder 1.
22. "Tally of Votes for Governor, Statewide Offices, Police Review Board and Judges," *New York Times*, November 10, 1966; "Harlem Went for Board, City Didn't," *New York Amsterdam News*, November 12, 1966.
23. Bernard Weinraub, "Police Review Panel Killed by Large Majority in City," *New York Times*, November 9, 1966; Dick Schaap, "Police Celebrate," *New York World Journal Tribune*, November 9, 1966. Joe Flaherty, writing in the *Village Voice*, witnessed Cassese's speech: "If there had been a speech teacher with a gun in the audience we would have had the Ford [sic] Theatre all over again." "Strange Bedfellows Bust Up a Board," *Village Voice*, November 17, 1966. John Garabedian, "The Review Defeat: An Analysis," *New York Post*, November 10, 1966.
24. Michael Stern, "Board's Defeat Elates Police, Saddens Negroes," *New York Times*, November 9, 1966; "News from NAACP—55 More Police in Suit Against PBA," December 17, 1966, Algernon D. Black Papers, Box 26, Civilian Complaint Review Board—4; John Sibley, "Negro Unit Suing P.B.A. Over Dues," *New York Times*, November 6, 1966; "Kheel Offers to Aid in Dispute by Police," *New York Times*, December 25, 1966.
25. "Sketches of Members of New Police Review Board," *New York Times*, November 23, 1966; "Thomas, Jackson Stay with Board," *New York Amsterdam News*, November 26, 1966.
26. Letter from Algernon D. Black, October 20, 1966, Algernon D. Black Papers, Box 26, Civilian Complaint Review Board—6; Letter from Harold Baer Jr. to Algernon D. Black, November 10, 1966, Algernon D. Black Papers; Box 26, Civilian Complaint Review Board—6.
27. The radio stations WINS and WMCA and TV station WCBS all broadcast multiple editorials supporting the hybrid board. See, for example, "The Barry Gray Show—Interview with Inspector Garelik," Lindsay Papers.
28. Letter from Harold Baer Jr. to Deputy Commissioner Sylvan Fox, November 2, 1966, Lindsay Papers, Box 366, Folder "The Board"; Memorandum from Jay Kriegel, Assistant to the Mayor—CRB, October Statistics, Lindsay Papers, Box 366, Folder "The Board"; Bernard Weinraub, "Few Poor People Accusing Police," *New York Times*, October 21, 1966. The all-police board, operating in November and December 1966, decided cases at the same rate—out of 123, five were recommended for discipline to the commissioner,

eighty-nine were unsubstantiated, twenty were sent to conciliation, three were referred to other city agencies for further investigation, and six resulted in a police official clarifying rules and regulations to an officer. The same rates would hold true through at least 1970. The number of complaints in 1968 had more than doubled from 1966, to 1,549, and almost doubled again by 1970, to 2,901. Report on Civilian Complaint Review Board activities in 1966, from Chairman Louis Stutman to Commissioner Howard Leary, January 31, 1967, Lindsay Papers, Box 367, Folder "Civilian Review Board—1966 Annual Report"; NYPD press release, February 12, 1967, Lindsay Papers, Box 367, Folder "Civilian Review Board—1968 Report"; NYPD press release, February 15, 1971, Lindsay Papers, Box 367, Folder "Civilian Review Board—Personnel Screening Commission, 1966–1971."
29. "Remarks by Commissioner Leary, Released Tuesday Afternoon, September 27," Lindsay Papers, Box 374, Folder "Statements—Police Civilian Review Board."
30. "Do New Yorkers Want a Police State?," Lindsay Papers, Box 371, Folder "Literature, Police Review Board, 1966."
31. John Corry, "The Man of That Board," *New York Times Magazine*, November 6, 1966.
32. NYCLU Staff Meeting report, November 14, 1966, ACLU Records, Box 491, Folder 1.

Epilogue: Insufficient Funds

1. Literacy tests and poll taxes persisted for several years after the Voting Rights Act. Despite the Supreme Court ruling in *Harper v. Virginia Board of Elections* that any and all poll taxes, not just those for federal elections, were unconstitutional, Maine retained its poll tax until 1973, when it repealed it in a nonunanimous vote, 26 to 2. "Maine Senate Votes Repeal of Poll Tax on Adult Males," *New York Times*, March 13, 1973.
2. Kate Taylor, "With Many Schools Thriving Nearby, Those in Harlem Are Left to Fail," *New York Times*, January 25, 2017.
3. Kate Taylor, "De Blasio Dismisses Past Efforts in Education," *New York Times*, May 11, 2017.
4. Alex Zimmerman, "Fariña to Parents: We Need 'Organic' Plans, Not Mandates, to Diversify Schools," *Chalkbeat*, February 24, 2016, http://chalkbeat.org/posts/ny/2016/02/24/farina-to-parents-we-need-organic-plans-not-mandates-to-diversify-schools.
5. Elizabeth A. Harris, "New Schools Chief Hurtles Into Integration Wrangle," *New York Times*, May 1, 2018; Sophia Chang and Jessica Gould, "NYC Schools Chancellor Richard Carranza Resigns," *Gothamist*, February 26, 2021, http://gothamist.com/news/nyc-schools-chancellor-carranza-resigns.
6. Kenneth B. Clark, *Dark Ghetto: Dilemmas of Social Power* (New York: Harper & Row, 1967), 115.
7. New York City Department of Education, "Demographic Snapshot," http://infohub.nyced.org/reports-and-policies/citywide-information-and-data/information-and-data-overview. Keep in mind that the federal poverty cutoff for a family of four in 2019 was $25,750, which is absurd for anywhere in the United States, much less New York City. See Office of the Assistant Secretary for Planning and Evaluation, Department of Health and

Human Services, "Prior HHS Poverty Guidelines and Federal Register References," http://aspe.hhs.gov/prior-hhs-poverty-guidelines-and-federal-register-references.
8. Elizabeth A. Harris, "Small Steps, but No Major Push, to Integrate New York's Schools," *New York Times*, July 5, 2016. John Kucsera, "New York State's Extreme School Segregation: Inequality, Inaction, and a Damaged Future," UCLA Civil Rights Project, March 26, 2014, http://civilrightsproject.ucla.edu/research/k-12-education/integration-and-diversity/ny-norflet-report-placeholder/Kucsera-New-York-Extreme-Segregation-2014.pdf.
9. Gary Orfield and Erica Frankenberg, with Jongyeon Ee and John Kuscera, "Brown at 60 Great Progress, a Long Retreat and an Uncertain Future," UCLA Civil Rights Project, May 15, 2014, http://civilrightsproject.ucla.edu/research/k-12-education/integration-and-diversity/brown-at-60-great-progress-a-long-retreat-and-an-uncertain-future/Brown-at-60-051814.pdf.
10. Eliza Shapiro, "New York's Most Selective Public High School Has 895 Spots. Black Students Got 7," *New York Times*, March 19, 2019. The city also operates the Fiorello H. LaGuardia High School of Music & Art and Performing Arts. Admission is done via audition and portfolio submission, not through the Specialized High Schools Admissions Test. Eliza Shapiro, "New York's Elite Schools Still Admit Few Black Students," *New York Times*, March 19, 2020.
11. Ingrid Gould Ellen, "Building Justice: New York City's Separate and Unequal Neighborhoods," *City Limits*, August 22, 2016, http://citylimits.org/2016/08/22/building-justice-new-york-citys-separate-and-unequal-neighborhoods. The Black-white dissimilarity index was 81.6 in 2010, the most recent year for which data are available.
12. Elise Gould, "A Close Look at Recent Increases in the Black Unemployment Rate," Economic Policy Institute, March 8, 2019, http://epi.org/blog/a-close-look-at-recent-increases-in-the-black-unemployment-rate/. The Black unemployment rate in February 2020, the last month before the economic calamity, was 5.8 percent, while the white unemployment rate was 3.1 percent. U.S. Bureau of Labor Statistics, http://bls.gov/news.release/empsit.t02.htm.
13. Office of the New York City Comptroller Scott M. Stringer, "Inside the Gender Wage Gap, Part I: Earnings of Black Women In New York City," August 2018, 5–9, http://comptroller.nyc.gov/wp-content/uploads/documents/BW-Equal-Pay-Day.pdf. The wage gap between Black women and white men is larger in the city than it is both statewide and nationwide, at 43 cents versus 34 and 37 cents, respectively.
14. Elise Gould, "Stark Black-White Divide in Wages Is Widening Further," Economic Policy Institute, February 27, 2019, http://epi.org/blog/stark-black-white-divide-in-wages-is-widening-further/. Elise Gould, "Black-White Wage Gaps Are Worse Today Than in 2000," Economic Policy Institute, February 27, 2020, http://epi.org/blog/black-white-wage-gaps-are-worse-today-than-in-2000/.
15. Emily Badger, "Whites Have Huge Wealth Edge Over Blacks (but Don't Know It)," *New York Times*, September 18, 2017, http://nytimes.com/interactive/2017/09/18/upshot/black-white-wealth-gap-perceptions.html.
16. Emily Badger, Claire Cain Miller, Adam Pearce, and Kevin Quealy, "Extensive Data Shows Punishing Reach of Racism for Black Boys," *New York Times*, March 19, 2018, http://nytimes.com/interactive/2018/03/19/upshot/race-class-white-and-black-men.html.

17. NYC Open Data, "Infant Mortality," http://data.cityofnewyork.us/Health/Infant-Mortality/fcau-jc6k. The non-Hispanic Black infant mortality rate in 2016, the last year for which data are available, was 8 per thousand. It was 3.8 for "other Hispanic," 3.4 for Puerto Rican, 2.9 for Asian and Pacific Islander, and 2.6 for non-Hispanic white.
18. Michael Schwirtz and Lindsey Rogers Cook, "In Map of Virus Deaths in New York, Lines of Race and Wealth Stand Out," *New York Times*, May 20, 2020. APM Research Lab, "The Color of Coronavirus: COVID-19 Deaths by Race and Ethnicity in the U.S." http://apmresearchlab.org/covid/deaths-by-race. In January 2021, Black Americans had died at a rate of 136.5 per 100,000 over the course of the pandemic thus far, compared to 97.2 for white people. Only Indigenous Americans had a higher death rate, at 168.4. NYC Health, "COVID-19: Data," http://www1.nyc.gov/site/doh/covid/covid-19-data-totals.page. In New York City in January 2021, since the first diagnosed case on February 29, 2020, the Black death rate was 261.34 per 100,000 versus 143.3 for white people. In the city, "Hispanic/Latino" people of any race had a death rate of 282.5, the only group with a higher mortality rate than Black people.
19. Sabrina Tavernise and Abby Goodnough, "Covid Effect: Life Expectancy in U.S. Shows Distress," *New York Times*, February 18, 2021.
20. African American adults are 60 percent more likely to carry a diabetes diagnosis than white adults and twice as likely to die from it. U.S. Department of Health and Human Services, Office of Minority Health, "Diabetes and African Americans," http://minorityhealth.hhs.gov/omh/browse.aspx?lvl=4&lvlid=18. African Americans have the highest incidence of high blood pressure in the world. American Heart Association, "African Americans and Heart Disease, Stroke," http://heart.org/en/health-topics/consumer-healthcare/what-is-cardiovascular-disease/african-americans-and-heart-disease-stroke. Poor or nonexistent data-collection practices at the federal and state levels, especially early in the pandemic, have made ever knowing the true death toll among African Americans impossible.
21. In January 1984, the Black unemployment rate was 17.3 percent. U.S. Bureau of Labor Statistics, http://data.bls.gov/timeseries/LNS14000006.
22. Federal Reserve Bank of St. Louis, "Unemployment Rate—White," http://fred.stlouisfed.org/series/LNS14000003. U.S. Bureau of Labor Statistics, "Employment Situation Summary," June 5, 2020. U.S. Bureau of Labor Statistics, "The Employment Situation—March 2021," April 2, 2021.
23. "Current NYPD Members of Service," New York City Civilian Complaint Review Board, http://nyc.gov/site/ccrb/policy/data-transparency-initiative-mos.page.
24. Graham Rayman, "The NYPD Tapes: Inside Bed-Stuy's 81st Precinct," *Village Voice*, May 4, 2010, http://villagevoice.com/2010/05/04/the-nypd-tapes-inside-bed-stuys-81st-precinct/. Benjamin Weiser, "Class-Action Lawsuit, Blaming Police Quotas, Takes on Criminal Summonses," *New York Times*, May 18, 2015. Saki Knafo, "The Education of Edwin Raymond," *New York Times Magazine*, February 21, 2016. Twelve officers of color sued the NYPD in 2015 over the use of quotas and discrimination in promotions for refusing to abide by them.
25. Hélène Barthélemy, "The Agency Designed to Protect Civilians from the Police Actually Protects Police from Civilians," *The Nation*, October 20, 2016, http://thenation.com/article

/the-agency-designed-to-protect-civilians-from-the-police-actually-protects-police-from-civilians/. Between 1998 and 2004, commissioners dismissed 63 percent of substantiated complaints the board forwarded to them, taking no action against officers found to have violated departmental policies, civil rights, or laws. It was substantiating complaints at about 5 percent a year, one of the lowest rates of any such body in the nation. Substantiated chokeholds, a potentially deadly use of force counter to departmental policy, had not led to a single firing in 2015, even after the 2014 killing of Eric Garner. Of those officers who are disciplined, a figure in the low hundreds, half are simply sent to additional training. A sizeable proportion of complaints is settled through mediation, or a meeting between the complainant and officer(s) in question, which terminates the complaint and removes any potential for departmental discipline. New York City Civilian Complaint Review Board, "Meet the Board," http://nyc.gov/site/ccrb/about/the-board.page.

26. Ray Suarez, "How Crime Rates in New York City Reached Record Lows," National Public Radio, December 30, 2017, http://npr.org/2017/12/30/574800001/how-crime-rates-in-new-york-city-reached-record-lows. There were more than 2,200 murders in 1990 versus 289 in 2018. Edgar Sandoval, "Murders Creep up in New York, but Crime Numbers Show Complex Trends," *New York Times*, January 8, 2020. Ali Watkins, "Violent Year in New York as Virus Fuels Crime Spike," *New York Times*, December 30, 2020. T. J. English, *The Savage City: Race, Murder, and a Generation on the Edge* (New York: William Morrow, 2012), xxi.
27. Algernon Black, *The People and the Police* (New York: McGraw-Hill, 1968), 163.
28. New York Civil Liberties Union, "Stop and Frisk Data," http://nyclu.org/en/stop-and-frisk-data.
29. "Stop and Frisk Data." The NYPD reported 13,459 stops in 2019 and 11,008 in 2018. Still only about 10 percent are white.
30. Jack Moore, "NYPD Officers Shot the Lowest Number of People Ever in 2017," *Newsweek*, December 24, 2017, http://newsweek.com/nypd-officers-shot-lowest-number-people-ever-2017-758205. J. David Goodman, "Report Documents a Rise in Fatal Shootings by the City's Police Officers," *New York Times*, November 20, 2013. Kimberly Kindy, Marc Fisher, Julie Tate, and Jennifer Jenkins, "A Year of Reckoning: Police Fatally Shoot Nearly 1,000," *Washington Post*, December 26, 2015, http://washingtonpost.com/sf/investigative/2015/12/26/a-year-of-reckoning-police-fatally-shoot-nearly-1000/. "Fatal Force," http://washingtonpost.com/graphics/investigations/police-shootings-database/. The NYPD lists fifty-two firearm "use of force" incidents for 2019: www1.nyc.gov/site/nypd/stats/reports-analysis/firearms-discharge.page.
31. Daniel Pantaleo, the NYPD officer who choked Garner, was fired in August 2019 and sued to get his job back two months later, a decision the Sergeants Benevolent Association enthusiastically supported. P. R. Lockhart, "The Officer Who Was Fired for Using a Chokehold on Eric Garner Is Suing to Get His Job Back," *Vox*, October 24, 2019, http://vox.com/identities/2019/10/24/20930842/daniel-pantaleo-lawsuit-nypd-eric-garner-chokehold.

Bibliography

Manuscript Sources

Brooklyn Historical Society, Brooklyn, New York.
Columbia Center for Oral History Archives.
Department of Rare Books and Special Collections, Princeton University Library.
Manuscripts and Archives, Yale University Library.
New York City Municipal Archives, New York, New York.
Papers of the Congress of Racial Equality.
Papers of the National Association for the Advancement of Colored People.
Rare Book and Manuscript Library, Columbia University Libraries.
Schomburg Center, New York Public Library, New York, New York.
Tamiment Library, New York University.

Government Documents

City of New York, Office of the Mayor. "For Immediate Release, Monday, July 20, 1964."
City of New York, Office of the Mayor. "For Release P.M. Papers, Wednesday, August 12, 1964."
City of New York, Office of the Mayor. "Remarks by Mayor Robert F. Wagner on CBS-TV, Channel 2." 1964.
City of New York, Office of the Mayor. "Statement by Mayor Robert F. Wagner."
Murphy, Michael J. *Civil Rights and the Police: A Compilation of Speeches*. New York: New York City Police Dept., 1964.
New York City Council. Committee on City Affairs. Subcommittee on Proposed Civilian Complaint Review Board. *Report to the Committee on City Affairs from Its Subcommittee on Proposed Civilian Complaint Review Board*. New York, 1965.
New York City Council. City Affairs Committee. Special Subcommittee to Study the Feasibility of Creating an Independent Civilian Complaint Review Board. *Report of a Special Subcommittee to Study the Feasibility of Creating an Independent Civilian Complaint Review Board to*

Investigate, Hear and Make Recommendations Concerning Allegations of Police Brutality of the City Affairs Committee of the Council of the City of New York. New York: The Subcommittee, 1965.

Report to Mayor-Elect John V. Lindsay. New York: The Task Force, 1965.

United States. *The Challenge of Crime in a Free Society: A Report.* 1967.

United States. *Equal Employment Opportunity: Hearings Before the Subcommittee on Employment and Manpower of the Committee on Labor and Public Welfare, United States Senate, Eighty-Eighth Congress, First Session, on S. 773, S. 1210, S. 1211, and S. 1937, Bills Relating to Equal Employment Opportunities. July 24, 25, 26, 29, 31; August 2 and 20, 1963.* Washington, DC: U.S. Government Printing Office, 1963–1964.

United States. *Nation's Manpower Revolution: Hearings Before the Subcommittee on Employment and Manpower of the Committee on Labor and Public Welfare, United States Senate, Eighty-Eighth Congress, First Session, Relating to the Training and Utilization of the Manpower Sources of the Nation.* Washington, DC: U.S. Government Printing Office, 1963–1964.

United States. *Task Force Report: The Police.* Washington, DC: U.S. Government Printing Office, 1967.

United States and Barbara Ritchie. *The Riot Report—A Shortened Version of the Report of the National Advisory Commission on Civil Disorders.* New York: Viking, 1969.

United States, Tom Wicker, and Otto Kerner. *Report of the National Advisory Commission on Civil Disorders.* New York: Dutton, 1968.

Periodicals

Brooklyn Daily
Chicago Daily Defender
Commentary
Congressional Quarterly Weekly Report
Daily News
Dissent
The Liberator
Muhammad Speaks
The Nation
National Review
New York Age
New York Amsterdam News
New York Courier
New York Herald Tribune
New York Journal American
New York Post
New York Review of Books
New York Times
New York World Telegram
New York World Telegram and Sun

Newark Evening News
Newark Star-Ledger
Newsweek
Paterson Evening News
Spring 3100
U.S. News and World Report
Wall Street Journal
The Worker

Books and Pamphlets

Abbott, David W., Louis H. Gold, and Edward T. Rogowsky. *Police, Politics, and Race*. Cambridge, MA: American Jewish Committee and the Joint Center for Urban Studies of the Massachusetts Institute of Technology and Harvard University; distributed by Harvard University Press, 1969.

Abdul-Jabbar, Kareem, and Peter Knobler. *Giant Steps*. Toronto: Bantam, 1983.

Abel, Roger L. *The Black Shields*. Bloomington, IN: AuthorHouse, 2006.

Abu-Lughod, Janet L. *Race, Space, and Riots in Chicago, New York, and Los Angeles*. Oxford: Oxford University Press, 2007.

Alex, Nicholas. *New York Cops Talk Back: A Study of a Beleaguered Minority*. New York: Wiley, 1976.

Armstrong, Michael F. *They Wished They Were Honest: The Knapp Commission and New York City Police Corruption*. New York: Columbia University Press, 2012.

Asinof, Eliot. *People vs. Blutcher: Black Men and White Law in Bedford-Stuyvesant*. New York: Viking, 1970.

Association of the Bar of the City of New York. "Report on the Referendum Question Concerning the New York City Civilian Review Board." New York: Association of the Bar of the City of New York, 1966.

Baldwin, James. *The Fire Next Time*. New York: Dell, 1963.

———. *Nobody Knows My Name: More Notes of a Native Son*. New York: Dial, 1961.

———. *Notes of a Native Son*. New York: Dial, 1963.

———. *The Price of the Ticket: Collected Nonfiction, 1948–1985*. New York: St. Martin's/Marek, 1985.

Banfield, Edward C. *The Unheavenly City Revisited*. Boston: Little, Brown, 1974.

Baraka, Amiri. *The Autobiography of LeRoi Jones*. New York: Freundlich, 1984.

Bellush, Jewel, and Stephen M. David, eds. *Race and Politics in New York City: Five Studies in Policy-Making*. New York: Praeger, 1971.

Benyon, John, and John Solomos, eds. *The Roots of Urban Unrest*. Oxford: Pergamon, 1987.

Berson, Lenora E. *Case Study of a Riot: The Philadelphia Story*. New York: Institute of Human Relations Press, American Jewish Committee, 1966.

Beschloss, Michael R. *Taking Charge: The Johnson White House Tapes, 1963–1964*. New York: Simon & Schuster, 1998.

Bessel, Richard and Clive Emsley, eds. *Patterns of Provocation: Police and Public Disorder*. New York: Berghahn, 2000.

Biles, Roger. *The Fate of Cities: Urban America and the Federal Government, 1945–2000.* Lawrence: University Press of Kansas, 2011.

Biondi, Martha. *To Stand and Fight: The Struggle for Civil Rights in Postwar New York City.* Cambridge, MA: Harvard University Press, 2003.

Black, Algernon. *The People and the Police.* New York: McGraw-Hill, 1968.

Bloom, Alexander, and Wini Breines, eds. *"Takin' It to the Streets": A Sixties Reader.* New York: Oxford University Press, 2003.

Bloom, Nicholas D. *Public Housing That Worked: New York in the Twentieth Century.* Philadelphia: University of Pennsylvania Press, 2008.

Boehm, Randolph, and Dale Reynolds. *Congress of Racial Equality Papers.* Frederick, MD: University Publications of America, 1983.

Boesel, David, and Peter H. Rossi, eds. *Cities Under Siege: An Anatomy of the Ghetto Riots, 1964–1968.* New York: Basic Books, 1971.

Boskin, Joseph. *Urban Racial Violence in the Twentieth Century.* Beverly Hills, CA: Glencoe, 1976.

Boustan, Leah P. *Competition in the Promised Land: Black Migrants in Northern Cities and Labor Markets.* Princeton, NJ: Princeton University Press, 2017.

Branch, Taylor. *Parting the Waters: America in the King Years, 1954–63.* New York: Simon and Schuster, 1988.

———. *Pillar of Fire: America in the King Years, 1963–65.* New York: Simon & Schuster, 1998.

Breitman, George, Ed. *Malcolm X Speaks.* New York: Grove, 1990.

Brown, Claude. *Manchild in the Promised Land.* New York: Macmillan, 1965.

Campbell, Angus, and Robert M. Fogelson. *Supplemental Studies for the National Advisory Commission on Civil Disorders.* New York: Praeger, 1968.

Cannato, Vincent J. *The Ungovernable City: John Lindsay and His Struggle to Save New York.* New York: Basic Books, 2002.

Capeci, Dominic J. *The Harlem Riot of 1943.* Philadelphia: Temple University Press, 1977.

Carmines, Edward G., and James A. Stimson. *Issue Evolution: Race and the Transformation of American Politics.* Princeton, NJ: Princeton University Press, 1989.

Caro, Robert A. *The Power Broker: Robert Moses and the Fall of New York.* New York: Knopf, 1974.

Cazenave, Noel A. *Impossible Democracy: The Unlikely Success of the War on Poverty Community Action Programs.* Albany: State University of New York Press, 2007.

Chafe, William H. *Civilities and Civil Rights: Greensboro, North Carolina, and the Black Struggle for Freedom.* New York: Oxford University Press, 1980.

Chevigny, Paul. *Cops and Rebels: A Study of Provocation.* New York: Pantheon, 1972.

———. *Edge of the Knife: Police Violence in the Americas.* New York: New Press, 1995.

———. *Police Power: Police Abuses in New York City.* New York: Pantheon, 1969.

Chicago Commission on Race Relations. *The Negro in Chicago: A Study of Race Relations and a Race Riot in 1919.* The American Negro, His History and Literature. New York: Arno, 1968.

Childress, Alice. *Wine in the Wilderness: A Comedy-Drama.* New York: Dramatists Play Service, 1969.

Citizens' Committee for Children of New York. *The Planning and Coordination of Services for Children and Youth in New York City.* New York, 1959.

Clark, Kenneth B. *Dark Ghetto: Dilemmas of Social Power.* New York: Harper & Row, 1967.

———. *Harlem, U.S.A.* New York: Collier, 1971.

———. *The Negro Protest: James Baldwin, Malcolm X, Martin Luther King Talk with Kenneth B. Clark.* Boston: Beacon, 1963.

Clark, Kenneth B., and Jeannette Hopkins. *A Relevant War Against Poverty: A Study of Community Action Programs and Observable Social Change.* New York: Harper & Row, 1969.

Clarke, John Henrik. *Harlem: A Community in Transition.* New York: Citadel, 1969.

Cohen, Norman S., ed. *Civil Strife in America: A Historical Approach to the Study of Riots in America.* Hinsdale, IL: Dryden, 1972.

Colburn, David R., and George E. Pozzetta. *America and the New Ethnicity.* Port Washington, NY: Kennikat, 1979.

Committee to Defend Resistance to Ghetto Life. *The Case of Bill Epton.* New York: Committee to Defend Resistance to Ghetto Life, 1966.

Community Council of Greater New York. *Brooklyn Communities: Population Characteristics and Neighborhood Social Resources.* New York: Bureau of Community Statistical Services, Research Dept., 1959.

Connolly, Harold X. *A Ghetto Grows in Brooklyn.* New York: New York University Press, 1977.

Cordasco, Francesco, and Eugene Bucchioni. *The Puerto Rican Experience: A Sociological Sourcebook.* Totowa, NJ: Rowman and Littlefield, 1973.

Countryman, Matthew. *Up South: Civil Rights and Black Power in Philadelphia.* Philadelphia: University of Pennsylvania Press, 2006.

Crawford, Alan Pell. *Thunder on the Right: The "New Right" and the Politics of Resentment.* New York: Pantheon, 1980.

D'Emilio, John. *Lost Prophet: The Life and Times of Bayard Rustin.* New York: Free Press, 2003.

DeLoach, Cartha. *Hoover's FBI: The Inside Story by Hoover's Trusted Lieutenant.* Washington, DC: Regnery, 1995.

Donner, Frank J. *Protectors of Privilege: Red Squads and Police Repression in Urban America.* Berkeley: University of California Press, 1990.

Dudziak, Mary L. *Cold War Civil Rights: Race and the Image of American Democracy.* Princeton, NJ: Princeton University Press, 2000.

Durr, Kenneth D. *Behind the Backlash: White Working-Class Politics in Baltimore, 1940–1980.* Chapel Hill: University of North Carolina Press, 2003.

English, T. J. *The Savage City: Race, Murder, and a Generation on the Edge.* New York: William Morrow, 2012.

Epton, William. *We Accuse: Bill Epton Speaks to the Court.* Brooklyn, NY: Progressive Labor Party, 1966.

Eskew, Glenn T. *But for Birmingham: The Local and National Movements in the Civil Rights Struggle.* Chapel Hill: University of North Carolina Press, 1997.

Farber, David R., and Beth L. Bailey. *The Columbia Guide to America in the 1960s.* New York: Columbia University Press, 2001.

Farmer, James. *Lay Bare the Heart: An Autobiography of the Civil Rights Movement.* New York: Arbor House, 1985.

Feagin, Joe R., and Harlan Hahn. *Ghetto Revolts: The Politics of Violence in American Cities.* New York: Macmillan, 1973.

Financing Government in New York City: Final Research Report of the Graduate School of Public Administration, New York University, to the Temporary Commission on City Finances, City of New York. New York, 1966.
Fitch, Robert. *The Assassination of New York.* London: Verso, 1993.
Flamm, Michael W. *In the Heat of the Summer: The New York Riots of 1964 and the War on Crime.* Philadelphia: University of Pennsylvania Press, 2017.
———. *Law and Order: Street Crime, Civil Unrest, and the Crisis of Liberalism in the 1960s.* New York: Columbia University Press, 2005.
Flanagan, Richard M. *Robert Wagner and the Rise of New York City's Plebiscitary Mayoralty: The Tamer of the Tammany Tiger.* New York: Palgrave Pivot, 2016.
Fogelson, Robert M. *Violence as Protest: A Study of Riots and Ghettos.* Garden City, NY: Doubleday, 1971.
Freeman, Joshua Benjamin, ed. *City of Workers, City of Struggle: How Labor Movements Changed New York.* New York: Columbia University Press, 2019.
———. *Working-Class New York: Life and Labor Since World War II.* New York: New Press, 2000.
Freeman, Lance. *A Haven and a Hell: The Ghetto in Black America.* New York: Columbia University Press, 2019.
Friedman, Milton, and Rose D. Friedman. *Capitalism and Freedom.* Chicago: University of Chicago, 1962.
Frymer, Paul. *Black and Blue: African Americans, the Labor Movement, and the Decline of the Democratic Party.* Princeton, NJ: Princeton University Press, 2008.
Gilbert, Richard L. *I Was a Mad Man: A Madison Avenue Memoir.* New York: Diversion, 2013.
Glazer, Nathan. *Affirmative Discrimination: Ethnic Inequality and Public Policy.* New York: Basic Books, 1975.
Glazer, Nathan, and Daniel P. Moynihan. *Beyond the Melting Pot: The Negroes, Puerto Ricans, Jews, Italians, and Irish of New York City.* Cambridge, MA: MIT Press, 1970.
Golland, David H. *Constructing Affirmative Action: The Struggle for Equal Employment Opportunity.* Lexington: University Press of Kentucky, 2011.
Goodman, James E. *Blackout.* New York: North Point Press, 2003.
Gottehrer, Barry. *The Mayor's Man.* Garden City, NY: Doubleday, 1975.
———. *New York City in Crisis: A Study in Depth of Urban Sickness.* New York: D. McKay Co., 1965.
Greenberg, Cheryl Lynn. *"Or Does It Explode?": Black Harlem in the Great Depression.* New York: Oxford University Press, 1991.
Gregory, James N. *The Southern Diaspora: How the Great Migrations of Black and White Southerners Transformed America.* Chapel Hill: University of North Carolina Press, 2005.
Gregory, Steven. *Black Corona: Race and the Politics of Place in an Urban Community.* Princeton, NJ: Princeton University Press, 1999.
Grimshaw, Allen Day. *Racial Violence in the United States.* Chicago: Aldine, 1969.
———. *A Social History of Racial Violence.* Somerset, NJ: Aldine Transaction, 2009.
Hackworth, Jason R. *Manufacturing Decline: How Racism and the Conservative Movement Crush the American Rust Belt.* New York: Columbia University Press, 2019.
Halstead, Fred, Anthony Aviles, and Don Charles. *Harlem Stirs.* New York: Marzani & Munsell, 1966.

Harris, Dianne Suzette. *Little White Houses: How the Postwar Home Constructed Race in America*. Minneapolis: University of Minnesota Press, 2013.

HARYOU. *Youth in the Ghetto: A Study of the Consequences of Powerlessness and a Blueprint for Change*. New York: Harlem Youth Opportunities Unlimited (HARYOU), 1964.

Hayden, Tom. *Rebellion in Newark: Official Violence and Ghetto Response*. New York: Vintage, 1967.

Heaps, Willard Allison. *Riots, U.S.A., 1765–1965*. New York: Seabury, 1966.

Heckscher, August. *Alive in the City: Memoir of an Ex-Commissioner*. New York: Scribner, 1974.

Helfgot, Joseph H. *Professional Reforming: Mobilization for Youth and the Failure of Social Science*. Lexington, MA: Lexington, 1981.

Hentoff, Nat. *A Political Life: The Education of John V. Lindsay*. New York: Knopf, 1969.

Hirsch, Arnold R. *Making the Second Ghetto: Race and Housing in Chicago, 1940–1960*. Cambridge: Cambridge University Press, 1983.

Horne, Gerald. *Fire This Time: The Watts Uprising and the 1960s*. Charlottesville: University Press of Virginia, 1995.

Horowitz, Irving L. *The New Sociology: Essays in Social Science and Social Theory, in Honor of C. Wright Mills*. New York: Oxford University Press, 1971.

Hunt, D. Bradford. *Blueprint for Disaster: The Unraveling of Chicago Public Housing*. Chicago: University of Chicago Press, 2009.

Institute of Public Administration. *The Administration of Services to Children and Youth in New York City*. New York, 1963.

Jackson, James E. *The Bold, Bad '60s: Pushing the Point for Equality Down South and Out Yonder*. New York: International Publishers, 1992.

Jargowsky, Paul A. "The Architecture of Segregation: Civil Unrest, the Concentration of Poverty, and Public Policy." The Century Foundation, August 9, 2015. http://apps.tcf.org/architecture-of-segregation.

Johnson, Marilynn S. *Street Justice: A History of Police Violence in New York City*. Boston: Beacon, 2003.

Joseph, Peniel E. *The Black Power Movement: Rethinking the Civil Rights–Black Power Era*. New York: Routledge, 2006.

Katznelson, Ira. *City Trenches: Urban Politics and the Patterning of Class in the United States*. New York: Pantheon, 1981.

Kearns Goodwin, Doris. *Lyndon Johnson and the American Dream*. New York: St. Martin's Griffin, 1991.

Kelley, Robin D. G. *Race Rebels: Culture, Politics, and the Black Working Class*. New York: Free Press, 1994.

Keppel, Ben. *The Work of Democracy: Ralph Bunche, Kenneth B. Clark, Lorraine Hansberry, and the Cultural Politics of Race*. Cambridge, MA: Harvard University Press, 1995.

Kessner, Thomas. *Fiorello H. La Guardia and the Making of Modern New York*. New York: McGraw-Hill, 1989.

Kim, Claire Jean. *Bitter Fruit: The Politics of Black-Korean Conflict in New York City*. New Haven, CT: Yale University Press, 2000.

Klein, Woody. *Let in the Sun*. New York: Macmillan, 1964.

———. *Lindsay's Promise: The Dream That Failed: A Personal Account*. New York: Macmillan, 1970.

Krosney, Herbert. *Beyond Welfare: Poverty in the Supercity.* New York: Holt, Rinehart, and Winston, 1966.
Kusmer, Kenneth L. *A Ghetto Takes Shape: Black Cleveland, 1870–1930.* Urbana: University of Illinois Press, 1976.
Lardner, James. *Crusader: The Hell-Raising Police Career of Detective David Durk.* New York: Random House, 1998.
Lawson, Ronald, and Mark Naison, eds. *The Tenant Movement in New York City, 1904–1984.* New Brunswick, NJ: Rutgers University Press, 1986.
Leuci, Robert. *All the Centurions: A New York City Cop Remembers His Years on the Street, 1961–1981.* New York: William Morrow, 2004.
Levy, Peter B. The Great Uprising: Race Riots in Urban America During the 1960s. Cambridge: Cambridge University Press, 2018.
Light, Jennifer S. *From Warfare to Welfare: Defense Intellectuals and Urban Problems in Cold War America.* Baltimore, MD: Johns Hopkins University Press, 2005.
Lindsay, John V. *The City.* New York: New American Library, 1970.
Lomax, Louis E. *The Negro Revolt.* New York: Harper, 1962.
Lynd, Staughton. *Nonviolence in America: A Documentary History.* Indianapolis, IN: Bobbs-Merrill, 1966.
MacLean, Nancy. *Freedom Is Not Enough: The Opening of the American Workplace.* Cambridge, MA: Harvard University Press, 2008.
Manoni, Mary H. *Bedford-Stuyvesant: The Anatomy of a Central City Community.* New York: Quadrangle, 1973.
Marable, Manning. *The Fire This Time: The Miami Rebellion, May, 1980.* Dayton, OH: Black Research Associates, 1981.
———. *How Capitalism Underdeveloped Black America: Problems in Race, Political Economy, and Society.* Boston: South End, 1983.
———. *Malcolm X: A Life of Reinvention.* London: Penguin, 2012.
———. *Race, Reform, and Rebellion: The Second Reconstruction in Black America, 1945–1990.* Jackson: University Press of Mississippi, 1991.
Marable, Manning, Ian Steinberg, and Keesha Middlemass, *Racializing Justice, Disenfranchising Lives: The Racism, Criminal Justice, and Law Reader.* New York: Palgrave Macmillan, 2007.
Margolis, Jon. *The Last Innocent Year: America in 1964: The Beginning of the "Sixties."* New York: Perennial, 2000.
Markowitz, Gerald E., and David Rosner. *Children, Race, and Power: Kenneth and Mamie Clark's Northside Center.* Charlottesville: University Press of Virginia, 1996.
Marx, Gary T. *Protest and Prejudice: A Study of Belief in the Black Community.* New York: Harper & Row, 1969.
Matlin, Daniel. *On the Corner: African American Intellectuals and the Urban Crisis.* Cambridge, MA: Harvard University Press, 2013.
McDonald, Brian. *My Father's Gun: One Family, Three Badges, One Hundred Years in the NYPD.* New York: Dutton, 1999.
McGreevy, John T. *Parish Boundaries: The Catholic Encounter with Race in the Twentieth-Century Urban North.* Chicago: University of Chicago Press, 1996.

Meier, August, and Elliott M. Rudwick. *CORE: A Study in the Civil Rights Movement, 1942–1968*. New York: Oxford University Press, 1973.
Meyer, Stephen Grant. *As Long as They Don't Move Next Door: Segregation and Racial Conflict in American Neighborhoods*. Lanham, MD: Rowman & Littlefield, 2000.
Meyerson, Martin, ed. *The Conscience of the City*. New York: G. Braziller, 1970.
Morris, Charles R. *The Cost of Good Intentions: New York City and the Liberal Experiment, 1960–1975*. New York: Norton, 1980.
Mumford, Kevin J. *Newark: A History of Race, Rights, and Riots in America*. New York: New York University Press, 2007.
Naison, Mark. *Communists in Harlem During the Depression*. New York: Grove, 1985.
——. *White Boy: A Memoir*. Philadelphia: Temple University Press, 2002.
National Association for the Advancement of Colored People. *NAACP Administrative File. General Office File. Civilian Review Board—New York*. Bethesda, MD: University Publications of America, 1996.
——. *Selected Branch Files, 1956–1965. Branch Department Files Geographical File [New York City, 1956–1957, 1959–1965]*. Bethesda, MD: University Publications of America, 2000.
Nelson, Jill, ed. *Police Brutality: An Anthology*. New York: Norton, 2000.
Nelson, Truman John. *The Long Hot Summer*. Berlin: Seven Seas, 1967.
——. *The Torture of Mothers*. Boston: Beacon, 1968.
New York (NY). *The Complete Report of Mayor La Guardia's Commission on the Harlem Riot of March 19, 1935*. Mass Violence in America. New York: Arno, 1969.
——. *The Knapp Commission Report on Police Corruption*. New York: G. Braziller, 1973.
New York City Youth Board. *Reaching the Unreached Family: A Study of Service to Families and Children*. New York, 1958.
New York County Lawyers' Association. "Civilian Complaints Against the Police: A Report with Recommendations on the Processing of Civilian Complaints Against Members of the New York City Police Department." New York, 1965.
Newfield, Jack. *Robert Kennedy: A Memoir*. New York: New American Library, 1988.
Niederhoffer, Arthur. *Behind the Shield: The Police in Urban Society*. Garden City, NY: Doubleday, 1967.
O'Brien, Gail Williams. *The Color of the Law: Race, Violence, and Justice in the Post–World War II South*. Chapel Hill: University of North Carolina Press, 1999.
O'Neil, Jim, and Mel Fazzino. *A Cop's Tale: NYPD: The Violent Years: A Detective's Firsthand Account of Murder and Mayhem*. Fort Lee, NJ: Barricade, 2009.
Orsi, Robert A. *The Madonna of 115th Street: Faith and Community in Italian Harlem, 1880–1950*. New Haven, CT: Yale University Press, 1985.
Osofsky, Gilbert. *Harlem, the Making of a Ghetto: Negro New York, 1890–1930*. Chicago: Ivan R. Dee, 1996.
Patterson, James T. *The Eve of Destruction: How 1965 Transformed America*. New York: Basic Books, 2014.
Pearson, Hugh. *When Harlem Nearly Killed King: The 1958 Stabbing of Dr. Martin Luther King, Jr.* New York: Seven Stories, 2002.
Pecorella, Robert F. *Community Power in a Postreform City: Politics in New York City*. Armonk, NY: M. E. Sharpe, 1994.

Perino, Justina Cintrón., ed. *Citizen Oversight of Law Enforcement*. Chicago: American Bar Association, 2006.
Pinkney, Alphonso, and Roger R. Woock. *Poverty and Politics in Harlem: Report on Project Uplift 1965*. New Haven, CT: College & University Press, 1970.
Plunz, Richard. *A History of Housing in New York City: Dwelling Type and Social Change in the American Metropolis*. New York: Columbia University Press, 1990.
Podair, Jerald E. *The Strike That Changed New York: Blacks, Whites, and the Ocean Hill–Brownsville Crisis*. New Haven, CT: Yale University Press, 2002.
Pratt Institute. *Stuyvesant Heights: A Good Neighborhood in Need of Help*. Brooklyn: Community Education Program, Planning Dept., Pratt Institute, 1965.
Pritchett, Wendell E. *Brownsville, Brooklyn: Blacks, Jews, and the Changing Face of the Ghetto*. Chicago: University of Chicago Press, 2002.
Purnell, Brian. *Fighting Jim Crow in the County of Kings: The Congress of Racial Equality in Brooklyn*. Lexington: University Press of Kentucky, 2013.
Purnell, Brian, Jeanne Theoharis, and Komozi Woodard, eds. *The Strange Careers of the Jim Crow North: Segregation and Struggle Outside of the South*. New York: New York University Press, 2019.
Race Relations in the USA, 1954–68. New York: Scribner, 1970.
Ralph Jr., James R. *Northern Protest: Martin Luther King, Jr., Chicago, and the Civil Rights Movement*. Cambridge, MA: Harvard University Press, 1993.
Reminiscences of James Farmer. 1979. Columbia Center for Oral History Archives, Rare Book & Manuscript Library, Columbia University in the City of New York.
Reminiscences of Kenneth Bancroft Clark. 1976, 1985. Columbia Center for Oral History Archives, Rare Book & Manuscript Library, Columbia University in the City of New York.
Reporting Civil Rights, Part Two: American Journalism, 1963–1973. New York: Library of America, 2003.
Rieder, Jonathan. *Canarsie: The Jews and Italians of Brooklyn Against Liberalism*. Cambridge, MA: Harvard University Press, 1985.
Roberts, Sam, ed. *America's Mayor: John V. Lindsay and the Reinvention of New York*. New York: Museum of the City of New York, 2010.
Rogers, David. *110 Livingston Street: Politics and Bureaucracy in the New York City Schools*. New York: Random House, 1968.
Ross, Arthur M., and Herbert Hill, eds. *Employment, Race, and Poverty*. New York: Harcourt, Brace & World, 1967.
Rothstein, Richard. *The Color of Law: A Forgotten History of How Our Government Segregated America*. New York: Norton, 2017.
Ruffini, Gene. *Harry Van Arsdale, Jr.: Labor's Champion*. London: Routledge, 2015.
Samuel, Lawrence R. *New York City 1964: A Cultural History*. Jefferson, NC: McFarland, 2014.
Sandburg, Carl. *The Chicago Race Riots, July, 1919*. New York: Harcourt, Brace & World, 1969.
Sanjek, Roger. *The Future of Us All: Race and Neighborhood Politics in New York City*. Ithaca, NY: Cornell University Press, 1998.
Satter, Beryl. *Family Properties: Race, Real Estate, and the Exploitation of Black Urban America*. New York: Metropolitan, 2009.

Sayre, Wallace S., and Herbert Kaufman. *Governing New York City: Politics in the Metropolis*. New York: Norton, 1965.

Schaffer, Richard Lance. *Income Flows in Urban Poverty Areas: A Comparison of the Community Income Accounts of Bedford-Stuyvesant and Borough Park*. Lexington, MA: Lexington, 1973.

Schelling, Thomas C. *Strategies of Commitment and Other Essays*. Cambridge, MA: Harvard University Press, 2007.

Schneider, Cathy L. *Police Power and Race Riots: Urban Unrest in Paris and New York*. Philadelphia: University of Pennsylvania Press, 2017.

Schneider, Eric C. *Smack: Heroin and the American City*. Philadelphia: University of Pennsylvania Press, 2008.

———. *Vampires, Dragons, and Egyptian Kings: Youth Gangs in Postwar New York*. Princeton, NJ: Princeton University Press, 1999.

Schwartz, Joel. *The New York Approach: Robert Moses, Urban Liberals, and Redevelopment of the Inner City*. Columbus: Ohio State University Press, 1993.

Sears, David O., and John B. McConahay. *The Politics of Violence: The New Urban Blacks and the Watts Riot*. Boston: Houghton Mifflin, 1973.

Sexton, Patricia C. *Spanish Harlem: An Anatomy of Poverty*. New York: Harper & Row, 1965.

Shapiro, Fred C., and James W. Sullivan. *Race Riots, New York, 1964*. New York: Crowell, 1964.

Shecter, Leonard. *On the Pad: The Underworld and Its Corrupt Police: Confessions of a Cop on the Take*. New York: Putnam, 1973.

Shefter, Martin. *Political Crisis/Fiscal Crisis: The Collapse and Revival of New York City*. New York: Basic Books, 1985.

Siegel, Frederick F. *The Future Once Happened Here: New York, D.C., L.A., and the Fate of America's Big Cities*. New York: Free Press, 1997.

Skrentny, John David. *The Ironies of Affirmative Action: Politics, Culture, and Justice in America*. Chicago: University of Chicago Press, 1996.

Sleeper, Jim. *The Closest of Strangers: Liberalism and the Politics of Race in New York*. New York: Norton, 1990.

Smethurst, James E. *The Black Arts Movement: Literary Nationalism in the 1960s and 1970s*. Chapel Hill: University of North Carolina Press, 2006.

Sugrue, Thomas J. *The Origins of the Urban Crisis: Race and Inequality in Postwar Detroit*. Princeton, NJ: Princeton University Press, 1996.

———. *Sweet Land of Liberty: The Forgotten Struggle for Civil Rights in the North*. New York: Random House, 2008.

Taylor, Clarence, ed. *Civil Rights in New York City: From World War II to the Giuliani Era*. New York: Fordham University Press, 2011.

———. *Fight the Power: African Americans and the Long History of Police Brutality in New York City*. New York: New York University Press, 2019.

———. *Knocking at Our Own Door: Milton A. Galamison and the Struggle to Integrate New York City Schools*. New York: Columbia University Press, 1997.

Thabit, Walter. *How East New York Became a Ghetto*. New York: New York University Press, 2003.

Theoharis, Jeanne, and Komozi Woodard, eds. *Freedom North: Black Freedom Struggles Outside the South, 1940–1980*. New York: Palgrave Macmillan, 2003.

Thomas, June Manning, and Marsha Ritzdorf. *Urban Planning and the African American Community: In the Shadows.* Thousand Oaks, CA: Sage, 1997.

Torres, Andrés. *Between Melting Pot and Mosaic: African Americans and Puerto Ricans in the New York Political Economy.* Philadelphia: Temple University Press, 1995.

Trotter, Joe William, and Eric Ledell Smith. *African Americans in Pennsylvania: Shifting Historical Perspectives.* University Park: Pennsylvania State University Press, 1997.

Tyson, Cyril D. *Power and Politics in Central Harlem, 1962–1964: The Harlem Youth Opportunities Unlimited Experience.* New York: Jay Street, 2004.

Tyson, Timothy B. *Radio Free Dixie: Robert F. Williams and the Roots of Black Power.* Chapel Hill: University of North Carolina Press, 1999.

Venkatesh, Sudhir A. *American Project: The Rise and Fall of a Modern Ghetto.* Cambridge, MA: Harvard University Press, 2000.

Viteritti, Joseph P. *Police, Politics, and Pluralism in New York City: A Comparative Case Study.* Beverly Hills, CA: Sage, 1973.

———, ed. *Summer in the City: John Lindsay, New York, and the American Dream.* Baltimore, MD: John Hopkins University Press, 2014.

Walker, J. Samuel. *Most of Fourteenth Street Is Gone: The Washington, DC Riots of 1968.* New York: Oxford University Press, 2018.

Walker, Samuel. *Popular Justice: A History of American Criminal Justice.* New York: Oxford University Press, 1980.

Wallace, Deborah, and Rodrick Wallace. *A Plague on Your Houses: How New York Was Burned Down and Public Health Crumbled.* London: Verso, 1998.

Watts, Jerry G. *Amiri Baraka: The Politics and Art of a Black Intellectual.* New York: New York University Press, 2001.

Wilder, Craig Steven. *A Covenant with Color: Race and Social Power in Brooklyn.* New York: Columbia University Press, 2000.

Wingate, Livingston L. *The Real HARYOU-ACT Story.* New York, 1966.

Woodard, Komozi. *A Nation Within a Nation: Amiri Baraka (LeRoi Jones) and Black Power Politics.* Chapel Hill: University of North Carolina Press, 1999.

Zeitz, Joshua. *White Ethnic New York: Jews, Catholics, and the Shaping of Postwar Politics.* Chapel Hill: University of North Carolina Press, 2007.

Zipp, Samuel. *Manhattan Projects: The Rise and Fall of Urban Renewal in Cold War New York.* New York: Oxford University Press, 2012.

Articles and Anthology Entries

Adams, John S. "The Geography of Riots and Civil Disorders in the 1960s." *Economic Geography* 48, no. 1 (1972): 24–42.

Avila, E., and M. H. Rose. "Race, Culture, Politics, and Urban Renewal: An Introduction." *Journal of Urban History* 35, no. 3 (2009): 335–47.

Bauman, Robert. "The Black Power and Chicano Movements in the Poverty Wars in Los Angeles." *Journal of Urban History* 33, no. 2 (2007): 277–95.

Bean, Jonathan J. "'Burn, Baby, Burn': Small Business in the Urban Riots of the 1960s." *The Independent Review* 5, no. 1 (2000): 165–87.

Biondi, Martha. "How New York Changes the Story of the Civil Rights Movement." *Afro-Americans in New York Life and History* 31, no. 2 (2007): 15–31.

Boesel, David. "An Analysis of the Ghetto Riots." In *Cities Under Siege: An Anatomy of the Ghetto Riots, 1964–1968*, ed. David Boesel and Peter H. Rossi. New York: Basic Books, 1971.

Brown, Claude. "Harlem, My Harlem." *Dissent*, Summer 1963, 378–82.

Cha-Jua, Sundiata Keita, and Clarence Lang. "The 'Long Movement' as Vampire: Temporal and Spatial Fallacies in Recent Black Freedom Studies." *Journal of African American History* 92, no. 2 (2007): 265–88.

Chronopoulos, Themis. "Police Misconduct, Community Opposition, and Urban Governance in New York City, 1945–1965." *Journal of Urban History* 44, no. 4 (2015): 643–68.

Davies, Tom Adam. "Black Power in Action: The Bedford-Stuyvesant Restoration Corporation, Robert F. Kennedy, and the Politics of the Urban Crisis." *Journal of American History* 100, no. 3 (2013): 736–60.

Davis, Natalie Zemon. "The Rites of Violence: Religious Riot in Sixteenth-Century France." *Past and Present: A Journal of Historical Studies* 59 (May 1973): 51–91.

Doyle, Arthur. "From the Inside Out: Twenty-Nine Years in the New York Police Department." In *Police Brutality: An Anthology*, ed. Jill Nelson. New York: Norton, 2000.

Edmond, Lez. "Harlem Diary—'The Long, Hot Summer.'" In *Reporting Civil Rights*, part 2: *American Journalism, 1963–1973*. New York: Library of America, 2003.

Eidson, Bettye. "White Public Opinion in an Age of Disorder." In *Cities Under Siege: An Anatomy of the Ghetto Riots, 1964–1968*, ed. David Boesel and Peter H. Rossi. New York: Basic Books, 1971.

Eisenstadt, Peter. "Rochdale Village and the Rise and Fall of Integrated Housing in New York City." *Afro-Americans in New York Life and History* 31, no. 2 (2007): 33–60.

Feagin, Joe R., and Paul B. Sheatsley. "Ghetto Resident Appraisals of a Riot." *Public Opinion Quarterly* 32, no. 3 (1968): 352–62.

Flamm, Michael W. "'Law and Order' at Large: The New York Civilian Review Board Referendum of 1966 and the Crisis of Liberalism." *Historian: A Journal of History* 64, no. 3 (2002): 643–55.

———. "New York's Night of Birmingham Horror: The NYPD, the Harlem Riot of 1964, and the Politics of 'Law and Order.'" In *Patterns of Provocation: Police and Public Disorder*, ed. Richard Bessel and Clive Emsley. New York: Berghahn, 2000.

Fogelson, Robert M. "From Resentment to Confrontation: The Police, the Negroes, and the Outbreak of the Nineteen-Sixties Riots." *Political Science Quarterly* 83, no. 2 (1968): 217–47.

Fogelson, Robert M., Gordon S. Black, and Michael Lipsky. "Review of the Report of the National Advisory Commission on Civil Disorders/Supplemental Studies for the National Advisory Commission on Civil Disorders." *American Political Science Review* 63, no. 4 (1969): 1269–81.

Fortner, Michael Javen. "The Carceral State and the Crucible of Black Politics: An Urban History of the Rockefeller Drug Laws." *Studies in American Political Development* 27 (April 2013): 14–35.

———. "The 'Silent Majority' in Black and White: Invisibility and Imprecision in the Historiography of Mass Incarceration." *Journal of Urban History* 40, no. 2 (2014): 252–82.

Frankel, Robert. "Notes on the Harlem Riots: The Civil Rights Movement in New York City." *The Activist*, 1964.

Freeman, Damon. "Kenneth B. Clark and the Problem of Power." *Patterns of Prejudice* 42, no. 4–5 (2008): 413–37.

Gellhorn, Walter. "Police Review Boards: Hoax or Hope?" *Columbia University Forum*, Summer 1964, 5–10.

Goldstein, Herman. "Police Policy Formulation: A Proposal for Improving Police Performance." *Michigan Law Review* 65, no. 6 (1967): 1123–46.

Gottehrer, Barry. "Urban Conditions: New York City." *Annals of the American Academy of Political and Social Science* 371, Social Goals and Indicators for American Society, vol. 1 (May 1967): 141–58.

Hahn, Harlan. "A Profile of Urban Police." *Law and Contemporary Problems* 36, no. 4 (1971): 449–66.

Hahn, Harlan, and Joe R. Feagin. "Riot-Precipitating Police Practices: Attitudes in Urban Ghettos." *Phylon* 31, no. 2 (1970): 183–93.

Hazirjian, Lisa Gayle. "Combating Need: Urban Conflict and the Transformations of the War on Poverty and the African American Freedom Struggle in Rocky Mount, North Carolina." *Journal of Urban History* 34, no. 4 (2008): 639–64.

Hill, Herbert. "Twenty Years of State Fair Employment Practice Commissions: A Critical Analysis with Recommendations." *Buffalo Law Review* 14, no. 22 (1964): 22–69.

Hirsch, Arnold. "Containment on the Home Front." *Journal of Urban History* 26, no. 2 (2000): 158–89.

———. "Massive Resistance in the Urban North: Trumbull Park, Chicago, 1953–1966." *Journal of American History* 82, no. 2 (1995): 522–50.

———. "Searching for a Sound Negro Policy: A Racial Agenda for the Housing Acts of 1949 and 1954." *Housing Policy Debate* 11, no. 2 (2000): 393–441.

———. "Second Thoughts on the Second Ghetto." *Journal of Urban History* 29, no. 3 (2003): 298–309.

Hudson, James R. "The Civilian Review Board Issue as Illuminated by the Philadelphia Experience." *Criminology* 6, no. 3 (1968): 16–29.

Hutchinson, John E. "The AFL-CIO and the Negro." In *Employment, Race, and Poverty*, ed. Arthur M. Ross and Herbert Hill. New York: Harcourt, Brace & World, 1967.

———. "Police Review Boards and Police Accountability." *Law and Contemporary Problems* 36, no. 4 (1971): 515–38.

Jacoby, Tamar. "The Uncivil History of the Civilian Review Board." *City Journal*, Winter 1993.

Johnson, Roberta Ann. "The Prison Birth of Black Power." *Journal of Black Studies* 5, no. 4 (June 1975): 395–414.

Joseph, Peniel E. "Black Liberation Without Apology: Rethinking the Black Power Movement." *Black Scholar* 31, no. 3 (2001): 2–19.

Jou, Chin. "Neither Welcomed, Nor Refused: Race and Restaurants in Postwar New York City." *Journal of Urban History* 40, no. 2 (2014): 232–51.

Kelley, Robin D. G. "'Slangin' Rocks . . . Palestinian Style': Dispatches from the Occupied Zones of North America." In *Police Brutality: An Anthology*, ed. Jill Nelson. New York: Norton, 2000.

Max Lerner. "The Negro American and His City." In *The Conscience of the City*, ed. Martin Meyerson. New York: G. Braziller, 1970.

Lieberson, Stanley, and Arnold R. Silverman. "The Precipitants and Underlying Conditions of Race Riots." *American Sociological Review* 30, no. 6 (1965): 887–98.

Loo, Dennis D., and Ruth-Ellen M. Grimes. "Polls, Politics, and Crime: The 'Law and Order' Issue of the 1960s." *Western Criminology Review* 5, no. 1 (2004): 50–67.

Mayer, Jeremy D. "LBJ Fights the White Backlash: The Racial Politics of the 1964 Presidential Campaign." *Prologue: The Journal of the National Archives* 33, no. 1 (2001): 7–19.

Mayer, Martin. "The Lone Wolf of Civil Rights—Bayard Rustin, July 1964." In *Reporting Civil Rights, Part Two: American Journalism, 1963–1973*. New York: Library of America, 2003.

McGregor, Alecia. "Politics, Police Accountability, and Public Health: Civilian Review in Newark, New Jersey." *Journal of Urban Health: Bulletin of the New York Academy of Medicine* 93, no. 1 (2016): S141–S153.

Mohl, Raymond A. "The Second Ghetto Thesis and the Power of History." *Journal of Urban History* 29, no. 3 (2003): 243–56.

Monti, Daniel J. "Patterns of Conflict Preceding the 1964 Riots: Harlem and Bedford Stuyvesant." *Journal of Conflict Resolution* 23, no. 1 (1979): 41–69.

Moynihan, Daniel P. "The President & the Negro: The Moment Lost." *Commentary* 43, no. 2 (1967): 31–45.

Neyer, Aryeh. "Civilian Review Boards—Another View." *Criminal Law Bulletin* 2, no. 8 (1966): 10–18.

O'Connor, Alice. "Community Action, Urban Reform, and the Fight Against Poverty: The Ford Foundation's Gray Areas Program." *Journal of Urban History* 22, no. 5 (1996): 586–625.

———. "The Privatized City: The Manhattan Institute, the Urban Crisis, and the Conservative Counterrevolution in New York." *Journal of Urban History* 34, no. 2 (2008): 333–53.

O'Reilly, Kenneth. "The FBI and the Politics of the Riots, 1964–1968." *Journal of American History* 75, no. 1 (1988): 91–114.

Packer, H. L. "Copping Out." *New York Review of Books*, October 12, 1967, 17–20.

———. "Who Can Police the Police?" *New York Review of Books*, September 8, 1966, 1–12.

Perlstein, Daniel. "The Dead End of Despair: Bayard Rustin, the 1968 New York School Crisis, and the Struggle for Racial Justice." *Afro-Americans in New York Life and History* 31, no. 2 (2007): 89–120.

Platt, Anthony M. "Social Insecurity: The Transformation of American Criminal Justice, 1965–2000." *Social Justice: A Journal of Crime, Conflict & World Order* 28, no. 1 (2001): 138–55.

Pritchett, Wendell E. "The "Public Menace" of Blight: Urban Renewal and the Private Uses of Eminent Domain." *Yale Law & Policy Review* 21, no. 1 (2003): 1.

———. "Race and Community in Postwar Brooklyn: The Brownsville Neighborhood Council and the Politics of Urban Renewal." *Journal of Urban History* 27 (2001): 445–70.

———. "Which Urban Crisis?" *Journal of Urban History* 34, no. 2 (2008): 266–86.

Pritchett, Wendell E., and M. H. Rose. "Introduction: Politics and the American City, 1940–1990." *Journal of Urban History* 34, no. 2 (2008): 209–20.

Purnell, Brian. "'Taxation Without Sanitation Is Tyranny': Civil Rights Struggles Over Garbage Collection in Brooklyn, New York During the Fall of 1962." *Afro-Americans in New York Life and History* 31, no. 2 (2007): 61–88.

Rasmussen, Chris. "'A Web of Tension': The 1967 Protests in New Brunswick, New Jersey." *Journal of Urban History* 40, no. 1 (2014): 137–57.
Rudé, George. "The Crowd and Its Problems." In *Civil Strife in America: A Historical Approach to the Study of Riots in America*, ed. Norman S. Cohen. Hinsdale, IL: Dryden, 1972.
Ryan, William. "Savage Discovery: The Moynihan Report." *The Nation*, November 22, 1965, 380–84.
Schwartz, Joel. "Tenant Power in the Liberal City, 1943–1971." In *The Tenant Movement in New York City, 1904–1984*, ed. Ronald Lawson and Mark Naison. New Brunswick, NJ: Rutgers University Press, 1986.
Seligman, Amanda. "'But Burn—No': The Rest of the Crowd in Three Civil Disorders in 1960s Chicago." *Journal of Urban History* 37, no. 2 (2011): 230–55.
Snyder, Robert W. "A Useless and Terrible Death: The Michael Farmer Case, 'Hidden Violence,' and New York City in the Fifties." *Journal of Urban History* 36, no. 2 (2010): 226–50.
Soskin, William F. "Riots, Ghettos, and the 'Negro Revolt.'" In *Employment, Race, and Poverty*, ed. Arthur M. Ross and Herbert Hill. New York: Harcourt, Brace & World, 1967.
Sugrue, Thomas J. "Revisiting the Second Ghetto." *Journal of Urban History* 29, no. 3 (2003): 281–90.
Taylor, Clarence. "Introduction to Special Issue: 'The Civil Rights Movement in New York City.'" *Afro-Americans in New York Life and History* 31, no. 2 (2007): 7–13.
——. "Robert Wagner, Milton Galamison, and the Challenge to New York City Liberalism." *Afro-Americans in New York Life and History* 31, no. 2 (2007): 121–37.
Terrill, Richard J. "Police Accountability in Philadelphia: Retrospects and Prospects." *American Journal of Police* 7, no. 2 (1988): 79–97.
Thale, Christopher. "The Informal World of Police Patrol: New York City in the Early Twentieth Century." *Journal of Urban History* 33, no. 2 (2007): 183–216.
Thompson, E. P. "The Moral Economy of the English Crowd in the Eighteenth Century." *Past and Present* 50, no. 1: 76–136.
Thompson, Heather Ann. "Making a Second Urban History." *Journal of Urban History* 29, no. 3 (2003): 291–97.
——. "Urban Uprisings: Riots or Rebellions?" In *The Columbia Guide to America in the 1960s*, ed. David R. Farber and Beth L. Bailey. New York: Columbia University Press, 2001.
Wacquant, Loic. "Deadly Symbiosis: When Ghetto and Prison Meet and Mesh." *Punishment and Society* 3, no. 1 (2001): 95–133.
——. "From Slavery to Mass Incarceration: Rethinking the 'Race Question' in the US." *New Left Review* 13, no. 1 (2002): 41–60.
Walker, Samuel. "The History of Citizen Oversight." In *Citizen Oversight of Law Enforcement*, ed. Justina Cintrón Perino. Chicago: American Bar Association, 2006.

Electronic Sources

Black, Algernon D. Interview by William H. Booth. 89.3 WYNC FM, October 1, 1968.
Buckley, William F., Al DeCaprio, and Theodore Woodrow Kheel. *Civilian Review Board, Yes or No?* Stanford, Calif: Hoover Institution Video Library, Stanford University, 2008.

Harlem: Test for the North. WNBC, July 26, 1964.
July '64. Dir. Carvin Eison. DVD. California Newsreel, 2006.
Marcus, Eric. "Bayard Rustin." *Making Gay History.* Podcast audio, January 10, 2019. http://makinggayhistory.com/podcast/bayard-rustin.
"Who Speaks for Harlem?" Moderated by Edwin Newman. WNBC, July 26, 1964.

Unpublished Works

Back, Adina. "Up South in New York: The 1950's School Desegregation Struggles." PhD diss., New York University, 1997.
Banks, Nancy Ann. "'The Last Bastion of Discrimination': The New York City Building Trades and the Struggle Over Affirmative Action, 1961–1976." PhD diss., Columbia University, 2006.
Bolden, Richard L. "A Study of the Black Guardian Organization in the New York City Police Department from 1943–1978." PhD diss., Columbia University, 1980.
Cowan, Ruth. "The New York City Civilian Review Board Referendum of November 1966: A Case Study of Mass Politics." PhD diss., New York University, 1970.
Darien, Andrew Todd. "Patrolling the Borders: Integration and Identity in the New York City Police Department, 1941–1975." PhD diss., New York University, 2000.
Guild, Joshua Bruce. "You Can't Go Home: Again Migration, Citizenship, and Black Community in Postwar New York and London." PhD diss., Yale University, 2007.
Lee, Sonia Song-Ha. "Between Boricua and Black: How the Civil Rights Movement Changed Puerto Rican Identities in New York City, 1950s–70s." PhD diss., Harvard University, 2007.
McClure-Walzenbach, Mary Louise. "Police Professionalism and the Civilian Review Board." Master's thesis, San Diego State University, 1991.
McGlashan, Diane M. "A Struggle for Power: Urban Racial Violence and the 1967 Newark Riot." Master's thesis, Temple University, Philadelphia, 1994.
Miller, Joel, and Cybele Merrick. "Civilian Oversight of Policing: Lessons from the Literature." Unpublished conference paper, Vera Institute of Justice, Global Meeting on Civilian Oversight of Police, Los Angeles, May 2002.
Podair, Jerald E. "The Ocean Hill–Brownsville Crisis: New York's *Antigone.*" Unpublished conference paper, Gotham History Festival, October 2001, New York.
Purnell, Brian. "A Movement Grows in Brooklyn: The Brooklyn Chapter of the Congress of Racial Equality (CORE) and the Northern Civil Rights Movement During the Early 1960s." PhD diss., New York University, 2006.
Silverman, Sondra Joyce. "Political Movements: Three Case Studies of Protest." PhD diss., Australian National University, 1966.
Wallace, Arthur J. "Policing the Police: An Analysis of Procedures for Investigating and Disposing of Charges, Complaints, and Grievances Against the Police with Special Reference to the Civilian Complaint Review Board Controversy in New York City." Master's thesis, John Jay College of Criminal Justice, 1970.

Index

Abram, Morris B., 222, 298–99n5
Advisory Committee on Human Relations and Community Tensions, 82–83
affirmative action, 3, 42, 61, 266n11
AFL-CIO (American Federation of Labor and Congress of Industrial Organizations), 41, 45–48, 56–60, 286n11
Ali, Muhammad, 37
Alicea, Victor, 148
Allen, Alexander, 143
Allen, Eddie, 189
American Bund, 226
American Jewish Committee, 170, 298–99n5
American Legion, 222
Anti-Defamation League of B'nai Brith, 214, 223
Arbeiter Zeitung (Austria), 162
Arbery, Ahmaud, 251
Arm, Walter, 165, 175, 179
Armstrong, Michael, 98
Association of the Bar of the City of New York, 234–35

Back, Adina, 271n33
Badillo, Herman, 220
Baer, Harold, Jr., 215, 236
Baker, Bertram L., 20
Baker, Ella, 3, 70

Baldwin, James, 18, 20, 22, 28, 37–38, 107, 201, 296n26
Baltimore, Maryland, 251
Banfield, Edward C., 181–82, 257n21
Banks, Nancy Ann, 268n40
Baraka, Amiri, 127
Barksdale, Barbara, 126–27, 193
Beame, Abraham, 297n1
Bedford-Stuyvesant, 2, 10–11, 19–20, 22–24, 36, 190
Bedford-Stuyvesant Youth in Action, 204
Belafonte, Harry, 37
Ben-Jochannan, Yosef, 131–32
Benson, Barbara, 146–47
Berlin Wall, 202
Bibuld, Jerome and Elaine, 73–74, 271n37
Biondi, Martha, 202
Birmingham, Alabama, 132
Birmingham Campaign (Southern Christian Leadership Conference), 57
Birns, Harold, 261n61
birth control, 230
Black, Algernon D., 212, 215, 218, 223, 236, 278n71
Black Cabinet (Roosevelt administration), 15
Black nationalism: Bayard Rustin and, 291n21; and Black Power, 254n11; and Harlem Uprising (1964), 109, 130–31, 133–34, 156, 177, 200; in New York City, 7, 134

Black Power, 7–8, 20, 133–34, 220, 240, 254n11–12
Black Power (Wright), 254n11
"Blame Hate Groups, Red & White, for Harlem Terror" (Mallon, Federici, and Lee), 202
Bland, Sandra, 250
blockbusting, 22–24. *See also* housing
Bloom, Nicholas D., 261n58
Bloomberg, Michael, 249
Board of Estimate, 27
Boesel, David, 135, 278n78
Booker, Cory, 266n5
Booth, William H., 231, 298–99n5
Boustan, Leah Platt, 182
Boycott Jim Crow Schools flier, 78
Breslin, Jimmy, 225–26
Broderick, Vincent, 300n15
Bronx Catholic Interracial Council, 212
Brooklyn Bar Association, 222
Brooklyn Navy Yard, 39
Brotherhood of Sleeping Car Porters, 60, 279n2
Brown, Claude, 95, 99, 104, 106–7, 160
Brown, Mike, 250
Brownell, Herbert, Jr., 209, 220, 223
Brownsville, 2, 11, 157
Brown v. Board of Education of Topeka, 1–2, 63, 65–66, 68, 74, 166
Brunetto, Frank, 185
Buckley, William F., Jr., 212, 229, 297n1
"Building a Better New York" (1960), 11
"Bulletin No. 1, July 1964. Harlem Freedom Fighters: How to Make a Molotov Cocktail" flier, 174
Bureau of Apprenticeship and Training, 55
Bureau of Real Estate, 12
busing, 65. *See also* school segregation

Callender, Eugene, 143, 170, 205–6
Carey, James B., 47–48
Carmichael, Stokely, 133, 254nn11–12
Carranza, Richard, 245
Carson, Sonny, 20

Carter, Robert, 210
Cassese, John J., 210–14, 222, 225–26, 232, 236, 299n7
Castile, Philando, 250
Catholic Interracial Council, 214
Cavanagh, Edward, Jr., 143, 171, 179, 268n43
Central Harlem Housing Committee, 14–15
Chandler, Frank, 189
Chaney, James, 289n4
charter schools, 270n16
Chevigny, Paul, 85, 124–25
Chicago Police Association, 300n13
Children's Rally for Freedom flier, 76
Childs, Alvin, 128
Chisholm, Shirley, 20
chokeholds, 307–8n25. *See also* New York Police Department (NYPD)
Citizens Union, 214
City Council, 234
City Planning Commission, 25
City Wide Committee on Housing Relocation Problems, 13
Citywide Coordinating Committee, 205–6
Civilian Complaint Review Board (CCRB): calls for reform, 169–71, 175, 179, 191, 196, 207; creation (1953), 208, 298n2; and Harlem Uprising (1964), 144, 198; referendum on 1966 reform, 4, 6–8, 220, 224–29, 232, 235–41, 301n1, 304n28; reform (1966), 207–10, 216, 217, 230–31, 238–39, 303n14; since 1987, 248–49, 307–8n25
Civil Rights Act of 1957, 209
Civil Rights Act of 1964, 1, 50, 52, 56, 62, 159, 239
civil rights movement: and interracial coalition, 6–8, 57, 134, 176–77, 219–28, 239; in North and South, 108–10, 243; white backlash, 3, 5, 8, 43, 158, 185, 189–91, 226, 239–40
Civil War and Reconstruction, 29, 241–43, 251, 288n3
Clark, Kenneth: on Adam Clayton Powell, 278n77; background, 20, 65–66, 67; and

CCRB reform, 298–99n5; on conditions in Harlem, 1, 4–5, 9, 95, 104; on Harlem Uprising (1964), 4–5, 192–93, 203–4; on job discrimination, 37; on racism, 5; and school desegregation, 65–66, 74, 245, 269n11
Clark, Mamie, 66, 67, 74, 269n11
Clark, Stephon, 250
Clarke, Walter, 167
climate change, 242
cocaine, 103. *See also* drugs
Cohen, Jack, 54
Cohn, Roy M., 199, 295n23
Cold War, 57, 162, 202
Cole, Marvin R, 303n18
Cole Fischer Rogow law firm, 232, 303n18
Columbus, Christopher, 293n15
Commissioner of Education of the State of New York, 71–72, 82–83
Commissioner of Investigation, 234–35
Commission on Integration, 63
Commission to Investigate Alleged Police Corruption (Knapp Commission), 84, 92–94, 98, 102, 105, 195
Committee of Religious Leaders, 170
Committee on Civil Rights (CCR, AFL-CIO), 46, 48
communism: and citizen review boards, 222–24, 232, 302n4, 302n6; Communist Party, 6, 71, 75, 201, 203, 266n7, 296n32; criminal anarchy, 194; and Harlem Uprising (1964), 199–204; Progressive Labor Party, 116–17, 146, 194, 201; Red Scare (1919), 194; Young Communist League, 272n45
Community Affairs Committee, 144
Community Council on Housing, 21, 259n37
Competition in the Promised Land: Black Migrants in Northern Cities and Labor Markets (Boustan), 182
Congress of Racial Equality (CORE): and Black Power, 20, 254–55n12; Brooklyn chapter of, 20, 190; and CCRB, 214; and confrontation, 68; and Harlem Uprising (1964), 108, 115–18, 153–57, 164, 170, 172–73, 178, 183–85; and Hunts Point Terminal Market campaign, 54, 56–58; and Thomas Gilligan, 198–99; and white people, 117, 152–53, 185–86
Conservative Party, 212, 234, 297n1
Cook, Fred J., 268n43
Cossacks, 282n82
Cost of Good Intentions, The (Morris), 182
cover charges, 124–25. *See also* New York Police Department (NYPD)
COVID-19, 247–48
Cox, Anna, 12
criminal anarchy, 194. *See also* communism
Crutcher, Terence, 250
Cuban Missile Crisis, 202
Cumberbatch, Edward, 125–26

Dandridge, Frank, 140
Davis, Edward Mills, 191
Davis, Edward "Pork Chop," 130–31
Davis, Sammy, Jr., 37
de Blasio, Bill, 249
Democratic National Convention (Atlantic City, 1964), 253n4
Department of Civil Rights (AFL-CIO), 46
Department of Housing and Buildings, 14
"Desegregating the Public Schools of New York City: A Report Prepared for the Board of Education of the City of New York" (Advisory Committee on Human Relations and Community Tensions), 82–83
Detroit, Michigan, 146
diabetes, 307n20
Diallo, Amadou, 250
Diaz, Manuel, Jr., 212
Dinkins, David, 248, 300n14
District 65 of the Retail, Wholesale, and Department Store Employees Union, 145
Donovan, James, 75
Downstate Medical Center (State University of New York), 43, 271n37
Drug Enforcement Administration, 99

drugs, 87–88, 99–103, 242, 248
Drummond, Melvin, 124–25
Du Bois, W. E. B., 198, 302n6
Dudley, Edward, 143
Dudziak, Mary, 202
Dukes, Nelson C., 117–18
Dwight, Minnie, 193

Eastland, James O., 201–2
Edmond, Lez, 200
Eisenhower, Dwight D., 55, 223
Ellison, Ralph, 37
Emmett Till Antilynching Act, 266n5
England, Marshall, 130
Epton, William, 194, 199, 201
Equal Employment Opportunity Commission, 46
Esposito, Meade, 276n32
Ettman, Rodney, 213–14
Executive Order 8802 (U.S., 1941), 31
Expressen (Sweden), 122
extraordinary rendition, 274n3

Fair Employment Practices Committee, 31, 46
Fard, W. D., 289–90n11
Fariña, Carmen, 245
Farmer, James: background, 3, 126, 279n2; on Black ghetto formation, 9; on FBI investigation, 163; and Harlem Uprising (1964), 132, 134, 137–38, 143, 152–53, 163, 170, 191, 203–4, 284n13; and Hunts Point Terminal Market campaign, 58; on Malcolm X, 282n88; on Martin Luther King, Jr., 153; on National Guard, 146; on Nation of Islam, 160; and nonviolence, 134, 152; pacifism of, 126, 134; photo, *109*; on police brutality, 126, 193; on Robert Wagner, 175; and school desegregation, 75–76, 82; and Watts Uprising (1965), 153
Farrell, Thomas R., 212
Federal Bureau of Investigation (FBI), 113, 158–60, 163, 192, 203–4, 298n2
Federal Bureau of Narcotics (FBN), 99, 103

Federated Associations for Impartial Review (FAIR), 214, 232–33, 233, 238–39
Federici, William, 202
Ferguson, Missouri, 251
Fiore, Ernest, 184
Fiorello H. LaGuardia High School of Music & Art and Performing Arts, 306n10
Fischer, Arthur A., 225–26, 232, 303–4n18
Fitzgerald, Ella, 37
flaking, 100–101. *See also* New York Police Department (NYPD)
Floyd, George, 250–51
Forest Hills Conservative Party Club flier, *211*
Fraiman, Arnold, 235
Francke, Max, 113–14
Frank, Norman, 214, 222, 225–26, 235–36, 300n13
Fraternal Order of Police, 302n4
Frazier, E. Franklin, 65
Free Choice Transfer Plan (1966), 80
Freedom Riders, 1, 57, 75, 126, 135
Freeman, Joshua, 45
Friedman, Milton, 34, 262n17

Galamison, Milton, 74–75, 82, 137, 163, 190
Gamblers Part (Municipal Court), 98
gangs, 157, 188–89
Garelik, Sanford, 209, 231, 237
Garner, Eric, 250–51, 307–8n25, 308n31
Garvey, Marcus, 3, 20, 134, 198, 254n11
General Order No. 14 (NYPD, 1966), 208–9
Gilligan, Thomas: after Harlem Uprising (1964), 193, 195–99; background of, 111, 280n21; community leaders call for suspension and arrest of, 137–38, 143–44, 169, 195; demonstrations demand suspension and arrest of, 117–18, 132, 150–52, 165–66, 172, 175, 183, 191; killing of James Powell, 111–15, 126, 191
Glazer, Nathan, 34
Gleason, Gene, 268n43
Glendale Taxpayers Association, 73

Godfrey Nurse Houses, 12–17. *See also* urban renewal
Goldwater, Barry: and Harlem Uprising (1964), 117, 145–46, 162–63, 174; program of, 6, 158–59, 288n2; support for, 185, 190, 198, 200
Golland, David, 60
Goodman, Andrew, 289n4
Gottehrer, Barry, 268n43
graft and bribery by police, 84, 91–94. *See also* New York Police Department (NYPD)
Graham, Ramarley, 250
Grant, Oscar, 250
Gray, Freddie, 250
Gray, Jesse, 20–23, 79, 130, 145–46, 199, 201, 283n6
Great Depression, 37
Great Pacific Garbage Patch, 242
Great Society, 161
Gregory, James, 293n10
Gross, Calvin, 74, 82
Guardian (Britain), 162
Guardians Association, 214, 220, 236
guerrilla warfare, 109, 130–34, 283n6
Gurley, Akai, 250

Hamill, Pete, 302n6
Harlem: conditions in 1950s and 1960s, 2, 9–11, 35–36, 88, 258n28, 278n78; geographical definition of, 11; national political importance, 22, 190; uprisings in 1935 and 1943, 141, 149
Harlem Defense Council, 146, 194, 199, 281n50
Harlem Estates, 12–17
Harlem Neighborhoods Association, 74, 144
Harlem Parents Committee, 74–79, 164
Harlem solidarity march for voting rights and racial justice (March 14, 1965), *110*
Harlem Uprising (1964): arrests and prosecutions, 187, 193–94; and Black leadership, 107–9, 135, 145, 190; and Black nationalism, 109, 130–31, 133–34, 156, 177, 200; and Black police, 136, 142, 169–70, 179, 194–95; causes of, 3–5, 119, 191; East Harlem peace patrols, 148; events of July 16, 110–15; events of July 17, 115–16; events of July 18, 116–27; events of July 19, 128–40; events of July 20, 141–57; events of July 21, 164–68; events of July 22, 169–78; events of July 23, 178–81, 183–87; FBI investigation of, 163; international coverage and implications of, 122, 141, 161–63; killings and brutality by police, 110–13, 187–88, 193; and nonviolence and pacifism, 107–9, 132–35; photos, *121*, *139*, *150*, *156*; property damage, 187–88, 190–91, 193; and street gangs, 188–89; white hostility to, 164, 172–73, 178, 180–81, 183–85, 189–90; white people injured by Black people, 123, 287n27, 289n4
Harlem Youth Unlimited, 76
Harper v. Virginia Board of Elections, 305n1
Harrington, Donald S., 298–99n5
Harrington, Michael, 293n17
Harris, Kamala, 266n5
HARYOU (Harlem Youth Opportunities Unlimited), 144, 175
HARYOU-ACT (Harlem Youth Opportunities Unlimited-Associated Community Teams), 170
"Has Giligan [sic] Been Cleared of the murder of James Powell" flier, *197*
health care, 2, 45, 61, 201, 247–48, 258n28, 307n20
heaving, 90–91. *See also* New York Police Department (NYPD)
Henderson, Vivian W., 34
Herman, Alexander, 115
heroin, 99–103. *See also* drugs
high blood pressure, 307n20
Hildebrand, Richard A., 129–30, 175, 180
Hill, Arthur B., 179
Hill, Herbert, 52, 60
Hirsch, Arnold, 260n57
Hogan, Frank, 54
Holocaust, 226. *See also* Jews

homosexuality, 75, 132, 241, 272n45, 287–88n36
Hoover, J. Edgar, 75, 159–60, 168, 199–200, 204, 289n4
Horne, Gerald, 279n1
Hotel Theresa, 10, 117, 132, 178
House Un-American Activities Committee, 202
housing: mortgages, 2, 5, 23–24, 36, 264n38; private housing, 18–19, *19*; public housing, 24–27; racial and economic discrimination in, 5, 23–28, 36–37, 61; segregation in, 2, 16–17, 22–24, 36, 244–46; urban renewal, 11–18, 20, 25–27, 38, 257n21
Housing Act of 1949, 16–18, 260n57
Housing Act of 1965, 25
Houston, W. Eugene, 14
Howell, Judith, 117
Humber, Charles, 123
Hunt, Haroldson Lafayette, Jr., 296n26
Hunts Point Terminal Market construction project, 53–61

immigrants and immigration: Asians, 245; Black people as, 182–83, 292n6, 292n8; Irish, 65, 182, 293n15; Italians, 51, 182, 189–90, 293n15; Jews as, 51, 65, 182; Puerto Ricans as, 157, 292n6; white people, 43, 65, 181–86, 240
Immigration and Nationality Act of 1965, 245
incarceration, 242–43
Independent Citizens Committee Against Civilian Review Boards, 213–14, *221*, 222, 232, 238–39
infant mortality, 247
Innis, Roy, 183, 213
International Harvester, 33
International Hod Carriers and Building Laborers Union, 51–52
International Ladies' Garment Workers' Union, 46, 50–51, 258n31
International Union of Electrical, Radio and Machine Workers, 47, 266n7

International Union of United Brewery, Flour, Cereal, Soft Drink, and Distillery Workers of America, 46
Irish, 65, 182, 209, 275n12, 293n15, 301n1. *See also* immigrants and immigration
"Is Harlem Mississippi?" meeting, 130–33
Italians, 51, 67, 173, 180–84, 189–90, 275n12, 293n15, 301n1. *See also* immigrants and immigration
Ives-Quinn Law (Law Against Discrimination), 39–40
Izvestia, 162–63

Jack, Hulan, 20
Jackson, Bernard, 215
Jackson, Blyden, 58, 115
James, Ed, 118, 125
Javits, Jacob, 222
Jean, Botham, 250
Jefferson, Atatiana, 250
Jenkins, Jay, 123
Jews: and civil rights coalition, 83, 219, 231, 253n9, 301n1; as immigrants, 51, 65, 182; and Nazi persecution, 130, 226; and NYPD, 209, 275n12; as white people, 253–54n9, 293n15
Jim Crow system, 108, 242
jobs and job discrimination, 2, 29–43, 48–61, 246–48, 264n47
John Birch Society, 198
Johnson, Lyndon B.: and Harlem Uprising (1964), 141–42, 158–63, 168, 199–200, 202–3, 288n3, 296n26; and housing, 25; and job discrimination, 50, 52, 55–59, 61; and urban rebellions of 1960s, 6, 192
Johnson, Marilynn S., 85, 274n3
Johnson, Robert H., 136
Johnson, William, 236
Joint Apprenticeship Committee, 48–49
Jones, LeRoi, 127
Jones, Madison, 143
Joseph, Peniel E., 254n12
journeyman, 42, 48, 264nn46–47

Katzenbach, Nicholas, 296n26
Kearns, Doris, 159, 288n3
Kennedy, John F., 45, 55–57, 61, 281n49, 289n4
Kennedy, Robert F., 159, 222, 231, 235
Kennedy, Stephen P., 96–97, 194, 211, 295n11
Kerner Commission (National Advisory Commission on Civil Disorders), 192
Kerrison, Theodore, 137
Kheel, Theodore W., 222, 236
King, Martin Luther, Jr.: and Black Power, 254–55n12; on communists, 202; and Harlem Uprising (1964), 163, 195, 199, 203–4; influence in New York City, 279n2; murder of, 293n17; on nonviolence, 134; photo, *109*; on policing, 87; Poor People's Campaign (1968), 293n17; on racial and social progress, 243–44; and Watts Uprising (1965), 135, 287n31
Knapp, Whitman, 92, 298–99n5
Knapp Commission (Commission to Investigate Alleged Police Corruption), 84, 92–94, 98, 102, 105, 195
Koch, Ed, 297n1
Korea, 202
Ku Klux Klan, 171

La Guardia, Fiorello, 285n4
law and order: Barry Goldwater on, 6, 288n2, 291n6; and CCRB referendum, 225, 239; James Rea on, 147; Kenneth Clark on, 192; Lyndon B. Johnson on, 158–59; Robert F. Wagner, Jr., on, 166, 169, 171–72
Lawson, James, 117, 128
Leary, Howard, 208–9, 213, 229, 236–37, 298n3
Lee, Henry, 202
Lenox Terrace, 12–17, 256n4. *See also* urban renewal
Lerner, Max, 4–5
Leuci, Robert, 93, 98, 104, 278n79
Lewis, John, 22, *109*, 163, 279n2
Liberal Party, 214
Lincoln, Abbey, 75–76

Lindsay, John V., 4, 39, 207–9, 212–14, 220–21, 229–31, *230*, 239–40
literacy tests, 49, 305n1
Little Rock school integration crisis (1957), 146, 209
Little Wagner Act (1958), 45
Local 1 (United Association of Plumbers and Pipefitters), 52, 61
Local 2 (United Association of Plumbers and Pipefitters), 49, 53–61
Local 3 (International Brotherhood of Electrical Workers), 55, 267n27
Local 10 (International Ladies' Garment Workers' Union), 51
Local 28 (Sheet Metal Workers Union), 42, 52, 55, 264n47
Local 32-B (Building Service Employees International Union), 205
Local 373 (United Association of Journeymen and Apprentices of the Plumbing and Pipe Fitting Industry), 41–42
Logan, Waverly, 94, 100, 104, 276n35
Lomax, Louis, 52, 128
London Daily Sketch, 162
lotteries, 95
Louis, Joe, 258–59n34
Lowell, Stanley, 54, 61
Lower Harlem Tenants Council, 21
Lucchese crime family, 102
Lumumba, Patrice, 149
Lynch, Patrick, 111–12, 114, 196
lynching: in 1960s, 1, 162, 171; after Reconstruction, 242; antilynching legislation, 46, 266n5; today, 251
Lyons Residence Law (Local Law No. 40 of 1937), 278n73

Maine, 305n1
Malcolm X: background, 3, 20, 149, 286n13, 289n11; and Black Power, 254n11; and Harlem Uprising (1964), 116, 125–26, 137, 163, 282n88; and school boycotts and rent strikes, 21, *79*; and self-defense, 134

Mallon, Jack, 202
Manhattantown development, 17–18
March Against Fear (1966), 220
March on Washington for Jobs and Freedom (1963), 47, 56, 75, 111, 145, 177, 279n2
March on Washington Movement (1941), 31, 60, 279n2
Martin, Trayvon, 250
mass shootings, 242
McCabe, Edward, 213, 236
McCarthy, Joseph, 199, 202
McConnell, Mitch, 266n5
McCoy, Rhody, 253n9
McDonald, Laquan, 250
McFadden, James J., 52
Meany, George, 46–49, 58–61
Medicare, 185
Meredith, James, 57, 146, 220
Messenger, The, 60, 198
Metropolitan Life Insurance Company, 257n19
Meyerson, Martin, 37
Michaux, Lewis, 130, 149, 202
Miller, Edward O., 229–30
Miller, Herman, 33
Miranda rights, 86, 274n3
Mitchell, Harold, 41–42
Mobilization for Youth, 212
Molotov cocktails, 119, 123, 147, 168, 174
Monaghan, George, 298n2
Montgomery Bus Boycott, 1, 57
Montgomery Improvement Association, 57
Moore, Queen Mother Audley, 20
Morris, Charles R., 182, 265n51, 292n8
mortgages, 2, 5, 23–24, 36, 264n38. *See also* housing
Moses, Robert, 15–17
Moslem World & the U.S.A., 289n11
mounted police, 175–76. *See also* New York Police Department (NYPD)
Muhammad, Elijah, 161, 289n11
Muhammad Speaks, 160–61
Murphy, Michael: and CCRB, 171, 211, 213; and Harlem Uprising (1964), 118, 128–29, 143–44, 175, 184, 194–95

Murphy, Patrick, 276n25
Murray, Walter Isaiah, 212, 217, 223

Naeem, Abdul Basit, 161, 289n11
Naison, Mark, 203
Narcotics Division (NYPD), 100. *See also* New York Police Department (NYPD)
Nation, The, 92, 96–97, 268n43
National Advisory Commission on Civil Disorders (Kerner Commission), 192
National Association for the Advancement of Colored People (NAACP): and Black Power, 254n12; and CCRB, 210, 229; and communists, 296n32; and Harlem Uprising (1964), 108, 112, 114, 135, 174–75; and housing, 19; and job discrimination campaigns, 42, 47, 56–57, 60, 69, 71; and school desegregation, 68–74; and white allies, 185–86
National Guard, 146
National Labor Relations Act (Wagner Act), 44–45, 253n3, 256n8
National Labor Relations Board (NLRB), 45, 47, 50
National Maritime Union, 231–32
National Memorial African Bookstore, 131, 149, 202
National Renaissance Bulletin, 226, 228
National Renaissance Party, 226–29
National Tenants Organization, 258–59n34
Nation of Islam (NOI), 20, 126, 131, 160–61, 174–75, 254n11, 289n11
Nazi and neo-Nazi groups, 222, 226–29, 227
Negro American Labor Council (NALC), 143, 286n11
Negro Teachers Association, 71
Neier, Aryeh, 214, 239
nepotism, 48–49
Newark, New Jersey, 146
New Deal (1930s), 2–3, 13
Newfield, Jack, 20
Newsom, Gavin, 272n45
New York Amsterdam News, 16, 123–24, 141, 237, 298–99n5

New York City Board of Education, 2–3, 63–64, 68–83
New York City Commission on Human Rights (CCHR): and CCRB, 215, 234, 298–99n5, 300–301n15; and Harlem Uprising (1964), 115, 128, 143; and job discrimination, 53–54, 61; origin, 285n4
New York City Department of Commerce and Industrial Development, 38
New York City Department of Education, 245–46
New York City Department of Health, 12–13
New York City Housing Authority, 17, 25–27, 261n58, 261n62, 269–70n11
New York City Industrial Development Corporation, 38
New York Citywide Committee for Integrated Schools, 74–75, 79
New York City Youth Board, 189
New York Civil Liberties Union (NYCLU), 115, 210, 214, 222, 239, 300–301n15
New York Daily News, 202, 210, 223
New York Federation of Reformed Synagogues, 170
New York Herald Tribune, 124, 237
New York Police Department (NYPD): composition by race, gender, and ethnicity, 85, 88–89, 205, 209, 248, 275n12; corruption and misconduct in, 84–106, 124–25, 147, 191, 195, 216, 248–51, 274n3, 280n21, 298n2, 307–8n25; organization of, 89–91, 95–100, 175–76, 275n12, 276–77n43, 276n33; Patrolmen's Benevolent Association (PBA), 8, 90, 207, 210–14, 219, 222, 232, 234–38; and racism, 50, 103–4, 188, 307n24
New York Post: and Civilian Complaint Review Board reform referendum, 226, 237, 302n6; and Harlem Uprising (1964), 118, 122, 125–26, 139; on NYPD corruption, 97
New York Society for Ethical Culture, 212

New York State Commission Against Discrimination, 39–42, 51
New York State Commissioner of Education, 74
New York State Commission for Human Rights, 40–42, 285–86n4
New York State Department of Commerce, 38
New York State Employment Service, 40, 264n41
New York Supreme Court, 212
New York Times: and Civilian Complaint Review Board reform referendum, 236–37; and Harlem Uprising (1964), 123, 126, 138, 148; and Hunts Point Terminal Market campaign, 61
Niederhoffer, Arthur, 87
night riders, 171
Nkrumah, Kwame, 149
Nobel Peace Prize (1963), 134
nonviolence: Black Power and, 254–55n12; and Downstate Medical Center campaign, 43; and Harlem Uprising (1964), 107–9, 117–18, 128, 132–35, 145, 148, 152, 190; James Farmer and, 134, 152; Martin Luther King, Jr., and, 134
Notasulga, Alabama, 147
numbers (gambling), 87–88, 95–99, 168, 276n40

O'Carroll, William, 139
Ocean Hill–Brownsville school decentralization struggle (1968), 6–7, 22, 83, 190, 220, 270n20
Olnick, Robert, 12–16, 256n4, 256n10
O'Neil, Jim, 167, 293n19
Open Enrollment plan (1959), 80. *See also* school segregation
opioids, 242. *See also* drugs
Organization of African Unity, 137
Organization of Afro-American Unity, 116, 178
Other America, The (Harrington), 293n17
Overton, L. Joseph, 143, 152, 287n29
Owen, Chandler, 198

pacifism, 126, 132, 134, 177, 230, 272n43
pad, the, 97–98. See also New York Police Department (NYPD)
Pantaleo, Daniel, 308n31
Parents and Taxpayers Coordinating Council, 73, 81, 222
Parents' Workshop for Equality in New York City Schools, 73–74
Parker, Theodore, 243
Parker, William H., 146
Park Slope, 271n38
Paterson, Basil, 66, 106, 269n11
Paterson, David, 269–70n11
Patrolmen's Benevolent Association (PBA), 8, 90, 207, 210–14, 219, 222, 232, 234–38
Patterson, William L, 201
Paul, Rand, 266n5
Pendergast, Thomas, 118, 200, 281n50
Philadelphia Black Uprising (1964), 298n3
Phillips, Bill, 93–95, 98, 100, 104
Phipps, Mamie, 66. See also Clark, Mamie
Pickett, Nathaniel, II, 250
Pittsburgh Courier, 198
Planned Parenthood, 212
Poitier, Sidney, 37
Police Advisory Board (Philadelphia), 223, 298n3
Polier, Justine Wise, 72
poll tax, 46, 305n1
Poor People's Campaign (SCLC), 185, 293n17
Poverty Council, 172
Poverty Operations Board, 172
Powell, Adam Clayton, Jr.: background, 20, 37, 75, 104, 278n77; and Black Power, 254n11; and Harlem Uprising (1964), 137, 169–70; on NYPD corruption, 97, 105
Powell, Annie, 137, 142
Powell, C. B., 298–99n5
Powell, Harold, 142
Powell, James, 3–4, 110–14, 116–17, 128, 136–38, 142, 196
Present, Harris L., 13–14
President's Committee on Equal Employment Opportunity, 57

Princeton Plan, 80. See also school segregation
Progressive Labor Party, 116–17, 146, 194, 199, 201. See also communism
Prude, Daniel, 250
PS 130, 74
PS 200, 73, 271n37
PS 258, 68–69, 270n22
PS 282, 73, 271–72n38
Public Morals Division (PMD), 95–99. See also New York Police Department (NYPD)
Puerto Rican Community Development Project, 212
Puerto Ricans, 67, 148, 157, 236, 273n53, 292n6, 301n1

Randolph, A. Philip: background, 3, 20, 60, 109, 198, 258n31, 279n2; and CCRB referendum, 220; on Civil War and Reconstruction, 29, 242; and Harlem Uprising (1964), 145, 163; and labor movement, 47, 59–60, 279n2, 286n11, 287n29; and March on Washington for Jobs and Freedom (1963), 279n2; and March on Washington Movement (1941), 31, 60, 279n2
rape, 249
Ray, Sandy F., 298–99n5
Rea, James, 147
Receivership Law (1962), 261n61
Reconstruction. See Civil War and Reconstruction
Redding, George, 295n11
Red Scare (1919), 194. See also communism
rent strikes, 6, 18, 20–22, 130, 259n37
Reuther, Walter, 46–47, 56, 286n11
Rice, Tamir, 250
Richardson, Gloria, 140
Rick, Abe, 123
Rieder, Jonathan, 240
Riverton Houses, 257n19
RKO Alhambra movie theater, 149
Robert Taylor Homes (Chicago), 26

Robinson, Cleveland: and Harlem Uprising (1964), 143, 145, 176, 185, 200; and labor movement, 145, 286n11, 287n29; and March on Washington (1963), 145, *177*
Robinson, Isaiah, 164
Robles, Ava, 139
Rochdale Village, 268n42
Rockefeller, Nelson: and CCRB referendum, 222; and Harlem Uprising (1964), 146, 200, 203; and housing conditions, 21, 27, 261n61; and job discrimination, 39, 42–43
Roosevelt, Franklin D., 15, 30–31, 44–45, 56
Rose, Antwon, 250
Rosenman, Samuel I., 234
Ross, Arthur M., 36
Russell, Ernest, 118
Russo, Anthony, 104
Rustin, Bayard: background, 3, 155, 258n31, 287n36, 296–97n32; on Black nationalism, 291n21; and Harlem Uprising (1964), 132–34, 137–38, 152–55, 176–77, 188, 284n15, 287n27; homosexuality of, 75, 132, 272n45, 287–88n36; and integration, 291n21; and March on Washington (1963), *177*; and nonviolence, 188; on NYPD corruption, 106; pacifism of, 132, 272n43; on racism, 241; and school desegregation, 75
Ryan, William, 231

same-sex marriage, 241. *See also* homosexuality
Sam's West Side Bar and Grill, 154–55
Santora, Al, 184–85, 293n15
Schimmel, Gertrude, 276n25
school segregation: and *Brown v. Board of Education of Topeka*, 1–2, 63, 65–66, 68, 74, 166; campaigns against segregation, 68–81; causes and consequences of, 2, 62–68, 81–83, 244–46; and Eurocentric models of history, 77; integration objectives and African American attitudes, 64, 107–10; northern laws against, 1–2, 63; school pairing and rezoning for integration, 63–65, 68–69, 71–74, 80–83; in southern schools, 272n41; white opposition to integration, 66, 71, 73–81
Schuyler, George S., 198
Schwerner, Michael, 289n4
Scott, Tim, 266n5
Scott, Walter, 250–51
Screvane, Paul R., 143–44, 163–64, 172, 199, 206, 268n43
Sealy, Lloyd, 179, 194–95, 208, 231, 236–37, 295n12
self-defense, 108, 116, 118, 133–34, 148, 161, 180, 254n11
Sergeants Benevolent Association, 308n31
Shack, Donald D., 222
Shanker, Albert, 68, 270n20
Shecter, Leonard, 85–86, 90–91
Silver, Charles, 65, 70
sit-ins, 1, 58, 73–75, 83, 108, 126, 135
slavery, 4–5, 29, 230, 241–43, 251
Smith, Louis, 124, 284n13
Social Security, 45, 185, 253n3, 256n8
Solivan, Anibal, 148
Southern Christian Leadership Conference (SCLC), 57, 68, 70, 75, 185–86, 254n12, 296n32
Sprowal, Chris, 115–17
Stansbury, Tim, 250
Sterling, Alton, 250
stop-and-frisk, 147, 249. *See also* New York Police Department (NYPD)
Student Nonviolent Coordinating Committee (SNCC), 3, 22, 68, 163, 185, 253n4, 254–55n12, 300–301n15
Stuyvesant Heights, 23
Stuyvesant Town, 257n19
Sutton, Percy, 143

Tactical Patrol Force of NYPD, 118–19, 123, 136, 155, 167, 281nn49–50, 293n19

Taft-Hartley Act (1947), 53
Tass news agency, 162
Taylor, Breonna, 250
Taylor, Clarence, 85
Taylor, Harry, 119
Teachers Union, 71
Theobald, John, 71–72
"This is home???" photograph, *19*
Thomas, Franklin, 213, 236
Thompson, Robert, 201
Thurmond, Strom, 75
Till, Emmett, 116, 266n5
Tocqueville, Alexis de, 4–5
Transit Authority, 120–21, 138, 167
Tri-Line Offset Company, 199
Truman, Harry, 46
Twenty-Eighth Police Precinct, 96, 102, 117–18, 125, 137–38, 169, 195, 200
Tyson, Timothy, 254n12

Union of American Hebrew Congregations, 214
United African Nationalist Movement, 117, 128, 174–75
United Automobile Workers, 46, 57
United Electrical, Radio and Machine Workers of America, 266n7
United Federation of Teachers, 68, 79, 231, 298–99n5
United Mine Workers of America, 46
United Steelworkers, 46, 57
Universal Negro Improvement Association, 198. *See also* Garvey, Marcus
Urban League: and CCRB, 215; and Harlem Uprising (1964), 143, 160, 163, 170, 174–75; and job discrimination, 42, 48, 54–55; and school desegregation, 65, 69, 71, 74
urban rebellions, 108, 135, 141, 146, 159, 192, 279n1. *See also* Harlem Uprising (1964)
urban renewal, 11–18, 20, 25–27, 38, 257n21. *See also* housing
U.S. Department of Defense, 39, 235

U.S. Department of Justice, 161, 208, 266n11, 298n2
U.S. Department of Labor, 50, 55, 263n23, 266n11
U.S. Supreme Court, 63, 74, 166, 194, 269n11, 274n3, 305n1

Van Arsdale, Harry, Jr., 55, 267n27
Vaughan, John, 139
Vietnam War, 293n17
Voting Rights Act, 52, 159, 240, 242

Wagner, Robert F., Jr.: after Harlem Uprising (1964), 192–93, 195–96, 204–6; and CCRB, 171, 179; during Harlem Uprising (1964), 137, 142–44, 164, 166, 171–72, 179; and housing, 11–17, 21, 27–28; and jobs and job discrimination, 38–39, 42–43, 52, 54, 61; political career, 3, 13–14, 206; and school desegregation, 64–65, 69–70; and unions, 45, 265n4, 299n8
Wagner, Robert F., Sr., 3, 44
Waist and Dress Pressers Locals 60 and 60-A, 51. *See also* International Ladies' Garment Workers' Union
Waith, Eldridge, 179
Wallace, George, 174, 190
Walsh, Philip, 128
"Wanted for Murder—Gilligan the Cop" poster, 151, *151*, 165–66, 199
War on Poverty, 159, 185, 293n17
War on Terror, 274n3
Watts Uprising (1965), 135, 146, 279n1
Weaver, Robert C., 15
Weiss, Theodore, 231, 297n1
white flight, 259n41
Wilder, Craig Steven, 7
Wilkins, Roy: and CCRB referendum, 225; and Harlem Uprising (1964), 82, 135, 163, 204; photo, *109*; and school desegregation, 69, 72
Williams, Robert F., 116, 254n12
Wirtz, W. Willard, 55

World's Fair (Queens, New York, 1964–1965), 55, 258n34
"World's Worst Fair" (Central Harlem, 1964), 258n34
Wright, Richard, 254n11

Yorkville, 4, 110–11, 226–27, 279n3

Young, Whitney, Jr., *109*, 163, 204, 279n2
Young Communist League, 272n45. *See also* communism
Young Democrats, 214
Young Republicans, 214

Zongo, Ousmane, 250

GPSR Authorized Representative: Easy Access System Europe, Mustamäe tee
50, 10621 Tallinn, Estonia, gpsr.requests@easproject.com

www.ingramcontent.com/pod-product-compliance
Lightning Source LLC
Chambersburg PA
CBHW021933290426
44108CB00012B/821